Gifted Education

Gifted Education

A Comprehensive View

Margie K. Kitano
Darrell F. Kirby

New Mexico State University

LITTLE, BROWN AND COMPANY BOSTON/TORONTO

Library of Congress Cataloging-in-Publication Data

Kitano, Margie.
Gifted education.

Bibliography: p.
Includes index.
1. Gifted children—Education—United States.
I. Kirby, Darrell F.   II. Title.
LC3993.9.K57   1985   371.95′0973   85-19890
ISBN 0-316-49677-4

Library of Congress Catalog Card No. 85-19890

ISBN 0-316-49677-4

9 8 7 6 5 4 3 2 1

ALP

Published simultaneously in Canada by Little, Brown & Company (Canada) Limited

Printed in the United States of America

Acknowledgments

Photographs
Chapter opening photographs by Frank Smith, except Chapters 1, 9, and 14 photos by Gary Waynick, © Barbara Fuhrmann, 1984.

Figures
Figure 3.1: J.P. Guilford, "Theories of Intelligence" in *Handbook of General Psychology*, Benjamin B. Wolman, ed., © 1973, p. 636. Reprinted by permission of Prentice-Hall, Inc., Englewood Cliffs, N.J.   *Figure 5.1:* From Baldwin, Gear, Lucito (eds.), *Educational Planning for the Gifted: Overcoming Cultural, Geographic, and Socioeconomic Barriers* (Reston, Va.: Council for Exceptional Children, 1978), p. 34.   *Figure 6.2:* From *Curriculum Development: Theory and Practice* by Hilda Taba, copyright © 1962 by Harcourt Brace Jovanovich, Inc. Reproduced by permission of the publisher.   *Figure 7.3:* From J.R. Suchman, "A Model for the Analysis of Inquiry," in H.J. Klausmeier and C.W. Harris (eds.), *Analysis of Concept Learning* (New York: Academic Press, 1966), pp. 177–187. Reprinted by permission.   *Figure 13.1:* From F. Karnes and J.P. Parker, "Teacher Certification in Gifted Education: The State of the Art and Considerations for the Future," *Roeper Review*, 6 (1983):19. Copyright © 1983 by *Roeper Review*. Reprinted by permission of the authors and *Roeper Review*, 2190 North Woodward Avenue, Bloomfield Hills, MI 48031.

(continued on page 413)

This book is affectionately dedicated to our parents—
Tad and Kimi, Fred and Mae

Preface

Many future leaders, scientists, artists, and musicians are gifted children today. What can our society do to increase the likelihood that such potential for excellence will be developed and enhanced? One major step is to provide stimulating educational experiences for the children. Our book, *Gifted Education: A Comprehensive View*, was designed specifically to help teachers, prospective teachers, school administrators, and parents create the milieu in which the potential of the gifted and talented is nurtured.

Providing rich educational experiences is a sobering challenge. We maintain that those entrusted with the task must have a broad and informed outlook, familiarity with pertinent theories and research findings, and a keen knowledge of instructional techniques and curriculum in a variety of subject matter areas.

Broad Perspective. As with most significant challenges, meeting the educational needs of gifted and talented children can be achieved only through creative and energetic efforts. Leaders seeking solutions to troublesome international problems, for example, must examine the economic, political, social, and cultural aspects of the situation. Anyone working with the gifted, must similarly possess a broad, even a multi-disciplinary, outlook. We have included in this book information on historical, legal, psychological, educational, and social perspectives on the gifted and gifted education.

Theory and Research. Because widespread attention to the educational needs of gifted children is so recent, many programs have been started without solid theoretical or empirical bases. Theories and research findings already exist that can tell us much about learners and effective programs and teaching methods. This book provides current information about the theoretical foundations and research support for effective programs.

Methods and Curriculum. Ideally, all teachers and parents of gifted children would be experts in every subject area. Realistically, however, we know that most individuals can expand their repertoire of teaching skills. We devote much attention in this book to developing comprehensive curricula for gifted learners, and we examine teaching methods and techniques appropriate for use in a variety of content areas.

To achieve these goals we have selected material and sequenced it in a way that provides a broad survey of the field. We begin with a look at the historical and legal aspects of gifted education. We then consider the concept of giftedness as we find it in this country and in others. The nature of giftedness and the characteristics of gifted and talented learners are examined in two chapters.

Upon that foundation, we then turn our attention to the process of educating the gifted. In Chapter 5, we consider the key topics of referral, assessment, selection, and placement of children. The next chapter, Curriculum Development, devotes attention to a number of topics including models for curriculum design and individualized educational programs. Chapters 7, 8, and 9 are "methods" chapters in which we consider how to enhance inductive, creative, and evaluative thinking. The ninth chapter also includes a discussion of affective development. We end this substantial segment of the book with two chapters on content teaching: the arts and leadership and selected academic areas.

The next portion of the text is called "Ecological Perspectives." Here we examine special groups of gifted learners, such as young gifted children, gifted handicapped, and underachievers. The task of implementing programs is addressed in Chapter 13. Involving parents and families are the key topics in Chapter 14.

The book ends with a look at current issues and future trends. In this chapter and throughout the book, we seek to stimulate divergent thinking about important topics.

Several individuals inspired our work, provided examples of excellent teaching, and generally offered their support. Nancy Tafoya, Ann Stile, Elaine Paredes, and Polly Walker served as model gifted teachers of gifted students. Frank Smith's artistic abilities are reflected in much of the photographic work. Reviewers who read our manuscript in several drafts gave freely of their criticisms and suggestions. We wish to thank: Reuben Altman, University of Missouri-Columbia; Daryl Basler, Central Washington University; Helen E. Jones, Fairmont State College; and Juanita Roderick, Youngstown State University. Finally, the efforts of Sylvia Dovner of Technical Texts, Inc., were indispensable to the project. We hope that gifted students everywhere have the fortune to interact with similar talent.

Margie Kitano
Darrell Kirby

Brief Contents

Contents

SECTION IV: PERSPECTIVES ON INSTRUCTIONAL METHODS   169

CHAPTER SEVEN
Enhancing Inductive Thinking   171

CHAPTER EIGHT
Enhancing Creative Thinking

CHAPTER NINE
Enhancing Evaluative Thinking and Affective Development

SECTION VI: ECOLOGICAL PERSPECTIVES   285

CHAPTER TWELVE
Special Populations   287

CHAPTER THIRTEEN
Implementing Programs for the Gifted   331

SECTION I

The Gifted in Historical and Legal Perspective

Chapter One

INTRODUCING
THE GIFTED

CASE STUDY 1

Boy, age six; head large at birth. Thought to have had brain fever. Three siblings died before his birth. Mother does not agree with relatives and neighbors that child is probably abnormal. Child sent to school—diagnosed as mentally ill by teacher. Mother is angry—withdraws child from school, says she will teach him herself.

— Goertzel and Goertzel, 1962, p. xiii

Postscript: This child grew up to invent the incandescent lamp, the phonograph, and the microphone. His name was Thomas Alva Edison.

CASE STUDY 2

Girl, age five; in public school kindergarten. Self-taught to read at age two and a half. Parents, both professional engineers, are in their late fifties. Child tests at third or fourth grade level in all areas of academic achievement, but keenest interest is in reading maps and creating maps of local terrain. Teacher reports defiant behavior, such as breaking crayons to avoid coloring.

Postscript: This child is now ten and in the fifth grade. A psychologist is attempting to help her learn to control her enuresis and defiant behavior in school.

CASE STUDY 3

Boy, age four; not yet in school. Reads *Wall Street Journal*, but favorite pastime is computer programming. Mother (divorced) states that son completely taught himself to use the computer by reading manuals and practicing each day at five in the morning until mother arose.

Postscript: This boy will be eligible by age to enter public school kindergarten next year. His future is unknown.

Although these three cases are not typical of all gifted children, they serve to illustrate several current concerns in the field: Do gifted children generally succeed without special attention? How much potential is wasted through failure to recognize talent at an early age? What happens to gifted children when their special needs are not met? This chapter sets the groundwork for answers to these questions by providing a rationale for gifted education and by examining the historical treatment of gifted individuals.

WHY GIFTED EDUCATION?

Services for handicapped children were organized on a state and a national level in this country long before the special needs of gifted and talented children became widely recognized. Delayed acknowledgment of gifted children's needs stemmed from several sources. First, the American sociopolitical philosophy of equality has been manifested in public education largely through an effort to improve the lot of the disadvantaged (poor, minority, handicapped, female) to permit more people greater access to the American dream. Any concentration of efforts on the gifted and talented has been challenged as elitist and therefore antithetical to the ideal of a classless, equality-based democratic society. A second, related obstacle to the recognition of gifted children's needs has been their lack of emotional appeal. Plainly stated, the picture of the "poor gifted child" is as unconvincing to the American public as is the idea of the "miserable rich." Like the economically advantaged, the beautiful, and the renowned, the gifted arouse little sympathy.

Why, then, should there be special programs for the gifted? Several arguments favor gifted education, and in the remainder of this chapter each of the following points is discussed.

1. The concept of equal opportunity applies to gifted children as well as to the educationally disadvantaged.
2. The gifted need extra support and often fail to achieve their potential on their own.
3. The gifted gain from special services.
4. Appropriately served, the gifted can benefit humankind; failure to meet their needs may result in tremendous losses not only to gifted individuals but to society as a whole.

Equal Opportunity for the Gifted

Equal educational opportunity refers not to providing the same education for every child, but to providing the means by which every child can strive to meet his or her individual potential. It would be unfair and unrealistic, for example, to have the same educational expectations, standards, methods, and materials for both a moderately retarded child and a child of average intellectual ability. In this case, the retarded child would not be receiving an equal opportunity to meet his or her potential. By the same token, a child of superior ability would suffer if given the same education as an average child. The practice of identifying and making special provisions for those with exceptional abilities continues unquestioned in many fields, including athletics and the performing arts. Rather than requiring that everyone receive exactly the same education, equality refers to equal opportunity to maximize individual potential. For the gifted, as for the disadvantaged, equal opportunity may mean the provision of services different from those normally provided by the schools.

Need for Special Support

A commonly held belief among many educators and the public is that gifted children do not require special services because they can succeed on their own. For this reason, where funds are limited, many education agencies give first priority to the handicapped. Appropriations at local, state, and federal levels, in fact, favor the handicapped. Yet the available literature does not support the assumption that children of high ability succeed independently. In too many cases the opposite is true. When no attention is paid to their unique needs, gifted students all too frequently become underachievers with low aspirations. Some gifted learners never even complete high school.

In their appeal for increased federal support for the gifted and talented, Zettel and Ballard (1978) cited three studies that had disturbing findings. In a 1957 investigation of the achievement of 251 gifted children, Miner reported that 54.6 percent were working at levels below those at which they were intellectually capable. More significantly, the majority were achieving at levels at least four grades below their potential. A second study, by Green in 1962, provided an analysis of Iowa's high school dropouts: 17.6 percent of the gifted students (those with an IQ of 120 and above) did not finish high school. Finally, data from Project Talent, a longitudinal study of over 400,000 high school students begun in 1960, indicated that more than 13 percent of the gifted students did not aspire to postsecondary education. Less than 20 percent of these students' parents reported having aspirations of education beyond high school for their children.

More recently, Lajoie and Shore (1981) examined the representation of gifted children among dropouts, delinquents, and suicides. Their review of the literature suggested that the proportion of gifted among high school dropouts is about the same as the proportion of nongifted. Although they could state little of a definitive nature in connection with suicide, the authors speculated that the idea of overrepresentation of the college-age gifted among suicide victims is consistent with suicide statistics and theories about suicide causes. Gifted youth, for example, might be more aware of the world's problems and the human limitations for solving those problems. Lajoie and Shore also found that the gifted may be underrepresented among delinquents. Seeley (1984), however, found a substantial number of gifted youths in a study of one Colorado juvenile justice system. His analysis of the literature further indicated that, because gifted delinquents tend to do less well than their nondelinquent peers in achievement and verbal measures of ability, they are less likely to be identified as gifted. Hence, a larger number of gifted may exist in the delinquent population than was previously thought. Despite the inconsistencies in the literature, it is obvious that there are gifted children among dropouts, delinquents, and suicides; that gifted youth need special help; and that many do not succeed on their own.

Even the most highly gifted require special attention. Feldman (1979), in his study of extremely gifted children, noted that early prodigious achievement will not occur unless the children have access to specialized resources and receive intensive instruction. Mozart, who composed at the age of nine or ten, grew up in a home where music was played, discussed, and written. John Stuart Mill (estimated IQ of 200) received a rigorous education from his father, who demanded that his son study Greek at age three and astronomy and physics by age ten (Cox, 1926). "No matter how remarkable are the feats of child prodigies, these feats are not achieved without intensive, prolonged, *educational* assistance" (Feldman, 1979, p. 351).

There are, of course, examples of gifted individuals who have been able to succeed despite unsympathetic educational institutions. Based on their fascinating study of the lives of four hundred eminent men and women, Goertzel and Goertzel (1962) reported that 60 percent had serious school problems. Their dissatisfactions stemmed from inflexible curricula, dull or irrational teachers, ridiculing or boring classmates, and school failure, in that order. The subjects' unhappiness in the classroom situation was true for many countries, for different types of schools, and for both sexes, as can be determined from the biographies of individuals such as Susan B. Anthony, Pearl S. Buck, Isadora Duncan, Leon Trotsky, Pope John XXIII, and Thomas Mann. Although three out of five subjects studied disliked schooling, four out of five evidenced exceptional talent at an early age. Prokofiev, for example, composed an opera at age seven. During his elementary years, Enrico Fermi designed electric motors. Marie Curie spoke German, French, and Russian as a child and in elementary school excelled in every subject. Expectedly, the teachers best liked by the eminent individuals studied were those who permitted self-pacing and the unimpeded pursuit of special-interest areas.

Goertzel, Goertzel, and Goertzel (1978) corroborated their earlier findings in subsequent studies of 317 eminent men and women. Of these subjects, 63 percent disliked school. Most of those who liked school became scientists or politicians. Writers were overrepresented among those who were unhappy in school. The authors observed in general that, as children, the eminent loved learning but had difficulty with school and with teachers who insisted on their pursuing a standard curriculum not designed for their individual needs. The individuals studied also disliked rote learning, repetition, and being forced to read required books. A small portion never went to school but had tutors, governesses, or parents who served as their teachers.

The eminent individuals whose lives were studied by the Goertzels succeeded despite insensitive teachers, teasing peers, and unchallenging curricula. One need ask, however, how many individuals of equal talent have been lost to the world because they could not overcome the frustrations of an inflexible formal educational system.

Benefits to the Gifted

In the absence of educational services geared to their needs, gifted children often function significantly below expectancy levels. A logical question, then, is whether special services have been effective in encouraging gifted and talented students to perform at levels more commensurate with their high abilities. Tuttle (1978) described a large-scale study, conducted in 1961 by Simpson and Martinson, of 929 gifted students in grades one through twelve, in California. The investigators reported that gifted students in special programs made significantly greater gains than did equally gifted students in regular programs. The academic achievement of those attending special classes increased by an average of two years as compared with an average increase of one year among peers in the regular classroom. In later chapters additional supportive research will be discussed with respect to different administrative arrangements for meeting gifted children's needs. It is sufficient at this point to conclude that many gifted students underachieve in undifferentiated regular programs but benefit when services are designed to meet their unique needs.

Benefits to Society

In times of personal and national need, people realize that the country's gifted and talented constitute a most valuable resource for solving a range of human problems. Humankind reaps many benefits—pragmatic and aesthetic—from its gifted: advances in science and technology; skills in medicine and human interaction; music, poetry, and visual entertainment. Now more than ever, the gifted and talented are needed as society faces complex problems concerning nuclear armament, human rights, pollution, and energy depletion on a global scale. Because the gifted have so much to offer, the loss of talent through educational neglect constitutes a tragic waste to both the individual and society. Gallagher noted that talent is not indestructible and can be suppressed or even eliminated by a chronically deprived environment; therefore, the benefits of gifted programs must be calculated in terms of the costs of not having such programs: "What is the cost of the medical discovery never made? Of the political compromise never reached to head off a war? Of the sonata that was never written?" (Gallagher, 1979, p. 39).

The profound nature of gifted children's potential contributions to society was recognized in Congress's declaration that

(1) the Nation's greatest resource for solving critical national problems in areas of national concern is its gifted and talented children,

(2) unless the special abilities of gifted and talented children are developed during their elementary and secondary school years, their special potentials for assisting the Nation may be lost, and

(3) gifted and talented children from economically disadvantaged families and areas often are not afforded the opportunity to fulfill their special and valuable potentials, due to inadequate or inappropriate educational services.

— P.L. 95–561, Title IX, Part A, Section 901

What does the future hold for the children described in case studies 2 and 3, introduced earlier? Without question, both children deserve and require special supportive services designed to meet their individual needs. The concept of equal opportunity should extend to these children, as to all children, in the form of provisions enabling them to attempt to meet their high potential. Available data indicate that without such provisions, these children and others like them may grossly underachieve. Yet, with appropriate services, they may grow as individuals and ultimately share the fruits of their gifts with all humankind.

Can we meet the challenge of nurturing our gifted and talented children? The next section examines this question within a historical perspective.

ROOTS IN THE PAST

In the history of gifted and talented education, we can find the roots of many current concepts and issues related to gifted and talented education. Attention to gifted individuals has varied over time and place according to the philosophy, values, and needs of society.

The major philosophical issue affecting treatment of the gifted is whether education should be aimed at elevating the masses (universal education) or at nurturing those who evidence the greatest potential. The issue has often been posed as a dichotomy between elitism and democratic equality. Another perspective, offered in recent Chinese history by Dr. Sun Yat-sen, is that the democratic practice of educating equally individuals of unequal intelligence—that is, having the same expectations and standards for the bright and the dull—is a false conception of equality that leads to mediocrity and wasted talent. True equality consists rather in providing each individual an "equal opportunity to profit by education according to his intelligence" (Tsuin-chen, 1961, p. 61). Throughout history the prevailing philosophy with regard to equality of opportunity has been manifested in the treatment of gifted individuals.

What society values has also helped determine the definition and identification of gifted individuals over time. When visual arts have been prized—for example, in Renaissance Europe—society has sought out and supported the artistically gifted. Acute needs based on emergencies such as war or famine, and chronic needs existing over time, have also influenced society's identification of gifted individuals. The warrior society of ancient Sparta, for instance, required and hence nurtured individuals gifted with military prowess.

It is logical that a society would channel support for its gifted and talented in the direction of culturally and experientially determined values and needs. An alternative view is that the aim of education is to help gifted individuals achieve personal self-fulfillment independent of the needs of the state. According to this view, a Spartan youth who desired to be a dancer rather than a warrior and who possessed natural gifts of coordination and strength that gave promise for either area would have been encouraged to follow his own inclination. Historical and modern practices indicate, however, that society has generally chosen to nurture its gifted in accordance with the state's values and needs.

Little has been written specifically about the historical treatment of the gifted; facts must be inferred from what is known about the history of education in general and the lives of gifted individuals during particular eras. This section examines the treatment of the gifted during major historical periods in both the West and the East: in ancient Greece and Rome, in medieval Europe, in Renaissance Europe, in early China, in feudal Japan, and in America from colonial times to the present.

Ancient Greece and Rome (700 B.C.–A.D. 476)

Greece. In two major cities of ancient Greece, Sparta and Athens, we can see how society's values and needs influenced the education of potential leaders. Spartan education was directed almost exclusively at military success. Hence, it can be assumed that those children who demonstrated superior abilities in combat and leadership were recognized as gifted. According to Meyer (1965), infants were screened at birth for body formation, health, and promise by a council of inspectors. Defective infants and those of dubious value were flung from the cliffs to their deaths. Boys who passed inspection were returned to their homes for seven years, after which they lived in public barracks and attended military school. Those who showed extraordinary competence became captains of their classes. Students who were able to endure the discipline, pain, and hardship of the schools were most admired. Military service was required until the age of thirty.

The girls accepted by the council of inspectors received public athletic training similar to the boys', but they lived at home. Their highest duty was to bear healthy children for the military state. Public education did not include reading and writing, although instruction in these areas was available to some through private schooling. Science and the arts were virtually ignored (Good, 1960).

The Athenian philosopher Plato (427?–?347 B.C.) argued that a better social order could be achieved if those who governed were selected from among the most intellectually able. In Athens, however, until the establishment of Plato's Academy, Athenian society and its educational system favored those born to position by virtue of social class or family name. As in Sparta, formal education began at age seven; however, Athenian education emphasized literacy and music as well as physical skills. The state did not provide or regulate education, but private schools existed for the education of sons (not daughters) of free Greeks who could afford the fees. Schooling continued until about age sixteen. In his chapter on genius in ancient Greece and Rome, Warmington (1961) noted that although details of the curricula have not survived, it is known that instruction included reading and writing, history, arithmetic, literature, the arts, and physical training. Students took written and oral tests, though there were no organized systems of examination and no rewards for passing. The students were not necessarily the intellectually elite; the purpose of their training was to foster good citizenship.

Higher education in Athens was controlled by the upper class, which consisted of wealthy and well-born citizens. Sophists, mostly foreign born, prepared young men for active citizenship, charging fees for their services. Their teachings included grammar, rhetoric, logic, and mathematics. Plato was the first to organize an institute of higher education at a fixed place, called the Academy. He accepted no fees and admitted on equal terms with men young women who possessed the necessary intelligence and stamina.

Rome. Roman education differed from the Greek by virtue of a stronger emphasis on law and administration, architecture, and engineering. A more important difference, perhaps, was Roman society's more liberal attitude toward women, an attitude that resulted in the emergence of gifted women such as Cornelia, celebrated mother of the Gracchi, statesmen and social reformers. Roman society held family and mother in greater esteem than did Greek society, and Roman women greatly affected the tone of their society (Good, 1960). Although girls were not admitted to higher education, they did attend elementary school (first level), and some went on to grammar school (second level).

The Middle Ages (500–1500)

Little can be said with regard to the education of the gifted during the Dark Ages (fifth and sixth centuries) and the latter part of the medieval period in Europe except that many of the early leaders of the Renaissance received preparation at the universities that arose during this period (Good, 1960). During the Dark Ages the Roman Catholic church was the prime educator of western Europe through monastery and convent schools. The curricula included grammar, rhetoric, logic, arithmetic, geometry, astronomy, and music—all designed to prepare the student for the highest subject, theology. Later, under Charlemagne's leadership during the eighth century, cathedral and parish schools were established and admitted many of the common people's children, who were not intended for monastic life.

Between 1100 and 1500, the growth of commerce and the rise of cities in Europe led to an increased number of schools, new and better books and instructional methods, and the creation of universities. Guilds organized by merchants and craftsmen established a system of vocational education as well as schools of liberal arts that permitted middle-class boys to prepare for the university. The earliest universities, popularly supported, arose during the twelfth century in Bologna, Paris, and Oxford. John Calvin, a leader of the Reformation, and Ignatius Loyola, founder of the Jesuits, both attended the University of Paris. Approximately eighty universities had been opened by 1500 and were preparing scholars and writers in many fields.

The Renaissance (1300–1700)

The Renaissance, the period during which the greatest revival of classical art, literature, and learning occurred, produced many outstanding writers, painters, sculptors, and architects. What caused this age to produce such gifted artists as Dante, Boccaccio, Michelangelo, and da Vinci? According to Good (1960), each state, with its concentration of wealth, strong government, and extensive public works, was able to reward its abler citizens with positions of honor, power, or wealth. Society, which valued aesthetics and learning as we today value science, sought out and supported its aesthetically gifted. Wealthy individuals, governments, and churches used private and public means to establish libraries, schools, and galleries to support scholars, teachers, and artists.

During this same period the Turkish Empire in southeastern Europe provided another example of early efforts in gifted education. The emperor Suleiman the Magnificent (1494–1566) was an ardent patron of the arts and literature. (Sinan, the greatest Turkish architect, was named court architect during Suleiman's reign.) Gifted Christian youths, slaves to Suleiman, were given intensive education in the Mohammedan faith, as well as in history, war methods, science, and art. They were considered prized assets in the building of the Ottoman Empire (Sisk, 1979).

Early China (618–1644)

During the thousand years of European advancement from the Dark Ages to the Renaissance, China was engaged in the identification and fostering of child prodigies (Tsuin-chen, 1961). From the beginning of the Tang dynasty (A.D. 618–906), noted for its literature and art and for the development of printing, through the beginning of the Ch'ing dynasty in 1644, when the Manchus came to power, giftedness was valued and actively fostered as a contributor to national prosperity. In accordance with the values of Chinese society, early literary ability, manifested in the composing of poems and essays, received most attention. Years before the establishment of the national examination system, local authorities sought out child prodigies and sent them to the imperial court for recognition and advancement. After the national examination system was introduced, special examination sessions were established for gifted children. Those who passed were awarded court positions or scholarships for further study:

> Take the renowned 'Divine Child', Liu Yen (died A.D. 780), for instance. A native of Nanhua, Shantung, he "at eight years of age, when the emperor Ming Huang worshipped Mount T'ai, distinguished himself by producing a sacrificial ode upon the occasion. He was then examined by Chang Yueh, and declared by him to be a portent of national prosperity. The ladies of the court caressed him; the nobles called him a 'divine child' and the 'thunder-clap of the age'. He was appointed tutor to the Heir Apparent."
>
> — Tsuin-chen, 1961, p. 58

According to Tsuin-chen, four modern ideas about the gifted were addressed by the early Chinese. First, they recognized many of the same characteristics of giftedness that we recognize today. In addition to literary ability, they valued perceptual sensitivity, reading speed, memory capacity, imagination, leadership, originality, and reasoning. The early Chinese also anticipated the modern concept of giftedness in manual or mechanical abilities; however, children who excelled in this area were sometimes suspect because the culture associated such abilities with cunning and deception. Tsuin-chen partially attributed China's slower development in science and technology to this belief.

A second idea emergent in early China was the need to distinguish between early developers (who grow up to be average adults) and prodigies (who continue to excel into adulthood). Early Chinese philosophers such as Liu Shao also recognized that some gifted children develop at later ages and may not be identified early.

The third idea recognized by the early Chinese was the importance of special educational services in the nurturing of gifted children. They understood that even a genius could not fully develop his or her innate talents without support. Chinese writings of the time contain mention of intellectually brilliant children whose capacities waned in the absence of education. The gifted were nationally supported in an effort to prevent the potential waste of talent and because of a prevailing belief that a child genius would not live long.

The fourth idea addressed by the early Chinese is attributed to Confucius (551?–?479 B.C.): Education should be available to all social classes without discrimination, but individuals of different intellectual capacity should be educated in different ways. As noted earlier, the idea of equal opportunity to profit from education according to one's intellectual ability was continued into the early twentieth century by Dr. Sun Yat-sen.

Feudal Japan (1604–1868)

During the feudal Tokugawa Society (1604–1868), several different types of school systems existed, all of which taught a Confucian curriculum aimed at the inculcation of moral values for character development (Anderson, 1975). As in the Western countries at this time, no national education system existed. The schools provided separate educational tracks for the samurai nobility and the commoners.

Clan schools served each clan government and provided education in Confucian classics for the children of the elite samurai, from whose ranks would come the future leaders of Japan. The curricula included moral training, martial arts, history, calligraphy, composition, and etiquette. As contact with the Dutch and British increased toward the end of the feudal era, the Western studies of medicine, military science, and foreign languages were added. Local schools were sometimes established as branches of clan schools to serve the youth of samurai stationed in outlying regions. Toward the end of the Tokugawa period, some local schools began to admit the sons of wealthy commoners (priests, farmers, and merchants), the youth who were destined for local leadership. Intellectually gifted samurai and commoners were also educated in private academies organized by individual scholars who desired to instruct according to their own philosophies. The academies represented opportunities for advancement based on talent rather than class. Still, poor villagers received only occasional moral teachings extolling the virtues of diligence, filial piety, humility, and loyalty in order to ensure their continued obedience. Writing and vocational schools were also available to wealthier commoners (Anderson, 1975).

America to the Present (1620–1980s)

Early History. The first 240 years of American educational history demonstrate little attention to gifted individuals. Gifted leaders certainly immigrated to America or were born to the first arrivals. Formal educational provisions for the gifted, however, were slow to emerge. The plantation/laborer system of the southern colonies led to the development of private schools for wealthy landowners. The New England colonies, with their skilled middle class and compact settlements, established semipublic schools; the culturally heterogeneous middle colonies established parochial and neighborhood schools (Good, 1960). Secondary schools established during the seventeenth century were Latin grammar schools that prepared boys for college. Although regarded as a training ground for prospective ministers, the colonial colleges also prepared students for entry into the professions and sciences. Because education was selectively based on high academic achievements as well as on the ability to pay the fees, these secondary schools and colleges probably provided for at least some of the colonies' gifted (Newland, 1976). Indeed, Thomas Jefferson and James Madison attended private grammar schools in preparation for William and Mary College and Princeton, respectively.

As education increasingly became a state responsibility, and as compulsory attendance laws were enacted, the school population became increasingly heterogeneous. Rather than focusing on the intellectually and economically elite, the schools were required to expand their services to include students representing a wide range of ability, social class, and economic status. Provisions made for gifted children during this period were spotty and noncontinuous—primarily because they depended on the interests of particular individuals at local educational levels, and the programs ended when these people left. In 1866, local schools in Elizabeth, New Jersey, introduced multiple-track plans to provide for the gifted and for slow learners. St. Louis followed suit in 1871. These efforts had little national impact, however, being locally initiated rather than formally legislated (Newland, 1976). Special classes for the gifted began to appear during the first three decades of the 1900s: in Cincinnati and Los Angeles, 1916; in Urbana, Illinois, 1919; and in Manhattan and Cleveland, 1922 (Newland, 1976).

Postwar Educational Efforts. World War I had little impact on gifted education. However, the major scientific advances of World War II led to American society's recognition of the need for gifted scientists and technicians in order for the nation to compete with other countries in a new technological era (Newland, 1976). Although educators at all levels called attention to the neglect of the gifted and to manpower shortages in the sciences during the early 1950s, it was not until the shock of *Sputnik* in 1957 that gifted education became a national concern. With the launching of *Sputnik* by the Soviet Union, the United States faced a tremendous loss of prestige and a threat to national security. Some of the post-*Sputnik* programs for the gifted were crash programs that did not survive; others had tremendous effect on subsequent curriculum developments —in math and science, for example—for all children.

As the space program got underway and the United States put a man on the moon, interest in the gifted declined. President Kennedy's program for civil rights and President Johnson's War on Poverty shifted attention during the sixties and early seventies to the economically and socially disadvantaged. Americans became concerned with the extension of equal opportunity to underprivileged minorities. However, the latter half of the 1970s witnessed a resurgence of interest in gifted education that was supported by federal legislation. Although the cause of this renewed interest is not yet known, one explanation proffered is backlash sentiment against campus revolutionaries and consequent university compromises that resulted in the lowering of academic standards (Tannenbaum, 1979).

Legislative Action. Whatever the reason, in 1970 Congress mandated that "Provisions Related to Gifted and Talented Children" (Section 806) be added to the Elementary and Secondary Education Amendments of 1969 (P.L. 91–230). As a result, gifted and talented children were added to those who could benefit from funds allocated for Titles III and V of the Elementary and Secondary Act and teacher education provisions of the Higher Education Act of 1965 (Jackson, 1979). The amendment also directed the U.S. commissioner of education to initiate a study to discover the extent to which special education provisions were necessary for gifted and talented children's needs; to identify whether federal programs were meeting these needs and, if they were not, how federal programs could more effectively meet the needs; and to recommend any new programs.

In 1971 Commissioner Sidney Marland fulfilled this legislative order in his report to Congress on gifted and talented children (Marland, 1972). Among his recommendations for actions to be taken under the existing legislative authority (*United States Code*, P.L. 91–230, Section 806) was the establishment of a staff for gifted education within the U.S. Office of Education. Four years later, under provisions of the Special Projects Act of P.L. 93–380, Title IV, Section 404, categorical funds were made available for gifted education for the first time. Two and a half million dollars were appropriated. Federal funding to stimulate local and state programs for the gifted and talented was also generated through Title IV–C, Educational Innovation and Support, of the Elementary and Secondary Act.

Finally, the Gifted and Talented Children's Education Act of 1978 (P.L. 95–561, Title IX, Part A) was signed into law on November 1, 1979, by President Carter. This act substantially increased the amount that could be authorized for gifted education, from $25 million for fiscal year 1979 to $50 million for fiscal year 1983. Unfortunately, the act was repealed toward the end of 1981 under the Reagan administration's policy of new federalism, which included the shifting of responsibility for many educational programs to the states through block grant provisions.

Projections for the Future. As in the post-*Sputnik* years, the recent renewed interest in gifted children may lead to lasting changes in education for all. The National Commission on Excellence in Education, created in 1981 by Education Secretary Bell of the Reagan administration, was charged with assessing the quality of American education and with making recommendations for improvement. In February 1982, the commission reported that "American education, in general, has sacrificed some key advantages of specialization to attain the equalitarian goal of general education for all" (Asian Pacific American Concerns Staff, March 1982, p. 4). It was noted that, unlike the United States, both Japan and the Soviet Union emphasize the study of mathematics and science in their elementary and secondary schools. Graduates of secondary schools in the Soviet Union, for example, possess far better training in mathematics and science than do their American counterparts. In 1983 the commission published its final report, entitled *A Nation at Risk*. The report cited as one indicator of risk that "over half the population of gifted students do not match their tested ability with comparable achievement in school" (National Commission on Excellence in Education, 1983, p. 8).

Findings of the commission included charges of diluted curricula, low expectations for students, ineffective use of school time, and the inability of the teaching field to attract bright students. To help remedy these problems, the commission made five major recommendations:

A. . . . that State and local high school graduation requirements be strengthened and that, at a minimum, all students seeking a diploma be required to lay the foundations in the Five New Basics by taking the following curriculum during their 4 years of high school: (a) 4 years of English; (b) 3 years of mathematics; (c) 3 years of science; (d) 3 years of social studies; and (e) one-half year of computer science. For the college-bound, 2 years of foreign language in high school are strongly recommended in addition to those taken earlier. . . .

B. . . . that schools, colleges, and universities adopt more rigorous and measurable standards, and higher expectations, for academic performance and student conduct, and that 4-year colleges and universities raise their requirements for admission. . . .

C. . . . that significantly more time be devoted to learning the New Basics. This will require more effective use of the existing school day, a longer school day, or a lengthened school year. . . .

D. This recommendation consists of seven parts. . . .

    1. Persons preparing to teach should be required to meet high educational standards, to demonstrate an aptitude for teaching, and to demonstrate competence in an academic discipline. . . .

2. Salaries for the teaching profession should be increased and should be professionally competitive, market-sensitive, and performance-based. . . .
3. School boards should adopt an 11-month contract for teachers. . . .
4. School boards, administrators, and teachers should cooperate to develop career ladders for teachers that distinguish among the beginning instructor, the experienced teacher, and the master teacher.
5. Substantial nonschool personnel resources should be employed to help solve the immediate problem of the shortage of mathematics and science teachers. . . .
6. Incentives, such as grants and loans, should be made available to attract outstanding students to the teaching profession, particularly in those areas of critical shortage.
7. Master teachers should be involved in designing teacher preparation programs and in supervising teachers during their probationary years.

E. . . . that citizens across the Nation hold educators and elected officials responsible for providing leadership necessary to achieve these reforms, and that citizens provide the fiscal support and stability required to bring about the reforms we propose.

— National Commission on Excellence in Education, 1983, pp. 24–32

The commission's report further emphasized the federal government's responsibility in identifying education as being in the national interest and in helping to fund and support efforts to promote that interest, including efforts to meet the needs of "key groups of students such as the gifted and talented." Hope is widespread that the commission's findings will provide the needed impetus for American schools to meet the challenge of excellence in education for all, including the gifted.

In fact, on May 3, 1984, Congressman Austin Murphy of Pennsylvania introduced H.R. 5596, the Education for Gifted and Talented Children and Youth Improvement Act. The bill called for (*a*) defining gifted and talented children and youth; (*b*) providing federal funds for programs for gifted and talented youth, training of personnel, and research; and (*c*) requiring the secretary of education to report on the status of education for the gifted and talented and to make recommendations for nationwide strategy. Unfortunately, H.R. 5596 was not heard by the Ninety-eighth Congress. However, with efforts such as H.R. 5596, considerable interest in improving education for the gifted and talented has been generated, and it is likely that new legislation will be passed within the next few years. At the beginning of the Ninety-ninth Congress, on January 3, 1985, Senator Daniel Inouye of Hawaii introduced a bill in the Senate (S. 134) to reestablish the Office of Gifted and Talented. On January 21, 1985, Senators Bill Bradley (D-NJ), Christopher Dodd (D-CT), and Claiborne Pell (D-RI) introduced the Jacob J. Javits Gifted and Talented Children's Education Act (S. 452). If passed, the bill will reestablish the Office of Gifted and Talented in the U.S. Office of Elementary and Secondary Education and provide funds to support gifted programs.

CHAPTER SUMMARY

The rationale underlying gifted education rests on four major assumptions. First, the concept of equal educational opportunity means the provision of services that will enable children of different capacities to strive to meet their individual potentials. It does not mean the same education for all. As is the case for educationally disadvantaged children, equal opportunity for the gifted translates into special services designed to meet individual needs. Second, contrary to popular educational mythology, gifted children do not succeed on their own; in the absence of special help, they often achieve at levels grossly below expectancy. Third, appropriate services do raise the achievement of gifted students. Fourth, providing programs for gifted and talented children constitutes a wise investment in the future of humankind.

The treatment of gifted individuals has varied over time and place according to each society's philosophy, values, and needs. The prevailing philosophy for many societies from antiquity to the twentieth century has been to concentrate educational efforts on the socially and economically elite and, frequently, on males. Thus, it can be assumed that some of the gifted in the elite classes were served by the prevailing educational institutions; lower-class gifted went largely unnoticed. Exceptions can be found in societies where specific values and needs dictated that certain types of gifts be recognized and nurtured despite social class—for example, in Renaissance Europe, where classical arts were valued; in early China, where society prized literary genius; in Sparta, where military prowess was needed; and in America, where manpower needs existed in science and technology. A consequence, however, of educating the gifted primarily in response to societal values and needs has been society's coming to view the gifted as instruments rather than as individuals.

The history of gifted education also demonstrates that several current concepts related to the gifted were being considered a thousand years ago. Early Chinese philosophers, for example, described the multifaceted nature of giftedness, the difficulty of early identification, the need for educational support to prevent deterioration, and the desirability of differentiated services for children of different capacities.

The history of the gifted in America clearly indicates the effects of prevailing viewpoints in focusing educational efforts on the economically elite (in the colonial period) or on the economically disadvantaged (in the 1960s). Similarly, the impact of social need has been reflected in the sudden upsurge of programs for the gifted in the aftermath of *Sputnik* and the national recognition of the United States' precarious position in the space race. Finally, recent American history suggests a renewed valuing of excellence in education, a valuing that, hopefully, will encompass more than science and technology.

ACTIVITIES FOR THOUGHT AND DISCUSSION

1. Construct a questionnaire or interview format to assess people's ideas about the need for special services for gifted and talented children. Administer the questionnaire to school teachers (regular and special education), school administrators, congressional representatives, civic leaders, and lay individuals. Summarize the results and make recommendations.

2. Assume that the local school board is considering budget requests for the next fiscal year. The board is hearing testimony from special-interest groups representing handicapped, bilingual, and athletic programs. Prepare a presentation representing the interests of the gifted.

3. Interview a gifted adult regarding his or her public education experiences. What recommendations might this person have for educators?

4. Is there evidence that the United States has learned lessons from the treatment of gifted individuals throughout history? How would you explain the relative lack of interest in gifted education prior to *Sputnik*? Why do you think there has been a recent resurgence of interest in the gifted?

5. Imagine that you are a historian in the year 2000 and are writing about the treatment of gifted children in the 1980s. How would you describe gifted education in this decade? How would you evaluate society's attitude toward gifted education and the values manifested therein?

Chapter Two

CONCEPTS OF GIFTEDNESS

As was indicated in the previous chapter, one overriding issue throughout the history of education in general and gifted education in particular has been the question of whether to serve the elite few or the entire populace. This chapter first presents three nations' views on the issue of elitism versus universal education as it affects gifted education; it then examines American definitions of giftedness.

INTERNATIONAL PERSPECTIVES

The objectives and types of programs for gifted children in other countries necessarily reflect the different societies' cultural values and sociopolitical philosophies. Yet several modern nations have a common conception of giftedness that applies to individuals who have exceptional abilities in academics, art, or music. It is apparent from the literature, however, that countries with conflicting political ideologies have confronted the issue of elitism and have resolved it in different ways. Japan, the Soviet Union, and Great Britain provide interesting examples of three different approaches.

Japan

Today, following the changes brought about as a result of the American occupation after World War II, Japan has a national system of universal education. Iwahashi (1961), however, has suggested that national efforts to democratize the school system and to raise the achievement of those below the average on nationwide exams have resulted in the neglect of the gifted. Attempts are being made to increase opportunities for the gifted through ability grouping and extracurricular activities. Japan's rigorous, fiercely competitive system of examinations to determine admission to prestigious institutions has been viewed as a way of identifying and educating the gifted. Graduates of the prestigious institutions are often recruited for leadership positions in government and business. Some observers, however, question whether the entrance exams actually assess cognitive ability (Clark and Davis, 1981).

Given the apparent lack of a national effort to serve the needs of the gifted and to focus instead on universal education, it is interesting to note that Japan has been described as providing "perhaps the best national climate for creativity and the development of giftedness of any country in the world" (Torrance, 1980, p. 11). Torrance has attributed much of Japan's remarkable technological, educational, and socioeconomic achievements to a widespread valuing of individual creativity, self-development, intuitive thinking, persistence, discipline, self-directed learning, group learning, and group problem solving. As an example, Torrance cited the annual awards of the *Yomiuri Shimbun*, one of Japan's largest newspapers, made to children and adults for creative writing, music performance and composition, art, and ballet.

The Soviet Union

During the nineteenth and the early twentieth century—until the Bolshevik Revolution in 1917—Russia served academically superior students from the upper classes through gymnasia, or secondary schools preparatory to the university. Fifteen years after the revolution, the Soviet educational system adopted the policy of heterogeneous grouping and prohibited special provisions for the academically talented (Brickman, 1979). Brickman has described the Soviet attitude toward gifted education since the 1950s as ambivalent, with some politicians, educators, and psychologists arguing that special schools result in snobbery, egoism, and anticollectivism. Moreover, adherents of Pavlovian psychology eschew the idea of innate ability in favor of the concept that almost everyone can excel given adequate preparation. However, other observers (Creighton, 1961a, b; Clark and Davis, 1981) point to the Soviet Union as a world leader in early identification of highly talented individuals, in provision of special services, and in rewarding the efforts of the gifted and talented.

Special schools and facilities for gifted and talented individuals do exist in the Soviet Union, and these institutions offer instruction in many areas, including mathematics, science, music, and ballet. Creighton (1961a) described the institutions for developing talent as consisting of full-time schooling and extracurricular activities. Specialized secondary schools, for example, offer two- to four-year courses to students between fourteen and thirty-five who have completed at least seven years of general schooling and have qualified by competitive examination. Although most of these schools train technicians in industry, agriculture, commerce, health, and education, a smaller number of schools specialize in music, ballet, theatrical, and circus training. For example, the Ballet School of the Bolshoi Theater in Moscow, begun in 1783, draws its students from children of the common people.

Similarly, higher educational institutions open to qualified applicants who succeed in competitive exams include special schools for music, art, architecture, theater, and cinema. Based on large-scale testing programs, or olympiads, designed to identify mathematically talented individuals, the Soviet Union has also established separate mathematical–scientific schools under the sponsorship of universities and the Academy of Sciences. Brickman (1979) noted that between ten and twelve thousand individuals participated in an all-Siberian olympiad in mathematics and physics held during the 1970s. An earlier literature olympiad held in Moscow in 1967 included all schools.

Extracurricular activities, generally sponsored by the Pioneers, provide access to scholastic, recreational, and guidance services that enrich the general school curriculum. (An extension of the Young Communist League, the Pioneer Organization is made up of children between eight and fourteen years of age.) According to Creighton (1961a), teachers in the general schools may also foster the development of gifted children through the provision of extra materials, individual attention, or, more usually, extracurricular activities.

England

England is a land of contrasts, a monarchy with a democratic government. Social class distinctions remain strong, yet the average worker and family have complete social security in health, education, and pension services.

School attendance is compulsory for children between the ages of five and sixteen. Primary schools are divided into infant schools (for children aged five to seven) and junior departments (for children aged seven to eleven). The latter have been described as notable for their spirit of experimentalism, inquiry, and innovation (King, 1973). Some local education agencies have also established middle schools, which serve children from the ages of eight, nine, or ten through twelve, thirteen, or fourteen. Traditional secondary schools continue primary education for children from eleven to eighteen. Until the beginning of the 1960s, secondary schools were of three types: grammar (college preparatory), secondary modern (more broadly academic, emphasizing modern languages rather than Latin), and technical. Entry into these schools was determined by examinations taken between the ages of ten and eleven. Comprehensive secondary schools began to be widely established during the 1960s and 1970s. Good comprehensive schools may offer academic preparation and extracurricular activities similar to those offered in the grammar schools, though with less rigorous expectations.

Some local education agencies have established sixth form colleges for students between sixteen and eighteen. The sixth form may be attached to schools or institutions of higher education and has traditionally been reserved for educating the able, as determined by examinations and teacher judgment (Brickman, 1979). The sixth form has been considered the "center of excellence" for the entire school system, especially in terms of preparing students for university admission examinations and in providing excellent services in academic, cultural, and sporting activities (King, 1973).

With regard to special provisions for academically or intellectually gifted students, the prevailing British philosophy seems to run counter to segregation and in favor of serving the needs of the gifted within the regular school system. The influential Plowden Report of 1967, a report of the Central Advisory Council for Education, continues to set the tone for policy on gifted education. Most members of the Central Advisory Council argued that the primary education system and comprehensive secondary schools can meet the needs of gifted children and, with the exception of those talented in music and ballet, such children need not be segregated in special schools (Brickman, 1979). This position has been reiterated more recently by Henry Collis (1981), former director of the British National Association for Gifted Children (NAGC) and coordinator of the First World Conference for Gifted and Talented Children. Describing NAGC's position against special schools, Collis argued that a consequence of segregation is that gifted children gain the impression that they represent the norm and that all others are intellectually inferior. The NAGC's concern is to promote teacher awareness of gifted children's special needs so that appropriate attention can be provided in the regular classroom situation. NAGC supports the idea that children gifted in music and ballet require special settings. Special schools have been established for such children and include the prestigious Royal College of Music and the Royal Ballet School, the latter established in 1947.

Summary and Prospectus

A brief overview of educational practices with regard to the gifted in Japan, in the Soviet Union, and in England reveals a similar valuing of excellence in the academics and arts despite the countries' differing political sentiments. Japan's incorporation of democratic values and popular education goals has focused attention away from the gifted. Yet a rigorous system of examinations and a national atmosphere supportive of creativity in the arts and sciences have served to promote the needs of many high-achieving students. Although some Soviet leaders have questioned whether providing special education for the gifted is consistent with the collectivist concept, the Soviet Union offers a variety of special facilities for its gifted students—facilities open to all through competitive examinations. Finally, despite England's prevailing educational bias against special schools, the British system of examinations and sixth form colleges remains a strong support for the academically superior.

It is interesting that leaders in both democratic and communist countries have assailed the notion of special services for the academically gifted as elitist. Evidently, countries with similar political inclinations do not necessarily agree on the elitism issue. During the Cultural Revolution of the late 1960s, Communist Chinese leaders, now known as the Gang of Four, labeled Chinese students and teachers as bourgeois intellectuals. The examination and grading systems were denounced as capitalistic relics, and the universities were required to select students from among workers, peasants, and soldiers who demonstrated ideological fervor (Clark and Davis, 1981). Consistent with this rejection of intellectualism, a writer for a Communist Chinese periodical in 1976 criticized the Soviet Union's establishment of special schools for talented students who hold themselves superior to the masses and who will be tracked to leadership positions (Brickman, 1979). The Gang of Four, however, lost the power struggle that ensued after Mao Tse-tung's death. Entrance examinations were reinstated in 1977, and intellectual ability again became an important quality (Clark and Davis, 1981). It appears that each country has resolved the elitism issue in its own unique way, perhaps reconciling its political ideology with its national needs to benefit from the contributions of its talented.

Indeed, evidence exists that many nations are becoming increasingly aware of the special needs of their gifted and talented children. The proceedings of the First World Conference on Gifted Children, held in London in 1975, briefly described provisions for gifted children in twenty-four countries (Gibson and Chennells, 1976). As a result of the conference, a World Council for Gifted and

Talented Children was formed, made up of representatives from many different countries. The council's goals and purposes are as follows:

— To focus world attention on gifted children and their valuable potential contribution to the benefit of mankind.
— To explore the nature of their talents and resultant problems in childhood and adolescence.
— To create a "climate" of acceptance of gifted children, not as a privileged elite but as a valuable global asset.
— To assemble, for an exchange of ideas and experiences, people from all over the world who are interested in the gifted and talented.
— To persuade the governments of the world to recognize gifted children as a category for special attention in normal educational programs.
— To establish a means for a continuing worldwide exchange of ideas, experiences, teaching, and teacher-training techniques in respect to gifted children.

— Collis, 1981, pp. 154–55

As more and more nations begin to adopt these objectives, increased numbers of gifted and talented children will be permitted to better realize their potential and to make positive contributions to international peace and prosperity.

THE GIFTED IN THE UNITED STATES

How do gifted children fare in the United States as compared to how they fare in other countries? The federal government has encouraged the development of special services to meet the needs of gifted students. The extent of such services varies according to individual states and, within each state, according to individual districts. An examination of the variations between federal and state definitions of giftedness raises several issues that require resolution.

Federal Perspective

In 1972 increased recognition of the schools' failure to serve gifted children and the consequent loss of benefits to humankind led to establishment of the Office of Gifted and Talented within the Bureau of Education for the Handicapped. In his report to Congress that year, Commissioner of Education Sidney Marland noted that less than 4 percent of the gifted were receiving adequate services. The definition of gifted offered by Commissioner Marland's report included those capable of high performance in six areas (authors' interpretation of each area is given in brackets):

Gifted and talented children are those identified by professionally qualified persons who by virtue of outstanding abilities are capable of high performance. These are children who require differentiated educational programs and services beyond those normally provided by the regular school program in order to realize their contribution to self and society.

Children capable of high performance include those with demonstrated achievement and/or potential ability in any of the following areas:

1. General intellectual ability [high intelligence]
2. Specific academic aptitude [high ability in a content area such as mathematics, science, language arts, or foreign language]
3. Creative or productive thinking [high ability to invent novel, elaborate, or numerous ideas]
4. Leadership ability [high ability to move others to achieve common goals]
5. Visual and performing arts [high talent in painting, sculpture, drama, dance, music, or other artistic endeavors]
6. Psychomotor ability [high ability in athletics, mechanics, or other skill areas requiring gross or fine motor coordination]

— Marland, 1972, p. 2

Commissioner Marland noted that identification of gifted children according to a definition that included all six categories would encompass 3 to 5 percent of the school-age population.

Seven years later President Carter signed into law the Gifted and Talented Children's Education Act of 1978, which carried a new federal definition of giftedness:

The term "gifted and talented children" means children and, whenever applicable, youth, who are identified at the preschool, elementary, or secondary level as possessing demonstrated or potential abilities that give evidence of high performance capability in areas such as intellectual, creative, specific academic, or leadership ability, or in the performing and visual arts, and who by reason thereof, require services or activities not ordinarily provided by the school.

— P.L. 95–561, Title IX, Part A, Section 902

The 1978 definition has four noteworthy components. First, while it de-emphasizes (but does not exclude) psychomotor ability as a talent area, it maintains the earlier concept of giftedness as multidimensional and as including a heterogeneous group. Second, it makes specific reference to a broader age range: preschool through high school. Third, the definition clearly includes children who have high potential (not necessarily manifested in current behavior) as well as those who have already demonstrated superior capabilities. Finally, the definition continues the requirement of differentiated services. That is, only those children whose demonstrated or potential abilities necessitate special services may be considered gifted. A corollary of this component is that services for gifted students should be different from those available in the regular school program and should be matched to the gifted child's individual needs.

The Gifted and Talented Children's Education Act declared that gifted children constitute the nation's greatest resource for solving critical national problems. The act also provided financial assistance to state and local education agencies, institutions of higher education, and other organizations for the planning, development, and operation of programs for gifted and talented children, with special attention to be paid to the identification and education of gifted children from economically disadvantaged families. Unfortunately, with the Reagan administration's repeal of P.L. 95–561 and the dismantling of the Office of Gifted and Talented, the major federal impetus supporting special education for the gifted and talented ceased to exist.

Federal programs for the gifted and talented were merged in the education block grant by the Education Consolidation and Improvement Act of 1981, which defined gifted and talented in terms similar to previous legislation. According to the act, gifted individuals are those who

> give evidence of high performance capability in areas such as intellectual, creative, artistic, leadership capacity, or specific academic fields, and who require services or activities not ordinarily provided by the school in order to fully develop such capabilities.
>
> — P.L. 97–35, Section 582 (3) (a)

Until leadership at the federal level becomes a reality, the responsibility for determining what constitutes giftedness and talent will be left to the individual states. However, heterogeneity of students, wide age ranges, potential as well as demonstrated ability, and differentiated services remain important factors in any definition of the gifted and talented.

Variations by State

A 1967 analysis of state legislation for exceptional children (Ackerman and Weintraub, 1969) indicated that as early as 1939, Florida's education code required county boards of education to provide, insofar as practicable, special facilities for children with unusual abilities. In 1945 Kansas authorized its Division of Special Education to encourage school districts to serve gifted children by adapting instruction to their needs and to waive restrictions that interfered with these children's development. By 1967, seventeen states recognized the gifted in some way, and seven of these states provided legal guidelines for determining the type of children to be served.

A more recent study on state policy and delivery of services for gifted children was conducted by the Council for Exceptional Children for the U.S. Office of Education (Zettel, 1979a, b; 1980). As of the latest report (Zettel, 1980), thirty-nine states have legislation that mentions or defines gifted and talented children. These states variously place the gifted and talented under the rubrics of exceptional, gifted, and/or talented (within general education statutes), handicapped, or children in need of special programs. Although most states administer their gifted and talented programs through departments of special education, some do so through their curriculum or instruction divisions or through special departments like technical assistance or program development.

The report also indicates that forty-four states presently have regulations or guidelines for screening and identifying gifted children. Another survey (Gallagher et al., 1983), to which forty-seven states responded, found that twenty-eight states use the federal concept of including as gifted those talented in the intellectual, academic, creative, leadership, and artistic areas. The majority of states define giftedness in terms of intellectual ability, although 75 percent include creativity, 67 percent include leadership, and 67 percent include artistic talent.

States also vary with regard to their specific definitional criteria within each category of giftedness. A survey of state departments of education (Mitchell, 1984) indicated that most states select gifted and talented students through multiple criteria and intelligence tests with cutoffs ranging from 1.5 to 2.0 standard deviations above the mean (for example, 122.5 to 130.0 would be the cutoff score for an intelligence test). Some states leave the responsibility for determining specific criteria to local education agencies (Zettel, 1979a).

Surveys by Zettel (1980) and Mitchell (1984) also indicated that, overall, the states have made significant strides in providing services to gifted children. In terms of numbers served, the states reporting indicated that programs were provided for 383,939 children during the 1975–76 school year. By 1979–80, this figure had risen to 766,759—an increase of approximately 100 percent. A recent national survey reported that for 1984, 1.14 million (2.9 percent) of the 39 million children of public school age were served in gifted and talented programs (Council of State Directors of Programs for the Gifted, 1984). Thus, services for gifted children nationwide have expanded dramatically over the last ten years. Yet individual states vary widely in the percentage of school-age children served in gifted programs—from a low of 0.8 percent in Washington to a high of 7.8 percent in Nebraska. Thirteen of the forty-two states reporting enrollment data in the Council of State Directors' survey indicated serving less than 2 percent of public school enrollment. If we take as correct Commissioner Marland's estimate that 3 to 5 percent of the school-age population is gifted, a significant number of children eligible for gifted programs are still not receiving services.

Analysis of state appropriations for gifted and talented education also showed a gain, from $56,206,608 in 1976 to $195,756,113 in 1984 (Council of State Directors of Programs for the Gifted, 1984). The total amount spent in 1984, however, masks a disproportionate spending pattern. Fifty percent of state funds for the gifted and talented were generated by only four states: California, Florida, North Carolina, and Pennsylvania. Despite tremendous progress, inequities in services to the gifted and talented continue and must be addressed.

Definitional Issues

The variations among states in definitions and availability of services for the gifted raise two related issues that require resolution. These issues concern (a) the categories or types of giftedness accepted by the states and (b) the concepts of legal and inherent giftedness.

Categories of Giftedness. As indicated by Zettel's (1980) survey, most states recognize the intellectually, academically, and creatively gifted. Fewer states include in their definition of gifted those children who demonstrate high potential in the visual and performing arts or in leadership. One concern with regard to the accepted categories of giftedness is that failure to recognize and serve artistically or socially gifted children may result in an irredeemable loss of talent both to society and to the children whose gifts remain undeveloped. Barriers to nationwide inclusion of the artistically gifted and children with leadership potential arise from (*a*) the understandable reluctance on the part of taxpayers to support music, dance, or art lessons, which traditionally have been secured by individual parents through private lessons, and (*b*) the difficulty in objectively identifying the gifted in these areas, especially when attempting to measure potential as opposed to demonstrated ability. However, the spiritual sustenance brought by an Aaron Copland or a Charles Ives and the peace and goodwill wrought by a Martin Luther King, Jr., may be considered as worthy to humankind as Enrico Fermi's contributions to the harnessing of nuclear power.

A second concern regarding the categories of giftedness included in various definitions is that the categories may be too limited and too arbitrarily selected. Getzels and Dillon noted that many qualities such as compassion, ability to cope, and love are conspicuously absent from the typical taxonomies of giftedness:

> What is striking about the talents listed is not their apparent diversity but their similarity; not that they are not useful and socially acceptable but that so many useful and socially acceptable talents are not included. The talents listed are utilitarian and operational; that is, they are talents of doing or performing in a strictly functional, not to say marketable, sense. Certain other talents which are readily and universally recognized in everyday life are almost wholly overlooked.
>
> — Getzels and Dillon, 1973, p. 705

An early definition proposed by Witty broadly encompassed all gifts valued by society: ". . . we consider any child gifted whose performance, in a potentially valuable line of human activity, is consistently remarkable" (Witty, 1958, p. 62). However, Witty's conception of giftedness was ahead of its time. Educators concerned with the pragmatics of identification and services could not put this definition to practical use.

Legal versus Inherent Giftedness. A second definitional issue concerns the possibility that, because of variations between and within states, a child qualifying as gifted in one system may not necessarily qualify as gifted in another. The child who moves from system to system remains the same; his or her qualities are inherent. Yet the availability of services changes for that child if he or she does not meet the legal criteria of the new place of residence.

Assuming an adequate environment, most children who initially qualify as gifted will continue to do so over time and place. Yet the plight of the few whose label is changed raises an unsettling issue: Is giftedness a real quality inherent in the child, or is it a legal abstraction determined externally? Obviously, institutions must establish eligibility criteria for special services (handicapped or gifted) to prevent abuses, to maximize homogeneity of the special group, and to promote equitable decision making. Even the most flexible school system must conform to some set of definitional criteria to maintain quality control.

A Working Definition of Giftedness. A different concept of giftedness—one that takes into consideration the issues we have discussed—has been proposed by Renzulli (1978). In his definition giftedness is an interaction of (*a*) above-average intellectual ability, (*b*) high task commitment, and (*c*) high creativity. Gifted individuals would be those possessing or capable of developing this set of traits and applying them to any socially useful area. As noted by Renzulli, high intellectual or academic ability does not itself lead to adult achievement. The results of several studies reviewed by Renzulli indicated that creative accomplishment in adult life is not related or is only slightly related to traditional measures of academic success (IQ scores, achievement test scores, school grades). Renzulli concluded that most productive individuals were not straight A or high-scoring students; they fell below the ninety-fifth percentile. Cutoff scores used as definitional criteria for gifted programs need to be reevaluated in light of these findings. Task commitment, the second trait found in productive individuals, refers to a drive for involvement in a problem over an extended time period. This trait seems to differentiate highly successful from less successful individuals of high intelligence.

Renzulli's definition has two advantages. First, it focuses on a combination of traits that may help identify the children who will most likely lead creative, productive lives. Second, it eliminates the need to identify categories of giftedness; at the same time it extends the applications of gifted potential to any area valued by society. The main caution about this definition is its emphasis on production. One might ask whether a highly intelligent but chronically unmotivated child would not still be inherently gifted.

The definition of giftedness continues to be problematic. Some authorities distinguish between gifted and talented by separating intellectual and academic from artistic and creative abilities. Others define as gifted the highly intelligent and the well rounded and define as talented those who possess high ability in only one area. Because of the practical difficulties in differentiating between the two terms, most definitions combine giftedness and talent under a single umbrella. We shall follow suit. For our purposes, the gifted and talented will be defined as *individuals of any age who possess superior ability in an area valued by society*.

This definition, similar to Witty's, supports a broader view than could be held during Witty's time. Today multifactor conceptions of intelligence have challenged earlier unitary ideas. This definition reflects our philosophy that gifted education includes more than an emphasis on academics for gifted and talented students.

CHAPTER SUMMARY

This chapter has examined some other nations' views on the gifted and talented as a basis for putting into perspective the position of our own country. Nations around the globe are recognizing that the gifted and talented have special needs that require attention if such children are to fulfill their potential for both their own benefit and society's. Countries with differing social and political values have confronted the charge that providing special services is elitist and have resolved the issue in different ways. Democratized Japan, for example, has attempted to raise the overall standards of popular education rather than focus on the gifted and talented. England has rejected the idea of segregated services for gifted children to avoid the development of feelings of superiority. However, the regular educational institutions of both countries have rigorous systems of examinations that essentially permit the identification and tracking of the academically superior. In contrast, the Soviet Union offers special schools and facilities in a wide range of arts and sciences to talented students who qualify by examination and school performance.

The United States falls between these two extremes. Federal efforts have encouraged differentiated services to the gifted and talented, but the types of programs to be offered have not been mandated. Individual states formulate their own definitions and establish their own means of serving gifted children's needs. As a result, states vary in terms of definitions used, funding provided, and types of programs initiated. One potential problem stemming from this variation is that children may meet the legal definition in one educational system but not in another. Although nearly all states recognize the intellectually and academically gifted and, perhaps, the creatively gifted, fewer include those excelling in leadership and the visual and performing arts as gifted. States and local education agencies have developed a variety of programs to serve the gifted. These programs range from changes within the regular school setting to special classes and schools. Surveys of states over the past five years indicate dramatic increases in the numbers of gifted children being served. Yet, using as a norm the 3 to 5 percent incidence of giftedness among the general population, we can estimate that between 37 and 61 percent of those eligible for gifted programs are still not receiving appropriate services.

Although there is currently no nationwide definition of gifted and talented children, such children clearly exist in all age categories, represent a heterogeneous group of talents, may have potential or demonstrated high abilities, and may require special services. Because we have been too limited in the types of giftedness we have recognized, many valuable human gifts may have been ignored.

Having explored concepts of giftedness in the abstract, in the next section we will examine the psychology, development, and characteristics of gifted children in more concrete terms.

ACTIVITIES FOR THOUGHT AND DISCUSSION

1. Investigate the concepts of giftedness and the provision of services for the gifted in another country. How has the country dealt with the issue of elitism? What might you expect the differences to be between established and developing countries regarding gifted education?

2. Interview your congressional representative about views currently held in Washington regarding federal involvement in gifted education.

3. Review the rules and regulations governing gifted education in your state. What types or categories of giftedness are included? What division administers gifted programs? How would you evaluate your state's definition of gifted and talented children? What definitional changes, if any, would you suggest?

4. Explore the gifted and talented programs offered by your local school districts. How much flexibility does the state allow them in determining definitional criteria and in prescribing special services?

SECTION II

Psychological Perspectives

Chapter Three

THE NATURE
OF GIFTEDNESS

Television talk shows and the popular press have focused national attention on the question of whether giftedness can be purposefully developed. In broadcast interviews some parents of gifted children have attributed their children's accomplishments to specific techniques such as reading to the fetus *in utero*. Some educators from private institutions have reported success in teaching preverbal infants to recognize correct responses to addition problems. Stories such as these prompt parents and teachers to ask whether they can "make" children gifted. The development of gifted children encompasses not only their intellectual growth but their social and physical maturity as well. This chapter explores the origins of giftedness, the nature of intelligence, and the development of cognitive, social, and physical abilities in gifted children.

ORIGINS OF GIFTEDNESS

Early researchers and theorists on the nature of intelligence agreed that intelligence was a fixed characteristic genetically determined at conception. However, especially following World War I, the American ideals of egalitarianism and self-determination came into conflict with the idea of predetermined limits. Several investigators began pointing to the environment as the principal influence on intellectual development. The highly explosive nature–nurture (heredity–environment) controversy was launched and remains a volatile issue today. This section describes the two opposing viewpoints and the current perspectives on this issue.

Intelligence as Hereditary and Fixed (The Nature Argument)

Hunt (1961) traced the roots of the nature viewpoint to Charles Darwin's theory of natural selection. Published in 1859, *On the Origin of Species* presented the thesis of evolution as the survival of adaptive inherited characteristics. Ten years later, influenced by the concept of evolution, Darwin's famous cousin, Sir Francis Galton, published a study of distinguished men of Great Britain and attributed their "genius" to heredity. Galton later developed measures to assess inherited individual differences. These measures consisted of simple sensory, motor, and memory tasks, which later research did not support as predictors of academic achievement. Convinced of the hereditary nature of intelligence, Galton founded the eugenics movement. This movement sought to improve society through such means as curtailing reproduction of "inferior" specimens—for example, the mentally handicapped.

The next significant event to further the nature viewpoint occurred in France in 1905, when Binet and Simon developed a test that differentiated between low and high achievers in school (Hunt, 1961). In 1904 the French minister of public education had appointed Binet to a commission whose task was to devise a method of identifying Parisian schoolchildren who were likely to fail and hence were in need of special services. Binet and Simon based their test on a conceptualization of intelligence more complex than Galton's, involving judgment, reasoning, memory, imagination, comprehension, and aesthetic appreciation. Although Binet argued against intelligence as fixed and suggested that the capacity to learn can improve with instruction, the influence of two other men combined to overshadow Binet's cautions against hereditary interpretations of test performance. First, Cattell, who brought to the United States in the late 1800s the idea of using tests in the schools, was a student of Galton and an ardent supporter of the hereditary perspective. Second, Goddard, the person who first brought the Binet–Simon test to the United States, also promoted the hereditary viewpoint (Hunt, 1961). Goddard translated the Binet–Simon test for use in his investigation of the mentally retarded and authored the well-known study of the Kallikak family, often cited in support of the eugenics movement. Goddard's study traced the descendants of the union of a Revolutionary War soldier, Martin Kallikak, with a feeble-minded girl and the descendants of his later marriage to a girl of normal intelligence. Goddard identified many of the descendants of the first union as feeble-minded and cited a high incidence of illegitimacy and criminality among them. In contrast, descendants of the later marriage included a number of professionals and individuals regarded highly by the local society. Goddard concluded that feeble-mindedness was hereditary and recommended segregation of feeble-minded individuals.

The findings of research on intelligence conducted during the first half of this century have been used as evidence of the inherited and fixed nature of intelligence. Five types of data have been interpreted as supporting the nature argument (Hunt, 1961):

1. Data indicating that the average (group) IQ remains relatively constant from age to age and group to group;
2. Positive correlations among different intelligence devices, suggesting that they all measure a common trait interpreted as intelligence (Findings of constancy of average IQ and intercorrelations among various intelligence measures, however, are probably artifacts of the way test items are selected. That is, test developers often choose items that will yield constancy in IQ over age groups and high correlations with other tests purporting to assess the same trait.);
3. Data indicating the relative stability of IQs of individual children over time;
4. Positive correlations between intelligence test scores and later school achievement;
5. Correlations among the intelligence scores of individuals who vary in degree of genetic material in common and/or degree of environmental similarity.

Studies producing these data have generally been of three types. The first type, holding environment constant, compares correlations of intelligence scores of closely related individuals to correlations of scores of more distantly related people. That is, the intelligence scores of identical twins (sharing identical genes) are correlated and compared to those of fraternal twins, nontwin siblings, and unrelated children reared together. For example, Jensen (1969) summarized data from studies of relatives conducted in the 1960s and reported median correlation coefficients of 0.87 for identical twins reared together, 0.56 for same-sex fraternal twins, 0.55 for nontwin siblings reared together, and 0.24 for unrelated children reared together. These data have been interpreted as indicating that the greater the genetic similarity between individuals, the more similar their IQ scores.

A second type of investigation attempts to hold degree of genetic relationship constant while varying the environment, as in comparing the IQ scores of twins and siblings reared together with the scores of those reared apart. Jensen's (1969) summary indicated a median correlation of 0.87 for identical twins reared together, 0.75 for identical twins reared apart, 0.55 for nontwin siblings reared together, and 0.47 for nontwin siblings reared apart. Such data have been interpreted as suggesting that even when environments differ, children with similar genetic makeup show little variation in IQ scores. If differences in environment determine differences in intelligence, a greater discrepancy would be expected between the correlations of the IQ scores of identical twins reared together and those reared apart, with twins reared apart having a lower correlation coefficient.

A third type of study compares the relationship between the IQs of adopted children and those of both their biological and their adoptive parents. Reviews of such investigations suggest that environment accounts for little variation in children's IQ scores (MacMillan, 1982) because the relationship between the IQs of children and their biological mothers is higher than that between the IQs of children and their adoptive mothers, even though the children were raised by their adoptive mothers.

Based on studies of correlations of IQ scores among relatives, attempts have been made to derive a heritability quotient statistically and thus provide a stable estimate of the variation in IQ attributable to genetic inheritance. Prior to World War II there was agreement in the literature that genetics accounted for 80 percent of the variance in intelligence, with environment accounting for 20 percent (Hunt, 1961).

Intelligence as Environmentally Determined (The Nurture Argument)

The environmentalist faction reacted to the nature argument by positing that differences in intelligence result entirely from differences in experience. The strict environmentalist position has been criticized for raising false hopes about the ability of parents and educators to make mentally retarded children intellectually normal and to make intellectually normal children gifted (Zigler, 1970). That genetic inheritance contributes to individual differences in intelligence cannot be denied. The issue today concerns the relative contributions of heredity and environment.

Evidence used to support the environmentalist position includes reinterpretations of data from studies of related individuals, changes in IQ over time, and studies of the effects of differing environments.

Reinterpretations of Studies of Relatives. Proponents of the nurture argument point out that heritability estimates of IQ based on studies of people who are related are not pure estimates of the variance in IQ attributable to genetic inheritance; the estimates also include variance attributable to environment. Bronfenbrenner (1972) argued that heritability estimates derived from studies of identical twins reared together versus studies of fraternal twins reared together assume that the environments for identical twins are no more similar than those for fraternal twins. However, the environments of identical twins may in fact be *more* alike; evidence indicates that identical twins are more often placed in similar situations and treated more similarly by parents than are fraternal twins. Hence, the higher correlation for identical twins may be due to more similar environments as well as to more similar genetic inheritance. Also, heritability estimates based on studies of identical twins reared together versus studies of those reared apart assume that the environments of twins reared apart are different. However, data suggest that when twins are separated—by adoption, for example—placement agencies make a concerted effort to place them in similar settings. Moreover, adoption studies suggest that even when twins are not selectively placed, the foster settings are fairly uniform (Bronfenbrenner, 1972). As a result, the relationship between correlations of twins reared together and twins reared apart may reflect similarity in both genetic inheritance *and* environment.

Changes in IQ. Longitudinal studies reported during the late 1940s indicated that children given intelligence tests periodically between infancy and eighteen years of age demonstrated significant upward or downward shifts in IQ score, rendering questionable the idea of fixed intelligence. Between the ages of six and eighteen, changes of 15 IQ points were common, with some children showing changes of 30 to 50 points. Shifts in IQ scores over time can be explained in part by differences in the test items used to measure intelligence at different age levels. However, changes in some children's scores may be attributable to environmental events such as illness and strained relationships (Biehler, 1981; Hunt, 1961). Studies of the same individuals over long periods of time also show gains in measured intelligence, at least until the fourth decade of life (Honzik, 1973).

Effects of Differing Environments. Proponents of environmental contributions to intelligence gain support for their theory from studies on the effects of animal deprivation, on institutionalization, and on parenting practices. Animal studies generally compare initially identical groups of animals that have been raised from birth in either deprived or enriched environments. In one classic example Krech (1971) found that rats raised in an enriched environment demonstrated superior problem-solving behavior and greater weight and density of the brain cortex. Despite having had an adequate food supply, rats raised in an unstimulating environment showed a relatively deteriorated brain structure. Similar experiments with dogs and primates corroborate the negative effects of an impoverished early environment on later cognitive, social, and parenting behaviors.

Although it is risky to apply the findings of animal research to humans, studies of children raised in drastically differing circumstances also point to the powerful influence of environment on development. Skeels and Dye (1939) compared the effects of a stimulating versus a deprived environment on young orphanage children. Children placed in the stimulating environment showed an average gain of 28 IQ points. A follow-up of the children twenty years later demonstrated that the enriched group's gain had persisted, with subjects having completed more years of schooling and having secured better employment than comparison subjects, several of whom were still institutionalized and unemployed (Skeels, 1966). More recent investigations of the effects of compensatory preschool programs for low-income children have also demonstrated at least short-term gains in IQ and evidence of longer-term school success (Darlington et al., 1980).

Several researchers have pointed to differences in language modeling and child-rearing attitudes and behaviors of parents as factors affecting their children's cognitive development. These studies will be discussed in more detail in Chapter 14, which deals with the role parents play in the development of children's intelligence and creativity.

Current Perspectives

Recent research regarding the heredity–environment issue and the nature of giftedness has encompassed four areas: (a) the nature of the heredity–environment relationship in producing individual differences in intelligence, (b) the origin of specific talents and abilities, (c) identification of environmental factors related to cognitive potential, and (d) neurophysiological correlates of intelligence.

Nature of the Heredity–Environment Relationship. Today there is no doubt that genetic factors account for a major portion of individual differences in mental ability (Bronfenbrenner, 1972; Scarr-Salapatek, 1975). However, recent studies of twins, nontwin siblings, and parent–offspring pairs using larger samples than were used in earlier investigations suggest that the heritability of intelligence is closer to 0.50 than to the 0.70 or 0.80 indicated in earlier studies (Plomin and DeFries, 1980). Yet even this lower estimate continues to indicate that genes play a major role in determining variation in IQ.

Several theorists have described models that attempt to explain how heredity and environment interact to produce an individual's current level of intellectual functioning. Jensen (1969) suggested a threshold hypothesis in which a certain minimum quality of environment is required for normal intellectual development. Above the threshold, variations in environment do not lead to major differences in intelligence. Thus, removing children from extremely deprived environments (below the minimum quality for normal development), such as those described in studies of early institutions and orphanages, would result in substantial IQ gains. However, moving children from a lower- to a middle-income environment would not, according to Jensen, result in dramatic increases in intellectual ability. The threshold hypothesis suggests that heredity sets limits for intellectual potential, while the quality of environment determines the extent to which that potential is achieved.

Scarr-Salapatek (1975) presented a reaction range model indicating that the same enriched or deprived environment affects individuals differently, depending on their genetic makeup. According to this model, people with lower inherited IQs have smaller reaction ranges—that is, smaller distances between their lower and upper limits of intelligence. Environmental factors, therefore, have less effect on the level of intellectual ability these individuals achieve. People with higher genetically determined intellectual potential have larger reaction ranges and therefore are more influenced by being moved from a restricted to an enriched environment. The major implication of the reaction range model is that no one-to-one correspondence exists between genetically determined potential and intellectual level ultimately achieved or between environmental condition and intellectual level achieved. Rather, a variety of heredity–environment combinations can produce the same IQ. Studies of "invulnerable" children, those who succeed in life despite extremely deprived or abnormal environments (e.g., Pines, 1979), provide support for the argument that the negative effects of a poor environment can be overcome, given the necessary combination of inherited abilities, personality characteristics, and fortuitous events.

Origin of Specific Talents and Abilities. Recent literature on the heredity–environment issue has revealed increased interest in the type of ability that is inherited. That is, do people inherit general intelligence only, specific abilities only (for example, math ability, creativity, or musical talent), or both general and specific abilities? It has been argued that genius can be neither suppressed nor improved, but talent can be fostered, its expression being contingent upon interest and instruction. Several authors (e.g., Mierke, 1962) have suggested that although genetic contribution does play a role, special abilities depend heavily on interest and opportunity to pursue the interest. Feldman's (1979) case studies of children extremely gifted in chess, music, and mathematics indicated that early achievement in these fields requires intensive education as well as gifted potential. Bobby Fischer learned to play chess at age six, but he also read hundreds of books about chess and had intensive formal instruction before reaching the rank of grand master at fifteen. Feldman argued that early prodigious achievement does not occur spontaneously but requires motivation and the opportunity to acquire the accumulated knowledge of the field. Large-scale investigations of gifted pianists, swimmers, and mathematicians have concluded that environmental factors contributed greatly to their success (Bloom, 1982; Bloom and Sosniak, 1981). Parents played a major role in supporting talent development by encouraging the child's interest, by providing special instruction, and by guiding and reinforcing practice.

Research attempting to sort out the relative contributions of genetics and environment to specific abilities has not been conclusive. DeFries, Vandenberg, and McClearn (1976) reviewed several investigations of the heritability of specific cognitive abilities. Data from twin studies lend support to the idea that some abilities (for example, spatial ability) may be more heritable than others (for example, word fluency). However, results of other studies suggest that a single genetic component underlies specific cognitive abilities. Family studies indicate greater resemblance between members of parent–offspring and sibling pairs for verbal than for nonverbal tasks. This resemblance may be due to higher heritability of verbal ability and/or to similarity in environment. DeFries and coauthors concluded that additional research with larger sample sizes is needed in this area.

Specific Environmental Factors. Evidence is fairly consistent that a positive relationship exists between socioeconomic status and cognitive performance. Yet not all upper-income children perform well on cognitive tasks, nor do all lower-income children perform poorly. In fact, a great amount of variability exists within each socioeconomic group. One trend apparent in the literature is the identification of specific factors within the environment that affect intelligence and achievement. For example, what specific events within a given child's home helped produce the child's particular ways of responding to academic tasks? Investigators have pointed to differences among home environments in (*a*) language modeling (mothers' specificity of instruction, use of praise versus criticism, and tendency to reason with their children rather than to command); (*b*) physical environment (number of individuals residing in the house, quality of nutrition and medical care, adequacy of housing structure, proportion of adult models, and availability of educational materials); and (*c*) parental attitudes (level of aspirations for children, values placed on education and individual achievement, and willingness to work directly with children on academic tasks). Differences among families in these areas and corresponding effects on achievement will be discussed in more detail in Chapter 14, which explores the influence of parent behaviors on gifted and talented children. It should be emphasized that children are not passively shaped by their parents, as was Galatea by Pygmalion, or by their physical environment. Rather, parents also *respond* to and are influenced by their children's initiatives. A substantial amount of variance in cognitive ability occurs *within* families, variance that is not reduced by eliminating environmental differences *between* families (Willerman, 1979).

Neurological Correlates of Intelligence. Sir Russell Brain (1960) speculated that the genius differs from ordinary individuals in the organization of his or her central nervous system. The genius, according to Brain, does not necessarily possess a greater number of nerve cells. Instead, the nerve cells are grouped into functional patterns called schemas, and the genius is richer in schemas. Brain offered as an analogy the difference between a child's reader and a Shakespearean play; both are composed from the same twenty-six letters, but how the letters are organized results in vastly different products.

More recent scientific efforts to demonstrate a neurophysiological basis for differences in intelligence provide preliminary support for the hypothesis that intellectually gifted individuals differ biologically from individuals of normal intelligence. Based on her review of animal and brain/mind research, Clark (1983) suggested that gifted individuals may (*a*) demonstrate accelerated synaptic activity, resulting in more rapid information processing; (*b*) have biochemically richer neurons, permitting more complex thought patterns; (*c*) make more use of prefrontal cortex activity, allowing increased planning, insight, and intuitive thinking; (*d*) enter more quickly and remain longer in the alpha state of brain-wave activity, thereby enjoying more relaxed learning, improved memory, and better integration of hemispheric functioning; and (*e*) have more and more frequent coherence and synchronicity of brain rhythms, permitting increased concentration and deeper inquiry.

Research on the relationship between brain functioning and learning is just beginning and may have exciting implications for educators of the gifted. Evidence supporting neurological differences between gifted and nongifted individuals will not, however, end the nature–nurture controversy. Biological differences may result from genetic inheritance and/or from the quality of the environment. Until there are definitive findings on both issues, Sir Russell Brain's words are appropriate: "Can anyone doubt that these differences between geniuses and ordinary folk and between one type of genius and another depend on differences of neural organization, partly innate and partly developed by use?" (Brain, 1960, pp. 14–15).

NATURE AND DEVELOPMENT OF INTELLIGENCE

In the preceding section we discussed the theories that general intelligence (and, perhaps, special abilities) originates both in genetic inheritance and in environmental experience. We also discussed the theory that intellectually gifted individuals may evidence superiority in the quality of their neurological processing. Any discussion of the origins of intelligence and other abilities assumes that intelligence exists as a measurable human characteristic that manifests itself to a greater or lesser degree among different individuals. Yet despite the volumes of philosophical, theoretical, and empirical literature on intelligence dating from the beginnings of recorded history, no consensus definition exists. In fact, some writers argue that intelligence is only a hypothetical construct invented by early theorists to explain and predict individual differences in behavior. These theorists have generally described intelligence in three ways: (*a*) the capacity to learn, (*b*) the totality of knowledge acquired, and (*c*) the ability to adapt to new situations in the environment (Robinson and Robinson, 1976). More recent conceptualizations of intelligence can be organized for purposes of discussion into factor, developmental, and information-processing theories.

Factor Theories

Factor theories attempt to describe intelligence in terms of its structure—that is, as being composed of one or more independent traits. Recent factor theories were developed from data using the statistical process of factor analysis. Factor-analytic procedures help researchers identify the traits or abilities (factors) that make up the construct being investigated. The general procedure permits the researcher to determine the number and nature of variables underlying a set of measures, such as intelligence subtests (measures may also be the individual items of a single test or may be several different tests). When different subtests correlate with one factor but not with any other, the subtests that correlate most highly with each factor are examined to determine what the factor represents. For example, assume that vocabulary, reading, and spelling subtests are highly correlated with factor A only, while mazes, puzzles, and form copying correlate highly with factor B but not with factor A. Because the subtests correlated with factor A all require language skills, the investigator might label factor A a language factor. Similarly, the subtests related to factor B might be interpreted as forming a spatial relations factor. Factor analysis has been used by investigators attempting to discover whether intelligence can be accounted for by a single, general factor or by a number of specific, independent factors.

Early Factor Theories of Intelligence. The English psychologist Charles Spearman is credited with introducing factor analysis into psychology. During the first quarter of this century, he proposed a two-factor theory of intelligence (Spearman, 1927). According to Spearman, a single general factor (g) underlies all intellectual operations, from verbal analogies to spatial relationships. He suggested that all intellectual tests or activities have the g-factor in common, with the remaining elements of the activities composed of specific (s) factors independent of the g-factor. Positive correlations among many diverse tests of mental ability were cited as evidence supporting a g-factor. Spearman described this factor as the ability to perceive, manipulate, and use relations. Opposing Spearman's view, Thorndike (1925) argued that intelligence cannot be accounted for by a single general factor but instead is a function of many highly specific and independent abilities. During the next decade Thurstone (1938) conducted a series of factor-analytic studies that led to the identification of seven factors, or "primary abilities," underlying intelligence tests: verbal comprehension, word fluency, number (speed and accuracy of arithmetic computation), spatial relations, associative memory, perception, and reasoning.

Guilford's Structure-of-Intellect Model. Guilford (1959, 1967, 1973) extended Thorndike's multifactor theory and developed a unique three-dimensional model of intelligence based on multifactor-analytic procedures. Guilford's theory represents a comprehensive effort to incorporate the abilities underlying all cognitive behaviors. The model goes beyond factors derivable from existing tests by projecting previously unidentified factors. As illustrated in Figure 3.1, the structure-of-intellect (SI) model posits 120 unique abilities that compose the intellect. These discrete abilities are defined in terms of three parameters: operations, products, and contents. Combining the five types of operations, six types of products, and four types of contents yields the 120 abilities. When the model was first developed, almost 40 abilities had been discovered through factor analysis. By 1973 nearly 100 abilities had been demonstrated by additional tests

Figure 3.1   Guilford's structure-of-intellect model (Guilford, 1973, p. 636)

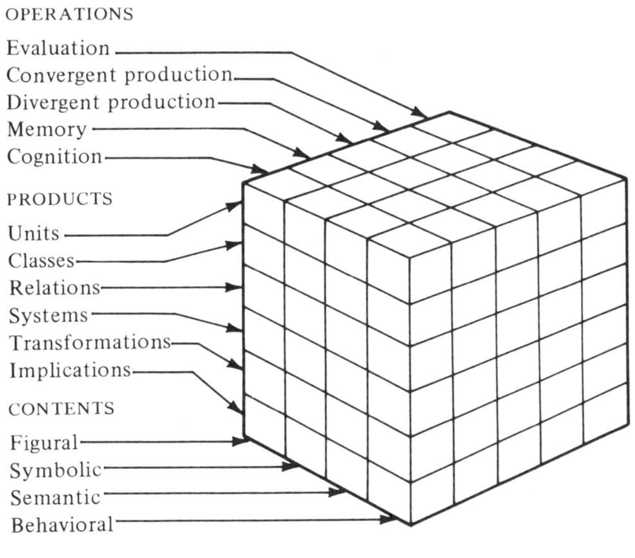

thought to represent those abilities. Guilford (1973) defined the three SI parameters and fifteen categories as follows:

1. *Operations* refer to major intellectual activities or processes, or to what the individual does with information.

   Cognition: the discovery or recognition of information, comprehension or understanding

   Memory: the process of storing information

   Divergent production: the generation of many and various ideas from given information (for example, naming as many birds as one can think of)

   Convergent production: the generation of information from given information, with emphasis on conventionally accepted best outcomes (for example, naming the state bird of California)

   Evaluation: the making of decisions or judgments based on logical criteria (not including judgments based on aesthetic and ethical values)

2. *Contents* describe broad classes or types of information operated upon.

   Figural: information in concrete form, as perceived from sensory input or recalled (a number of visual–figural, auditory–figural, and kinesthetic–figural abilities have been identified)

   Symbolic: information in the form of signs (letters, numbers, musical notations, codes, and words) when considered independent of meanings and form

   Semantic: information that communicates meaning

   Behavioral: information involved in the nonverbal interactions of individuals and transmitted through sensory cues such as body posture, facial expression, tone of voice, and choice of words

3. *Products* are the organizational forms that information takes in the individual's processing of it.

   Units: single entities or items of information

   Classes: sets of items grouped on the basis of shared attributes

   Relations: connections between items of information based on what they have in common (for example, a triangle is half of a diamond)

   Systems: organized collections of items of information; complexes composed of interrelated parts (for example, equations are symbolic systems, and a social situation is a behavioral system)

   Transformations: changes, redefinitions, or modifications in an existing item of information (for example, a pun is a semantic transformation)

   Implications: items of information suggested by other items of information; inferences

Each of the 120 potential abilities is defined by the intersection of the categories that lie along the three dimensions of operations, contents, and products. For example, the ability defined as divergent-figural-units may be assessed and practiced by having the student create many different designs out of squares.

Based upon analyses of methodological procedures used for factor derivation, Guilford's assumptions about the independence of the factors has been criticized. Eysenck concluded that Guilford's "attempt to construct a structure-of-intellect model has not been successful and cannot at the moment dethrone the paradigm originally set up by Spearman and Thurstone" (Eysenck, 1979, p. 182). Eysenck reconciled the disparate views about the nature of intelligence by suggesting a hierarchical model. According to this model, there exists a general intelligence (g) that underlies a number of correlated primary abilities, such as those identified by Thurstone. Eysenck gives Guilford credit for adding important new primary factors within the hierarchical model.

Implications of Factor Theories. Three implications of major import for gifted education stem from factor theories of intelligence. The first implication concerns the issue of single-factor versus multifactor theories of intelligence; the other two stem primarily from Guilford's SI model. The decision to accept a single or a multifactor theory has an impact on the definition of giftedness and hence on what type of individual is subsequently identified as gifted. Acceptance of a single-factor approach promotes the idea that giftedness is synonymous with high general intelligence as measured by a single IQ score. In contrast, adherence to a multifactor model of intelligence permits a definition of giftedness that includes individuals who excel in one or more of several different ability areas (for example, mathematics, the arts, or creativity). A multifactor theory is also consistent with the notion that a gifted individual may demonstrate superiority in some areas but perform at an average or below-average level in others.

Guilford's structure-of-intellect model already has had profound influence on the field of gifted education in two ways. First, although Guilford was not the first to introduce the concepts of divergent and convergent production, his distinction between these two types of operations within the SI model has generated tremendous interest in theory, research, and practice relative to creative thinking. Second, Guilford's model provided the basis for development of SOI Learning Abilities Tests (Meeker, 1977), which some educators describe as the most comprehensive tests of abilities for identifying gifted individuals; most other intelligence tests fail to assess creative and other nonconvergent abilities. Mary Meeker's Structure of Intellect Institute in California provides materials and training to help practitioners translate specific structure-of-intellect abilities into curriculum and instruction strategies.

Guilford's model will continue to be influential. It has potential to provide methods for identifying and working with children who possess talent in specific areas. For example, measures of abilities in figural content may ultimately aid in the identification of children gifted in the visual and performing arts. Similarly, tests of abilities in behavioral content may help educators discover socially gifted children.

Gardner's Theory of Multiple Intelligences. Psychologist Howard Gardner (1982, 1983) recently proposed a multifactor theory that human intelligence consists of seven semiautonomous domains: (*a*) linguistic, (*b*) musical, (*c*) mathematical–logical, (*d*) visual–spatial, (*e*) bodily kinesthetic, (*f*) social–interpersonal, and (*g*) intrapersonal. Gardner's theory is unique in two ways. First, drawing on data from individuals who sustained injury to different parts of the brain, Gardner posits that the seven types of competence have independent existences in the neural system—that is, each has its own neurological organization. Second, Gardner recognizes abilities not generally included as areas of cognitive competence: music, fine and gross motor skills, and the two "personal" abilities. Interpersonal intelligence refers to the ability to understand and interact with others. Intrapersonal intelligence is defined as one's ability to know oneself and to have a developed sense of identity.

Gardner's theory has implications for the definition, identification, and education of the gifted and talented. The theory supports a broad definition of giftedness that includes individuals who are socially, personally, and motorically gifted. If accepted, this definition would require that the assessment process, including the use of experiential and observational methods, be viewed anew. Gardner also suggests that areas of weakness can be improved if identified early. Educators could facilitate the development of strengths by broadening the definition of schooling to include the community. For example, students gifted in the spatial domain might work with an architect in a setting outside the classroom.

Developmental Theories

Hunt has argued that factor theories of intelligence, including those of Spearman, Thurstone, and Guilford, have produced categories that in all probability are unrelated to the natural structures and processes that compose human problem solving: "It might appear that factor-analytic studies of intelligence have revealed the roof, the walls, and the cupola of the intelligence barn but missed the basic structure of the barn itself" (Hunt, 1961, p. 304). He offers as an alternative Piaget's developmental theory of intelligence, which, he suggests, describes the natural structures of problem-solving processes.

Piaget's Theory of Cognitive Development. Jean Piaget, Switzerland's noted genetic epistemologist, proposed a more holistic model of the development of human cognition from birth to adolescence (Piaget, 1950, 1958). According to this model, cognitive development consists of progression through an invariant sequence of stages, with the child incorporating the structures (organized patterns for dealing with the environment) acquired at each stage into new, higher-order structures at each succeeding stage. The child's progression from stage to stage is a result of adaptation, or interactions between the child's maturational level and the environment. Adaptation consists of two complementary processes: (*a*) assimilation, or the incorporating of features of the environment into the child's existing structures, and (b) accommodation, the modifying of one's structures in response to environmental demands. For example, when an infant encounters a mobile dangling from the crib, the infant must *accommodate* his or her vision and movements to the distance. The infant also *assimilates* the mobile into already existing patterns of behavior—that is, structures for reaching and grasping.

As a result of assimilation and accommodation, new, qualitatively different structures are continually created out of previously acquired structures to assist the child in interacting with the environment. Piaget described the development of these structures in a series of stages. During the *sensorimotor* stage (birth to eighteen months), the child has not yet acquired language. The infant manifests intelligence through actions on objects, such as jiggling the crib to put the mobile in motion. The second, or *preoperational*, stage (eighteen months to seven years) is characterized by the use of language, symbolic behavior, and inability to conserve. The two-year-old evidences symbolic behavior by pretending that a can is a glass and "drinking" from it. However, the preoperational child has not yet acquired the structures necessary for conservation or the ability to recognize that matter is conserved despite superficial changes in shape or form. For example, when a three-year-old is presented with two equal balls of clay, one of which is subsequently rolled into a cigar shape, the child perceives the ball and the cigar as being unequal in size. When asked which is larger, the child may attend only to length and select the cigar or only to width and choose the ball. The two dimensions are not considered simultaneously. The preoperational child is also described as egocentric—that is, as having difficulty understanding another's point of view.

Children in the stage of *concrete operations* (seven to twelve years) have acquired the rules of conservation. The concrete operational child also demonstrates understanding of relational concepts, such as heavier and longer, and can order objects based on these relations. Finally, this child can produce a mental image of a series of actions, such as how to get from home to school. The last stage, *formal operations*, is entered at around the age of twelve. The adolescent who has achieved formal operations differs from the concrete operational child in that the adolescent can consider all possible ways of solving a problem, think in hypothetical terms, and use abstract rules in problem solving.

Piaget's theory suggests that although children may attain the different stages at varying ages, all children follow the same sequence. Progression from stage to stage is facilitated by two tendencies common to all organisms: organization and equilibrium. *Organization* refers to the movement toward increasingly integrated and higher-order structures. *Equilibrium* is the tendency of organisms toward a balance between self and environment. For example, at some point in midchildhood, maturity and experience will enable the child to reach a point when his or her available structures can no longer accommodate or reconcile the conflicting ideas that (a) the cigar-shaped clay must be made of more clay because it is longer than the ball and (*b*) the cigar-shaped clay was formed from an equivalent ball without any additions of mass. The child experiences disequilibrium and is naturally motivated to resolve the conflict. Resolution results in both renewed equilibrium and attainment of higher-order structures (for example, structures for conservation).

Several implications that psychologists and educators have drawn from Piaget's theory are relevant to the education of gifted children. First, the young child views the world in a qualitatively different way than adults do. Second, learning is based on the acquisition of higher-order structures built on previous structures and hence involves the acquisition of broad, general rules, or maps, rather than of specific, isolated facts. Third, progression through the stages is motivated by desire for competence and facilitated by the presentation of an optimally challenging task or discrepant event that predisposes the child to disequilibrium. Fourth, the child is an active seeker of new information rather than a passive responder to stimuli. Fifth, children learn best through interacting with and manipulating the environment. Finally, group interactions may present children with ideas that conflict with their own, thereby encouraging accommodation, assimilation, and new growth.

Several investigators have explored the stages of development of a variety of gifted and nongifted populations. In a recent review of research, Carter and Ormrod (1982) indicated that mentally retarded, average, and gifted children follow the same pattern or sequence of stage progression, supporting Piaget's view of sequence invariance. However, studies investigating differences between gifted and nongifted learners in terms of *rate* of progression have yielded conflicting results. The discrepant findings may be accounted for by investigators' use of different measures for assessing level of cognitive development and by differences in the age groups studied. Young gifted children may not show superiority over average peers in rate of cognitive development because such development, according to Piaget, is limited by maturation and experience. The rate of maturation and the amount and variety of experience may not differ for gifted and nongifted children in the early years. Based on their review, Carter and Ormrod also suggest that gifted children's rate of progression may depend on whether they have already attained a stage or whether they are in transition between stages. Some evidence suggests that gifted children progress more rapidly than nongifted children *within* a stage but achieve transitions to concrete and formal operations at about the same age as their average peers.

However, Carter and Ormrod's own research (Carter, 1985; Carter and Ormrod, 1982) indicates that gifted children both progress more rapidly than nongifted children within a stage and demonstrate earlier transition to succeeding stages. Based on a study of the cognitive development of 125 gifted and 98 average children aged ten through fifteen, Carter and Ormrod (1982) found that (*a*) the gifted outperformed their peers of average abilities at each age level and (*b*) the gifted achieved formal operational thought at earlier ages. The majority of average children, including fifteen-year-olds, had not attained the stage of formal operations but were in transition. The gifted subjects entered formal operations by age twelve or thirteen. Carter (1985) found that although the trend is not consistent across all age groups, gifted children are approximately two years ahead of average children in demonstrating certain cognitive operations.

Based on their findings, Carter and Ormrod suggest that, because gifted children enter formal operations at earlier ages than do average children, they require special curricular interventions to prevent boredom and frustration. However, teachers should not assume that every gifted twelve-year-old has achieved the stage of formal operations. Rather, every child should be assessed on measures designed to determine level of cognitive development.

Criticisms of Piaget's Theory. Piaget's developmental theory has been criticized on several grounds. First, several investigators (e.g., Eysenck, 1979) have interpreted correlational data as indicating that Piagetian tasks designed to assess cognitive development in reality measure general intelligence (g). However, Eysenck also notes that Piaget's work has helped to determine the precise nature of changes in cognitive thought as development progresses. Second, more recent studies of cognitive development in young children (e.g., Gelman, 1979) have indicated that preschoolers are not egocentric and unable to conserve. Rather, when simpler tasks are used to evaluate their thinking, preschool-age children demonstrate an ability to consider the perspectives of others and an ability to conserve. Other researchers (e.g., Urberg and Docherty, 1976) have counterargued that the simpler tasks measure lower levels of the cognitive structures being studied (for example, the ability to take another's perspective). While we await additional research that will yield more definitive answers, the contributions of Piaget's theory to our thinking about the learning *process* cannot be denied.

Information-Processing Theories

Information-processing theories attempt to define precisely the processes or operations individuals employ in solving particular problems. These operations include sensory processing, encoding and decoding strategies, and memory processing. Information-processing theories differ from factor theories in that the former analyze the sequence of steps individuals use to perform different tasks, whereas factor theories seek to determine the independent variables that make up individuals' performance on the same type of task (for instance, an intelligence test). Information-processing theories differ from developmental theories in that developmental theories describe changes in human problem-solving mechanisms from birth to adulthood, while information-processing theories describe events within a particular problem-solving situation.

One approach to information processing is computer simulation (e.g., Newell and Simon, 1972). Computer simulation involves (*a*) careful analysis of subjects' descriptions of their thought processes and behaviors while solving a problem, (*b*) specifying these behaviors as a computer program, and (*c*) testing the program on a computer to determine the closeness of the match. The assumption is that a close match between the subjects' descriptions of steps in successful problem solution and the computer's steps in reaching the same solution indicates the accuracy of the subjects' descriptions.

Another approach that has been applied directly to gifted individuals (mainly college-age adults) is Sternberg's (1977, 1981) componential theory of human intelligence. Sternberg analyzed human problem solving as involving elementary information processes, or components, that perform five functions: metacomponents and performance, acquisition, retention, and transfer components. According to Sternberg's (1981) theory of intellectual giftedness, giftedness can be understood in terms of the superior functioning of, activation of, and feedback from information-processing components and may be trainable.

Sternberg describes metacomponents as the executive functions of planning and decision making in problem solving. He identifies six metacomponents. The first, problem recognition, refers to the important function of recognizing that a problem exists and defining the nature of the problem to be solved. The second metacomponent is the generation and determination of steps for solving the problem. Next is the selection of strategies for problem solving. Strategy selection may involve sequencing the identified steps, knowing when to apply specific steps, and knowing what strategy is best for oneself. The fourth metacomponent is the selection of representations for information, or the best mode for conceptualizing the problem. For example, when attacking a physics problem, the student must know which part of the task requires linguistic representation and which part requires spatial representation. The fifth metacomponent consists of making decisions regarding the allocation of componential resources, or determining which of several tasks or which part of a single task merits the most resources in terms of time and energy. Solution monitoring, the final metacomponent, refers to using feedback to determine what steps should be taken next and being flexible in changing plans as the situation dictates.

Sternberg defines performance components as the seven processes used to execute the problem-solving strategy planned by the metacomponents. The performance components can be described in terms of the problem of writing a paper about the causes of the Vietnam War. *Encoding* the problem involves identifying the relevant facts. *Inference* refers to the drawing of relationships between objects or ideas—for example, between the Communist presence in Vietnam and American democratic ideals. *Mapping* requires the relating of the features in one domain to those in another—for example, comparing the causes of the Vietnam War to those of the Korean War. In *application*, predictions are made on the basis of one situation or event and are applied to what will happen in another situation. For example, if the student has inferred that the American military will become active in any country threatened by communism, he or she might predict American military involvement in Nicaragua. In *comparison*, the student compares the prediction made in the application process to other alternatives, such as those suggested by news analysts. *Justification* refers to the process of verifying which option is the best one. Finally, the student makes a *response*, communicating the solution of the problem through writing the paper. Sternberg suggests that metacomponents and some performance components are common to all tasks and may contribute to a general intelligence (g) factor, making componential theory compatible with factor theories.

Sternberg describes acquisition components as those skills used in learning new information. Retention components involve retrieving previously acquired information. Transfer components refer to generalizing information from one context to another. Sternberg indicates that the specific components that make up acquisition, retention, and transfer have not yet been identified through research.

Sternberg's componential theory of information processing has two major implications for the education of gifted individuals. First, componential theory provides a different way of perceiving or defining intellectual giftedness: It defines giftedness as superior access to and implementation of information-processing components (especially in the use of feedback to alter other components). Second, Sternberg suggests that success in training individuals in access and implementation should make it possible to "train individuals to become 'more intelligent,' if not to become truly gifted" (Sternberg, 1981, p. 92). Moreover, according to Sternberg, some evidence already exists that individuals can be trained in the components. Much of Sternberg's work was conducted with adults, and additional research with school-age gifted children is required. Alexander (1984) has described a training program for gifted students based on Sternberg's componential theory. Subjects (included fourth-grade children) are being taught to apply the components to nonlinguistic analogies, then to linguistic analogies developed in sentences, paragraphs, and stories; and finally to performance in content areas.

A recent refinement of Sternberg's information-processing approach (Davidson and Sternberg, 1984) posited that one major way in which the intellectually gifted differ from the intellectually average is in insight ability, which involves three separate but related processes. The first, selective encoding, refers to the ability to discriminate between relevant and irrelevant information, as in selecting the appropriate clues to solve a mystery. A second process is selective combination, or synthesizing pieces of information into a unified whole. Finally, selective comparison is the ability to relate new information to previously acquired information, as in using past experience to solve a current problem. From a series of studies on fourth- through sixth-grade children, Davidson and Sternberg (1984) reported finding that (*a*) performance is consistent with their information-processing theory of insight and (*b*) certain aspects of insight performance can be trained in both gifted and intellectually average children.

Consistent with the information-processing theory, though not definitive with regard to specific components or processes, some studies have indicated that bright children do process information differently than do children of average intelligence. Moller (1983) has suggested that intellectually gifted children take less time to retrieve information stored in long-term memory, as indicated by measures of reaction time. After examining the quality of information-processing strategies, Scruggs and Mastropieri (1984) reported that gifted students outperform their nongifted peers on recall tasks through their superiority in spontaneously producing recall strategies and in the complexity of those strategies. For example, to recall the word pair *king–table*, a complex strategy would be to use the word *Arthur* as a mediator; a simple, less effective strategy would be to repeat the word pair.

In sum, there are several approaches to defining intelligence, each suggesting a different conceptualization of giftedness. Single-factor theories (for example, Spearman's g-factor theory) are compatible with a definition of gifted individuals as possessing a high level of intelligence that underlies performance in a variety of areas. Multifactor models, such as Guilford's structure-of-intellect model, suggest that individuals may be gifted in some specific areas, such as mathematics, creativity, or the arts, and not necessarily gifted in other areas. Multifactor theories are more compatible with current definitions of giftedness. Information-processing approaches, represented by Sternberg's componential theory of giftedness, hypothesize that intelligence can be improved through the acquisition and efficient implementation of a set of problem-solving steps. According to this view, teachers will ultimately be able to "make" children gifted. Developmental theories, in contrast, imply that intelligence cannot be taught as a series of skills but can only be encouraged by providing optimally challenging opportunities matched to each child's level of maturation and experience.

Thus, depending on the theory of intelligence used, gifted individuals may differ from their nongifted peers in such areas as neurological functioning, cognitive development, or information processing. The next section addresses whether gifted individuals can be considered unique in their physical and social development.

PHYSICAL AND SOCIAL DEVELOPMENT

Prior to the 1920s, popular conceptions of gifted individuals stereotyped such individuals as male, physically frail, bookwormish, bespectacled, and eccentric in behavior. Nineteenth-century psychiatrist Cesare Lombroso (1895), reflecting the ideas of his time, argued that genius was closely related to insanity (albeit insanity of a special type). In 1921 Lewis Terman began his pioneering longitudinal study of gifted children at Stanford University, called the Stanford Studies of Genius. Terman's findings were instrumental in dispelling the prevailing stereotype and produced the most comprehensive data on the characteristics of intellectually gifted individuals over time. This section begins with a description of Terman's studies, focusing particularly on his findings on physical and emotional status. More recent literature on gifted children's physical and social development is then examined in relation to Terman's findings.

The Stanford Studies of Genius

Selection of Participants. Terman (1926) focused his search for participants for his study of genius mainly in the California cities of Los Angeles, San Francisco, Oakland, Berkeley, and Alameda. The selection process began with teachers nominating one to five children as their most intelligent students. A group intelligence test was administered to these children, and those scoring in the top 10 percent were given an abbreviated form of the Stanford–Binet Intelligence Test (Terman's revision of the Binet–Simon test). Children who achieved an IQ of 130 or above on the abbreviated version were given the complete scale. The major criterion for inclusion in the study was an IQ of 140 or above on the complete Stanford–Binet test, although lower cutoffs were used for children older than ten.

By May 1924, Terman's files contained 1,444 subjects. The main experimental group consisted of 657 girls and boys, two through thirteen years old, with most in the eight-to-twelve-year age range. An additional 356 children were included from cities outside the main target cities. A third group consisted of 378 high school students. A small number of children who did not qualify for any other group but who demonstrated special abilities in art and music also were added to the sample. Additional children who scored close to the cutoff levels were included for follow-up. The final sample numbered 1,528 (856 boys and 672 girls).

Initial Findings. Data on the physical history, status, and health of the main experimental group were collected through the administration of thirty-seven anthropometric measures for each child (for example, height, weight, chest circumference, breathing capacity) and through questionnaires given to parents, school personnel, and medical doctors. The findings can be summarized as follows (Terman, 1926):

1. As a group, the gifted children were physically superior to comparison groups, evidencing greater height and weight for their age and better breathing capacity.
2. The gifted children as a whole weighed more at birth than did comparison children.
3. On the average, the gifted children had learned to walk a month earlier and to talk three and one-half months earlier than comparison children.
4. Substantially fewer gifted children were reported as suffering from frequent headaches and general weakness, although more of the gifted group had undergone tonsillectomies and evidenced visual defects.
5. The children in the gifted group appeared to have superior nutritional status to those in control groups.

To assess gifted children's character development, participants were administered a battery of tests, including measures of trustworthiness, emotional instability, social attitudes, types of characters and story lines preferred, and tendency to overstate abilities (a measure of honesty). Again, as a whole, the gifted children evidenced superiority to unselected controls for both sexes and all age groups. Gifted children were described as reaching high levels of character development earlier than unselected children. Finally, with the exception of honesty measures, gifted girls appeared to achieve higher scores than gifted boys.

Follow-up Results. Follow-up studies were conducted with the greater sample of children in 1927–28, 1939–40, and 1951–52 and are being continued by Terman's colleagues (Oden, 1968; Sears and Barbee, 1977; Sears, 1977). In general, the follow-up studies suggest that gifted children maintain their superiority into adulthood. The twenty-five-year follow-up (Terman and Oden, 1947) indicated that compared to the general population, the gifted group evidenced (*a*) a lower mortality rate; (*b*) equal or superior general health; (*c*) a normal or below-normal incidence of juvenile delinquency, personality disorders, insanity, alcoholism, and homosexuality; (*d*) equal or superior marital adjustment; and (*e*) no higher divorce rate.

Summary and Implications of the Stanford Studies. The longitudinal studies begun by Terman have generated a positive picture of gifted individuals as beginning with and maintaining superiority to nongifted peers in physical and emotional health as well as in intellectual capacities. However, the original sample generally consisted of white, middle-class children from well-educated, semiprofessional or professional families. Hence, it is unclear whether the sample's initial and continued superiority can be attributed to high intelligence or to highly advantaged home environments. Moreover, the findings can be generalized only to gifted children identified on the basis of intelligence tests and may not reflect characteristics of the creatively gifted.

More Recent Findings

The Stanford Studies of Genius constitute landmark investigations in the field of gifted education, and their contributions to continuing research and practice have been phenomenal. One potentially negative effect, however, has been the creation of a new myth: Intellectually gifted children excel in every domain (Whitmore, 1980). This section reviews the evidence for and against the "Terman myth" with regard to gifted children's physical development, social cognitive development, peer relations, and self-concept.

Physical Development. Although Terman's data indicate a moderate advantage for gifted children in reaching such developmental milestones as walking and talking, developmental psychologists generally agree that early physical maturation and motor development are not strongly related to intelligence during the school years (Musser, Conger, and Kagan, 1969). For example, evidence that children in Uganda, Brussels, and Stockholm walk earlier than do children in Paris, London, and Zurich does not indicate that children from the first three cities are more intelligent. Body build, rate of maturation, and rate of motor development are not reliable predictors of intellectual giftedness. Body build and physical development can be influenced by quality of nutrition, health practices, emotional factors, opportunities for exercise, amount of encouragement, and genetic inheritance (Biehler, 1981).

Social Cognitive Development. We will define social cognition as children's logical understanding of other individuals, as opposed to their feelings and emotions about others. Areas of children's interpersonal behavior in which social cognition has theoretical importance include development of moral judgment, role taking, rule implementation, play, and communication.

Much of the theoretical basis for examining children's social cognition stems from Piaget's work. According to Piaget, *cognitive development* proceeds through an invariant sequence of four stages: sensorimotor, preoperational, concrete operational, and formal operational. Descriptive of the differences among stages is the child's development from egocentrism (centering on the self) to decentration (the ability to separate the self from others) to the ability to accommodate several views or ideas simultaneously. Children's development of social cognition (summarized in Table 3.1) can be conceptualized as occurring in a manner parallel to intellectual development.

The development of *moral judgment* refers to the child's ability to make increasingly higher levels of decisions about the propriety of human behavior. Children in the stage of objective morality (parallel with preoperational thought) base their judgments about behavior on objective criteria such as magnitude of damage. Take, for example, the story of two children who spill ink on a tablecloth. The first child makes a small blot in playing with the ink bottle. The second child makes a large blot in attempting to tidy the table. At the objective morality stage, children tend to determine that the second child was more in error because more damage occurred. Good intentions do not count. In contrast, children in the higher stage of subjective morality (corresponding to concrete operations) consider motivation and judge the first child as the more guilty. Lawrence Kohlberg has developed a six-stage theory of moral judgment development based on Piaget's stages. Kohlberg's theory is described in detail in Chapter 9.

Role or perspective taking is defined as the ability to consider another person's point of view. Again, preoperational children differ from operational children in this capacity. For example, when very young children are asked to select a birthday present for Daddy, they may select something desirable from their own perspective (for example, a teddy bear). Young children may also have difficulty anticipating how a physical scene might be viewed from a geographical position different from their own.

Children also evidence consistent developmental patterns in their *implementation of rules* in games. Preoperational children demonstrate their egocentricity in their lack of knowledge about the rules of the game they are playing,

Table 3.1 Social cognitive development

AREA OF DEVELOPMENT	STAGE			
Cognitive	*Sensorimotor* (0–1½): does not display representation, but demonstrates intelligence via actions	*Preoperational* (1½–7): has language; begins to represent; engages in symbolic play; lacks conservation	*Concrete operational* (7–12): can conserve in concrete situations, can classify, and can seriate	*Formal operational* (12+): can generate and explore all possible solutions, including hypothetical
Moral judgment		*Objective morality or realism* (3–7): can make moral judgments based on objective criteria	*Subjective morality* (8–10): sees intention as the criterion of guilt	*Interpretation of the act* (11+): has developed a sense of moral responsibility for his or her behavior
Role/perspective taking	*Egocentric*: is completely centered about the self; makes little differentiation of self and others	*Egocentric* (2–5): does not recognize that others may have perspectives different from own; (6–7): begins to realize existence of other views	*Sequential* (7–8): can reflect on own behavior as seen from another's view and vice versa but only sequentially	*Simultaneous* (9+): can consider multiple perspectives at the same time

although they may insist that they know the rules. They play together in the sense of physically sharing space and/or materials but do not play interactively —that is, by a common set of rules. By the stage of incipient cooperation, corresponding to concrete operations, children know the rules of the game and attempt to win. Formal operational children who have reached the stage of genuine cooperation display legalistic fascination with rules, often devoting most of the recess period to rule development and elaboration and leaving little time to play.

In general *play*, sensorimotor children often can be found playing by themselves or engaging in parallel play. Parallel play refers to children sharing physical proximity but acting independently. For example, preschool-age children often work on separate puzzles next to each other. As they enter the preoperational stage, they begin to share and take turns.

Development of *communication* follows a pattern similar to play development. Preoperational, egocentric children are often found talking to themselves

Table 3.1 (continued)

AREA OF DEVELOPMENT		STAGE		
Rule implementation		*Egocentric* (4–7): does not know or follow rules; plays "together" with other children (each having own set of rules); has little notion of winning	*Incipient cooperation* (7–11): has mastered basic rules; can agree with partner on common set of rules (since not all rules have been mastered, conflicts still occur.)	*Genuine cooperation* (12 +): has thorough mastery of rules; has legalistic fascination with rules; enjoys settling differences, inventing, elaborating
Play	Alone or parallel	(age 3): still likes parallel play but begins to share and take turns		
Communication		*Egocentric* (4–7): is centered about the self; fails to take into account listener's view; engages in repetition, talking to self at early ages	*Decentered* (7 +): begins to take into account an external point of view; tries to anticipate what the listener needs to know	

or to one another about something meaningful only to the speaker: "Bring me the dish that looks like my sister's." With increased maturity and experience, the child becomes decentered and begins to anticipate what information the listener needs to have in order to understand or respond appropriately.

The research on social cognition has been well summarized by Shantz (1975), especially with regard to role taking. First, preschool children are not profoundly egocentric but demonstrate simple levels of competence in role taking and communication. Second, investigators have produced conflicting results with regard to relationships among various types of social cognition and cognitive development. While some children are consistent in their levels of development in such areas as cognition, moral judgment, and perspective taking, others may be advanced in one area but may lag behind in another. Third, correlational and training studies indicate moderately positive relationships between role taking and such prosocial behaviors as helping and sharing. However, the relationships must be considered tentative in light of contradictory findings. Finally, correlations between social cognition and intelligence range from low to moderately positive, giving scant support to the idea that intellectually gifted children necessarily show correspondingly high levels of social cognition.

Consistent with Shantz's review of general populations, recent research targeted specifically at studying the social cognition of gifted children does not provide firm evidence that intellectually gifted children are superior to average children in social cognition or prosocial behavior. Austin and Draper (1981) reviewed a study by Roedell indicating that IQ is more related to social cognition than to social behavior among preschool children. Abroms and Gollin (1980) concluded from their study of gifted preschool children that neither role taking nor intelligence test scores reliably predict prosocial behavior, suggesting that social giftedness develops independently of intelligence and the social cognitive factor of role taking.

Karnes and Brown (1981) found significant but low correlations between level of moral reasoning and IQ on the Stanford–Binet Intelligence Test (0.31) and the Wechsler Intelligence Scales for Children—Revised (0.14). Tan-Willman and Gutteridge (1981) presented evidence that academically gifted adolescents do not demonstrate higher levels of moral judgment development than do their age peers in the general population, despite suggestions that gifted children express an earlier concern about morals and values. Bear (1983) reported a correlation of 0.33 between moral reasoning and the vocabulary scale of the Stanford Achievement Test for sixty gifted and nongifted children in the sixth grade. Bear also found that the moral judgment scores of the gifted children were significantly higher than those of their nongifted peers, with the gifted as a group appearing to be one-third of a stage more advanced. However, not all the gifted subjects scored above the nongifted on moral reasoning. The gifted children demonstrated fewer conduct problems in the classroom than did the control group, a finding Bear attributed to higher intelligence rather than to higher levels of moral reasoning. Discrepancies between the findings of Tan-Willman and Gutteridge and those of Bear may be due in part to differences in the measures used to assess moral judgment development and differences in the procedures used to identify subjects as gifted.

More research is obviously required to determine the relationships among giftedness, social cognition, and prosocial behavior. The idea that intellectually gifted individuals possess correspondingly high levels of social cognition is intuitively appealing and inherently logical because intellectual thought and social cognition both seem to require perceptive problem-solving abilities. It would not be surprising if high levels of social cognition—for example, in the development of moral judgment or role taking—were not found sufficient to produce prosocial behavior. Making sound moral decisions is a cognitive act; *behaving* in a moral manner demands more than social or academic intelligence.

Peer Relations. Austin and Draper's (1981) review of peer relations among gifted children indicates that although intellectually gifted children tend to be socially popular, the relationship between intelligence and popularity is affected by age, level of giftedness, sex, and socioeconomic status. Most studies of elementary-age gifted children suggest, on the basis of sociometric questionnaires, that gifted children tend to be chosen as friends more often than their average and retarded peers. However, a sizable minority of gifted children are perceived on sociometric measures and teacher ratings as having few friends. Some gifted children may appear to be loners in the classroom because their friends are older and hence attend other classes. Although a minimum level of intelligence appears to be necessary for popularity, possessing intelligence above a maximum (for example, 150 IQ) may be a social liability. Highly gifted children often have different interests, a higher level of language proficiency, and more knowledge and insight than their intellectually average peers. These characteristics can adversely affect their social acceptance. Such children often choose solitary activities and thus may be perceived as less socially adept. Some data suggest that, whether or not they are removed from the regular classroom for part of the day, children with high intelligence tend to prefer as friends children of equal intelligence.

Austin and Draper (1981) found fewer studies conducted with gifted adolescents. Those available indicated that high achievement is perceived more positively by boys from middle-class backgrounds than by boys from lower-class backgrounds because such achievement is seen by middle-class students as preliminary to professional training. Although boys value athletics more highly than scholarship, high achievement does not harm their popularity with the same or with the opposite sex. However, girls view high ability as detrimental to popularity with the opposite sex. Counseling may be important in encouraging bright girls to demonstrate their abilities through high achievement.

Self-Concept and Social Adjustment. Although some contradictory findings have been reported, the bulk of recent research on the self-concept and social adjustment of intellectually gifted children has been positive. Studies using comparison groups of nongifted peers generally indicate that gifted children evidence higher scores on various measures of self-concept and adjustment. Some data suggest that placement in special programs may affect gifted children's self-concepts, although findings are inconsistent. Even when special class placement reduces gifted children's self-concepts, their self-concepts remain high in comparison to those of average children.

Consistent with Terman's findings of superior social adjustment among intellectually gifted individuals, most studies on secondary-school- and college-age gifted describe these students as more self-sufficient, independent, and internally controlled and as having a more positive self-concept than their intellectually average peers (Lehman and Erdwins, 1981). Kelly and Colangelo

(1984) found that gifted students in grades seven through nine had significantly higher academic and social self-concepts than did their intellectually average peers. Lehman and Erdwins (1981) reported similar findings for gifted third-grade children tested with the California Test of Personality and Children's Social Attitude and Value Scales. The gifted children were reported as feeling comfortable with themselves and their interpersonal relationships and as showing negligible evidence of maladjustment. Compared to their age peers, the gifted demonstrated fewer complaints of physical symptoms and bad dreams, were less destructive, possessed higher social skills, and were more likely to value cooperation and democratic group interaction, although they also showed less willingness to compromise.

Gifted children's self-concepts may be affected by placement in special programs. Maddux, Scheiber, and Bass (1982) found that placement of fifth- and sixth-graders in special programs, whether segregated from the regular class or integrated as part of the regular class, did not result in lower self-concepts or lower peer acceptance. However, two studies by Coleman and Fults (1982, 1985) indicate that in special programs children make comparisons between themselves and other children that may result in lower self-concepts.

In their 1982 study Coleman and Fults suggested that self-concept is dynamic and changing, influenced to a large extent by the particular context in which an individual interacts and by the persons within that context who serve as a standard with which the individual can compare his or her performance. Although the study was confounded by failure to equalize comparison groups, it provided some evidence that the self-concepts of gifted children in a pullout program were lower than those of high-achieving children who remained in the regular program full time. When retested eight months after their return to the regular classroom, the pullout group no longer evidenced a difference in self-concept from the group who had remained in the classroom. The investigators interpreted the lower self-concept of gifted children in the special group as due to self-comparisons with other gifted children. After returning to the regular class, where they compared their performance with those of nongifted students, the gifted children showed improved self-concepts. It should be noted that the average self-concept scores of the gifted and high-achieving students far exceeded the mean scores for standardization samples, indicating that although placement may have affected gifted students' self-concepts, these students continued to demonstrate higher-than-average self-concept scores.

In their 1985 investigation Coleman and Fults compared the self-concept scores of 102 elementary-age gifted children assessed prior to their participation in a one-day-per-week segregated enrichment program with the self-concept scores of 92 gifted children assessed during program participation. The children assessed prior to program participation evidenced higher self-concept scores. Coleman and Fults interpreted this finding as support that self-comparison with other gifted students in a special class decreases some children's evaluations of their own abilities. A second finding was that gifted students of lower-ability assessed during program participation evidenced the lowest self-concept scores. Again, the self-concept scores for gifted students of both lower and higher ability were superior to mean scores for the standardization sample (that is, the general population).

Although the recent research supports Terman's findings regarding the superior social adjustment of gifted individuals, the limitations that applied to Terman's studies also apply to the recent studies. That is, most investigations have continued to use white, middle-class children identified by standardized IQ or achievement measures. The studies generally have not included significant representation of those populations of gifted students who are more likely to demonstrate less positive self-concepts: the minority, low-income, and under-achieving gifted. Moreover, researchers have tended to limit their investigations to intellectually and academically gifted individuals, excluding the creatively gifted. Getzels and Dillon's (1973) review indicated that most studies show no relationship between creativity and emotional maladjustment. However, Taft and Gilchrist (1970) found that while high creative attitudes correlated with such positive social traits as extroversion and enthusiasm, creative production was related to lack of self-control, daydreaming, unhappiness in childhood, and emotional disorders requiring medical attention.

Clearly, then, not all gifted children should be characterized as having high self-concepts and superior social adjustment. Experience dictates that some gifted children have difficulty forming realistic self-appraisals, often setting high expectations for themselves and becoming frustrated when they do not achieve their goals. Their frustration increases when they find that their level of motor or artistic development limits their ability to reproduce the perfect image they have created in their mind's eye. Intellectually gifted children may also experience feelings of inadequacy when moved from a regular class, where they maintain first-place status with little effort, to a setting where they must compete with children of equal or better abilities. Highly gifted children who recognize early that they function at a level different from the level at which others function may feel out of place and insecure around their peers. Finally, gifted children who have focused their energies on academic achievement may feel less confident in their ability to interact socially. Ross and Parker (1980) found that gifted boys and girls in grades five through eight demonstrate higher academic than social self-concepts. One explanation may lie in the disproportionate amount of attention and approval gifted children receive from teachers and parents for their excellence in academic as opposed to social pursuits.

CHAPTER SUMMARY

We began this chapter with questions about how gifted children develop and whether teachers and parents can "make" an average child gifted. The literature on the origins of intelligence suggests that although the environment provided by parents and teachers can certainly affect intellectual performance, genetic inheritance plays a major role in determining intellectual capacity. The relationship between heredity and environment is a complex one; many combinations of genetic endowment and environmental quality can produce the same IQ. It is clear that removing children from severely deprived conditions can lead to substantial gains in the children's IQ. However, it is questionable whether providing additional enrichment to children being raised in average environments will produce significant increases in their intellectual capacity. The environment does appear to play a large part in supporting the development of specific talents, such as in music and mathematics. Whether induced by heredity or environment, intellectual giftedness appears to have physiological correlates in the form of superior brain functioning.

Intelligence is a term widely accepted and commonly used in our society to describe individual differences in observed behavior. Yet there is no single agreed-upon definition of intelligence. Difference theorists have variously conceptualized intelligence as (a) a single general factor underlying a broad range of behaviors; (b) a composite of a few to many different types of abilities; (c) a developmental progression through increasingly complex stages, each built upon the preceding stage; and (d) a series of steps in the process of problem solving. The selection of a particular definition of intelligence influences how giftedness is conceptualized and how gifted individuals are identified.

The physical and social development of intellectually gifted children over time has been described by Terman in terms of superiority commensurate with intellectual abilities. However, precocious physical development does not have a one-to-one correspondence with later intelligence and may not in itself constitute a useful predictor of intellectual giftedness. The literature on social development of gifted children is less clear. Although some evidence shows that bright children exhibit higher levels of social cognition, they may not demonstrate superior social behavior. Intellectually and academically advanced children tend to be more socially accepted and popular than their average peers, especially at elementary school ages. Some, however, are perceived as loners, perhaps because they prefer older friends or more mature activities.

The intellectually gifted also seem to possess positive self-concepts and good social adjustment, but this generalization is limited to white middle-class children. The picture of self-assurance and social adeptness may or may not be appropriate for minority, low-income, underachieving, or creatively gifted individuals, who have largely not been targeted for investigation. Moreover, even intellectually gifted children may experience self-doubt about their abilities, especially in the social arena. Teachers need to consider that (a) not all gifted children are superior in social knowledge and behavior; (b) high-achieving children can feel frustrated in academic situations; and (c) some high achievers feel socially inadequate and need opportunities and encouragement to develop social skills.

ACTIVITIES FOR THOUGHT AND DISCUSSION

1. How would you describe the relative contributions of heredity and environment to intellectual giftedness? As a parent or teacher, how could you try to increase a child's intellectual potential?

2. Investigate additional theories of intelligence not described in this chapter; for example, Cattell's theory of fluid and crystallized intelligence (1963); Jensen's two-level theory (1970); and Bruner's developmental theory (1964). What implications do these theories have for the definition of giftedness and for the identification of gifted individuals?

3. Which theory of intelligence do you find most appealing or satisfying? Why?

4. Is it logical to assume that the intellectually gifted should evidence higher levels of moral reasoning and behavior than do individuals of average intelligence? Why or why not?

Chapter Four

CHARACTERISTICS OF GIFTED AND TALENTED LEARNERS

One of the questions most frequently asked of educators in the field concerns the signs or characteristics that might be helpful in identifying gifted and talented children. Often the first person to suspect that a child has exceptional potential is the parent, the preschool or primary school teacher, or a specialized instructor (for example, a piano, dance, or religion teacher). Only if someone recognizes his or her potential for giftedness can a child be referred for individual assessment to confirm the diagnosis and provide appropriate educational planning. The formal identification and assessment process will be detailed in Chapter 5. This chapter describes frequently observed traits and concomitant educational needs of intellectually, academically, and creatively gifted individuals and individuals gifted in leadership and in the visual and performing arts. Each section begins with illustrative biosketches of two gifted individuals: one an adult who has achieved eminence and one a child whose potential is yet to be fulfilled.

INTELLECTUAL GIFTEDNESS

CASE STUDY 1

Bertrand Russell (1872–1970)

Bertrand Russell, British philosopher, mathematician, teacher, writer, and political rebel, is considered one of the greatest thinkers of the modern age. In his many books he ranged over the subjects of philosophy, mathematics, science, ethics, sociology, education, history, religion, and politics. It is said that he generally wrote three thousand words per day. The winner of several awards, including a Nobel Prize for literature, he was born an aristocrat, grandson of one of Great Britain's most distinguished prime ministers. His father died when Bertrand was one year old, and the boy was subsequently placed in the custody of his paternal grandparents, Lord John Russell and Lady Russell. Lady Russell was an outspoken opponent of imperialist wars and the government's attitude toward Ireland. She disliked the public schools, and Bertrand was educated for college at home.

Although famous for his three-volume *Principia Mathematica*, it is said that Bertrand wept over his first efforts to learn the multiplication tables and initially disliked algebra. At age eleven he questioned Euclidian geometry, demanding proof for axioms that were to be accepted without proof (Ewart, 1972). Bertrand grew up a silent and shy boy, yet he was considered extremely intellectually precocious (Goertzel and Goertzel, 1962). At fourteen he contemplated suicide because he was tormented by questions concerning religion, but he resolved the issue by becoming an agnostic like his late father. He read voraciously from his grandfather's library; however, at sixteen he was forbidden to continue this practice because of eye strain. He filled in the hours by memorizing poetry. By the time he was ready for college, he was fluent in German, French, and Italian.

Although his prevailing interest until the age of thirty-eight was mathematics, Bertrand's genius was evident in many areas. At thirty-five he ran for Parliament as a candidate of the National Union of Women's Suffrage Societies, but he lost. With the advent of World War I, he achieved notoriety as a supporter of conscientious objectors and was imprisoned for six months for pacifist writings. The war also contributed to his conversion to socialism of a type favoring industries run by those working in them. He visited Russia and China and continued bidding unsuccessfully for political office. In 1927 he established a progressive school that subsequently failed because of financial and staffing difficulties. During the 1930s he produced many noted philosophical works, and at age eighty he turned to writing fiction. He spent the final decades of his life actively opposing nuclear armament and the Vietnam War.

CASE STUDY 2

Sandy

Sandy is the only child of a career naval officer and his homemaker wife. Having no basis for comparing Sandy's development, Sandy's parents did not recognize her exceptional potential until she was three years old, when they were alerted to it by Sandy's preschool teachers. Her mother could not determine the precise age at which Sandy began to read; sometime during her third year Sandy seemed to go from memorizing stories to reading, without any clear distinction. Sandy also seemed to crave information, demanding answers to her many questions. A friend of her father presented Sandy with a piece of coral when she was four years old, and she began a coral collection and developed an interest in marine polyps that continues today.

Sandy began kindergarten at age five but was almost immediately accelerated to first and then second grade. She is now nine years old and attends a regular sixth-grade class. Although Sandy is physically the smallest child in her grade, her mother reflects that the decision to accelerate her was a good one because Sandy remains at the top of her class. She scores at eleventh-grade level or above in all subject areas, although she prefers mathematics.

According to her teacher, Sandy's only weakness is penmanship. Sandy explains that her hand will not write as fast as she thinks. Her relationships with her peers are excellent. She has been elected to the student council for two consecutive years and is a leader in her classroom and in her neighborhood. She has pitched for a girls' softball team for three years. Sandy seems to enjoy establishing goals for group projects and delegating responsibilities to get the goals accomplished. Her mother recalls that when the softball team needed three more players and a sponsor, Sandy instructed: "Mom, you get the sponsor and I'll get the players." When Sandy and several other children became discouraged about a project assigned in class, she announced to her peers: "I'm not going away until this gets done."

Sandy has also played the violin for two years and would like to begin flute lessons. Her mother muses that Sandy's only limitation is finding the time to pursue all her interests. In addition to sports and music, Sandy enjoys being a Girl Scout and reads voraciously about coral and reef life. She wants to be either a marine biologist or a professional baseball player.

Characteristics and Needs

Much of what we know about the characteristics of intellectually gifted children comes from Terman's longitudinal studies (described in Chapter 3) of 1,528 children with IQs above 130 (average IQ was 150). Terman's (1926) findings with regard to schooling and achievement can be summarized as follows:

1. Compared to the controls, the gifted were less likely to display negative attitudes toward school.
2. Nearly half of the gifted learned to read before starting school (at least 20 percent learned before age five), and most learned with little or no formal instruction.
3. One-half of the gifted were reported by their parents to have superior ability in arithmetic, and one-third were reported by their parents to have superior ability in music.
4. The gifted evidenced their high ability at an early age, exhibiting such characteristics as a desire to learn to read, quick understanding, insatiable curiosity, possession of extensive information, superior memory, early speech, and an unusually advanced vocabulary. They also tended to prefer playmates older than themselves.
5. The average gifted child scored 40 percent above his or her chronological age expectancy level on achievement measures but was at a grade level only 14 percent above the norm for his or her chronological age. In other words, the gifted tended to be held in grade placements at levels two to three years below their level of mastery.
6. The gifted tended to be superior in all areas of achievement. Although they exhibited unevenness in abilities, children of average intelligence displayed similar unevenness.
7. Gifted children were more interested than unselected children in abstract subjects, such as literature and dramatics, and less interested in pragmatic subjects, such as penmanship, sewing, and manual arts. Both groups exhibited the same preference for games and sports.
8. The gifted expressed more interests than did control children; one and three-fourths times as many gifted children as control children had begun collections, especially in areas connected with science.
9. Compared to the controls, the gifted read more and covered a wider range of topics, preferring science, history, biography, travel, folk tales, informational fiction, poetry, and drama. Gifted children read less adventure, mystery, and emotional fiction than did the controls.

Follow-up studies (Terman, 1954) indicated that close to 90 percent of the gifted group entered college, and 70 percent graduated. Midlife achievement reports of 800 men (average age of forty) showed that they had published 67 books; over 1,400 technical and professional articles; more than 200 short stories, novelettes, and plays; and 236 miscellaneous articles. They had authored over 150 patents and hundreds of newspaper articles and radio and television scripts.

Based on the findings of Terman and others, several checklists have been developed (e.g., Karnes and Associates, 1978b; Renzulli et al., 1976) that list characteristics of intellectually gifted children. These characteristics may be summarized as follows:

— advanced vocabulary for age
— early interest in books and reading
— early reading ability; self-taught reading at an early age (two to three years)
— independent reading, frequent preference for adult-level books
— rapid learning and easy recall of factual information
— quick perception of cause–effect relationships
— high level of curiosity evidenced by many "how" and "why" questions
— enjoyment in being with older children
— pursuit of interests and of collecting things
— long attention span for age
— self-imposed high standards
— mature sense of humor for age
— preference for new and challenging experiences
— retention of information
— high level of planning, problem solving, and abstract thinking compared to peers
— ability to generalize quickly from principles and to look for similarities and differences
— possession of an unusually large storehouse of information about a variety of topics
— tendency to become easily bored with routine tasks
— concern for ethical issues, questions of right and wrong, and adult topics such as religion and politics

Intellectually gifted individuals' receptivity to the unusual, interest in problem solving and cause–effect relationships, and analytic prowess may exist concomitantly with several negative characteristics. These include gullibility, perfectionism, resistance to authority, omission of detail, difficulty in accepting the illogical (as in children's stories and news events), dislike of routine and drill, boredom with the regular curriculum, impatience with waiting for the larger group of average students to catch up, tendency to dominate discussions, refusal to participate in activities where they do not excel, and a critical attitude toward others (Clark, 1983; Seagoe, 1975). Given these children's unique combinations of abilities and traits, programs for the intellectually gifted must consider these children's needs for (a) obtaining new and challenging information, (*b*) pursuing special interests, (*c*) having opportunities to communicate knowledge, (*d*) receiving appropriate (accelerated) pacing, (*e*) engaging in inductive thinking and problem solving, (*f*) applying knowledge to realistic problems, (*g*) learning to respect individual differences, (*h*) setting realistic goals for themselves and others, and (*i*) dealing with moral and ethical issues.

ACADEMIC GIFTEDNESS

CASE STUDY 3

Marie Curie (1867–1934)

Marie Curie, Polish scientist, codiscoverer of radium and winner of two Nobel Prizes, was born Manya Sklodovska. She was the youngest daughter of a Warsaw math and physics teacher who was dismissed for his refusal to teach in Russian during the Russian domination of Poland. Her mother and her oldest sister died when she was a young child, leaving Marie and her remaining sister to find work at early ages to support themselves and their father. While working as a teacher, Marie secretly participated in the nationalist free university by reading in Polish to women workers. At eighteen Marie became a governess.

As a young child, Marie demonstrated outstanding abilities. At four years of age, she was memorizing the names of pieces of technical equipment used by her physicist father. In elementary school she was at least two years ahead of her peers in all subjects and spoke German, French, and Russian (Goertzel and Goertzel, 1962). Upon completion of her secondary education at the Russian lycee at sixteen, she won a gold medal. Science held a fascination for her from childhood, partly because it was one of the subjects the Russians forbade Poles to study (Collier, 1972). Marie moved to Paris, where her sister lived, to study science. There she quickly earned master's degrees in physics and mathematics. Determined to work in research, she obtained a contract for conducting investigations on the magnetic properties of various steels. While seeking a suitable laboratory, she met and married Pierre Curie, a French scientist. Their first daughter, Irene, would also win a Nobel Prize.

Marie became interested in scientist Henri Becquerel's experiments with uranium. In collaboration with Pierre over the next twelve years, Marie succeeded in isolating the element radium. When radium began to be manufactured on a large scale, the Curies refused to take out a patent because they felt that radium belonged to the world. In 1903 the Curies and Becquerel shared the Nobel Prize for physics for the discovery of radioactivity. During the same year Marie received her doctorate of science.

Pierre died in 1906, and Marie succeeded to his position and became the first female director of the physics laboratory at the Sorbonne. She continued her research, and in 1911 she received the Nobel Prize for chemistry for the discovery of radium and polonium and for the isolation of pure radium. In Paris during World War II, Marie organized and equipped X-ray stations and X-ray care for the wounded and trained others in the use of X-rays and radium therapy. She died from anemia caused by the destruction of bone marrow from prolonged exposure to radiation (Collier, 1972).

CASE STUDY 4

Donald

Donald is the oldest child (by ten years) in a family of three children. Both parents are mathematicians by training, although the mother currently manages a retail computer outlet. Donald's father recalls that one day the three-year-old Donald asked how many days were left until his birthday. When told that his birthday was in seven weeks and five days, Donald immediately calculated the correct number of days. At age four he played dominoes with adults and often pointed out better plays to his opponents. At the same age Donald took piano lessons and could read the lyrics in the songbooks. His favorite reading material, however, was humorous poetry.

At five years of age, Donald reacted to media coverage of the manned space program with a sudden and zealous interest in astronomy. Over the next several years he read everything he could on the subject, borrowing books from the public library until his father had to turn to the local university's library and its bookstore for more advanced sources. Meanwhile Donald's school achievement, initially weak, became increasingly poor. His kindergarten teacher conferred with Donald's parents about his potential "dullness" because Donald frequently refused to participate in coloring and other activities and often disrupted the other children's efforts. As Donald progressed through the elementary years, he demonstrated increasing defiance in the classroom and rarely completed assignments. His teachers continued to believe that he had a learning or behavior problem.

Frustrated with the increasing misunderstanding between themselves and the school, Donald's parents took him to a child psychologist. In addition to providing therapy, the psychologist made arrangements for Donald to participate in a university program designed to give prospective special education teachers opportunities to interact with gifted children. Donald's tutor introduced him to an internationally renowned astronomer working at the university. At the first meeting the astronomer explained how he made his discoveries, and he was impressed by the level of Donald's understanding. Donald was subsequently permitted to take a freshman course in astronomy, and he came out at the top of the class. At age eleven Donald continues to work below his ability level in school, although the psychologist has helped Donald to accept his own abilities and to recognize concomitant responsibilities.

Characteristics and Needs

Academic giftedness refers to special talent in a particular academic field, such as science, mathematics, social science, or the humanities. Most investigations of gifted individuals who have achieved eminence in a specific academic area have focused on the fields of science and mathematics. Roe (1951) studied the life histories of twenty-two eminent physical scientists nominated by their peers. She identified patterns of traits characteristic of these individuals, including deep absorption in work, driving persistence and curiosity, independence, and self-sufficiency. As children, the scientists tended to be avid readers, to enjoy school and studying, and to have an interest in gadgets and hardware. Roe also described her subjects as having exhibited high, but not exceptionally high, performance on aptitude and intelligence measures. Their career success appeared to be more a function of hard work than of inherent brightness.

Based on several studies, Taylor and Barron (1963) summarized the traits of creative scientists as including high autonomy and self-direction, detached attitudes in interpersonal relations, preference for intellectually as opposed to socially challenging situations, high ego strength and emotional stability, a liking for precision, high impulse control, independence as opposed to conformity of judgment, superior intelligence, and early interest in intellectual activities. Examining similar biographical and assessment studies, Michael (1977) concluded that the eminent physical scientists and mathematicians have in common the traits of high intelligence, independence, introversion, and flexible working style. However, scientists differ from mathematicians in being more self-assertive, dominant, and striving but somewhat less oriented toward humanitarian concerns and need for order.

A large-scale retrospective study conducted by Bloom and his associates (Bloom, 1982, 1985) offers the most recent and comprehensive information available on the characteristics of persons in specific talent areas. Investigators identified approximately 150 individuals between seventeen and thirty-five who achieved world-class standing in one of six fields: concert piano, sculpture, research mathematics, research neurology, Olympic swimming, and tennis. The purpose of the study was to identify characteristics and environmental influences that had enabled these outstanding individuals to reach such high levels of achievement. Information was collected through extensive interviews with the talented individuals, their parents, and some of their outstanding teachers.

Bloom's (1982) analysis of data on Olympic swimmers, research mathematicians, and concert pianists yielded three characteristics common to each group. The first characteristic was an unusual willingness to devote large amounts of time and effort to achieve a high standard. This characteristic was not predominant during the early years (ages five to eight) but became increasingly apparent after the achievers had received several years of instruction. The second notable characteristic was competitiveness with peers in the talent field and a determination to do one's best. The third trait was the ability to rapidly learn new techniques, ideas, and processes in the talent area. Although some subjects displayed rapid learning in many achievement areas, for most individuals this facility was restricted to their particular talent area. Bloom suggested that these characteristics were probably influenced by early socialization in the home and by early training from teachers.

Bloom identified four characteristics specific to research mathematicians—two present before age eight and two most evident during adolescence. First, as children (beginning at age three), the subjects frequently asked substantive questions of parents and other adults and then made use of the answers. Second, even at very young ages, the subjects often engaged in solitary activities for long periods of time. Initially these activities involved playing with blocks, toys, and puzzles; later the subjects graduated to science projects and reading. As Terman had found in studying the intellectually gifted, Bloom found that some of the research mathematicians had, as children, preferred working on projects by themselves to playing with peers. Parents reported that these children were often lost in thought, contemplating some event.

Third, as adolescents, Bloom's subjects demonstrated a large measure of independent learning gained from reading books and from observing others. Much of their learning in science and math at the secondary level derived from working through textbooks by themselves. Many subjects regarded classroom learning as an unenjoyable duty and preferred to learn by reading or by observing others attacking a problem. Fourth, subjects were identified as unusually able in math and science during their high school years. The research mathematicians did not report being outstanding in the elementary grades or in junior high school, and some recalled having had difficulties in reading and in other areas during their early school years.

Extrapolating from Bloom's findings and from the observations of other researchers, characteristics of individuals gifted in specific academic areas include the following:

— long attention span for activities related to a specific academic area
— advanced understanding of concepts, methods, and terminology of the specialized field
— ability to apply concepts from the specialized field to activities in other subjects
— willingness to devote large amounts of time and effort to achieve high standards in a specific academic field
— competitiveness in a specific academic area and motivation to do one's best
— rapid learning in the specialized field

Additional characteristics can be listed, depending upon the specific academic area in which the talent is manifested. For example, Bartz (1982) listed a number of traits that describe linguistically gifted students, including field independence, tolerance for ambiguity, extroversion, risk taking, active seeking of opportunities to use the target language, quick adjustment to the target language, attention to form as well as meaning, empathy, and ability to guess. Based on a survey of foreign-language teachers, Carlson (1981) developed separate lists of characteristics of students gifted in learning French, German, and Spanish.

In sum, individuals whose giftedness is manifested in a specific academic area can be characterized as persistent and goal-directed in their field. They demonstrate high motivation and powers of concentration in their area of interest. Some of these individuals evidence similar strengths in many academic areas; other are not so well rounded. Their positive characteristics may be accompanied by resistance to and resentment toward interruption, by stubbornness, and by a lack of interest in social activities. Students gifted in specific academic areas require opportunities to (a) acquire fundamental competencies, technical vocabulary, and advanced knowledge in a given field; (b) interact with leaders in the field; (c) apply their knowledge to current problems; (d) communicate their knowledge; and (e) develop their abilities in other academic and social areas.

CREATIVE GIFTEDNESS

CASE STUDY 5

R. Buckminster Fuller (1895–1983)

R. Buckminster Fuller, architect, engineer, inventor, philosopher, and poet, is best known as the creator of the geodesic dome, used worldwide in the design of theaters, defense facilities, and residences. Although he had no formal architectural training, Buckminster was awarded the Royal Gold Medal for Architecture in 1968 by Queen Elizabeth II, and during the same year the Gold Medal Award of the National Institute of Arts and Letters. He is considered one of the most original thinkers of the second half of the twentieth century, an optimist who believed that humankind can control the environment worldwide through comprehensive anticipatory design. The problems of shelter, nutrition, transportation, and pollution could, he believed, be solved efficiently with minimal energy resources through careful long-range planning.

Buckminster Fuller, born in Milton, Massachusetts, was descended from a long line of nonconformists. His great-aunt, Margaret Fuller, was a friend of Emerson and Thoreau and cofounded the *Dial*, the literary journal of the transcendentalist movement. Another Fuller ancestor was the Massachusetts delegate to the Federal Constitutional Assembly who argued passionately against acceptance of the Constitution in absence of a clause specifically prohibiting slavery. When his plea went unheeded, he refused to sign the Constitution.

Buckminster was born with a visual defect that was not discovered until he was four years old, at which time he was fitted with thick, owlish glasses. His corrected vision suddenly enabled him to see the wonder and beauty of the world, awaking in him an awe of nature that he would possess throughout his life. Buckminster enjoyed school and especially enjoyed studying mathematics, although his questioning brought him into constant conflict with his teachers. For example, when his teacher explained that a cube is composed of imaginary planes constructed from imaginary lines and points, Buckminster asked how she could draw a cube if it were imaginary (Rosen, 1969). With the exception of Latin, he excelled in all subjects but did especially well in science.

Buckminster's creative genius was evident early. When he was six years old, his kindergarten teacher gave him toothpicks and dried peas to play with, and with intense concentration he built a tetrahedronal octet truss—three squares combined to make eight triangles—patented by Buckminster in 1961 as Octetruss (Hatch, 1974). Buckminster spent several summer vacations at Bear Island in Maine, where at age ten he invented a way to propel his boat with an umbrella to solve the problem of having to face backward when rowing a boat without an engine. His invention was inspired by his observations of the jellyfish in the bay, which moved by opening and closing like an umbrella. At Bear Island, he also invented a record holder much like those sold commercially today. Buckminster enjoyed sports and made quarterback on the football team during his junior year in high school.

Buckminster's father, an importer, died when Buckminster was thirteen. His mother worried that Buckminster would be a failure because of the trouble he caused in school and his tendency to spend money foolishly. Buckminster followed the family tradition and entered Harvard, but he was expelled twice and never completed his formal education. He left Harvard the first time disillusioned by his lack of social acceptance, which was probably due to his stubborn individualism and "oddball" thinking and appearance (Hatch, 1974). He withdrew the money his family had provided for his semester expenses and spent it entertaining Ziegfeld chorus girls in New York City. When funds ran out, he charged his purchases to the Fuller family. His family then sent him to Quebec, where his cousin owned a cotton mill, and Buckminster there became intimately acquainted with technology. Buckminster served in the U.S. Navy during World War I as commander of a crash-boat flotilla and was recognized for his inventions of life-saving equipment.

In 1922 Buckminster's first daughter died at the age of four from a series of illnesses that her father blamed on the inadequacies of the environment. After five years of depression, he began a period of high creativity. In 1927 he invented the Dymaxion house, a factory-assembled, easily transported structure with its own utilities. In 1933 he invented the Dymaxion car, the first streamlined car and one that could handle like a jeep, accelerate to 120 miles per hour, make a 180-degree turn in its own length, carry twelve passengers, and average 28 miles per gallon. In 1943 he produced a new model that averaged 40 to 50 miles per gallon. All wheels were steerable, enabling the car to move sideways and park in a minimum of space. Neither version of the Dymaxion car was put into commercial production. Perhaps due to his early experiences with plane geometry, Buckminster developed a vectorial system of geometry from which he invented the geodesic dome. The dome maximizes strength without internal supports and covers a great deal of space with minimum material. Buckminster also developed the Dymaxion map, which depicts all land areas of the world without distortion.

CASE STUDY 6

Anna

Anna is the youngest in a family of five children. Her parents were divorced when she was three, and Anna lives with her mother, who works as a waitress. Anna's exceptional creativity was first noticed by her kindergarten teacher. During music time, when children were asked to "move the way the music makes you feel," Anna's movements showed an uncommon depth of expression and sensitivity to tempo and rhythm. She concentrated on coordinating all parts of her body, whereas other children ran, skipped, twirled, giggled, and fell. Her individuality and independence were evident in her fondness for hats. One day she came to school with a paper napkin decorated with crayon and made into a visor held to her head by a rubber band. She insisted on wearing the visor despite teasing from her peers. While the other children drew flowers, houses, and suns, Anna's pictures were filled with strange animals such as "kangaraffes," long-necked jumping beasts.

Anna's kindergarten teacher referred her to the school psychologist for assessment. She scored in the gifted range on measures of creative thinking and problem solving but only in the high-average range on general intelligence. Anna was not placed in the school's gifted program, which was designed for intellectually and academically gifted children. During her elementary school years Anna's academic achievement was good but not outstanding. Her teachers noted in her a tendency to ignore directions in completing assignments. For example, when asked to write a formal book report, Anna handed in a story written from the perspective of one of the book's minor characters.

After a guest presentation by a local physicist, Anna became fascinated with mechanical tools and electronics equipment. From parts left for the children by the physicist, she independently put together a circuit that rang a bell. After being introduced to the computer, she spent hours designing graphics, coming to school early and staying as late as her teacher would allow. Today, in the sixth grade, Anna spends most of her free time reading at the library or tinkering with broken clocks and appliances at home. Her refusal to participate in peer group activities (dances, fashion shows) has left her with few friends.

Characteristics and Needs

Highly creative individuals can be defined as those who exhibit strong abilities in generating new ideas that have potential value to society. A pattern of attitudinal and personality traits associated with creativity has emerged from research comparing highly creative individuals to less creative ones. A review of the literature (Getzels and Dillon, 1973) indicates that creative scientists, architects, and art students tend to hold high theoretical and aesthetic values. Regarding interpersonal relations, creative individuals in general demonstrate self-sufficiency, more interest in ideas than in people, disinterest in social activities, independence, lack of inhibition, and low extroversion. The literature also suggests a common pattern of perception and cognition among creative individuals that includes a preference for complexity, independent judgment, resistance to group pressure, humor in free association, the expression of nonconforming ideas, a tendency to be stimulus-free versus stimulus-bound, and high risk taking.

Taft and Gilchrist (1970), investigating creativity among art and architecture students, distinguished between creative attitudes and creative production. Creative attitudes were measured by a creative interest scale, while productivity was assessed by ratings of the quality and quantity of self-reported creative activities. The investigators found that those possessing creative attitudes alone tended to show extroversion, enthusiasm, quick-wittedness, and high theoretical and academic interests. In contrast, creative productivity was related to such traits as being disorderly and impractical, lacking in self-control, daydreaming, using imagination, desiring to retreat from reality, and having less emotional participation in the environment. Moreover, creative production showed some correlation with unhappiness in childhood and with neurotic disorders requiring medical attention. In general, Taft and Gilchrist's study, as well as other studies, suggests that children with high creative potential may exhibit the following characteristics:

— inquisitiveness
— tendency to do things in their own way
— preference for working alone
— experimentation with whatever is at hand
— active imagination
— ability to think up many ways to accomplish a goal or solve a problem
— tendency to respond with unexpected, clever, or smart-aleck answers
— production of original ideas
— uninhibited expression of what may be nonconforming opinions
— adventurousness and willingness to take risks
— possession of a keen sense of humor
— sensitivity to beauty
— nonconformity and lack of interest in detail
— lack of concern with social acceptability

The creative individual's inventiveness and independence may result in a tendency to reject the known, to insist on inventing for himself or herself, to resist pressures toward conformity, to become frustrated with externally imposed deadlines, and to engage in rejecting or rebellious behavior (Seagoe, 1975). Program planners must consider these students' needs for encouragement of their creative efforts, for opportunities to pursue their interests without unnecessary time limitations, for guidance in applying their talents to appropriate social goals, and for help in recognizing situations where social conformity is valuable.

LEADERSHIP AND SOCIAL GIFTEDNESS

CASE STUDY 7

Martin Luther King, Jr. (1929–1968)
Before his assassination, Martin Luther King, Jr., led the first mass civil rights movement in the United States. The black Baptist minister won the Nobel Peace Prize in 1964 for his application of Gandhi's techniques of nonviolence to problems of racial prejudice in this country. He was born in Atlanta, Georgia, and is described by Goertzel and Goertzel (1962) as having come from an ideal home, with parents who were devoted to each other and who held a common philosophy and common interests. Both parents were respected and prominent members of the black community. Martin Luther King, Sr., was pastor of the

Ebenezer Baptist Church in Atlanta. In a region that enforced segregation of services by race, he set an example for his children by insisting that he and his family be treated with courtesy. He refused to patronize establishments (bus lines, stores) that relegated black customers to separate areas. When Martin and his two sisters were all in school, their mother returned to college to complete her degree.

Martin went to nursery school and from the beginning demonstrated good peer relations. His hobbies included making kites and model airplanes, and he readily involved others in play. He earned money from an early age; he sold weekly newspapers at eight, he had his own paper route at thirteen, and a few years later he worked himself up to assistant manager in charge of thirty boys. He had a close group of friends, belonged to the debate club, and was popular with his teachers. He skipped three grades and entered Morehouse College at age fifteen under a special program for gifted students. He received his bachelor's degree in 1948 and spent the next three years at Crozer Theological Seminary in Chester, Pennsylvania. There he was elected student body president and graduated with the highest academic average in his class. He earned his Ph.D. at Boston University at the age of twenty-six.

In 1955, while pastor of Dexter Avenue Baptist Church in Montgomery, Alabama, Martin was elected by black activists to lead the boycott of the city's transit system, which segregated black passengers. As spokesman for this group, Martin demonstrated his skillful rhetoric, inspiring personality, and strong faith. Although his home was dynamited, he refused to give up his principles. Just over a year later, Montgomery desegregated the city buses. Recognizing the need for national efforts in civil rights, King organized the Southern Christian Leadership Conference. He began to lecture in all parts of the country, meeting with national and international leaders, including India's Prime Minister Nehru.

In 1960 King returned to Atlanta to become copastor, along with his father, of Ebenezer Baptist Church. In this position he devoted most of his time to civil rights activities. During the period from 1960 to 1965, he actively supported nonviolent demonstrations (sit-ins and protest marches) against segregation in restaurants, public parks, and other facilities, as well as discrimination in hiring practices. He won the allegiance of many blacks and liberal whites on a national level. With other civil rights leaders, he organized the March on Washington in 1963 to call national and international attention to demands for equal rights under the law. The civil rights movement resulted in passage of the Civil Rights Act of 1964, requiring desegregation of public facilities and outlawing employment discrimination.

CASE STUDY 8

Karen

Karen, seventeen, is president of the senior class in high school, student body president, and editor of the school paper. Her father is an engineer and her mother an attorney. Karen's mother recalls that Karen's gregarious nature was evident early in life. Even as an infant, she seemed to enjoy attention from new adults and rarely minded being left with a sitter. As a preschooler, she often directed the activities of other children in the neighborhood, even though some were older. She was not a "bossy" child, but she seemed to put others at ease. For example, when a new child joined the group (playing barber shop), Karen created a role for the newcomer, including him as the hair dryer salesman. When a child fell and scraped his knee, Karen coordinated the first-aid operation, comforting the injured child and sending another for help.

Karen earned A's and B's throughout elementary school. Although she was motivated to achieve academically, her interests were more directed at extracurricular projects, such as scouting activities. Through the scouts she helped organize fund raisers, charity drives, and sporting events. When Karen was thirteen, her father was transferred for two years to South America and took his family with him. Karen rapidly acquired fluency in Spanish and adjusted readily to her new school. Conditions in the poorer rural areas of South America affected her deeply. Upon her return to the United States, Karen became an avid reader of periodicals describing social, political, and economic conditions in Latin America. She resolved that she would one day join the Peace Corps.

In high school Karen demonstrated a talent for vivid expression in oral and written modes and used her powers of persuasion to rally the student body to work against drug abuse and alcoholism on campus. She debated with her teachers issues like human rights and foreign aid in developing countries and the effects of multinational cartels. One of her teachers, interested in encouraging Karen's development in world politics, helped her obtain a scholarship to participate in a summer leadership institute in Washington, D.C. Karen now looks forward to college, where she plans to major in international relations as background for a career with the State Department.

Characteristics and Needs

Although many definitions exist, leaders have been conceptualized in the field of gifted education as individuals who actively maintain and change social processes (Foster, 1981). Devising a list of characteristics indicative of potential leadership presents difficulties because leaders cannot be identified in isolation; their status as leaders depends on other individuals within the social context. One can be intelligent, achieving, creative, or artistic in the absence of other individuals because these gifts are inherent and generally stable over time. Leadership is a relationship that exists among members of a group and is not a passive status or a simple combination of traits (Bass, 1981). Leadership can be situationally dependent. An individual may emerge as a leader under conditions of stress (for example, war or external threat to the group) and may lose leadership status when conditions have returned to normal. Leaders acquire their status by active participation and by demonstrating the capacity to carry acts to completion.

In his comprehensive review of theory and research on leadership, Bass (1981) reported several findings relevant to the identification of leadership potential. First, the characteristics and skills required of a leader are determined largely by the demands of the situation. For example, athletic ability and physical prowess are traits of leaders in boys' gangs and play groups. However, intelligence and integrity are the salient features of excellent leaders in government. Second, individuals do not become leaders by virtue of their possession of certain traits; rather, their characteristics must be relevant to the characteristics, goals, and activities of the group they are to lead. Third, although the best predictor of leadership is prior leadership success, individuals who are leaders in one situation may not necessarily be leaders in other contexts. Fourth, and most important to our discussion, leadership does not emerge haphazardly; the patterns of traits and abilities that differentially characterize leaders and nonleaders appear to be persistent and stable and therefore can be useful in the selection of potential leaders. Studies of leadership characteristics indicate that, compared to other members of the group, leaders tend to be higher in intelligence, scholarship, dependability, social participation, sociability, initiative, persistence, knowing how to get things accomplished, self-confidence, insight into situations, cooperativeness, popularity, adaptability, and verbal facility.

Leadership may be considered a specialized form of social giftedness. Although not specifically recognized by legislated definitions of giftedness, social talent constitutes a resource at least as important as scientific or intellectual giftedness. Socially gifted individuals are those who possess an exceptional capacity for mature, productive relationships with others (Jarecky, 1959). Such individuals exhibit mature social conscience and ethics. They help improve social relations among people by encouraging more realistic and sympathetic perceptions of one another and by stimulating positive behavior.

Jarecky (1959) investigated social giftedness in a sample of middle- to upper-middle-class adolescents (aged thirteen to fifteen). He found that those designated socially gifted by a battery of sociometric questionnaires, teacher ratings, and adaptive behavior scales were characterized by ten traits:

1. physical attractiveness and neatness of appearance
2. acceptance by an overwhelming majority of peers and adults
3. involvement in some social enterprise to which they contribute positively and constructively
4. tendency to be viewed as arbiters and policymakers by peers
5. egalitarian rather than insincere, artificial, or patronizing relationships with peers and adults
6. nondefensive behavior and lack of facade
7. freedom from emotional tension and free but relevant emotional expression
8. ability to maintain enduring relationships with peers and adults, with no rapid turnover in friendships
9. ability to stimulate productive behavior in others
10. unusual capacity for coping with social situations with intelligence, humor, and insight

A checklist of characteristics that may indicate leadership potential and social giftedness in school-age children includes the following:

— frequent involvement in some social enterprise, contributing actively and positively to it
— popularity among peers
— easy interaction with children and adults
— tendency to adapt easily to new situations
— tendency to dominate others and direct activities
— tendency to be looked to by others for ideas and decisions
— tendency to be chosen first by peers
— ability to carry responsibility well and be dependable
— knowledge of how to get things done
— ability to express self well
— enjoyment in being around others
— ability to stimulate positive behavior in others

Children with high leadership potential may also display a need for success and recognition, vulnerability to rejection, and frustration with inactivity and lack of progress toward desired ends. Based on their characteristics and the requirements of modern society, the educational needs of potential leaders include opportunities for group interaction, encouragement in learning to be effective followers as well as leaders, experience in setting realistic goals, guidance in perceiving alternative approaches to goal attainment, help in clarifying personal values and priorities, help in learning to work with individuals who have different values, help in acquiring an awareness of the complex and interdisciplinary nature of human problems, and help in acquiring an appreciation for individual differences and the value of human life.

GIFTEDNESS IN THE VISUAL AND PERFORMING ARTS

CASE STUDY 9

Isadora Duncan (1877–1927)

Isadora Duncan is considered one of the greatest dancers who has ever lived. A pioneer in modern dance, she effected changes in dance from more formal ballet movements to more meaningful movements that incorporated the simple motions of running, walking, and leaping as direct expressions of the human soul. She has been credited with starting an artistic revolution in dance and noted for her vivid, moving portrayals (Stoddard, 1970).

Isadora was born in San Francisco, California. She began her dance career at an early age. When she was six, she gathered neighborhood infants, lined them up on the floor, and had them wave their arms like swaying flowers. The artificial and highly stylized movements taught in ballet school (for example, balancing on tiptoe) irritated her, and she left after her third lesson. Isadora's mother divorced her husband for desertion and struggled to keep the family together by teaching music and knitting mittens. Isadora often went to school hungry and without proper attire for the weather. She did not like school and at age ten gave up schooling with the permission of her parents to devote herself full-time to the teaching of dance (Goertzel and Goertzel, 1962).

When Isadora was twelve, she and her sister started a dancing school in a house lent to the family by her father. She taught natural movements, beginning with children's play actions such as skipping, running, and jumping. Her brother opened a theater in the barn, and the plays became so popular that the Duncan children gave performances up and down the Pacific coast. However, the house had to be sold because of debts, and the family entered upon a period of forced mobility. Isadora's mother brought the piano along on each move and in the evenings played Schubert, Chopin, Mozart, and Beethoven. Isadora composed dances to the music, often improvising into the early hours of the morning (Stoddard, 1970).

At eighteen Isadora called a family council, and the Duncans decided to move East. Isadora found work dancing in Chicago and later in New York, where she was received well. However, she thought her future lay in Europe, so she left for England and later moved on to Paris. Her barefoot dancing and filmy costumes, scant for the age, were considered by some as refreshingly innocent, by others as scandalous. When asked to add a chemise under her veils, she replied that she would dance her own way or not at all. In Paris she began a thirteen-year rise to fame that would be unmatched by that of any American woman overseas. She danced in several European countries and in Russia, where she opened a school of dance and received acclaim as the first to *dance* the music rather than dance *to* the music. During curtain speeches she frequently asked for funds to support her dance schools, and she once antagonized an American audience by waving a red scarf and shouting that she was also red. When changes in Russian governmental policies ended liberal support for her school, Isadora returned to France (Stoddard, 1970).

CASE STUDY 10

Jason

At twelve Jason is an accomplished pianist and composer. His piano teacher suggests that Jason could be even further along in music if his lessons had begun earlier than at age five. Jason's parents, however, are not musicians and discovered his potential only by accident. One day when they were visiting some friends, five-year-old Jason entertained himself by playing at the piano keyboard. After familiarizing himself with the location of the various notes, Jason surprised his parents by picking out the melody from a Mozart concerto that had been played on the stereo during dinner. At their hosts' suggestion, Jason's parents purchased a piano and hired a private teacher. Both parents worked with the piano teacher to understand and demand the amount and type of practice required of Jason and to reinforce his progress.

Jason's precocity extends to academic areas as well. His father recalls that at twenty months of age, Jason was sitting on the lap of a house guest who was reading the morning paper. Jason spontaneously read the headlines and half the words in the articles out loud. Over the next year several individuals who had had contact with Jason commented that interacting with him was like "talking to a thirty-year-old three-year-old." Motivated by Jason's ability to read and his extensive vocabulary, Jason's parents consulted a psychologist, who evaluated Jason as gifted. Jason's parents, both of whom are vitally interested in their son's development, began reading extensively in the area of gifted education. They investigated options within the state and relocated to an area that provided quality programs for gifted children.

When Jason turned ten, his family moved to another state, where programs for gifted children, especially the musically gifted, had not yet been established. During the first few months of regular class, Jason proved to have little patience with his less accomplished peers. For example, he had difficulty controlling his sarcasm when other children made errors in arithmetic. He frequently lectured his classmates on the stupidity of their mistakes, with the result that one day several children grouped together and stomped on his carefully perfected science project. However, the new school district soon recognized Jason's intellectual talents and promoted him to junior high school.

Jason, now twelve, currently attends junior high part-time for social studies and English, high school part-time for mathematics and science, and college for music instruction. He will attend college full-time when he turns fourteen. Jason does not appear to be uncomfortable with the discrepancy in age and physical stature between himself and his classmates. In fact, he uses the discrepancy as an excuse to avoid participation in athletics, which he abhors. During the past few summers his parents have provided financial support for him to participate in music camps (where admission is gained through competition) in the United States and Europe. His ambitions are to go to Julliard and to play at Carnegie Hall.

Characteristics and Needs

Much of the work done on the characteristics of individuals talented in the arts has been retrospective in nature—that is, it has examined biographical correlates of high-school-aged or older subjects who have been identified as creative in an artistic field. Schaefer and Anastasi (1968) compared creative–artistic (strong in graphic arts and literary expression) and creative–scientific (strong in science and math) high school boys with controls matched for school attended, class, and grade point average. Students were identified for these groups based on teacher nomination and on scores on a creativity measure. All students completed a biographical inventory covering physical characteristics, family history, educational history, leisure-time activities, and miscellaneous items. Schaefer and Anastasi found that, compared to controls, creative students in science and art were more likely to evidence pervasive and continuing enthusiasm for the chosen field, singleness of purpose in pursuit of the field, ownership of field-related equipment, membership in field-related organizations outside of school, broad interests, and a stronger drive toward novelty and diversity. The creative students reported more frequent creation of new games, mechanical or electronic objects, poems, stories, or other art products; receipt of more awards in their special field outside of school; less interest in sports; more interest in reading;

more and unusual hobbies and collections (for example, of road signs and spider webs); and a preference for both older and younger friends. As children, the creative–artistic students were more likely than their controls to daydream, to have imaginary companions, to have unusual experiences (for example, travel), and to have unusual abilities (for example, eidetic memory). Anastasi and Schaefer's (1969) investigation of artistic and literary creativity in high school girls found essentially the same characteristics as their earlier work had found for creative boys.

More recently, Ellison et al. (1976) characterized artistically talented high school students as responsible and dependable; preferring literary classics to novels and mysteries; having outstanding sensitivity to and awareness of the environment; preferring classical music; being highly competitive, confident, and ambitious; preferring to work alone; and considering themselves outstanding in speed and completion of artistic and academic work and in the possession of good knowledge and techniques in their special field. The authors suggested that such biographical information can help in the identification of students most likely to achieve in artistic pursuits.

Finally, Getzels (1979) reported that talented male and female art school students differ from the norm on personality measures; they demonstrate higher aesthetic and lower social values and more aloofness, introspection, alienation, imagination, self-sufficiency, and willingness to experiment. Moreover, the female artists tend to be more dominant (a typically masculine trait) than other women, while the male artists tend to be more sensitive (a feminine trait) than other men their age. Getzels interpreted this finding as a suggestion that artists may possess a fuller range of feelings and emotions than average individuals.

These findings were supported and expanded by Bloom's (1982) work on gifted scientists, athletes, and musicians. In addition to the characteristics of willingness to work, competitiveness, and rapid learning ability, Bloom found three traits most frequently reported for concert pianists. Responsiveness to music at an early age was the first trait. Parents reported that, beginning in the crib, these children displayed a natural feeling for music, great sensitivity to music, and great emotional responsiveness to music. The children were described as being calmed by singing and other music, moving to the rhythm, and listening intently. However, it is not clear whether these children's musical responsiveness was greater in infancy than the responsiveness exhibited by nongifted children. A second characteristic Bloom identified was the ability to play by ear. By age six most subjects could listen to simple tunes and harmonies and pick them out on the piano. Authorities do not agree on whether the ability to play by ear is an unlearned characteristic or the result of early musical experience. Third, Bloom found that about half of the pianists demonstrated perfect pitch by age six or seven; they were able to hear a note and then sing or play the same note accurately without hesitation. Perfect pitch is generally found among only 1 percent of children; however, it is not clear whether perfect pitch is an inborn or a learned characteristic.

The following lists that characterize children with potential giftedness in music, art, and drama were synthesized from the works of Bloom (1982), Chetelat (1981), Karnes and Associates (1978b), Luca and Allen (1974), Renzulli et al. (1976), and Szekely (1981).

Children who are potentially gifted in music tend to demonstrate the following behaviors and attitudes:

— make up original tunes
— enjoy and seek out musical activities and opportunities to hear and create music
— respond sensitively to music and move body in accord with tempo and mood changes
— easily remember and reproduce melodies and rhythm patterns
— pick out and discuss background sounds, chords, and individual instruments played
— play a musical instrument or express a strong desire to do so
— have perfect pitch

Children who are potentially gifted in art tend to demonstrate the following behaviors and attitudes:

— fill in extra time by drawing, painting, or other art activity
— demonstrate extraordinary imagination
— draw a variety of things—not just people, houses, and flowers
— remember things in detail
— take art activities seriously and derive satisfaction from them
— have long attention spans for art activities
— plan the composition of artwork
— willingly try out different media, materials, and techniques
— arrive at unique solutions to artistic problems
— produce highly original work with distinctive style, balance, and unity
— demonstrate accelerated development of technical skill in art
— show adeptness at representing movement
— ask for explanations and instruction
— respond to unusual subjects in art
— are keen observers of the world around them
— set high standards of quality and rework their creations to achieve these standards
— show interest in other children's products by spending time studying and discussing them

Children who are potentially gifted in drama tend to demonstrate the following behaviors and attitudes:

— show interest in dramatic activities and volunteer for plays and skits
— easily relate stories with effective use of gestures and facial expressions

— are adept at role playing, improvising, and imitating others
— are able to evoke emotional responses from listeners, get others to laugh or frown, and hold the attention of the group
— handle their bodies with ease and poise
— create original plays
— maximize effects by good timing and create suspense

As is true for students talented in specific academic areas, the persistence and goal-directedness of students gifted in the visual and performing arts may result in resistance to interruption and lack of interest in activities unrelated to the talent field. Educational needs other than specific instruction in the talent area include encouragement in developing knowledge in other fields and help in integrating abilities and sensitivities with other aspects of life. Although hotly debated in public education, a need of all children may be the opportunity to develop skills in one or more artistic areas. Lacking such opportunity, many children's potential in the visual or performing arts may go unrecognized. It appears that achievement in the arts requires not only ability but also experience and encouragement in an area where opportunities are frequently limited by lack of exposure to the arts and by an absence of resources in the home and at school.

OTHER CONSIDERATIONS

Not every potentially gifted child displays all or even most of the characteristics discussed in this chapter. The positive traits usually considered possible signs of giftedness may go unnoticed in the presence of more salient negative behaviors that can also be characteristic of the gifted. Individuals responsible for identifying potentially gifted students must be aware of both sets of traits. For example, an intellectually gifted five-year-old may be bored by typical kindergarten activities and display withdrawing or defiant behaviors that mask advanced development. A first-grader may unmercifully question the teacher about why names always have to be written in the upper right-hand corner of the paper, asking why they can't be written in the left corner, on the bottom, or on the back. A mathematically precocious adolescent may consistently fail to complete homework assignments in math because of self-satisfaction with his or her current level of mastery. In an unstimulating classroom, gifted students of all ages often learn to behave like average students to avoid extra busywork (a frequent reward for finishing assignments early) or to keep from being different. Such children's high potential may never be recognized.

Gifted children of culturally diverse backgrounds also may go unnoticed if they express their talents in ways different from children in the majority culture. Based on interviews with members of three Hispanic communities in Texas, Bernal (1978) characterized gifted Hispanic children as being able to rapidly acquire English; exhibiting leadership in a sometimes unobtrusive manner;

being street-wise; accepting responsibilities generally reserved for older children (for example, helping with another child's homework); and designing imaginative games from simple toys or household objects. Torrance (1977) described other characteristics variously shown by gifted black, Native American, and Hispanic children. These include ability to express feelings and emotions in storytelling, movement, and visual arts; ability to improvise with commonplace materials; use of rich imagery; skill in group activities; responsiveness to the concrete (for example, conceptualizing problems in practical terms); a keen sense of humor; originality of ideas; persistence in problem solving; understanding of others' feelings; and ability to adapt quickly to change.

A final consideration concerns the uniqueness of all children, gifted and nongifted. Our discussion of characteristics is intended to aid those responsible for initial referral of potentially gifted children, not to create new stereotypes or myths. Each gifted child is different from every other, and his or her characteristics may or may not be consistent with those described here. When a child's characteristics suggest potential giftedness, initiation of referral–placement procedures is in order. The next chapter details these procedures.

CHAPTER SUMMARY

A knowledge of typical characteristics of gifted children and youth can help teachers and parents recognize high potential and plan appropriate instruction. Several checklists are available for identifying gifts and talents in intellectual, specific academic, creative, leadership, and artistic fields. Although these lists are helpful, users should keep several considerations in mind. First, many gifted individuals do not fit neatly into any one specific category of giftedness. Second, some gifted individuals will not display the typical characteristics described and may in fact demonstrate more negative than positive behaviors. Third, the ways in which characteristics of the gifted are identified may vary across cultural groups.

ACTIVITIES FOR THOUGHT AND DISCUSSION

1. Read and analyze biographies of some famous individuals, such as Alexander Graham Bell, Elizabeth Barrett Browning, Adolf Hitler, Abraham Lincoln, Margaret Mead, and Marilyn Monroe. Would you classify each of these people as gifted? Would each have been recognized by schools as gifted? Why or why not?

2. Interview an individual whom you consider gifted, or interview that person's parents. When was the person first recognized as exceptional? What characteristics of giftedness were present in his or her childhood, and how were they manifested?

3. Consider the ten individuals presented in the biosketches in this chapter. What types of programs and services would you have recommended for each of them?

4. Should individuals gifted in specific areas (academic, creative, or artistic) be urged to acquire additional strengths, or should the majority of instructional time be focused on developing their full potential in their specific talent area? Give a rationale for your opinion.

SECTION III

Perspectives on Educational Process

Chapter Five

THE REFERRAL-
PLACEMENT PROCESS

School districts that provide programs for gifted and talented children generally have established formal procedures for admitting children to these special programs. The procedures vary from district to district, depending on the definition of giftedness being used and whether the state administers gifted programs under special or general education regulations. Despite the variety of procedures, four basic steps are common: (*a*) referral, (*b*) assessment, (*c*) selection, and (*d*) placement.

REFERRAL

The first step in having a child considered for a gifted program is to refer the child through some kind of screening process. Ideally, every child in the district would be periodically assessed by a certified school psychologist or diagnostician using a battery of individually administered assessment devices sensitive to all types of giftedness. Unfortunately, individually assessing every child on just one type of test is prohibitive in terms of time and money. Considering that many districts define gifted learners numerically as the top 1 to 5 percent of school-age children, individually assessing all students would constitute an inefficient use of scarce resources. Therefore, most school districts employ a screening process that permits consideration of all students by using one or several easily administered mechanisms as a basis for nominating specific children for further individual assessment. Screening methods typically include (*a*) teacher judgment, (*b*) parent nomination, (*c*) group test scores, and (*d*) combinations of these and other indicators.

Teacher Judgment

Historically the subjective judgment of teachers has been a primary criterion for identifying gifted students, and surveys of current screening procedures continue to show frequent reliance on teacher referrals (Gear, 1976). Asking teachers to select children in their classrooms for further assessment has practical value because (*a*) all students are seen by teachers and (*b*) teachers are familiar with their students' work and observe their behaviors in a variety of academic, social, and artistic settings. Although several studies have questioned the accuracy of teacher judgments in identifying gifted children, recent investigations indicate that teacher referral can be a valuable screening resource, provided that teachers have received training on the identifying characteristics of gifted students.

Based on her review of literature on the accuracy of teacher judgment in identifying gifted children, Gear concluded that "teachers are relatively poor at the task" (Gear, 1976, p. 486). Accuracy indexes included (*a*) effectiveness, or the percentage of confirmed gifted who are nominated by teachers as gifted, and (*b*) efficiency, or the percentage of students nominated who actually achieve criteria for giftedness. Gear reviewed six studies, four on children of primary school age and one each on elementary students and junior high students. These investigations yielded effectiveness ratings from 9.5 to 61.2 percent and efficiency ratios of 4.3 to 57.0 percent. The effectiveness data suggest that teachers correctly identify about 50 percent of those actually gifted and fail to recognize the remaining 50 percent. The efficiency data indicate that a high percentage (43.0 to 95.7 percent) of students nominated by teachers are of average ability. Jacobs (1971) found that at the kindergarten level the children of average ability who were nominated by teachers as gifted were generally verbally adept and cooperative. Other researchers (see Gear, 1976) have suggested that teachers tend to identify as gifted students those who are conforming, pleasant, motivated, and achieving. Without specific training, teachers' difficulty in recognizing giftedness in creative, underachieving, and culturally different students increases.

More recent investigations (Borland, 1978; Gear, 1978) demonstrate that accuracy of teacher nominations can be significantly improved with specific training. Gear (1978) compared the accuracy of control teachers with that of experimental teachers who participated in five two-hour training sessions in the terminology and definitions of, and selection criteria for, giftedness and in the characteristics of gifted and talented children and the role of IQ tests in identifying these children. Following the training, teachers were asked to nominate children from their classrooms who might be gifted, after which the gifted children were confirmed through intensive assessment. Gear found that teachers who received the training identified over eight of every ten confirmed gifted, for an effectiveness ratio of 85.5 percent. Control teachers identified less than half of the confirmed gifted (40.3 percent). There were no significant differences between teachers in efficiency ratios; both groups nominated as gifted a substantial percentage of average students. These findings strongly suggest that, given training, teachers can use their judgment as an effective screening instrument for identifying potentially gifted students.

Several rating scales have been developed to help teachers become more effective identifiers of gifted students. Probably the most widely used teacher rating scale is Renzulli and Hartman's (1971) Scale for Rating Behavioral Characteristics of Superior Students (SRBCSS). The scale asks teachers to rate students on eight to ten items in each of four areas: (a) learning (for example, "Has quick mastery and recall of factual information"), (b) motivation (for example, "Is easily bored with routine tasks"), (c) creativity (for example, "Is a risk taker; is adventurous and speculative"), and (d) leadership (for example, "Seems to be well liked by classmates"). Ratings are made in terms of the frequency of observed behaviors on a scale of 1 to 4. The items making up the scale were derived from a review of characteristics of superior students and field tested by teachers and counselors in several school districts. Renzulli, Hartman, and Callahan (1971) reported interrater reliability coefficients for a sample of fifth- and sixth-grade children as 0.89, 0.85, 0.91, and 0.67, respectively, for the four scales. Test–retest reliability ratings were 0.88, 0.91, 0.79, and 0.77. Renzulli and coauthors also found that the learning and motivation scales correlated well with measures used to select students for academically oriented gifted programs and that the creativity scale correlated positively with verbal scores of the Torrance Tests of Creative Thinking. The leadership scale compared favorably to peer ratings on sociometric measures. Renzulli and coauthors recommended that the SRBCSS be used only as an aid for teachers in conjunction with other measures and not constitute the only criterion for determining giftedness. The scales can also be used to help plan programs consistent with the individual student's strengths. Although field tested primarily on students of elementary school age, the scales have been used at the secondary level as well.

It should be cautioned that a recent factor-analytic study of the 1971 SRBCSS (Burke, Haworth, and Ware, 1982) suggested that scores on the four scales could be accounted for by one major factor—learning—because teachers tend to rate students on the basis of achievement as opposed to creativity and leadership. The authors concluded that although the SRBCSS represents a good start, a need exists for more empirical support for use of the scales in identifying characteristics in four distinct areas.

The 1976 version of the SRBCSS (Renzulli et al., 1976) includes six additional scales: (*a*) artistic (for example, "Produces balance and order in art work"), (*b*) musical (for example, "Eagerly participates in musical activities"), (*c*) dramatics (for example, "Handles body with ease and poise for his or her particular age"), (*d*) communication precision (for example, "Speaks and writes directly and to the point"), (*e*) communication expressiveness (for example, "Is an interesting storyteller"), and (*f*) planning (for example, "Organizes his or her work well"). Teacher ratings of first-, third-, fourth-, and fifth-grade students on art, music, and dramatics were found to correspond to the identification of talented students by specialists in art and music.

Similarly, Karnes and Associates (1978a, b) have developed Preschool Talent Checklists consisting of six scales rated with a Likert format: intellectual, academic (reading, math, and science), creative, leadership, visual and performing arts (art and music), and psychomotor. The Preschool Talent Checklists were standardized on preschool handicapped children aged three to six but can be used with young nonhandicapped children as well.

Parent Nomination

As parents' sophistication in recognizing children's special needs increases, parents are taking a more active role in initiating referral procedures. Because of a prevailing belief that all parents think their children are gifted, some school districts are skeptical of parent nominations as a referral source for gifted programs. Many districts, however, are becoming increasingly aware of the value of parents as a referral source. Parents are the first teachers of their children and have many insights about their children's learning speed and accuracy, as well as their interests, abilities, and needs, which in some cases may not be expressed in formal academic situations. Jacobs (1971) reported an effectiveness ratio of 76.0 percent for parent referrals as compared to a ratio of 9.5 percent for teachers. Efficiency ratings for parents (61.0 percent) were also higher than for teachers (4.3 percent). Jacobs concluded that parents, who nominated fewer children than did teachers, were more conservative and did not overestimate their children's abilities. Ciha et al. (1974) also found parents more effective than teachers in nominating children as gifted, although parents nominated more children of average ability than did teachers. These findings support the use of parent nominations as a referral source.

Martinson (1975) suggested that one-page inventories be sent to all parents during their children's early school years to help screen for indications of high abilities. A brief introductory statement on the form would indicate that the teacher is interested in learning about the child in order to plan appropriate learning experiences. A simple checklist based on the characteristics described in Chapter 4 could be devised, or parents could be asked to give a brief description of their children's special hobbies and interests, problems and needs, unusual accomplishments and talents, past opportunities, preferred activities, and favorite books. Martinson (1975) and Taylor (undated) have developed several sample parent inventories.

Group Tests

Scores from standardized measures administered on a districtwide basis in large group settings provide data that permit all students to be considered for gifted programs. Some districts routinely administer group intelligence measures, and virtually every district requires group achievement testing. Although neither measure alone provides a valid indicator of giftedness, a combination of scores can serve as a fairly accurate screening device for intellectual giftedness. Pegnato and Birch (1959) found that combining a group intelligence test and a group achievement test into one screening procedure resulted in the identification of eighty-eight of ninety-one (96.7 percent) junior high students determined as gifted on an individual intelligence measure. Using a group IQ cutoff score of 130 alone located only 21.9 percent of the gifted children. A criterion of 115 IQ resulted in identification of 92.3 percent of the gifted. However, over 81.0 percent of children scoring 115 or above were not identified as gifted on the individual test. A criterion of three grade levels above grade placement on averaged reading and arithmetic subtests located 79.2 percent of the gifted students, but 78.5 percent of students selected by this criterion were not identified as gifted on the individual test.

It should be cautioned that limiting referrals to students who score well on group intelligence and achievement tests may eliminate children who are gifted in creativity, leadership, and the visual and performing arts. Moreover, group tests should not be used with preschool-age children. Scores in all age ranges can be affected by language differences, reading deficiencies, and motivation problems.

Multiple Measures

Using a comprehensive battery of easily administered instruments permits the consideration of many types of giftedness and constitutes the most effective screening mechanism. Frequently a screening committee is established within a particular school to consider children for further testing. The committee may include parents, the principal, the counselor, the teacher of the gifted program, regular class teachers, and, as needed, experts in special areas. As many sources of information as possible are collected for each child. These sources may include teacher judgment, scores from group intelligence and achievement tests, creativity measures, grade point average, parent or peer nominations or self-nominations, biographical information, anecdotal records, student products (such as artwork), organizational membership (for example, in student government or science, language, debate, or chess clubs), and expert nomination (for example, by an orchestra conductor). After reviewing all available information, the committee makes a group decision to refer the child for individual assessment.

Peer nominations can be determined by having students list several of their peers whom they consider to be the most imaginative, sensitive, organized, productive, or creative, depending on the type of giftedness under consideration. Although potentially gifted children may hide their talents from their peers, in some cases children are more aware of their friends' unique abilities than are teachers and parents. Biographical information can be useful because past behavior, experiences, and self-descriptions may give indications of future performance. Autobiographies may be written or taped and may include topics such as the student's interests, hobbies, projects, unique experiences, life philosophy, and relationships with family, friends, and organizations. Ellison et al. (1976) presented evidence that biographical information such as that collected through the Alpha Biographical Inventory (Institute for Behavioral Research in Creativity, 1968) can be used effectively to predict academic achievement, leadership ability, and artistic talent. Form R consists of three hundred multiple-choice items that individuals complete to describe themselves and their backgrounds. Ellison et al. found correlation coefficients of 0.65, 0.58, and 0.72 for artistic, leadership, and academic keys with criterion scores. The biographical keys were unrelated to sex and less racially biased than traditional measures. The authors concluded that the biographical information approach is superior to traditional identification measures and should be used more frequently in identifying students gifted in art, music, leadership, and academic areas. The most recent revision, Form U Biographical Inventory, consists of one hundred and fifty multiple-choice items and yields four scores: academic performance, creativity, leadership, and artistic potential (Taylor and Ellison, 1983).

In some districts parents may refer a child directly to the agency responsible for individual assessment. More commonly, parents are asked to discuss the nomination of their child with the child's teacher, who then refers the child to the principal or to the assessment agency, depending on the district's chain of command. In many cases parents of potentially gifted children are not aware of their children's special abilities and needs and/or are not aware that the district offers special services for such children. Hence, a major share of responsibility for recognizing potential giftedness and making referrals through the appropriate channels falls to teachers.

ASSESSMENT

Assessment is the second step in the referral–placement process and involves determining the referred child's level of abilities on a battery of tests. Many of these tests are individually administered by a person specially trained and certified in test administration and interpretation, often referred to as the school psychologist or the educational diagnostician. The types of tests used to determine a child's eligibility for gifted programs depend on the type of programs offered. For example, in states where the definition of giftedness and program options are limited to students with exceptional potential in intellectual and academic areas, the test battery generally consists of intelligence, achievement, and/or problem-solving measures. The following sections describe the types of measures that might be included in a comprehensive battery aimed at identifying gifted potential in a variety of areas.

Individual Intelligence Tests

Individual intelligence tests are superior to group intelligence tests because they allow the examiner to establish rapport, encourage motivation, and observe the quality of a child's performance as well as correctness of response. One educational diagnostician recently reported that a first-grade child given the analogy "Snow is white; coal is . . ." responded, "Coal is a black combustible mineral produced from decomposition of vegetable matter with the application of heat and pressure over millions of years in the absence of air." The diagnostician's recording of a simple " + " for a correct answer would not have communicated the quality of this child's response. When asked, "Why do we have houses?" the preschool-age daughter of a wealthy real estate investor replied, "It's none of your business why we have houses." Further exploration of the child's perceptions suggested that the child understood the question in a personal rather than a general sense because her family owned several houses.

Individual intelligence tests generally sample abilities associated with discrimination, generalization, motor behavior, general information, vocabulary, induction, comprehension, sequencing, detail recognition, analogies, abstract reasoning, memory, and pattern completion (Salvia and Ysseldyke, 1981). Two tests widely used in the assessment of gifted children are the Stanford–Binet

Intelligence Scale and the Wechsler scales. Many authorities prefer the Stanford–Binet for use with potentially gifted children because of its wider range. The Wechsler scales do not accommodate extremely low or extremely high IQs. There is also some evidence that the IQs of gifted individuals average 10 points lower on the full-scale IQ of the Wechsler than on the Stanford–Binet (Martinson, 1975; Rellas, 1969).

The Stanford–Binet includes items appropriate for testing individuals ranging from two years of age to adulthood. In general the test emphasizes verbal abilities, with the exception of preschool items, which require predominantly motor responses. The Stanford–Binet yields both a mental age and an IQ score with a mean of 100 and standard deviation of 16. Although this test has enjoyed a long history of use and acceptance, the creators of the most recent (1972) edition have been criticized for failure to include reliability and validity data, making, instead, the assumption that the new edition is reliable and valid because previous editions were (Salvia and Ysseldyke, 1981).

Three Wechsler scales have been constructed for three age groups: the Wechsler Preschool and Primary Scale of Intelligence (WPPSI) for children aged four through six and a half, the Wechsler Intelligence Scale for Children —Revised (WISC–R) for children aged six through sixteen, and the Wechsler Adult Intelligence Scale (WAIS) for individuals over sixteen. All three scales differ from the Stanford–Binet in that the Wechsler scales provide both verbal and performance subtests, yielding separate verbal, performance, and full-scale IQ scores (with a mean of 100 and standard deviation of 15). Some examples of problems on verbal subtests would be identifying similarities between two items, solving arithmetic problems, defining words, and answering general-information questions. Performance subtests include problems such as manipulating blocks to reproduce a visually presented design, completing puzzles, identifying missing parts of objects in pictures, and sequencing pictures to tell a story. The Wechsler scales are considered technically adequate, offering good reliability and satisfactory validity (Salvia and Ysseldyke, 1981).

The Kaufman Assessment Battery for Children (K–ABC), recently available from the American Guidance Service, offers a third alternative for measuring the intelligence of preschool and elementary children. The K–ABC provides both intelligence and achievement scores for children from the ages of two and a half to twelve and a half and is derived from neurological and cognitive psychology views on intelligence. Intelligence is defined as the ability to solve problems using simultaneous and sequential mental processes. An important feature of the K–ABC is its attempt to separate out intelligence (problem solving) and achievement (acquired knowledge). The instrument provides four global scales, each yielding standard scores with a mean of 100 and standard deviation of 15: (a) sequential processing; (b) simultaneous processing; (c) mental processing component, a global estimate of intellectual functioning; and (d) achievement. In addition, to promote less biased assessment of minority and low-income children, the K–ABC provides sociocultural norms based on a sample of black and white children for the four global scales and for other scales. Reliability coefficients and validity data for the K–ABC appear adequate. The norming sample was stratified based on 1980 census data and included representative proportions of white, black, Hispanic, Asian, Native American, and exceptional children (including the gifted). A Spanish version of the K–ABC is also available. Validity studies have been conducted with exceptional children, including the gifted. However, the fact that the K–ABC has been only recently published (1983) indicates the need for additional support for the measure's use with gifted children. One preliminary study (McCallum, Karnes, and Edwards, 1984) indicated that the K–ABC yields significantly lower scores for gifted children than do the Stanford–Binet and WISC–R scales; therefore, using the K–ABC processing scores for placement could result in fewer placements than if scores from the other two intelligence measures are used. Kaufman (1984) reported that minority children (black, Hispanic, and Native American) score higher on the K–ABC mental processing scales than on the WISC–R at all ranges of intelligence and therefore the K–ABC may be useful in identifying gifted minority children. However, the improved performance of culturally different children on the K–ABC may be due more to this instrument's failure to assess complex intellectual content on the mental processing scales, especially verbal reasoning and problem solving, than to increased cultural fairness (Hessler, 1985).

Other, more specialized individual intelligence devices appropriate to gifted children are the Leiter International Performance Scale, Raven's Progressive Matrices, and Piagetian measures of cognitive development. The Leiter was developed to assess the intelligence of children who experience difficulty responding verbally (for example, the hearing or speech impaired and the non-English speaking). The 1948 edition covered the age range of two through eighteen; the 1950 edition covered ages two through twelve only. The test requires that the child place blocks in a frame to match colors and forms, complete patterns, make analogous designs, and classify. Resulting scores include mental age and IQ. Raven's Progressive Matrices are also nonverbal measures of intelligence; one is designed for use with children from four and a half to eleven and a half. The child being assessed is presented with a series of colored designs, each of which has a section omitted. The child selects from six alternatives the one that best fits the shape of the missing section. The test yields a percentile rank rather than an IQ score.

Piagetian measures of cognitive development may be useful as a data source for identifying gifted children from populations that are missed by traditional psychometric tests. Although children's level of cognitive development can be assessed by performance activities described by Piaget, several attempts have been made to develop standardized measures. The Concept Assessment Kit–Conservation (Goldschmid and Bentler, 1968) was designed to assess the attainment of conservation principles by children aged four to seven. The tests consist of several tasks for measuring acquisition of various types of conservation, including mass, liquid, number, and weight. The kit does not measure attainment of other Piagetian concepts, such as seriation, classification, and transitivity, and requires additional research to support its validity and reliability.

The Social Science Piagetian Inventory (Carter and Ormrod, 1982) is a thirty-item, group-administered, multiple-choice paper-and-pencil test developed to assess performance on a variety of concrete and formal operational tasks. Resulting scores classify the respondent as concrete, transitional, or formal operational. Validity and reliability studies were conducted on upper-elementary and junior high students. Carter and Ormrod reported that scores are significantly related to age, as would be suggested by Piaget's theory of cognitive development, and that IQ accounts for only a small portion of the variance (0.29). The authors concluded from their research that the inventory discriminates between the cognitive abilities of gifted and nongifted individuals and measures something other than psychometric intelligence.

DeAvila and Havassy (1975) described a battery of "neo-Piagetian" measures, including the Cartoon Conservation Scales, designed as quantifiable versions of Piagetian tasks. DeAvila and Havassy (1974) reported from their research on Mexican-American children that these measures appear to be valid indicators of cognitive development and to be unbiased with regard to sex, ethnicity, and language spoken; hence, the measures provide a viable alternative to traditional standardized intelligence measures.

Individual Achievement Tests

Achievement tests are intended to measure directly skill development in academic content areas. Unlike intelligence tests, which are designed to assess a student's potential to benefit from instruction, achievement tests evaluate the extent to which a student has profited from schooling compared to other students of the same age or grade. Two widely used individual achievement tests are the Peabody Individual Achievement Test and the Wide Range Achievement Test.

The Peabody Individual Achievement Test (PIAT) is a norm-referenced instrument intended to assess achievement in five academic areas: mathematics, reading recognition, reading comprehension, spelling, and general information. The mathematics, reading recognition, reading comprehension, and spelling subtests consist of multiple-choice or other types of items presented to the student on an easel format that permits eye-level viewing. For the general-information subtest, the administrator asks questions that the student answers orally. The PIAT can be used with students from kindergarten through twelfth grade and gives age and grade equivalents, percentile ranks, and standard scores. The PIAT's standardization is considered excellent, although low subtest reliabilities limit use of the test to screening purposes (Salvia and Ysseldyke, 1981).

The Wide Range Achievement Test (WRAT) is a norm-referenced, paper-and-pencil test that measures a student's performance in reading (letter recognition, letter naming, and pronunciation of words in isolation), arithmetic (counting, solving oral problems, and performing written computation), and spelling (copying, writing one's name, and writing dictated words). Level 1 was developed for students below the age of twelve; level 2 is for students over twelve. The test yields grade ratings, percentile ranks, and standard scores. The WRAT is easily administered, but it provides limited behavior sampling and insufficient reliability and validity data (Salvia and Ysseldyke, 1981).

Although major educational decisions should not be made on the basis of the WRAT or the PIAT alone, each can serve as a screening device to provide a global index of achievement for identifying students who demonstrate high performance compared to their peers. Neither test yields enough information to specify academic objectives, especially where test content is inconsistent with the local curriculum. As alternatives to the WRAT and the PIAT, group achievement tests can be administered individually. Some group tests, like the Stanford Achievement Test and the Metropolitan Achievement Tests, contain more complete batteries than do some individual achievement tests (Salvia and Ysseldyke, 1981) and can yield useful information when administered individually.

The Stanford Achievement Test (SAT) for children in grades 1.5 to 9.5, the Stanford Early School Achievement Test for children in kindergarten and first grade, and the Stanford Test of Academic Skills for high school students are norm- and criterion-referenced tests with good standardization, reliability, and validity. Subtests include vocabulary, reading comprehension, word study skills, math concepts, math computation, math application, spelling, language, social science, science, and listening comprehension. Not every subtest is included at every grade level. Two special editions of the SAT have been developed for evaluating the achievement levels of visually impaired and hearing-impaired students.

The Metropolitan Achievement Tests (MAT) offer two sets of measures designed for different purposes. The MAT survey test was developed to assess general skill development in reading comprehension, mathematics, language, social studies, and science and provides both norm- and criterion-referenced information for kindergarten through twelfth grade. The instructional component of the MAT is intended for instructional planning and contains batteries for evaluating performance in reading, mathematics, and language, with norm- and criterion-referenced information for kindergarten through ninth grade. Standardization, reliability, and validity data for the Metropolitan Achievement Tests are adequate. In selecting a test to assess the achievement of potentially gifted students, the district should consider (a) the extent to which the test reflects the content of the school's curriculum, (b) the similarity of the district's students to the students who make up the standardization sample, and (c) the test's reliability and validity.

Measures of Creativity

The measurement of creative potential constitutes a complex problem in that (a) standardized testing that demands on-the-spot creative production is antithetical to the creative process; (b) standardized measures in general have not produced convincing evidence of predictive validity—that is, high test scores do not guarantee that a student will be a creative producer in adulthood; and (c) tested creativity may not be distinct from general intelligence. These issues will be discussed in more detail in Chapter 8. The most widely used tests of creative abilities are the Torrance Tests of Creative Thinking, the structure-of-intellect tests based on Guilford's model, and the Wallach–Kogan battery. Educators should be cautioned that these tests generally were developed for research rather than for instructional purposes, although they are frequently used in batteries to identify gifted students.

The Torrance Tests of Creative Thinking (TTCT) are available from Scholastic Testing Service, Inc. (Bensenville, Illinois) in two forms: verbal and figural. Both forms were designed to measure four aspects of divergent thinking—fluency, flexibility, originality, and elaboration—although norms are not provided for verbal elaboration. A figural item might, for example, ask students to sketch interesting pictures or objects by adding lines to incomplete figures. Fluency refers to the ability to generate many solutions or responses and is scored by counting the number of figures completed. Flexibility, which involves the ability to change mind sets, is scored by counting the number of different categories into which responses fall. Originality is defined as uniqueness of response and is determined by rating the frequency with which other individuals give the same response. Elaboration refers to the ability to embellish or add more detail to a concept, idea, or design and is measured by counting the number of meaningful details given.

The TTCT can be administered individually or in groups (the verbal test can be given orally to students in kindergarten through third grade). Although recommended for use with kindergarteners through adults, much of the reliability and validity data were derived from studies with elementary and secondary students. One limitation of the TTCT is the time required for scoring, which must be done by hand (a scoring service that provides standard scores and percentiles is available). Although interscorer reliability coefficients appear adequate, the novice scorer lacking training and experience may encounter difficulty. Inconsistent test–retest reliabilities are attributed to the tendency of creativity to be affected by level of motivation at the time of testing and by situational variables. The author suggests that the TTCT can be used to assess the gifted and talented in terms of both identifying potential and providing information for programming.

For younger children (aged three to eight), Torrance has developed Thinking Creatively in Action and Movement (TCAM), which provides standard scores for fluency, originality, and imagination. Scores are based on children's oral or performance responses. Scoring children's responses can be a highly subjective task, so children who feel inhibited when asked, for example, to "move like a rabbit" may be penalized by the scorer's assessment of their imaginative abilities.

Probably the most elaborate battery of creativity measures was developed by Guilford and his associates. Guilford's structure-of-intellect (SI) model (discussed in Chapter 3) defined 120 abilities in terms of three parameters, each involving several processes: operations (cognition, memory, evaluation, convergent production, divergent production), contents (figural, symbolic, semantic, behavioral), and products (units, classes, relations, systems, transformations, implications). Guilford (1975) gave the following examples of items from tests of divergent production in the semantic–content area. Each item corresponds to a different type of product:

— Name all the things you can think of that are white and edible (units).
— Regroup, in sets of three, ten given familiar words (classes).
— Describe several different ways in which a father and daughter are related (relations).
— Write as many sentences as possible that contain all three of the words *desert*, *food*, and *army* (systems).
— Suggest clever titles for a given short story (transformations).
— List all possible occupations for a person who wears a bell on his clothing (implications–products).

The SOI Learning Abilities Tests (Meeker, 1984), based on Guilford's SI model, were designed to evaluate individual students' strengths and weaknesses with regard to a variety of specific learning abilities. Several forms of SOI tests have been developed, including measures for preschoolers, a screening instrument designed specifically for gifted children, and a diagnostic device for reading, arithmetic, and creativity skills. The tests can be administered by teachers in a group setting, although individual administration may be required for nonreaders.

The SOI Learning Abilities Tests do not provide a single score relative to the general population, but rather a profile of strengths and weaknesses for each child relative to his or her own test performance. The profile permits individualized instructional planning through field-tested methods and materials available in the form of SOI workbooks. The SOI Institute, located in El Segundo, California, offers computer scoring and curriculum programming services. The general instructional procedure is to combine a weakness in an ability within one parameter (for example, symbolic content) with strengths in the two other parameters (for example, evaluative operation and class product). The child could thus work, for example, on the evaluation of symbolic classes through exercises and activities prescribed by SOI curriculum materials.

Pearce (1983) found few significant correlations between SOI abilities and intelligence. She suggested that use of the SOI tests for screening or identification be approached carefully and that its major value was in curriculum planning rather than in identification of levels of ability. O'Tuel, Ward, and Rawl (1983) also cautioned against use of the SOI tests as an identification tool.

Wallach and Kogan (Wallach, 1970) based their measures on the associative conception of creativity developed by Mednick (1962), defining creativity in terms of associative production that is abundant and unique. The Wallach–

Kogan battery has been used for elementary and secondary students and has been adapted for preschool children. It consists of three verbally presented and two visually presented tasks. The "instances" task requires the subject to generate possible instances of a class concept, such as round things. The "alternate uses" task asks the subject to think of as many uses as possible for a specified object, such as a cork. For "similarities" the subject generates possible similarities between two objects, such as a mouse and a cat. The "pattern meanings" task requires the subject to think of many interpretations in response to a number of abstract visual designs. In the "line meanings" task the subject must again think of many interpretations, this time in connection with visually presented line forms. Each task is scored for number and originality of responses. The Wallach–Kogan battery has been evaluated as being less related to intelligence than is the TTCT (Crockenberg, 1972).

An alternative to standardized assessment of creativity is the use of expert judgment of students' creative products. This method has the advantage of directly evaluating creative production as opposed to assessing creative thinking. Moreover, as suggested by Martinson (1975), expert judgment of creative products stimulates involvement of the community with the schools and brings students into contact with accomplished producers.

Measures of Critical Thinking

Measures of critical thinking and problem solving have been developed in an effort to assess individuals' logical thinking abilities in a more specific way than can be determined from tests of general intelligence. The Ross Test of Higher Cognitive Process (Ross and Ross, 1976) was designed to evaluate abstract and critical thinking skills among gifted and nongifted children in grades four to six in individual or group settings. The standardization sample included both populations. The authors report good test–retest reliability (0.94) and adequate construct validity based on correlations with age and IQ and ability to differentiate gifted from nongifted children. Test items are multiple choice, and they assess levels of higher cognitive processes within the areas of analysis, synthesis, and evaluation. Raw scores can be converted to percentiles. An investigation by Callahan and Corvo (1980) suggested that the Ross test discriminates between gifted and nongifted elementary students and measures cognitive abilities rather than general intelligence. Beckwith (1982) found the Ross test to be a useful evaluation instrument for measuring gifted student performance in programs emphasizing critical thinking.

The Watson–Glaser Critical Thinking Appraisal (Watson and Glaser, 1964) was developed for high school students and adults. It measures performance in such skills as drawing inferences, recognizing assumptions, drawing deductions, interpreting data, and evaluating arguments. The Cornell Critical Thinking Tests (Ennis and Millman, 1971) are available for two levels—for grades seven to twelve and for adults.

Measures of Artistic Talent

In addition to biographical data, measures of artistic judgment and criteria for expert appraisal of art products have been developed as means for assessing artistic potential. Measures of artistic judgment do not evaluate individuals' creative production; rather, they evaluate the individuals' artistic perceptions. The Barron–Welsh Art Scale (Welsh and Barron, 1963) was developed for use with individuals aged six and older, although norms below adult level are available for children aged six to eight only. The scale consists of eighty-six black-and-white figures, for each of which the subject indicates a liking or a disliking. However, the predictive validity of the scale has not been established, and biographical information may be a better indicator of potential for artistic productivity.

The Meier Arts Tests (Meier, 1942, 1963) include a measure of art judgment (for grades seven to sixteen and for adults) and a measure of aesthetic perception (for grades nine to sixteen and for adults). The test of art judgment consists of one hundred items, each depicting two black-and-white pictures, alike except for a small portion that has been altered on one. Subjects are asked to select the better of the two pictures. Correct responses are determined by agreement of experts in art. Percentile ranks are provided. According to Schultz (1953), the art judgment test is the most satisfactory of all art tests for evaluating sensitivity to design and is statistically reliable. The second test, aesthetic perception, contains fifty items from painting, sculpture, and abstract designs. Each item is presented in four versions, only one of which is the original work of art. The subject ranks the four choices according to his or her aesthetic judgment.

Because the reliability and validity of measures of art judgment have been criticized, efforts have been made to develop a means of assessing artistic potential based on student products. The Advanced Placement Program in Studio Art (Dorn, 1976) provides an examination for secondary students that requires them to submit portfolios of their original work: four works of a specific size and several slides. Judges examine the work based on specified criteria, such as the work's quality, its concentration within a particular mode, and the student's ability to handle the formal, technical, and expressive means of an artist. The Arts Recognition and Talent Search Program (ARTS) of the National Foundation for Advancement in the Arts uses a similar procedure to identify Artistically Talented high school students for the purposes of providing recognition and support. In collaboration with the Educational Testing Service, ARTS has developed an adjudication process to identify youth talented in dance, music, theatre, visual arts (including film and video), and writing. The adjudication process relies on expert evaluation of student products and/or performance. (For a description of the application and adjudication process, see Wenner, 1985.)

A review of research on the identification of students gifted in the visual arts (Clark and Zimmerman, 1983) indicated that no single measure is more effective or efficient than any other and that no criteria exist that have been empirically confirmed as reliable and valid for general use. Clark and Zimmerman suggested that a battery of standardized tests, informal instruments, and nontest measures be used to identify artistically talented students.

Measures of Musical Talent

Dorhout (1982) recently reviewed standardized measures for assessing three areas related to musical talent: musical aptitude, musical achievement, and musical performance. According to Dorhout, musical aptitude is a product of innate potential and early experience and is not affected by drill or practice. Items measured by musical aptitude tests include sense of pitch, sense of time, sense of loudness, and sense of timbre. For example, Gordon's Primary Measures of Music Audiation provide reliable and valid indicators of the aptitudes of children in kindergarten through third grade with regard to sensitivity to pitch and rhythm. Gordon's Music Aptitude Profile for children in grades four and higher consists of a battery for assessing tonal imagery, rhythmic imagery, and musical sensitivity and is rated the best of its kind available. Bentley's Measures of Musical Abilities for children aged seven through twelve contain four tests for pitch discrimination, tonal memory, chord analysis, and rhythmic memory. Some of the subtests have limitations due to a low ceiling. The Seashore Measures of Musical Talent evaluate pitch, loudness, rhythm, time, timbre, and tonal memory of children in grades higher than third grade.

Musical aptitude tests generally have not been extended for use with preschool-age children. However, Gordon (1980) described the nature of musical aptitude for very young children and a way of assessing children's musical strengths and weaknesses.

In contrast to musical aptitude tests, measures of musical achievement evaluate students' abilities after training—for example, the ability to differentiate between major and minor, to recognize tonal center, and to read music (Dorhout, 1982). Colwell's Music Achievement Test is a comprehensive test assessing achievement on a wide variety of skills. It is the most widely used standardized test battery in music (Dorhout, 1982). Gordon's Iowa Tests of Music Literacy for grades four through twelve and grades seven through twelve evaluate students' perceptual and notational skills.

Musical performance measures directly evaluate students' performing abilities in singing and playing instruments. The Belwin–Mills Singing Achievement Test assesses sight-singing skills for grades five through sixteen and requires qualified judges. The Watkins–Farnum Performance Scale identifies an individual's current level of performance, can be used for all band instruments, and possesses adequate reliability and validity (Dorhout, 1982). Kreitner and Engin have cautioned that tests of musical talent should not constitute the final authority in identifying musically gifted students: ". . . they are no substitute for a flexible program and a keen ear for talent" (Kreitner and Engin, 1981, p. 203).

In sum, a number of standardized tests are available to aid in the identification of potentially gifted individuals. However, standardized test scores alone should not be considered the best indicators of giftedness. Users should carefully examine the appropriateness of selected measurements in terms of content, age range, standardization sample, validity, and reliability. Type of tests selected (for example, creativity, musical aptitude) should be matched to the type of program offered. For example, if the gifted program will not provide opportunities for the musically talented, use of musical aptitude tests may not be appropriate. Standardized assessment devices are best used in combination with other indicators, such as teacher observation and expert nomination. It is not recommended that a single criterion, such as an IQ test score, be used to identify gifted individuals. Table 5.1 summarizes data sources that may be used to assess various types of giftedness.

Table 5.1 Data sources for specific types of giftedness

	TYPE OF GIFTEDNESS				
DATA SOURCE	INTELLECTUAL	ACADEMIC	CREATIVE	LEADERSHIP	ARTISTIC
Teacher rating	X	X	X	X	X
Cumulative records/ grade point average	X	X			
Parent nomination	X	X	X	X	X
Peer nomination	X	X	X	X	X
Self-nomination	X	X	X	X	X
Biographical information		X	X	X	X
Anecdotal records		X	X	X	X
Student products		X	X	X	X
Organization membership		X		X	
Expert nomination		X	X		X
Tests:					
Group intelligence	X	X		X	
Group achievement	X	X			
Individual intelligence	X	X		X	
Individual achievement	X	X			
Creativity			X		X
Critical thinking	X	X	X		
Specialized (art, music)				X	X

SELECTION

Once a child has been referred as potentially gifted and assessed to determine his or her areas of high ability and levels of ability, two decisions must be made. First, based on screening and assessment data, is the child gifted? Second, should the child be selected for participation in a special program? In some districts, being labeled gifted automatically makes the child eligible for special services. In others a gifted child is considered eligible only if the child's abilities cannot be appropriately accommodated within the regular classroom. Data gathered from both screening and assessment provide a basis for making these decisions (see Table 5.1). Three frequently used models for determining giftedness and program eligibility are (*a*) the set criterion, (*b*) the matrix, and (*c*) the case study approaches. A fourth model, Renzulli's Revolving Door Identification and Programming Model, also merits discussion.

The Set Criteria Approach

Some states and districts require a common battery of individual assessment devices for all types of giftedness, usually including one each of individual intelligence, achievement, creativity, and critical thinking measures. The results of this assessment are evaluated in conjunction with screening and specialized data (for example, art products) that are appropriate. To be considered gifted, the child must demonstrate superior performance on one, two, or three of the measures given. Cutoff criteria depend on the types of scores given by the particular measurement device. For example, the common criterion for individual intelligence tests is 2.0 standard deviations above the mean (132 for the Stanford–Binet and 130 for the Wechsler tests). For achievement, creativity, and critical thinking tests, the criterion frequently used is placement in the ninety-fifth or ninety-sixth percentile and above or achievement three grade levels above the child's grade expectancy. Students who meet the established criteria are designated as gifted. Then a committee, generally including the diagnostician, the principal, the teacher of the gifted, the referring teacher, the parents, and, as appropriate, special services personnel meets to determine the most appropriate placement for the student. The committee bases its recommendation on both the standardized assessment data and other accumulated information.

Establishing flexible standards, such as meeting set criteria on any two of four measures, has the advantage of including children who are gifted in specific areas but not gifted in every area. One disadvantage of the set criteria approach is that children from low-income or culturally diverse populations, who may not perform well on standardized measures, may be virtually excluded from participating in programs for the gifted. Another disadvantage is that the number of children admitted to the program may vary from year to year, with many children meeting the criteria one year and few meeting them the next.

The Matrix Approach

The matrix approach constitutes an alternative to establishing set criteria based on standardized assessment devices and provides a method for ranking students within a single classroom, grade level, school, or district. This approach allows school personnel to derive a total score from a variety of assessment data (for example, standardized test data, subjective nominations, intelligence scores, musical ability scores).

One example of the matrix approach is the Baldwin Identification Matrix, illustrated by the sample form in Figure 5.1. Devising such a matrix involves the following steps:

1. Select and list the data sources to be used (for example, specific tests, teacher ratings).
2. For each data source, determine the range of scores that will describe six categories (for example, below average, average, high average, above average, gifted, and high gifted).
3. Assign a weight value to each category (for example, 0 for below average to 5 for high gifted).
4. Count the number of data sources for which a student falls into each category.
5. Multiply the number for each category by the corresponding weight value.
6. Add each product to determine a total score for the student.

A cutoff criterion can be established for the total score, or, as is more common, students can be ranked according to total score and the top 1 to 5 percent designated eligible for special services. The matrix approach has the advantages of providing a total score from disparate sources of information, providing a profile of individual strengths and weaknesses, and permitting the inclusion of students in special programs based on their rankings relative to other students of similar status. For example, a gifted program in a school serving primarily low-income students would admit students who ranked at the top on the matrix compared to other students in the same school. These students would not be competing for admission to the gifted program with students from a school that serves children from highly advantaged homes.

Matrices can also be designed to identify students for specific types of programs. For example, Dorhout (1982) has suggested a matrix for identifying musically gifted students. Total scores for Dorhout's matrix are calculated from measures of musical aptitude, musical achievement, judgment of performance, attitude toward music, and teacher recommendations. Parents', peers', guidance counselors', and the student's own comments are included separately for consideration.

The Case Study Approach

Whether a district decides to use a set criteria or a matrix approach, evidence indicates that methods that consider a variety of information sources are more effective than the traditional procedure of basing judgments on group and/or

Figure 5.1 Sample form for Baldwin Identification Matrix (Baldwin, 1978)

Student _Joseph Matrix_ School _Loman Elementary_
Age _9_ Grade _3_ Sex _M_ Date _5/6/78_ School District _Eastern_

Assessment Items	Scores					B-NA
	5	4	3	2	1	
1. Standardized Intelligence Test	140+ ( )	130-139 ( )	120-129 (✓)	110-119 ( )	100-109 ( )	
2. Achievement Test Composite Score	95%ile ( )	90-94%ile ( )	85-89%ile (✓)	80-84%ile ( )	75-79%ile ( )	
3. Achievement Test–Reading Score	Stan 9 (✓)	Stan 8 ( )	Stan 7 ( )	Stan 6 ( )	Stan 5 ( )	
4. Achievement Test–Math Score	95%ile ( )	90-94%ile ( )	85-89%ile (✓)	80-84%ile ( )	75-79%ile ( )	
5. Learning Scale Score	32 (✓)	28-31 ( )	24-27 ( )	20-23 ( )	16-19 ( )	
6. Motivational Scale Score	36 (✓)	32-35 ( )	28-31 ( )	24-27 ( )	16-23 ( )	
7. Creativity Scale Score	40 (✓)	36-39 ( )	32-35 ( )	28-31 ( )	20-27 ( )	
8. Leadership Scale Score	40 ( )	36-39 (✓)	32-35 ( )	28-31 ( )	20-27 ( )	
9. Various Teacher Recommendations	Superior ( )	Very Good (✓)	Good ( )	Average ( )	Below Average ( )	
10. Psychomotor Ability	( )	(✓)	( )	( )	( )	
11. Peer Nominations	( )	(✓)	( )	( )	( )	
12.	( )	( )	( )	( )	( )	
Column Tally of Checks	4	4	3	0	0	
Weight	x5	x4	x3	x2	x1	
Add Across	20	16	9	0	0	
Total	45					

individual intelligence measures alone. The case study approach consists of having a selection committee identify gifted students based on a variety of easily obtainable data, such as aptitude or achievement test scores, teacher ratings, information from cumulative files, parent and peer ratings, and the student's self-rating. The case study approach can be used both to identify gifted students and to recommend appropriate services or placements.

Renzulli and Smith (1977) compared the efficiency (in terms of time and money) and the effectiveness of the traditional IQ procedure with the efficiency and effectiveness of the case study approach for identifying academically gifted students in the elementary grades. Results indicated that the case study method was superior to the traditional method in terms of (*a*) teacher ratings of appropriateness of placement for identified students, (*b*) dollar costs (the case study approach cost one-third as much as the traditional), and (*c*) sensitivity to gifted minority children. Three of four districts using the case study approach rated intelligence and achievement tests as most useful. However, the fourth district, which served mainly minority students, rated intelligence test data as least useful.

The Revolving Door Identification and Programming Model

The Revolving Door Identification and Programming Model (RDIM) is an approach for selecting students for participation in gifted programs that provides a mechanism for allowing students to enter and exit the resource room as their needs dictate (Delisle and Renzulli, 1982; Renzulli and Smith, 1980). The model is based on Renzulli's (1978) definition of giftedness as a combination of above-average ability, creativity, and task commitment. It assumes that a number of people manifest gifted behavior under certain conditions and at different times. Therefore, the RDIM permits the identification of a relatively large percentage (for example, 25 percent) of a school's students who have above-average ability and designates them as part of the talent pool.

Delisle, Reis, and Gubbins (1981) described the application of the RDIM in one district. Students in the talent pool participate in exploration and enrichment experiences (for example, research skill development, creativity training, and visits with guest experts) to stimulate pursuit of independent projects. Students who elect to work on a project spend several hours per week in the resource room over a period of several weeks. Upon completion of the project, the students revolve out of the resource room, creating space for other children. The RDIM increases the number of students receiving special services and decreases the elitism associated with programs that designate gifted and non-gifted as discrete categories.

PLACEMENT

After a student has been referred, assessed, and formally identified as potentially gifted, a decision based on the accumulated information must be made regarding the type of placement or special services that will most appropriately meet the student's needs. This section describes three general administrative arrangements for providing services (enrichment, acceleration, and grouping) and includes specific types of programs offered at elementary and secondary school levels. Problems and issues in placement practices are also discussed. Readers desiring more detailed descriptions of placement options and working examples should consult Fox (1979) and Morgan, Tennant, and Gold (1980) for general programs, and Arnold et al. (1981), Feldhusen and Reilly (1983), Keating (1979), and Silverman (1980) for secondary programs.

Enrichment

Although enrichment (meeting individual needs through broadening, deepening, or accelerating the regular curriculum) should be included in all types of programs for gifted students, we will use the term to designate the provision of differentiated learning experiences *within the regular classroom*. According to Getzels and Dillon (1973), enrichment became popular for gifted students during the 1930s, when it was considered important for proper socialization to maintain children with their chronological-age peers. Despite increases in the number of special programs available to gifted students over the past decade, many gifted children continue to be served in their regular classrooms. Getzels and Dillon's review of the few studies available on the efficacy of enrichment programs suggests that enrichment is superior to undifferentiated regular classroom programs. However, enrichment does not appear to produce superior performance when compared to other administrative arrangements, such as acceleration.

Many teachers and administrators favor enrichment because it avoids segregation and resulting charges of elitism while permitting all teachers to work with a few star pupils. However, appropriate enrichment may severely tax the energy and resources of regular classroom teachers and require special training for them. A real danger with enrichment is that individual teachers may define it as giving gifted students more of the same work, using gifted students as tutors for other students, requiring independent study projects without appropriate support and monitoring, or providing unique experiences (such as dissecting a heart) that are not integrated into a comprehensive plan and are therefore meaningless. Enrichment can be effective and stimulating when teachers provide differentiated instruction for the gifted in terms of well-articulated activities that require higher cognitive processing, in-depth investigation of content, wider ranges of content, and challenging modes of communication. The following methods for enriching the regular curriculum have been used at both elementary and secondary levels.

1. *Independent study*. Students conduct self-directed research projects that are carefully planned with the teacher and are monitored frequently. Prerequisites include instruction in library research skills, the scientific method, and other types of inquiry. The Management Plan for Individual and Small Group Investigations (Renzulli and Smith, 1979a) provides an excellent format for

planning and evaluating an independent study. The form requires the student to specify (*a*) the general area of study (for example, architecture), (*b*) intended audiences (for example, librarians, historical societies), (*c*) intended products (for example, a presentation to community group, a photography display, a model of a building), (*d*) steps for getting started (for example, writing letters to specific individuals, obtaining maps, visiting specific sites), (*e*) description of the specific problem to be investigated and objectives to be completed (for example, how to preserve historical structures), and (*f*) lists of resources/ activities (for example, specific resource persons, books, periodicals, and necessary equipment). Reis and Cellerino (1983) provided additional suggestions for guiding gifted students through independent study.

2. *Opportunities for rapid pacing and testing out of units of instruction in advance.* Such opportunities permit the student to engage in new learning activities and avoid the boredom of repeating instruction in skills already mastered. The time saved can be used for learning more about a regular unit of study or for pursuing interests in other subject areas.

3. *Applying higher-level thinking processes.* Teachers in the regular classroom can provide several activities for the same curriculum area that permit each learner to participate at a level appropriate to his or her intellectual abilities. For example, in the same reading assignment lower-level students can be asked factual questions whose answers require knowledge and comprehension, while higher-level students may be asked to give the story a different ending—a skill that requires analysis, synthesis, and divergent thinking.

4. *Guest speakers.* Guest speakers can provide information on topics beyond the regular classroom teacher's expertise. University faculty, parents, leaders in business and industry, and other teachers often are willing to share their expertise in specific areas. For example, one program brought in a local gemologist who demonstrated diamond cutting as part of a geology unit.

5. *Mentors.* A mentor is an adult expert who meets with an individual student for discussion and work in a field of mutual interest. The mentor may share readings and ideas and involve the student in actual field activities (for example, an archeological dig or an orchestra rehearsal). Where many mentors are available, it may be helpful to provide a match in terms of ethnicity and sex so that the mentor can serve as a role model. Mentors can be recruited by sending brief questionnaires to university faculty, public school faculty, hospitals, community organizations, and scientific and art centers.

6. *Higher-level materials.* Teachers may wish to provide higher-level materials and books to students who excel in specific areas. Coordination with teachers at the next higher grade level is necessary to ensure that undue repetition will be avoided.

At the secondary level, four additional methods of enrichment are appropriate. Each of these methods involves out-of-school activities.

1. *College-level resources.* Arrangements might be made to permit gifted students access to a university's library and laboratory facilities.

2. *Community-based career education.* As part of a career awareness program, individual students could apprentice with professionals in the student's area of interest (for example, in hospitals, businesses, industries, schools, government agencies). A variation of this model is the junior or senior work semester.

3. *Exchange programs.* Individual students may attend school in a different type of community (for example, a student from a rural community might attend school in an urban setting) or in a foreign country.

4. *The International Baccalaureate and United World Colleges.* The International Baccalaureate (IB) is a two-year diploma (eleventh and twelfth grades) that meets international standards for admission to colleges and universities throughout the world and is administered through the International Baccalaureate Office in Geneva (Cox and Daniel, 1983). High schools that offer the IB require candidates to take nine academic requirements over the two years, including first and second languages, a social science, experimental science, mathematics, art or music, and interdisciplinary studies. Candidates are also required to participate in some form of creative, aesthetic, or social service activity and to submit an independent research project. The United World Colleges (UWCs) encompass the last year of secondary school and the first year of college, providing a rigorous program focused on international understanding and academic achievement (Cox and Daniel, 1983). The curriculum incorporates the requirements of the International Baccalaureate. One UWC is the Armand Hammer United World College of the American West, located in Montezuma, New Mexico.

Grouping

Grouping refers to placing students of like ability together in homogeneous arrangements, such as in special classes. Most experts in the area of the gifted agree that the gifted should be grouped together for some period of time to stimulate each other and to make them aware that other students have equal or superior intellectual ability. Gifted students in the regular classroom may become overconfident about their ability to learn when they can compare themselves only with classmates of lower abilities. Being with their intellectual peers challenges such students to higher levels of production. It should be cautioned, however, that gifted children with fragile self-concepts may have difficulty making the adjustment from a regular class, where they have been the acknowledged social and academic stars, to a special class.

Research conducted throughout the 1960s indicated that special classes are generally superior to regular classes as a placement for gifted students, although special secondary programs, such as honors classes, may not be more effective than comprehensive high schools in preparing students for college (Getzels and Dillon, 1973). More recent research suggests that grouping arrangements appear to be helpful but not automatically effective in improving achievement. Grouping must be accompanied by quality instruction and enriched programming. Tremaine (1979) compared seventy-four gifted high school graduates who had participated for at least one year in special programs (the enrolled gifted) with fifty-nine gifted graduates who had not participated in the programs. She found no significant differences between the two groups on IQ. However, results indicated significant superiority for the enrolled gifted in grade point average and in number of advanced and gifted courses taken. These findings suggest that the gifted who have had special class experience earn higher grades while taking more demanding classes. Significant differences in favor of the enrolled gifted were also evident in SAT verbal and math scores and in number of scholarships and awards received. Finally, the enrolled gifted appeared to possess higher educational goals and more regard for high school and teachers and were more involved in school activities than gifted students in the comparison group. Both groups were equally involved in community projects and had numerous friends.

More recently Evans and Marken (1982) compared forty-three elementary-age gifted students who had participated in one, two, or three years of special class placement with thirty-eight eligible students who had elected to remain in the regular classroom. The investigators found no significant differences between the groups on measures of higher cognitive processing, personal autonomy, attitude toward school, self-concept, or extracurricular leadership and participation. The groups were not compared on academic achievement. The findings may have been due to failure of special-classroom teachers to implement the specified program goals or to excellent instruction in the regular classroom.

Although additional research is needed on the efficacy of grouping, it appears that bringing gifted students together is the strategy most preferred by educators and parents. In a national survey of teachers, administrators, and parents, Gallagher, Weiss, Oglesby, and Thomas (1983) found that respondents favored a resource room or a pullout strategy for elementary students. Special classes constituted the second most preferred arrangement. At the secondary level, advanced special classes and independent study were first and second choices, respectively. Three methods for grouping gifted elementary school children are listed in the following paragraphs.

1. *Self-contained special classes*. The special class enables gifted students to be challenged in every area throughout the day, to be stimulated by their intellectual peers, to have guidance from specially selected teachers, and to have an orderly sequenced, well-integrated curriculum. Critics of the special class point out that it establishes an elite group, depriving regular classes of the contributions that the gifted might make and providing the gifted students with poor preparation for real life.

2. *Pullout programs*. Pullout programs combine the advantages of regular class integration and special class grouping by bringing gifted students together

part-time on a regular basis. Like resource rooms, pullout programs may provide specialized services for an hour or so every day or for a full day once a week. Scheduling one full day a week permits uninterrupted, in-depth work on special projects. Pullout programs require careful coordination and communication between the special classroom teacher and teachers in regular classrooms to prevent unnecessary duplication of effort and to determine what will be required of the gifted student. For example, one issue that must be resolved is whether the gifted child will be asked to make up the assignments missed while he or she is participating in the gifted program. A well-coordinated pullout program can incorporate in the special activities the same skills being covered in the regular classroom during the time missed. The regular teacher can facilitate flexibility in scheduling by providing opportunities for self-pacing and testing out of specific units.

3. *Cluster grouping.* Cluster grouping provides an option for bringing gifted students together in small schools that cannot provide separate special classes. In cluster grouping, gifted students at the same grade level are placed in the same regular classroom, permitting the teacher to group the gifted homogeneously for some activities (for example, accelerated math) and at other times to group children heterogeneously according to other areas of interest and achievement.

Several additional grouping methods, described in the following paragraphs, are more commonly found at junior high and high school levels.

1. *Special schools.* Special schools have the same advantages and disadvantages as full-time special classes. Although special schools can concentrate more resources on the gifted, they create an even more segregated environment and are feasible only in major population centers. New York City has six schools for gifted students, including the Bronx High School of Science and two schools for adolescents gifted in the visual and performing arts (Morgan, Tennant, and Gold, 1980). Some special schools have achieved high rates of success because of their ability to provide specialized instructors, continuous acceleration, well-coordinated enrichment, and articulation among programs. For example, the Bronx High School of Science has demonstrated its efficacy through its young students' achievements, including discovery of a new species of fruit fly and of a new type of mold and innovations with regard to microscopes and protozoology (Silverman, 1980). Cities with several high schools can organize according to the magnet school concept, in which each high school specializes in one field, such as science and math, language arts, or fine arts. Students select the school that emphasizes their interest area. A language arts school, for example, can provide advanced classes in creative writing and journalism and give students the experience of writing, editing, and producing magazines and learning materials for the entire district. This type of school may also serve students interested in vocational arts related to printing, photography, and commercial art.

2. *Honors classes.* Honors classes that provide opportunities for practicing higher-level thinking skills, for creativity, and for broadening or deepening of content can be useful in meeting the needs of some gifted adolescents.

3. *Cluster scheduling for core courses.* The schedules of gifted students can be arranged so that they take required core courses together and thus form a homogeneous class that provides more rapid pacing, less drill, and greater depth.

4. *Seminars.* Through cluster scheduling, gifted students can be grouped for a period or two every day (or for one full day per week) in seminars aimed at research, interdisciplinary studies, visual and performing arts, or academic subjects. Seminars provide students with opportunities to interact with specialists who can guide them on in-depth projects within a specific area. Topics frequently presented through seminars for the gifted include computer programming, values clarification, leadership, Great Books, and archeology. Counseling and guidance can be provided through the same vehicle.

Several grouping methods, described in the following paragraphs, are applicable to both elementary and secondary programs.

1. *Resource centers.* A school or district can establish a learning, media, or interest center available to all students but reserved for gifted students at specific times. Districtwide centers enable gifted students to meet other gifted students from a broader geographical area.

2. *Special classes outside the school day.* Gifted students can meet in special classes or interest groups before school hours, after school hours, or on weekends.

3. *Summer institutes.* Many school districts, universities, and other agencies organize programs during the summer for gifted students. Some of these programs are residential, while others are day schools. The University of Denver's University for Youth (Katz and Seeley, 1982) offers a six-week summer program for gifted children from preschool through high school. Courses range from French to jazz improvisation to aerodynamics and are taught by university faculty. Indiana University has organized two residential summer programs, one a two-week academic program for students entering fifth through ninth grades, called the College for Gifted and Talented Youth (Spicker and Southern, 1982). A second two-week program, the Indiana University Summer Arts Institute (Clark and Zimmerman, 1982) serves students in sixth through ninth grades who are seriously interested in studying the visual arts, music, and dance. Many states offer summer camps for specific fields, such as computers, and music institutes open to a select few through rigorous competition.

4. *Summer expeditions.* Some school districts and universities offer intensive field studies conducted on site. These expeditions are led by experts who serve as instructors, guides, and resource personnel for topics such as oceanography, California missions, and Alaskan wildlife.

5. *Outreach programs.* Gifted students can be brought together at study centers in museums, universities, science laboratories, and industries to learn about and participate in the research and service being conducted at those sites. For example, several museums provide opportunities for gifted students to help with the cleaning and cataloging of fossils and shards; others provide training programs for the gifted to serve as docents and tour guides.

Acceleration

Acceleration involves changing the rate of presentation of the regular curriculum to enable apt students to complete the program in less time than is usual. Research conducted from the 1930s through the 1960s produced data clearly favoring the acceleration of gifted students in terms of early admission to elementary, secondary, and college levels. Gifted students who were accelerated generally demonstrated equal or better achievement and social adjustment compared to students of equal ability who were not accelerated (Braga, 1971; Getzels and Dillon, 1973; Paulus, 1984). Recent research corroborated these findings. For example, Alexander and Skinner (1980) conducted a follow-up study of eleven students in grades six to eight who had been permitted early entrance to kindergarten. Ten of the eleven had maintained A or A/B grade point averages throughout their school history. All eleven participated in a wide range of extracurricular activities and demonstrated outstanding achievements. Although two students indicated some disadvantages in being the youngest in their classes and excluded by age from some activities, their reservations were far outweighed by their positive remarks. Parents reported several advantages to acceleration: The students were no longer bored, and they learned to work to remain in the upper portion of their classes; learning had previously come too easily to them.

Fox (1979) has argued that early admission to kindergarten or first grade can provide a better match between gifted children's learning needs and program content. Grade skipping may be mandatory for meeting the needs of extremely gifted students who are very advanced in academic learning. Although rapid acceleration produces practical difficulties in terms of exclusion (owing to age or size) from some extracurricular activities (for example, driving a car, dating, athletics), most gifted children understand and adjust to these realities. It is important to compare these relatively minor inconveniences with the social and emotional problems that can emerge when very advanced gifted children are held back in the regular grade levels and forced to wait for their peers to catch up. Moreover, as indicated in our earlier discussion of the characteristics of gifted children, such children frequently prefer the company of older students.

Despite the abundance of evidence favoring acceleration at all age levels, acceleration—especially early entrance to kindergarten or first grade—is the least used option. One reason may be the opposition of teachers. Jackson, Famiglietti, and Robinson (1981) found that kindergarten teachers express a bias against early entrants unrelated to their experiences in teaching early entrants. When considering early admission, teachers, as well as parents and administrators, frequently express concern about gifted young children's lack of social and emotional maturity, need for interaction with chronological-age peers, physical and motor immaturity, and ability to work independently. All individuals involved in making decisions regarding acceleration may need training in the characteristics and needs of gifted young children. One obstacle is the lack of clear guidelines for determining which children can best benefit from acceleration programs. Teachers and administrators can become involved in exploring the creation of such guidelines.

An important consideration in employing acceleration as a method for meeting gifted students' needs is the requirement of careful articulation among programs. If a student is permitted to complete course work in a shorter amount of time than is usual, some provision must be made for either continuing acceleration or using the extra time for high-level enrichment. Without some means for well-planned continuation, efforts at acceleration are wasted.

Modes of acceleration generally used for elementary students include those listed in the following paragraphs. Keep in mind the need for program articulation in each.

1. *Early entrance to kindergarten or first grade.* Each child eligible for early entrance should be evaluated in terms of (a) degree of advancement in relation to peers, (b) number of areas in which the child shows advanced achievement, (c) the child's self-concept, and (d) ability of the regular teacher to provide individualized enrichment.

2. *Grade skipping.* Considerations are the same for grade skipping as for early entrance.

3. *Part-time grade skipping.* For children who demonstrate superiority in some areas but not in every area, an option would be placement at a higher grade for just the areas in which they are advanced. For example, in many elementary schools children in one grade move to another classroom at a higher grade level for instruction in reading or mathematics.

4. *Combined classes.* Classes in which children from two grade levels are combined (for example, fifth/sixth) permit the younger children to interact with the older students both socially and academically. Ungraded classrooms also permit acceleration through self-pacing.

5. *Telescoping.* Telescoping refers to a form of acceleration in which part of the curriculum is covered in a shorter amount of time than is usual (for example, two semesters' or two years' work in one). Self-paced, programmed instruction can aid in telescoping but should not constitute the only method of instruction for gifted students. Most programmed workbooks do not involve the student in different thinking processes. Computer-aided instructional packages also permit self-pacing.

The types of acceleration listed in the following paragraphs are frequently found at the secondary levels.

1. *Multilevel enrollment.* Gifted students with uneven ability or interest levels may take some courses at the junior high and others at the senior high school.

2. *College course work.* Many high schools permit qualified juniors and seniors to take college courses for college credit while completing the high school degree. College courses might also be taken during the summer. Some school districts with large numbers of gifted students have college professors come to the high school to teach college-level courses. In rural areas isolated from universities, correspondence courses might be arranged. Cox and Daniel (1983) provide additional information regarding concurrent enrollment in high school and college.

3. *Early admission to college.* Districts may permit early graduation from high school through a variety of acceleration methods (for example, grade skipping, testing out of courses, telescoping), thereby permitting early admission to college. In rare instances students may go on to college without receiving a high school degree. A survey of 190 colleges and universities (Karnes and Chauvin, 1982) revealed that a large number of public and private institutions have established policies for early admission, but few students avail themselves of these opportunities, perhaps due to lack of specialized advice or counseling.

4. *Advanced Placement Program (APP).* The APP, run by the College Entrance Examination Board, combines advanced courses with other forms of acceleration to allow students to graduate early from college.

5. *College-Level Examination Program (CLEP).* The CLEP tests, administered by the Educational Testing Service, permit students to earn college credit by exam.

6. *Accelerated classes outside the school day.* Special accelerated classes for gifted students can be held after school or on weekends to enable students to complete programs earlier than is usual. For example, students gifted in the sciences or mathematics might take advanced courses in these areas on Saturdays in order to begin college-level science and mathematics courses earlier in their school careers.

Julian Stanley's Study of Mathematically Precocious Youth (SMPY), conducted at Johns Hopkins University, demonstrates accelerated programming at its best (Stanley, 1977; Stanley and Benbow, 1983). Begun in 1971, SMPY identifies and serves mathematically gifted students in junior high school. The Scholastic Aptitude Test is the primary identification tool. SMPY has developed a variety of accelerated programs aimed at curricular flexibility. These include (*a*) statewide talent searches, (*b*) fast-paced classes held on Saturdays or during summers, (*c*) grade skipping, (*d*) Advanced Placement Program exams, (*e*) early entrance to college, and (*f*) fast-paced college-level courses (two and one-half hours once a week for thirty weeks) that cover a year of high school calculus concurrently with the first year of college calculus. The effectiveness of these programs has been validated longitudinally (Stanley and Benbow, 1983). The evaluation of fast-paced Saturday classes has indicated that students completed between two and four and one-half years of math in twelve to fourteen months. Case studies document phenomenal accomplishments of SMPY graduates. One received his bachelor's degree at Johns Hopkins at age seventeen, after only five semesters. He received his master's and doctoral degrees by age twenty-two and was an assistant professor at Northwestern University at twenty-one.

Problems and Issues in Placement

The preceding discussion suggests the existence of a great range and variety of enrichment, grouping, and acceleration options. However, most school districts can afford only a limited number of options. Few, if any, districts offer all the alternative placements we have described. Many problems associated with placement stem from the limited variety of options realistically available. Although ideally the most appropriate placement for a given child is determined by that child's individual characteristics, abilities, and needs, more often the placement decision is a compromise between these characteristics and what is available in the district.

A second problem is related to district procedures for monitoring placement appropriateness over time. For example, a gifted elementary-age child may be accelerated into the junior high and achieve successfully during the first year. During the second year, however, grades may decrease from A's to B's and C's and may be accompanied by a lessening of motivation. The junior high teachers, unaware of the student's history, may not perceive these grades as a problem. Regularly scheduled monitoring of gifted students' placement by district personnel can prevent such situations.

A third, related pitfall is the too prevalent assumption that a program labeled gifted or advanced necessarily is the most appropriate placement for a child identified as gifted. Many parents and teachers who refer a child for potential giftedness are satisfied to find that the child is subsequently placed in a program for the gifted. Yet the particular program may be one of low quality—or one of high quality but not appropriate to the specific child's needs. For example, an extremely intelligent child with uniformly high achievement and a need for radical acceleration may be placed in an excellent enrichment program whose focus is not on faster pacing but on broadening experiences.

These problems can be avoided by (a) having a concerned, knowledgeable placement team or committee meet with the parents (and the child, if appropriate) to establish the most appropriate setting based on the student's characteristics and the district's alternatives; (b) having the same committee monitor and evaluate the student's progress in the prescribed setting at least annually (more frequently if indicated); (c) having district personnel who seek and create additional placement alternatives; and (d) helping parents become informed advocates for their children by providing parent training in the characteristics and needs of gifted children and information on the range of placement options nationally available. Many districts have established procedures to review and correct, if necessary, placement decisions with which parents or school personnel are dissatisfied.

It should be noted that some states mandate procedures for ensuring that gifted students receive free, appropriate services through the development of individualized education programs (IEPs) and due process procedures. The Education for All Handicapped Children Act of 1975 (*United States Code*, P.L. 94–142) revolutionized special education for the handicapped by requiring that every such child be given a free, appropriate public education in the least restrictive setting, nondiscriminatory evaluation, and individualized education programs. Under the same law parents of handicapped children were given the right to (*a*) participate in the planning of their children's educational program, (*b*) give or withhold consent to initial evaluation/assessment and placement, (*c*) have access to school records, and (*d*) challenge the accuracy of their child's assessment, program, and placement through due process procedures (Turnbull, Turnbull, and Wheat, 1982). Although the law's guarantees to handicapped children and their parents do not extend to gifted children and their parents, as of 1980 eleven states required and six suggested use of IEPs for gifted and talented students. Seventeen states required and two states suggested use of due process procedures in identification, assessment, and placement of gifted and talented students (Zettel, 1980). New Mexico, not included in these figures, also mandates IEPs and due process for gifted students.

Where required, IEPs must include (*a*) a statement of the student's present levels of performance, (*b*) a statement of annual goals and short-term instructional objectives, (*c*) a statement of specific special education and related services to be provided and the extent of the student's participation in regular education, (*d*) projected dates for initiation of services and expected duration, and (*e*) criteria and evaluation procedures for determining whether the objectives are being met (Michaelis, 1980).

In states mandating due process, parents who are dissatisfied with assessment, program, or placement procedures for their child can request an impartial hearing. If dissatisfied with the decision of the hearing officer, they have a right to appeal the decision and have it reviewed. The decision on the appeal can be challenged through civil action in court. The school district can use the same process to challenge a parent's decision—for example, refusal to permit testing or placement, which results in denying a student services appropriate to his or her special needs.

Resorting to appeals or to court action frequently creates antipathy and distrust between parents and schools and may not result in improved services to the student (Strickland, 1982). In most cases, involving parents as partners early in the referral–placement process and communicating effectively at each step will lead to mutually satisfying placement decisions. In turn, active, informed parents frequently become the school's most avid supporters. It is the ethical responsibility of the schools, whether or not IEPs and due process are mandated, to invite parent participation and joint planning to create the best possible program for each child.

FUTURE TRENDS

The inconsistent quality of programs for the gifted nationwide has resulted in efforts to reconceptualize traditional procedures for identification and placement. Movement is toward a more inclusive approach to providing services through individualized education. For example, Birch argued that "identification of gifted students, as generally practiced in the United States, is neither desirable nor necessary" (Birch, 1984, p. 160) and suggested that identification be replaced by an assessment designed to provide information that can be used to develop individual education programs for every student. Schools can begin by assessing children prior to school entry.

The recent Richardson Study, a national survey of 1,572 school districts with programs for the gifted, reported that current efforts to serve gifted students are inadequate to those students' needs. Survey results indicated that part-time special pullout classes and regular classroom enrichment constitute the most common program options. Only 47 percent of the pullout programs and 16 percent of the enrichment programs were evaluated as substantial based on minimal criteria for hours per week, number of students, and adequacy of curriculum and materials. The Richardson Study proposes as a solution a pyramid of options at each grade level. At the base would be enrichment activities in the regular classroom for a large number of students; fewer, more specialized programs (for example, outside classes and special schools) would be included at the top of the pyramid and would be aimed at serving the most able students. The pullout program would be eliminated as an option. The pyramid system encourages opening the services to a broader population of students and moving the students ahead on the basis of mastery. The model discourages the identification and labeling of children as gifted (Olson, 1985).

CHAPTER SUMMARY

Procedures for admitting students to school programs for the gifted and talented include four steps: referral, assessment, selection, and placement. Actual procedures vary from district to district, depending on the definition of giftedness used, the resources available, and whether gifted students are considered as part of special education.

Some schools do not formally identify gifted students but attempt to meet their needs in the regular classroom. Some automatically place students referred by teachers or screening committees into special programs. Still others, especially those in states where the gifted are defined as exceptional or special education students, specify distinct referral, assessment, selection, and placement procedures.

Referral involves nominating a student for consideration through some kind of screening mechanism that theoretically permits all children the opportunity to be referred. Screening methods typically include teacher judgment, parent nomination, group testing, or combinations of several formal and informal indicators. Assessment refers to the evaluation of the student's abilities, generally according to standardized measures of intelligence, achievement, creativity, critical thinking, and specific abilities, depending on the type of giftedness suspected and the type of gifted students served in the district. Selection consists of evaluating the formal and informal data collected through screening and assessment to determine (a) whether the student is gifted and (b) whether the student should be selected for special services.

After the student has been referred, assessed, and identified as gifted, a decision must be made concerning the most appropriate type of placement or special services for that student. Three general options are (a) enrichment within the regular classroom, (b) grouping gifted students together, and (c) using acceleration to permit students to complete the program in a shorter amount of time than is usual.

About one-third of the states mandate due process in referral–placement to ensure delivery of an appropriate education to gifted and talented students. In all states, meeting the individual needs of gifted and talented students can be facilitated by having committees (including the parents, if possible) review assessment results, determine the appropriate placement based on each student's individual needs, monitor the implementation of placement decisions, continually investigate additional program options for the district, and keep parents informed.

Future trends include a movement away from formal identification of children as gifted and toward assessment and programming designed to individualize instruction for all students.

ACTIVITIES FOR THOUGHT AND DISCUSSION

1. Write a definition of gifted and talented that is acceptable to you. Then design referral–placement procedures appropriate to your definition. Include specific methods and criteria for determining whether a given student is gifted.

2. What referral–placement procedures are mandated or suggested by your state? In general, how are these procedures implemented in the local school districts? What suggestions would you make if you were invited to participate in revising state and local procedures?

3. Develop one of the following types of referral instruments: (a) a teacher rating scale, (b) a parent nomination form, (c) a peer nomination form, (d) a biographical inventory.

4. Discuss the advantages and disadvantages of enrichment, grouping, and acceleration as general administrative arrangements. Suggest additional methods of enrichment, grouping, and acceleration.

Chapter Six

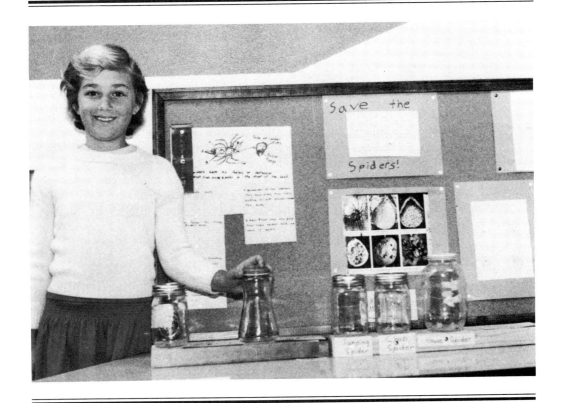

CURRICULUM
DEVELOPMENT

$\mathbf{B}$oth the 1972 Marland report and the 1978 Gifted and Talented Children's Act declared that gifted and talented children are children who, by reason of their exceptional abilities, require services different from those provided by the regular program. The rationale for the provision of differentiated services is the fact that without special attention to their unique needs, many gifted and talented children underachieve. As in the case of other special needs children, such as handicapped and bilingual, identification without special programming is an unproductive endeavor.

Chapter 5 described three administrative arrangements that permit the provision of differentiated services to gifted students: enrichment within the regular classroom, grouping, and acceleration. This chapter suggests ways in which educators can differentiate curricula to meet the needs of gifted students in any administrative setting. The first part provides an overview of curriculum development theory and process. The following sections discuss structured models for curriculum design, and the chapter closes with some suggestions regarding individualized education programs (IEPs) for the gifted.

CURRICULUM DEVELOPMENT THEORY AND PROCESS

Even after a decade of heightened interest in gifted students, educators exhibit little apparent concern with undertaking basic curriculum development processes as the first step in gifted education. Examination of the literature on gifted education reveals few references to curriculum per se. Hundreds of articles in a dozen journals, several of which are devoted exclusively to gifted education, have been written in the past few years, and few of them contain even a mention of curriculum. For example, neither the fifty-seventh yearbook (Part II) of the National Society for the Study of Education, *Education of the Gifted* (1958), nor their seventy-eighth yearbook, *The Gifted and Talented: Their Education and Development* (1979), addressed curriculum. In fact, only one mention of curriculum occurs in both tables of contents, and neither volume contains the word *curriculum* in its index. Only recently has curriculum as a comprehensive plan been addressed by a few pioneering writers (Kaplan, 1975, 1979a, 1979b, 1980, 1981; Kaplan et al., 1982; Maker, 1982; Roberson, 1984).

It is essential that curriculum be defined in terms that promote intelligent discourse. *Curriculum is a comprehensive educational plan designed to maximize instructional interactions in achieving and potentiating behavior change.* A comprehensive curriculum should designate the main elements of a subject matter area over a number of years. Thus, a comprehensive curriculum could cover the courses in elementary school, those in secondary school, or both. Comprehensive curriculum development outlines the content for the target population.

Two important points should be noted. First, our definition is not concerned with post facto descriptions of instructional activities, as are some curriculum definitions (for example, curriculum is all the experiences the learner has at school). Second, our definition is not concerned with a microcurriculum approach, which focuses attention on the daily lesson plan or on instructional units. The need for comprehensive, long-term planning of educational experiences for the gifted is imperative. This same need has been generally recognized in regular education for half a century or more. Comprehensive curriculum development is a process that can serve gifted education very well. The following subsections provide an analysis of the state of the art of curriculum development in gifted education and suggest a theoretical basis and procedures for comprehensive curriculum development.

The State of the Art: A Critique

A review of representative writings in gifted education yields a number of reasons why educators of the gifted have not addressed some of the crucial issues of curriculum development. The reasons are valid.

1. *Most writers in gifted education address the problem of "programs" for the gifted.* The use of the term *program* most probably is rooted in the fact that for a decade following the 1972 Marland report, education of the gifted was a category in the federal designation of special education. However, it should be pointed out that several writers in gifted education (e.g., Kaplan, 1979) use the term *program* in the sense of a scheme for implementing curriculum or organizing instruction rather than as an overall plan of intended outcomes.

2. *Curriculum as a field of study suffers from different interpretations and definitions.* Terminology used by curriculum specialists is not standardized, nor are the processes of curriculum development. Variability in the curriculum field is a mixed blessing.

3. *Most writers in gifted education appear to believe that the gifted are well served if standard subject offerings are changed in some way.* Just what changes are made often appears unimportant. The seemingly crucial task is to make the programs different. The result is window dressing that often does not achieve the objective.

4. *Many believe that the typical curriculum in the schools is acceptable if it is enriched or if the gifted student is accelerated or grouped with other gifted students.* This idea is implicit in the rather general failure to address comprehensive curriculum development for the gifted.

5. *Many writers in the field of gifted education suggest that modifying typical teaching methods is the same as changing the curriculum.* Granted that teaching modes for gifted learners should differ in some instances from teaching modes for typical youngsters, this difference is instructional, not curricular.

6. *Most school districts and certainly most schools lack trained curriculum specialists.* Furthermore, most curriculum specialists probably are trained in the traditional subject areas and have had little experience with the problems of gifted education curriculum development.

7. *The curricular needs of small numbers of gifted students are easier to ignore than are the needs of the majority of students.* In financial situations that include tight budgets and inflation, school officials generally cut back instructional programs that affect the fewest pupils.

8. *Many gifted "programs" are apparently being set up according to the dictates of dynamic but misguided workshop organizers and other educational opportunists.* School districts are frequently settling for novelty and superficial cosmetic program changes with questionable instructional materials. Literature on education for the gifted clearly reveals that many writers seem to prefer instructional innovation—games, logic problems, puzzles, mind-benders, and other intriguing abstractions—to basic curriculum development.

9. *A sufficient number of trained leaders in gifted education curriculum development has been lacking at the federal and state levels.* Too few people have been expected to service too many teachers and school districts. Because education for teachers of the gifted has only begun to be a concern at the college level, the quick and easy in-service and conference approach to gifted education for teachers has been favored until recently.

10. *The complexities of designing curriculum to include elements of enrichment, grouping, and/or acceleration are formidable obstacles.* Those who would improve education for gifted and talented students are dissuaded by such complexities.

11. *Tackling the complex and expensive task of developing comprehensive curricula for the gifted is sufficient deterrent for many school administrators.* Some of these administrators are beset by more easily visible problems, such as minimum competency concerns and eroding financial resources.

12. *Curriculum development personnel at all levels, including those at universities and colleges, have been noticeably reluctant to involve themselves in the gifted education movement.* One probable reason is that the early federal definition placed gifted education outside the areas of expertise of most college curriculum professors. Moreover, the number of college students interested in taking courses in curriculum development for the gifted is limited. Thus, colleges and universities have been slow to respond to the needs of educators of the gifted.

Philosophical and Theoretical Bases of Curriculum for the Gifted

In this country, curriculum for the gifted is unquestionably tied to a philosophy that must address a basic question: What should be the goals of education in our democratic society? This philosophic question contains some implications. First, the question is, what *should be* the goals? not, what *are* the goals? Thus, the emphasis is on attainable societal ideals, or at least some hoped-for improvements of the status quo. Second, the question implies a plurality of valid goals, including educational goals, personal/individual goals, and societal goals. These categories raise further questions: What should be the intellectual/

cognitive purposes of education? The affective/attitudinal purposes? The career/vocational purposes? The answers to these questions are based on a particular view of the world—in short, on a philosophy or a value system. Historically, answers to such questions are always tentative, even though the questions are relatively stable.

In 1860 Herbert Spencer asked the following question: What knowledge is of most worth? Roughly seventy-five years later, curriculum writers extended the question: What knowledge and *experiences* are of most worth? Rational attempts at answers must extend the question even further: Of most worth to whom? For what purposes?

Ralph Tyler, one of the foremost writers in curriculum, dealt with the question of educational goals in a democratic society by developing a rigorous rationale that pointed out that attempts to answer the question must be based on studies of society, of the learner, and of the subject matter. He then posed his famous four questions (Tyler, 1950):

1. What educational purposes should the school seek to attain?
2. What educational experiences can be provided that are likely to attain these purposes?
3. How can these educational experiences be effectively organized?
4. How can we determine whether these purposes are being attained?

Hilda Taba, a contemporary of Tyler, responded to the basic question of educational goals with a rationale that involved the following seven steps: (*a*) diagnose needs, (*b*) formulate objectives, (*c*) select content, (*d*) organize content, (*e*) select learning experiences, (*f*) organize learning experiences, and (*g*) evaluate (Taba, 1962). These steps do not by themselves answer the question of what educational goals should be, but they do provide guidelines for considering goals.

Public education as a social institution is an attempt to answer the questions related to educational goals and to provide learning experiences that will satisfy both the individual and society in terms of survival, growth, and progress. Such objectives are never easy to achieve, but they nonetheless constitute the constant aim of public education. All education is rooted in the culture it is intended to serve. Furthermore, as Johnson pointed out, the source of all curriculum is the available culture, and "learning is the process by which an individual invests cultural content with meaning" (Johnson, 1967, p. 136).

Over the past three-quarters of a century, various groups have developed educational objectives for this country. What their endeavors had in common was an attempt to provide basic goals for students in this society. Two of the more well-known sets of objectives are those published by the Commission on Reorganization of Secondary Education in 1918 and by the Educational Policies Commission of the National Education Association in 1938. The goals of the Commission on Reorganization of Secondary Education were (*a*) health, (*b*) command of fundamental processes, (*c*) worthy home membership, (*d*) vocation, (*e*) citizenship, (*f*) worthy use of leisure time, and (*g*) ethical character. In 1938 the Educational Policies Commission used the following four headings for its goals: (*a*) self-realization, (*b*) human relationships, (*c*) economic efficiency, and (*d*) civic responsibility.

Neither of the two groups mentioned gifted education per se, yet the point is obvious, although sometimes overlooked by current educators: Gifted students exist and conduct their lives in the same social milieux as the nongifted. The problem of developing a philosophical position on curriculum for the gifted is precisely the same as the problem of developing a tenable philosophical position on curriculum for typical students. The question is how best to serve each student in relation to individual needs as well as societal goals.

Providing for the unique needs of the gifted is a responsibility of public education, just as is providing for the needs of typical students. Gifted education should form an integral part of public education. The gifted require a differentiated curriculum, one that does not create an elitist attitude or an elite group and does not promote a segregated group that ultimately isolates itself from the mainstream of society.

All students—all citizens, for that matter—are unique if analyses of traits and comparisons of abilities and interests are carried far enough. There is a danger in subscribing to and supporting gifted education in an uncritical manner, just as there is a danger in uncritically crusading for industrial arts classes, interscholastic athletics, or advanced science curricula. The danger is in fragmenting or overbalancing the curriculum. Education is rooted in society and must reflect the needs of society. One unassailable fact emerges: All education in the formal, institutional sense exists to conserve and improve the society in which it operates. Society will not long tolerate educational practices that operate against this axiom.

Educators of the gifted have a fundamental responsibility to include citizenship education for their students. It is in the best interests of the gifted and all others to recognize and respond in humane ways to the radical ambiguities the gifted find in a world peopled largely by "average" individuals. Citizenship education can best be achieved through a comprehensive curriculum that is sensitive to differences and diversities and that accommodates both variability and commonality.

We must not assume, however, that the only aim of institutional education is the preservation of society. The transformation of culture and society must also be considered. It is reasonable to expect that the initial hoped-for breakthroughs in all areas of human endeavor, such as medical research, conflict resolution, and social reorganization, will be accomplished first by the gifted. But this fact does not argue for differentiation carried to extremes; rather, it shows clearly that the gifted operate in the total social milieu. "All decisions about education, including those about curriculum, are made within the context of a society. The values and forces of that society determine not only what manner of man exists but also to some extent what manner of man is needed" (Taba, 1962, p. 25).

Curriculum Development Procedures

In the process of curriculum development for any student population, curriculum modifications will build on, enhance, or extend certain elements already in place in the typical K–12 curriculum. Take, for example, the current interest in developing computer literacy. These efforts should be labeled computer applications because the computer will not discover any new mathematics or grammar or social science per se. Rather, the computer will be used in new ways to help achieve new objectives necessary for a technological society. In short, except where new knowledge is generated, there is little chance of anything totally new being added to the public school curriculum. Developing differentiated curriculum appropriate to the gifted is the primary task. For the most part, differentiation will be accomplished through adaptations in content, process, products, resources, learning environment, and the interactive elements of all of these components. In this section we describe general considerations for developing curricula for the gifted.

Since 1971 the emphasis on gifted education has created an ongoing demand for identifying gifted students and finding satisfactory means of meeting their needs. Even though large numbers of progressive school districts have developed programs and curricula for the gifted, these programs require constant evaluation and revision. Also, there is a tendency on the part of public school educators to jump too quickly on academic bandwagons and then to realize that some of the fundamental procedures for building strong programs have been slighted. In districts where gifted education has been in place for any significant length of time, both formal data collection and informal impressions and assessment have taken place or are taking place, and these can serve as valid bases for curriculum revision.

The necessity for constant concern with identification of the gifted population and redefinition of need is illustrated by the fact that since the mid-seventies many school districts, encouraged by federal special education funds and further pressured by state departments and local vested-interest groups, have launched programs for gifted students. However, it is doubtful that many of these districts had the resources and expertise to develop comprehensive curricula for gifted students. Early efforts were probably piecemeal endeavors that need modification now, as experience has accumulated. Consider the following example. District R–2–J (a fictitious name) initiated a program for intellectually gifted students at the primary level only, reasoning that as the years passed, these gifted students would be channeled into the intermediate and secondary levels. Placing the emphasis at the primary level was based in part on the rationale that as the students matured, they would be better able to progress on their own. Furthermore, the reasoning went, teachers at the upper-elementary and secondary levels have more depth of knowledge in specialized subject matter areas and thus are able to individualize learning for gifted students.

After the gifted program in District R–2–J had been in place for three years, the school department found that students from the gifted program became bored in grades four, five, and six and consequently underachieved. When these students went on to junior high, their discontent increased, and several became discipline problems and eventually dropped out.

A second problem with the gifted program in R–2–J became apparent when a group of parents organized for the purpose of having the gifted program expanded to include talented and creative students. As a result, school district officials recommended redefinition of the program in terms of the target population to be served.

After the administrative officers of a school district accept the need for curriculum development in gifted education, the next activity is the formation of a districtwide committee composed of a reasonable cross-section of the district involved. This committee will ordinarily be initiated by a superintendent for curriculum and instruction, a district curriculum director, a director of elementary or secondary education, or a combination of these or similarly titled personnel. The district comprehensive curriculum committee has as its major responsibility guiding the various subject matter, grade level, and special population committees to ensure the best possible articulation, correlation, coordination, and integration of educational experiences for the learner.

Interrelationships of various subject matter, grade level, and special population committees are shown in Figure 6.1. Each of these committees includes in its membership building administrators and counselors. Note that the special population labeled "gifted and talented" includes pupils with special ability in music, dance, drama, art, literature, and interpretation as well as in the academic areas.

Typically, school districts have a written philosophy that applies to the entire educational range for which the district is responsible. Therefore, it is more productive generally for districtwide curriculum committees to develop a succinct and rigorously derived rationale. The statement of the major purposes and underlying beliefs may be called a philosophy, a rationale, or a position statement. The important thing is that it be written.

A philosophy of gifted education provides the following: (a) a basis for policy decisions; (b) fundamental guidelines for curriculum development; (c) guidance for instructional activities; (d) a rational means for resolving value conflicts among interested parties; (e) stability during unexpected change in community, administration, or teachers; (f) a backdrop for evaluation of programs, student progress, and materials; (g) necessary protection against self-serving special interest groups; (h) an impetus for proactive educational endeavors; (i) basic elements to help integrate the efforts of teachers, administrators, guidance personnel, and others; and (j) a means for continued communication and interaction among teachers, administrators, students, and other interested parties. In general, a philosophy/rationale is a consensus declaration subscribed to by the committee members and others. It is an agreed-upon set of basic beliefs about gifted education.

Figure 6.1   Interrelationships of curriculum committees

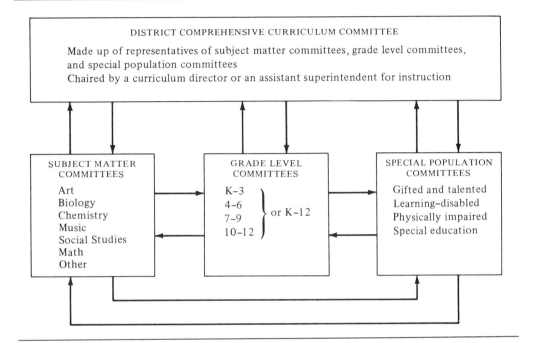

A rationale need not be—and for practical purposes, should not be—lengthy and verbose. A detailed treatment is hardly necessary as a preface for developing comprehensive curriculum for the gifted. Note the following example:

> The Board of Education of R–2–J recognizes that gifted education is an integral and important part of the educational services of the District. It is further recognized that in accordance with democratic principles and with the philosophy of this District, it is the responsibility of the District to provide the opportunities necessary for the greatest academic and personal fulfillment of every student. To these ends, the Board of Education of R–2–J commits the resources—human and material—necessary to carry out a comprehensive program of gifted education, kindergarten through grade twelve.
>
> Gifted education will be administered according to applicable R–2–J School District policies as set forth in the official R–2–J School District Policies and Procedures Handbook. These policies will govern curriculum planning and implementation, staffing, supervision, and evaluation.

One of the more workable models that curriculum committees can follow is the model developed by Taba (1962) and based on eight steps for developing a teaching–learning unit (see Figure 6.2). It is not intended that any committee

Figure 6.2   Taba's model for curriculum design and steps for developing a teaching-learning unit (Taba, 1962)

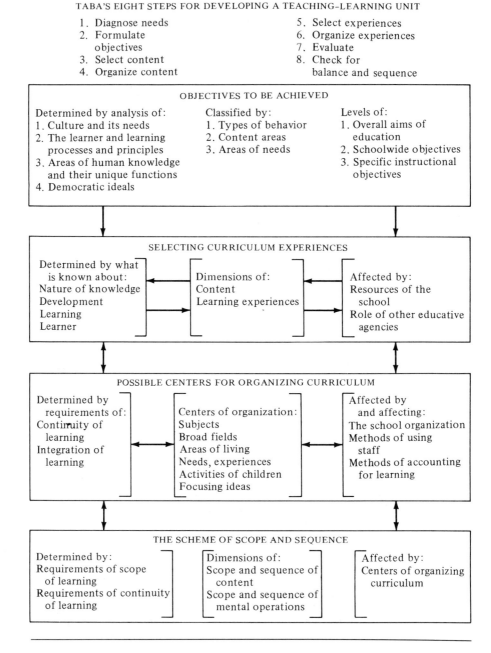

TABA'S EIGHT STEPS FOR DEVELOPING A TEACHING-LEARNING UNIT

1. Diagnose needs
2. Formulate objectives
3. Select content
4. Organize content

5. Select experiences
6. Organize experiences
7. Evaluate
8. Check for balance and sequence

OBJECTIVES TO BE ACHIEVED

Determined by analysis of:
1. Culture and its needs
2. The learner and learning processes and principles
3. Areas of human knowledge and their unique functions
4. Democratic ideals

Classified by:
1. Types of behavior
2. Content areas
3. Areas of needs

Levels of:
1. Overall aims of education
2. Schoolwide objectives
3. Specific instructional objectives

SELECTING CURRICULUM EXPERIENCES

Determined by what is known about:
Nature of knowledge
Development
Learning
Learner

Dimensions of:
Content
Learning experiences

Affected by:
Resources of the school
Role of other educative agencies

POSSIBLE CENTERS FOR ORGANIZING CURRICULUM

Determined by requirements of:
Continuity of learning
Integration of learning

Centers of organization:
Subjects
Broad fields
Areas of living
Needs, experiences
Activities of children
Focusing ideas

Affected by and affecting:
The school organization
Methods of using staff
Methods of accounting for learning

THE SCHEME OF SCOPE AND SEQUENCE

Determined by:
Requirements of scope of learning
Requirements of continuity of learning

Dimensions of:
Scope and sequence of content
Scope and sequence of mental operations

Affected by:
Centers of organizing curriculum

would follow Taba's curriculum scheme step by step. However, allowing for modifications any given committee might make, it is our qualified professional opinion, based on two decades of curriculum experience, that following Taba's general outline will yield the desired results.

GENERAL MODEL FOR CURRICULUM DEVELOPMENT

One of the best ways to maintain the perspective necessary in comprehensive curricula building with its vast array of subject matter content is to arrange a planning flowchart (Figure 6.3) that shows the major developmental aspects of the effort. The crucial components of curriculum development are (*a*) subject area, (*b*) pupil population, (*c*) broad aims, (*d*) enabling skills, (*e*) instructional concerns, and (*f*) major concept clusters. Interactions of these components are both relational and operational and thus provide the basis for comprehensive curriculum development.

For example, curriculum development of social studies for the gifted relates concepts from the social sciences with instructional concerns and with skills and processes that students will need to apply. The basic concepts determine the content parameters at the various grade levels. That is, set I concepts are utilized at the primary level, set II concepts at the intermediate level, and set III concepts at both levels. Specific applications of the basic concepts are determined by logical relationships between and among basic concepts and would depend on the knowledge, interests, and readiness of the learners.

Thus, clusters of integrated concepts would control to a reasonable degree the instructional methods used to communicate the subject matter. For example, with *citizenship and individual attainment* as the broad aim, and with *rational inquiry skills, social science methods*, and *communication processes* as enabling social science skills, we might select *cultural diversity* as an appropriate area of instructional concern. As a result, we might arrive at a set I cluster of integrated concepts labeled *interaction*. Set II clusters that would fit would be *society* and *institutions*, while appropriate set III clusters would be *value clarification* and *self and society*. In essence the flowchart establishes a curricular context within which selected concepts and knowledge of the social sciences become integrated. This is the best way to manage the selected aspects of the universe of knowledge upon which social studies are based. The logic of the subject matter will determine the development of content, and learner needs will influence the articulation of concept clusters—for example, *man, other primates, human differences, cultural traits, tools and inventions, value systems, coping mechanisms*, and *environment*.

All content used in schools represents an attempt to design a model of the outside world with the hope that the learner can use the understanding thereby gained for personal benefit as well as benefit to society. For elementary-age gifted students, typical social studies content will be extended, broadened, and

Figure 6.3   Planning flowchart for curriculum development of social studies for the gifted

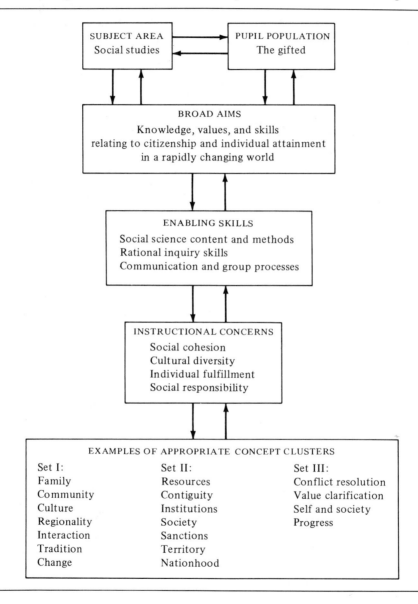

deepened. In addition, teachers of the gifted will be expected to employ inquiry and heuristic methods when desirable and appropriate.

After the basic concept structure has been designed, fluid elements of the curriculum can be shown by grade level, as in the curriculum outline for intermediate-level social studies that follows. Although the outline is for social studies, keep in mind that for each subject area, the comprehensive plan should include (a) a rationale, (b) broad goals for each grade level, (c) the major categories of subject matter content, and (d) activities designed to produce specific learner behaviors.

SOCIAL STUDIES: GRADE FOUR

Broad Goals

1. To understand and appreciate salient features of state government and history
2. To understand citizenship, ethnicity, race, and belief and value systems
3. To respect various lifestyles and cultures
4. To understand that to the people in it, each culture is logical and valuable
5. To begin to relate the state to the region and to the nation
6. To become aware of and to understand the importance of environmental problems

Grade Four Student Performance Objectives

I. To learn about the state (for example, New Mexico)

   A. Early habitation
   B. Life of early inhabitants: homes, family life, food, shelter
   C. Indian tribes of the state
      1. Apache
      2. Navajo
      3. Other
   D. Influence of Indian heritage on the state
      1. Place names
      2. Foods
      3. Ceremonies
      4. Occupations
      5. Art, music, literature
      6. Religion
   E. Spanish presence
      1. Don Juan Onate and early explorers
      2. Missionaries and missions
      3. Spanish influence and contributions: religion, foods, dress, language, music, architecture

 II. To learn the legal and ethical bases of equality
    A. Sovereignty
    B. Citizenship
    C. Cultural awareness
    D. Biculturality
    E. Multiculturality

III. To understand human variability
    A. Common human traits
    B. Unique human traits
    C. Ethnocentrism and prejudices
    D. Being different as not being better or worse
    E. Value of contributions of all kinds of people during a long history

IV. To examine culture
    A. Universals, language, beliefs, rituals
    B. Differences, values, tools, inventions
    C. Sanctions and taboos

 V. To see the state as a part of a large region
    A. Characteristics of a region
        1. Weather and climate
        2. Crops
        3. Occupations
        4. History
        5. Language and culture
    B. The different rules to which the state has been subject
        1. Indian
        2. Spanish
        3. United States
    C. Statehood and nationhood as a set of interactive, reciprocal relationships

VI. To become aware of various kinds of pollutions affecting the state and the region
    A. Causes of various kinds of pollution
    B. Solutions to some environmental problems
    C. Crucial issues in environmental deterioration

SOCIAL STUDIES: GRADE FIVE

Broad Goals

1. To acquire the basic knowledge relevant to the discovery of the New World
2. To understand the idea of exploration in geographical and other contexts
3. To realize and appreciate that people of diverse backgrounds and different beliefs have helped our nation grow
4. To acquire the basic knowledge that pertains to the growth of our nation
5. To learn about life in the United States and in North America today

Grade Five Student Performance Objectives

I. To acquire knowledge about early explorations and how North America was discovered
   A. Map and globe skills
      1. Size and shape of the earth
      2. Concept of location: absolute, relative, and natural
   B. Navigation inventions
   C. Why humankind has always explored

II. To understand the concept of colonization
   A. Importance of the New World to Spanish, French, English, Dutch
   B. Economic development
   C. Natural resources
   D. Government forms, structures, and functions

III. To learn about acquisitions of territory in the New World
   A. Louisiana Purchase
   B. Gadsden
   C. Texas
   D. Florida
   E. Oregon
   F. Alaska
   G. Hawaii
   H. Panama

IV. To interpret the human experience
   A. Historical time
   B. Probable cause and effect of historical changes
   C. History as culture change
   D. Human diversity as evolutionary problem solving
   E. Incompleteness of historical records and necessity for inferencing

V. To understand that change is a constant in human interactions
   A. People changing through evolution and revolution
   B. Social institutions changing as people wish them to change
   C. Social institutions changing slowly in ways that meet human needs, which remain the same
   D. Society developing through the contributions of individuals and groups

VI. To gain knowledge about customs and traditions
   A. The imprint that culture leaves on the individual
   B. Customs that continue to be observed even though the reasons for their existence are gone
   C. Change viewed as not always an improvement
   D. Response to change as dependent upon many factors

VII. To learn about advances in civilizations
   A. Development of law and the societal good
   B. Explorations and acculturation

    C. Institutions and inventions

    D. The effect of technology and science in producing civilizations different from pastoral societies

    E. Settlement of conflicts in a number of ways, not just with weapons

VIII. To understand the concept of nationhood

    A. Conditions under which people become a nation

    B. A society within every nation

    C. Many cultures within every society

    D. Many subcultures within every culture

SOCIAL STUDIES: GRADE SIX

Broad Goals

1. To learn fundamental concepts about other lands and peoples
2. To build on the indisputable fact that the earth is the home of all people
3. To understand the earth in its physical context
4. To learn about land and water distribution on the globe
5. To broaden the perception of students to include the world as we know it today
6. To realize that conditions in various parts of the world are due to various basic causes

Grade Six Student Performance Objectives

I. To understand fundamental concepts about other lands

    A. The role of natural resources in the ways that countries develop

    B. Climatic conditions as they help determine ways of life

        1. Location

        2. Precious metals

        3. Water power

        4. Temperature

        5. Land forms

    C. Culture: the shared way of life of a people

        1. Belief systems

        2. Tools

        3. Customs

        4. Traditions

        5. Institutions

        6. Economic systems

        7. Political systems

        8. Foods

        9. Dress

        10. Transportation

        11. Communication

        12. Language

D. International relations
   1. Interdependence
   2. Cultural constants
   3. Human variability
   4. Politics
   5. Government
   6. The United Nations
   7. Conflict resolution

II. To become aware of and seek solutions to current global issues and problems
   1. Environmental deterioration
   2. Toxic waste disposal
   3. War
   4. The Third World
   5. Unequal distribution of resources
   6. Population patterns and densities
   7. Food supply
   8. Communicable diseases
   9. Communication
   10. Understanding

The following lesson plan format is one that a teacher might use at social studies level four for the topic of environmental pollution.

Lesson Topic: Kinds of Pollution

Key terms and concepts

___ pollution
— environment
— atmosphere
— hazard
— air pollution
— water pollution
— noise pollution
— visual pollution

Discussion questions

___ What are the main causes of air pollution? Of water, noise, and visual pollution?
— What are some things you can do to prevent pollution?
— Why must we find solutions to pollution problems?

Instructional materials

___ pictures
— films

— tape recording of noise pollution
— jar of polluted water

Activities

__ Divide the class into four groups, each group to brainstorm the discussion questions.
— Have each group perform the following activities:
    write a short skit about pollution
    develop a poem or song
    develop a mural on butcher paper depicting pollution in their
        community
— Integrate activities with language arts, mathematics, and science.

Evaluation

__ recall of terms
— representation of concepts in final products

Each of the traditional subject matter areas must be differentiated to meet the criterion of appropriateness for gifted students. The area of intermediate-level social studies (for grades four, five, and six) can be used to illustrate several kinds of instructional adaptations essential to teaching gifted students. Any or all of the suggestions that follow may be used with typical students at different times and under the right circumstances. One or more of the following differentiation modes must be used with gifted students. Keep in mind that changes in content, process, product, and situation (environment) can and must be used at any level, preschool through senior high school. Thus, depending on factors such as intellectual maturity, background, readiness, and interest, students can engage profitably in the study of any topic. Or, as Bruner stated in *The Process of Education:* "We begin with the hypothesis that any subject can be taught effectively in some intellectually honest form to any child at any state of development" (Bruner, 1960, p. 33).

As an example at the fourth-grade level, let us take student performance objective VI: "To become aware of various kinds of pollutions affecting the state and the region." To make the content appropriate to gifted students, the unit can be developed along both interdisciplinary and multidisciplinary themes. First, some of the social sciences that might be studied to help us arrive at the solutions to environmental problems must be identified. These would include the disciplines of history, geography, political science, economics, anthropology, sociology, ethics, law, and psychology. Following identification of the social sciences might be a comparison and contrast of the various methods each of these disciplines utilizes to gather and interpret data. At this stage it seems essential to identify some fundamental concepts of each discipline to provide the student with an understanding of the parameters of knowledge, or the "turf claims," of each. Some examples of fundamental concepts are as follows:

— *History:* tradition, change, multiple causation, interpretation, ambiguity, progress
— *Geography:* site, resources, land forms, human–land relationships, location, climate
— *Economics:* scarcity, goods, production, consumption, profit, division of labor
— *Anthropology:* culture, culture transmission, culture transformation, acculturation, inventions and tools
— *Sociology:* society, group, institution, interaction, interdependence, status, role, sanctions
— *Political science:* state, power, authority, regulation, sovereignty, governance, laws
— *Ethics:* rights, responsibilities, common good, social progress, values, standards

It will soon become apparent that all the social science disciplines have much to contribute to the solution of environmental problems. As students gain insights about social sciences, they will develop high-level abstractions that integrate concepts. For example, the concept of resources will be viewed by economists, geographers, sociologists, political scientists, anthropologists, and historians in ways that will differ in some respects and will be convergent in some respects.

Extending the content differentiation one step further, it would be productive to inquire what disciplines other than those in social science might be used to help solve environmental problems. This adds a multidisciplinary dimension. For example, chemistry in various applications is certain to be named, as are physics, biology, and geology. Literature and philosophy would not be surprising entries, nor would statistics, accounting, range science, animal science, engineering, medicine, and computer science. Given time, the list could be continued. Gifted youngsters will group and extend disciplinary applications to real environmental problems and their solutions.

Out of these content considerations, ecology will emerge as the science with the most directly related central concepts:

Ecology: ecosystem; balance, biotic, abiotic, symbiotic, and reciprocal relationships; habitat; trophic structure; limitations; adaptations

Students will develop novel and innovative applications of these concepts from ecology as the students interact with the content relating to environmental deterioration.

As they acquire new insights from the concepts and content of the social sciences and other disciplines, gifted youngsters will be able to discover, develop, and apply the methods of investigation of disciplinary inquiry. In other words, it is appropriate that gifted students utilize various inductive approaches in the solution of real-life environmental problems. For example, students could be asked to engage in original research on an environmental problem. This research could be done either individually or in teams of two and would involve the students in the entire process, from identifying the problem to reviewing the literature, hypothesizing, collecting data, testing, and drawing inferences. The results of these investigations could be used in several ways. First, students could present their papers in a classroom setting designed to be similar to a professional conference, complete with questions from and interactions with their colleagues. Second, students could present their papers to high school or college classes or to a group of teachers or professors, again responding to input or questions from the audience. Third, students could evaluate and select (upon derived criteria) several of the papers to be abstracted and submitted for publication in local journals or newspapers. Fourth, students could synthesize relevant conclusions, findings, and inferences in a "think tank" setting and publish the results in an appropriate medium.

From the foregoing discussion we have seen that with some careful planning, *content* has been differentiated in several important ways: (*a*) content outside the typical social studies has been included, (*b*) content outside social studies per se has been included, and (*c*) the contents have been interrelated, correlated, and integrated. The *processes* for dealing with the content have been expanded beyond the typical read-and-recite formula to include heuristic approaches, inquiry, problem solving, discovery, analyses, syntheses, and evaluation. The *product*, a scientific paper, is beyond the range of typical fourth-grade students, and the *environment* has been modified by making the learning situation much more open, flexible, and innovative than the typical classroom.

STRUCTURED MODELS FOR CURRICULUM DESIGN

Consistent with sound curriculum development procedures, planners of curricula for gifted students must consider (*a*) the philosophy of the program (for example, is the aim of gifted education to develop the individual or to serve society?); (*b*) learning, socioemotional, and cultural characteristics of the specific population; (*c*) parent and community perceptions of needs; and (*d*) historical precedent. Several models for planning curricula have been developed that assume certain philosophical notions about the gifted and their education. These models will be referred to as structured because they provide a philosophical base, general goals, and explicit frameworks that can be applied to a variety of geographic locations and content areas. Unstructured models, on the other hand, are developed in specific localities, including individual schools, as a response to particular pressures and follow the preferences of individual teachers, principals, curriculum coordinators, and central office personnel. We use the terms *structured* and *unstructured* recognizing that the degree of structure follows a continuum and that every model contains both structured and flexible elements.

Maker (1982) has described four features of programs that educators can modify to provide qualitatively different curricula for gifted students: content, process, product, and learning environment. These features have been utilized in our example of differentiating a social studies curriculum and will be elaborated upon here. Based on gifted students' superior cognitive abilities and needs for humanistic orientation, Maker's content modifications include (*a*) increasing the *abstractness* of content (for example, deriving higher-order concepts and generalizations), (*b*) increasing the *complexity* of concepts and generalizations, (*c*) increasing the *variety* of content presented, and (*d*) providing for the *study of people* (for example, through biographies). Process modifications refer to use of instructional methods designed to meet gifted students' needs for developing higher levels of thinking, inductive and deductive logic, and creative production. Modifications in product require gifted students to design more professional products that deal with real problems and that are communicated to real audiences. The products of gifted students should differ from those of students with lesser ability in an emphasis on transforming rather than on summarizing existing knowledge. Finally, Maker's learning environment modifications are those that encourage student centeredness, independence, openness, complexity, acceptance, and mobility.

The models to be discussed in the following subsections vary in their emphasis on content, process, product, and environmental modifications. Renzulli's enrichment triad model includes all four types of modifications. Meeker's structure-of-the-intellect model, Taylor's multiple talent approach, and Bloom's taxonomy of educational objectives emphasize changes in process. Our unit approach focuses on content and process modifications.

Enrichment Triad Model

Renzulli's (1977) enrichment triad model has two main objectives: (*a*) to provide students with opportunities to pursue their own interests and (*b*) to help students identify and pursue realistic, solvable problems consistent with their interests and find appropriate outlets for their products. The triad consists of three types of enrichment activities. Type I, general exploratory activities, encourages all students (not just the gifted) to develop and explore their interests through interest centers, field trips, and meetings with resource persons. Activities emphasize the methods of inquiry associated with each interest area rather than accumulated facts. For example, an interest center on historiography might include the tools and resources of historiographers—early maps, diaries, letters, newspapers—rather than descriptions of local history. Through Type I activities, students determine which areas they wish to pursue in depth.

Type II, group training activities, involves training exercises designed to help all students develop thinking processes. Types of processes include creative thinking, observing, classifying, analyzing, synthesizing, evaluating, comparing, and hypothesizing. Teachers provide process training using content areas that students have identified as interests during Type I enrichment.

Type III enrichment consists of individual and small group investigations of real problems. Students become investigators of real problems, use appropriate methods of inquiry, and communicate their findings to real audiences. For example, students in southern New Mexico investigated the effects of a dispute between Texas and New Mexico resulting from a court ruling that permitted Texas to drill for water in New Mexico. The students presented their findings and suggestions to citizens' political action committees.

The enrichment triad model is unique in two ways: (a) it encourages the integration of students with heterogeneous abilities (in Types I and II enrichment), and (b) it permits teachers to identify able and interested students—that is, those who have the ability and commitment to pursue the investigative activities of Type III enrichment. Moreover, the structure is self-selective in that all students have the opportunity to participate in independent or small group investigations, although a smaller number will actually identify manageable problems and see projects through to completion.

In sum, the enrichment triad model incorporates content modifications through the use of exploratory activities (Type I), process modifications through the training of thinking skills (Type II), and product and environment modifications through the assignment of independent projects aimed at real-life problems (Type III). The triad model is widely used at elementary and secondary levels for both comprehensive programs and specific programs (music, art, social studies). Before implementing the triad approach, program planners should consider whether the implicit assumptions of the model are consistent with their philosophy and goals and with the needs of the specific target population. The triad model includes these assumptions: (a) all children are capable of and can benefit from explorations of different topical areas and activities that require higher-order thinking, (b) gifted students will emerge through the triad process and should be permitted to self-select in or out, (c) content should be based on student interest, and (d) real-life problems should constitute a major curriculum emphasis.

Structure-of-the-Intellect Model

Guilford's structure-of-intellect (SI) model of intelligence (described in Chapter 3) postulates 120 different thinking abilities derived from five kinds of operations applied to four types of contents, resulting in six types of products. Operations include cognition, memory, divergent production, convergent production, and evaluation. Types of content are figural, symbolic, semantic, and behavioral. Products consist of units, classes, relations, systems, transformations, and implications. Each discrete ability combines one operation with one type of content and one product (for example, memory-semantic-unit). Meeker's structure-of-the-intellect (SOI) measures and materials translate Guilford's model into individual educational profiles and prescriptions (Meeker, 1977; Kester, 1982; Navarre, 1983). The SOI Learning Abilities Tests permit the identification of children's strengths and weaknesses in many of the 120 abilities. Computer programs are available for the analysis of individual profiles, and workbooks for students provide learning activities matched to strengths and weaknesses.

Teachers trained in the SOI approach can classify the available commercial and their own teacher-made materials according to SOI abilities. Teachers can also design activities that give students practice in specific abilities for any content area.

Multiple Talent Approach

Taylor's (1967, 1968) multiple talent approach stands on several philosophical premises: (a) most individuals possess talent in at least one area and often in several areas, (b) developing these talents results in better self-concepts and motivation in school, and (c) multiple talents relate to success in the world of work. Concerned that the Guilford SI model may overwhelm practicing teachers because of the number of elements that require training, Taylor suggested that many of these elements can be grouped into six manageable areas: productive thinking, decision making, planning, forecasting, communication, and academics. Table 6.1 provides a definition and a sample activity for each of these talent areas. Taylor (1985) recently noted three new talent areas: implementing, human relations, and discussing opportunities. Activities for the implementing talent area encourage students to implement a plan. Activities in the human relations talent area focus on obtaining and keeping a job or getting promoted. Finally, activities for the discussing opportunities area are designed to help students identify new opportunities.

Talents Unlimited (1974), a federally funded (Title III) project in Mobile, Alabama, developed a model of the multiple talent approach for classroom implementation. The project-designed *Talent Activity Packet* provides activities for grades one through six that integrate process training with subject areas (mathematics, science, language arts, music, art, physical education). Schlichter (1981) described evaluation results of the implementation of the Talents Unlimited project in heterogeneous classrooms over a three-year period and compared these classrooms to control classrooms that did not use Talents Unlimited. Schlichter reported significant differences favoring Talents Unlimited classrooms on measures of academic achievement (Stanford Achievement Test), on measures of creativity (Torrance Tests of Creative Thinking), and on project-developed measures of talent development. Schlichter also indicated that Talents Unlimited has potential for improving the identification and inclusion of rural, black, or disadvantaged youngsters whose talents may lie in less traditional areas.

Schlichter noted that the evaluation study did not provide data on use of the multiple talent approach with gifted students, although the model does provide some direction for the enrichment of regular classroom programs. Use of the multiple talent approach is most consistent with programs based on a philosophy that supports the idea that all students possess some talent and can therefore benefit from enrichment activities.

Table 6.1 Summary of Taylor's multiple talent model

TALENT AREA	DEFINITION	SAMPLE ACTIVITY
Productive thinking	To generate many varied and unusual ideas or solutions and to add detail to the ideas to improve or make them more interesting	Students working in a math unit on surveying and graphing are asked to think of a variety of unusual topics for a survey they will conduct and graph during the day.
Decision making	To outline, weigh, make final judgments; and defend a decision on the many alternatives to a problem	Students who are preparing to order materials through the Scholastic Books campaign are assisted in making final selections by weighing alternatives with such criteria as cost, interest, and reading level.
Planning	To design a means for implementing an idea by describing what is to be done, identifying the resources needed, outlining a sequence of steps to take, and pinpointing possible problems in the plan	Students who are studying the unusual characterstics of slime mold are asked to design experiments to answer questions they have generated about the behavior of the mold.
Forecasting	To make a variety of predictions about the possible causes and/or effects of various phenomena	Students who are conducting a parent poll on their school's dress code are encouraged to generate predictions about the possible causes for low returns on the survey.
Communication	To use and interpret both verbal and nonverbal forms of communication to express ideas, feelings, and needs to others	Fifth-graders studying the American Revolution role-play reactions of Loyalists and Rebels hearing the reading of the Declaration of Independence.
Academics	To develop a base of knowledge and/or skill about a topic or issue through acquisition of information and concepts	Students read from a variety of resources to gain information about the Impressionist period and then share the information in a discussion of a painting by Monet.

SOURCE: Schlichter, 1981, p. 146.

Taxonomy of Educational Objectives

Among the more significant educational developments of modern times was the appearance of *A Taxonomy of Educational Objectives, Handbook I: Cognitive Domain* (Bloom, 1956). As the title of the work denotes, Bloom and his colleagues sought to express in scientific, taxonomic form the major categories of educational objectives in the cognitive realm. Later volumes dealt with the affective and psychomotor domains. This division of objectives into the cognitive, affective, and psychomotor areas was not novel. For decades educators had used the terms *understandings, attitudes, and skills.* Bloom and his associates simply gave more formal names to these categories. Of monumental importance, however, was the building of the classification scheme (taxonomy).

The cognitive domain, concerned with acquiring information, is divided into six major classes arranged in a continuum from simplest to most complex. Table 6.2 illustrates the six major classes of the cognitive domain, which have become known as Bloom's taxonomy, as they may be applied to kindergarten art.

The most important implication of Bloom's taxonomy for gifted education is that it can be used to help students arrive at higher-order cognitive behaviors ordinarily expected of gifted children. Academically gifted students are recognized and identified in part by their intellectual acuity, their ability to acquire knowledge easily, and their ability to demonstrate with verbal facility their possession of large amounts of knowledge. As one moves up the levels of the taxonomy when building comprehensive and differentiated curricula, it is apparent that special care and effort are needed to include the levels of synthesis and evaluation—levels the gifted generally attain at earlier ages than do their intellectually average peers. Some gifted students normally operate at the levels of synthesis and evaluation, and curricula for them must be built accordingly. However, the curriculum developer must not presume that all gifted learners have mastered basic knowledge, comprehension, and application levels for every topic.

Table 6.2 Bloom's taxonomy applied to kindergarten art

OPERATION	DEFINITION	EXAMPLE: COLORS
1. Knowledge	Can recall specific facts, terms, concepts, principles	What color is this?
2. Comprehension	Can grasp *meaning* of material; understand, interpret, explain, summarize	How do we get the color green?
3. Application	Can use learned material in new situations	Paint a picture using the primary and secondary colors.
4. Analysis	Can break down material into component parts to understand the structure; can see similarities and differences	How does this painting make you feel? What colors did the painter use to make you feel that way?
5. Synthesis	Can put parts together to form a new whole; rearrange, reorganize	Paint a picture that conveys the feeling of anger.
6. Evaluation	Can judge the value of material based on definite criteria	How effective is the use of color in this picture?

SOURCE: Kitano, 1982, p. 20.

The Unit Approach

The unit approach to curriculum planning (Kitano and Kirby, in press) is based on the following assumptions: (*a*) content acquisition constitutes a major goal of education, and (*b*) educators' specialized knowledge renders them competent and responsible for selecting topics to be offered. The unit approach has long served regular education and can provide a flexible vehicle for developing curricula matched to gifted students' unique learning characteristics, needs, and interests. The unit approach offers a model for program development based directly on the individual program's philosophy, objectives, and target population.

Philosophy and Assumptions. Models such as the enrichment triad and the open classroom assume that gifted learners' own interests should determine curriculum content. For these models, teachers serve as guides and resources. In contrast, the philosophy most consistent with the unit approach purports that although gifted students often possess the maturity and motivation to select their own learning experiences, educators should design the curriculum. There exist bodies of knowledge that history and experience have determined are appropriate to the education of well-informed citizens. The teacher's role is to select the content to be mastered and to encourage high-level and creative thinking through appropriate instructional methods.

Steps for Developing Unit-Based Curricula. Given that the assumptions underlying the unit approach are congruent with program philosophy, a unit-

Table 6.3 Basis for selecting unit topics

CRITERION	RATIONALE
1. Stimulates interest	Fosters positive attitudes toward learning
2. Permits integration of several disciplines	Encourages multidisciplinary orientation
3. Encourages higher-level thinking; is problem oriented	Provides opportunities for creativity and problem solving
4. Expands general knowledge and related experiences	Provides a thorough foundation in content knowledge
5. Supports humanistic goals	Encourages sensitivity to human problems
6. Is consistent with present and future student needs	Meets needs for growth
7. Can be accomplished with available resources	Maximizes utilization of available resources and minimizes costs

based curriculum can be developed using the steps listed in the following paragraphs.

1. *Develop a rationale and criteria for selecting unit topics.* The rationale must be based on overall program goals and student characteristics. For example, characteristics often cited as common to gifted students include wide interests, a large store of general information, superior capacity for creative and high-level thinking, and potential for contributing to society, given high levels of task commitment and motivation. Taking into consideration these traits as well as societal needs for humanistic leaders with multidisciplinary perspectives, typical goals for gifted students should include (*a*) developing student interests; (*b*) increasing academic knowledge; (*c*) practicing creative and high-level thinking skills; (*d*) developing self-confidence, task commitment, intelligent risk taking, and positive attitudes toward learning; and (*e*) developing humanistic understanding. Consistent with these goals, the criteria for selecting unit topics can be specified as shown in Table 6.3. Topics can then be selected according to the specified criteria and rationales, which in turn match program goals and learner characteristics. Table 6.4 offers an example of unit topics in social studies

Table 6.4 Sample unit topics for social studies

	TOPICS	CONCEPTS	UNDERSTANDINGS
I.	Myself, family, friends	Self Family Friendship Helping Rules and laws Individual differences	I am unique and valuable. All people are unique and valuable. People are different but alike. There are many types of families. Helping is important. Rules and laws are needed for people to live in harmony.
II.	People	Needs Culture Careers Work and play Architecture Giving Problems	People live in different places. Different cultures have different foods, dress, festivals, and so forth, but similar needs, such as food, shelter, work, play, and friends. Differences are valuable. Sometimes people face problems, such as poverty or hunger. It is important to help others.

III.	Geography	Maps
		Weather
		Land forms
		Biospheres
		   Desert
		   Forest
		   Plains
		   Coast
			People and animals live in different kinds of places.
			The things people need (food, shelter, clothing, work, play) differ in different regions.
			Weather affects what people wear and what they do.
			There are different kinds of life in different biospheres.

Table 6.4 (continued)

TOPICS	CONCEPTS	UNDERSTANDINGS

IV. Plants and animals	Reptiles
	Mammals
	Plants
	Vegetables
		Plants and animals differ.
		People are animals.
		Some animals help each other.
		Different types of animals and
		    plants have lived over the history of the
		    earth.

V. Technology	Tools Machines Computers	Only people use tools. Tools have changed throughout history. Tools help people in many ways. Tools help people to help each other. Computers are tools.

VI. Travel	Walking
	Horses
	Boats
	Trains
	Automobiles
	Planes
	Space shuttle
	Earth
	Planets
	Solar system
		Traveling is important;
		    through travel people meet new friends
		    and learn about new places.
		Over history, people have used
		    different ways to travel.

VII. Ecology	Ecology
	Pollution
	Helping
		All living things affect and
		    are affected by each other.
		Natural resources contribute to
		    the well-being of people.
		Technology and use of resources
		    have resulted in diminishing supplies and
		    pollution.
		Pollution and resource loss
		    hurt plants, animals, and people.
		Each person can help conserve
		    resources and clean up pollution.

VIII. Transitions	Growing
	Being independent
	Change
	Seasons
	Metamorphosis
	Molting
		Living things change over time.
		Some changes are cyclic in nature,
		    such as seasons.
		People change in physical ways
		    and also become more independent.

selected for gifted children of preschool/primary school age. Each unit is intended to cover a four- to five-week period, with six to seven units presented over one academic year. Planning more units than will actually be used permits teacher flexibility in selecting those units that most meet student interests and needs, which change over time. (For each unit topic selected in this step, steps

2 through 7 apply. Figure 6.4 presents a completed unit development worksheet that offers a format for accomplishing steps 2 through 5.)

2. *List the concepts and understandings that students should acquire through their interaction with the unit.* It is useful to categorize these understandings as cognitive (content knowledge), affective (attitudes and values), and skill-related (thinking processes) to ensure that each unit includes attention to each of these domains. The understandings can also be considered as unit objectives.

3. *List content areas to be integrated into the unit.* The unit approach assumes that many gifted individuals will serve as the nation's future problem solvers. Because all human problems are by nature multidisciplinary, curricula for gifted students must also be multidisciplinary, integrating several fields of knowledge to demonstrate their interdependence.

4. *List potential resources that can be utilized in unit activities.* Free brainstorming of resources available in the community and related to the topic can trigger exciting ideas for activities. Resources include expert individuals, field sites, equipment, literature, and films.

5. *Brainstorm ideas for activities using a matrix format that ensures the integration of content areas listed in step 3.* The matrix in Figure 6.4 has content areas and goal areas as horizontal and vertical dimensions. Depending on the program's emphases, however, thinking processes, concepts, products, ability levels, or interests could be substituted as horizontal or vertical dimensions.

6. *Organize the understandings and activities developmentally.* After ideas for activities and resources have been gathered in steps 4 and 5, the understandings (or objectives) and activities can be sequenced in a logical order of presentation. Figure 6.5 presents an example of a unit outline on people that is consistent with the unit development worksheet (Figure 6.4).

7. *Develop specific lesson plans that permit flexibility to accommodate a variety of interests and ability levels.* If written daily lesson plans are to be included as part of the curriculum, they should permit flexibility for individual student needs while meeting stated content objectives for the lesson. Flexibility can be built in by permitting students to choose their own themes, methods of working (for example, individually or in groups, doing field research or library research), products (such as a photo display, written report, newspaper article, audiotape, book of poetry, model, or map), and audience (for example, teacher, peers, general public, professional organization, civic group). Lesson plan activities include instructional techniques that encourage high-level thinking. Figure 6.6 presents a sample lesson plan for the unit on people.

In sum, the unit approach can be useful in constructing curricula for the gifted in programs that emphasize (*a*) content acquisition as well as the development of thinking processes and (*b*) educator selection of topics that are flexible enough to meet individual student interests. Whether used in general education or in gifted education, the unit approach helps ensure that curricula will be

Figure 6.4 Sample unit development worksheet

Unit Topic __People__

Concepts	Content Areas	Resources
Needs	Social studies	Mrs. Green from Brazil
Culture	Science	Mr. George from New Zealand
Work	Mathematics	Mexican dance ensemble
Play	Language arts	Office of International Studies
Shelter	Visual/performing arts	Chinatown
Helping		
Human problems		

Understandings

Cognitive: 1. People live in different places.

2. People have different foods, dress, language, festivals, and housing but similar needs, such as food, clothing, shelter, play, friends.

3. Sometimes people have problems meeting these needs.

Affective: 1. Differences are valuable.

2. It is important to help others.

Skills-related: 1. Observe similarities and differences.

2. Make generalizations about similarities and differences.

3. Generate solutions to human problems.

<table>
<tr><td></td><td colspan="4" align="center">Content Areas</td></tr>
<tr><td></td><td>Social Studies</td><td>Science/Math</td><td>Language Arts</td><td>Fine Arts</td></tr>
<tr><td rowspan="2">Goal Areas — Cognitive</td><td>Have guest presenters representing different cultures.</td><td>Introduce the globe; have children list countries and locate them on the globe.</td><td>Read stories from different cultures.</td><td>Learn about the music, dances, crafts, and festivals of different cultures.</td></tr>
<tr><td>Select a critical human problem; brainstorm a project for helping to solve that problem.</td><td>Calculate the impact of the project, if quantifiable.</td><td>Brainstorm what it would be like if all people were alike; write a descriptive story.</td><td></td></tr>
<tr><td>Skill-related</td><td>Brainstorm contributions of different cultures to American society.</td><td>Identify the types of technology that can help solve problems of hunger, resource depletion, and so forth.</td><td></td><td>Create an artistic product depicting cultural richness or human problems.</td></tr>
</table>

Figure 6.5   Sample unit outline

UNIT: People

1. Children will understand that people live in different places.
   a. Introduce world map and globe.
   b. Have children brainstorm countries and have teachers locate the countries on the map and the globe.
2. Children will (*a*) understand the concept of culture, (*b*) understand that in different places there are different cultures, and (*c*) understand that different cultures have different foods, dress, languages, festivals, housing, and so forth.
   a. Hold a Brazil Day, presenting that country's traditional dress, food, language, arts, music, customs.
   b. Hold a New Zealand Day, including activities similar to those used for Brazil Day.
   c. Visit Chinatown.
   d. Analyze similarities and differences among cultures.
   e. Compare other cultures with American culture.
3. Children will understand that differences are valuable.
   a. Brainstorm the contributions of different cultures to American society.
   b. Write a story about what it would be like if all people were the same. Alternatives: write a play or a poem or produce some other artistic product.
4. Children will understand that people have needs that must be met if they are to survive and be comfortable, and that some people have problems meeting these needs without help.
   a. Analyze human needs and activities.
   b. Brainstorm human problems and technology that can help solve these problems.
   c. Select a problem and determine how the class can help solve or alleviate it.
   d. Organize a class project to help solve a human problem.
   e. Evaluate the project's effect.

---

designed in accordance with the program goals and the needs of the target population. Hence, unit-based curricula are differentiated for each population served. Finally, although the examples given were designed for young gifted children, the same approach is equally appropriate for gifted students from the upper-elementary level through high school.

Figure 6.6   Sample lesson plan

UNIT: People

Objectives

Content: Children will understand that all people have needs that must
be met if people are to survive.

Skills: Children will analyze needs and create an original product.

Materials

Chalkboard, chalk, wide variety of art materials, musical instruments,
and recorded music.

Activities

1. Children are asked to consider what they learned about the different
cultures presented throughout the unit.
2. Children brainstorm freely the needs people must meet to survive; the
teacher lists these needs on the board.
3. Children analyze the list they have made, categorizing those items that
are essential to life and those that, although not essential, provide comfort or pleasure.
4. Children discuss how needs are met in the different cultures previously
observed.
5. Children are asked to create an original product depicting something
about common human needs.

Evaluation

1. Do children list essential needs?
2. Do they differentiate between essential and nonessential needs?
3. Do they discuss similarities and differences among cultures in providing
for these needs?
4. Do their products suggest something about human needs?

INDIVIDUALIZED EDUCATION PROGRAMS

As noted in Chapter 5, Public Law 94–142, the Education for All Handicapped
Children Act, requires among other services that each handicapped student have
an individualized education program (IEP). Although gifted students are not
currently included in this federal legislation, a number of states have passed
regulations that recommend or require IEPs for gifted students. Federal law
describes IEPs for the handicapped as follows:

> . . . a written statement for each handicapped child developed in any meeting
> by a representative of the local educational agency or an intermediate educa-
> tional unit who shall be qualified to provide, or supervise the provision of,
> specially designed instruction to meet the unique needs of handicapped chil-

dren, the teacher, the parents or guardian of such child, and whenever appropriate, such child, which statement shall include (A) a statement of the present levels of educational performance of such child, (B) a statement of annual goals, including short-term instructional objectives, (C) a statement of the specific educational services to be provided to such child, and the extent to which such child will be able to participate in regular educational programs, (D) the projected date for initiation and anticipated duration of such services, and (E) appropriate objective criteria and evaluation procedures and schedules for determining, on at least an annual basis, whether instructional objectives are being achieved.

— *United States Code*, P.L. 94–142

In planning an IEP for a gifted student, an education, appraisal, and review (EA&R) committee generally determines, prior to IEP development, whether the student qualifies as gifted and what services shall be provided. Plans include the amount of time to be spent in the regular classroom and projected dates for initiation and completion of services, as in parts C and D of the law quoted above. The EA&R committee frequently includes teachers, parents, diagnosticians, and administrators and may also serve as the IEP committee.

Purpose of IEPs

The intent of IEPs is to help ensure that each exceptional student has a program individualized to meet his or her unique needs and to communicate in writing to all key individuals the nature of the student's program. When applied to the gifted, IEPs help teachers adapt the general and/or gifted program to each student's strengths, weaknesses, and interests. IEPs encourage teachers to assess each student's learning characteristics and to focus efforts on meeting individual needs. Team construction of IEPs by parents, other teachers, administrators, and the student promotes parent-teacher collaboration and provides a vehicle for effecting a smooth transition from the IEP to other current and future programs. The IEP also serves as a way of adapting the general curriculum to individual students.

Design of IEPs

Although the IEP concept evolved particularly for facilitating the appropriate education of handicapped learners, IEP guidelines developed for the handicapped are appropriate, with modifications, to gifted students. The major modification concerns the amount of flexibility in the stated instructional objectives. Educating handicapped learners requires specific, precise, quantitatively stated objectives (for example, "Given a nickel, a dime, a quarter, and a penny, the student will identify the nickel with 100 percent accuracy over four consecutive trials"). In contrast, appropriate objectives for gifted learners are open-ended and flexible to allow for the spontaneous changes and developments that should occur continuously throughout the year (for example, "The student will identify and pursue one interest area in depth").

The major steps in designing an IEP include (*a*) forming the IEP committee; (*b*) assessing the student's strengths, weaknesses, and interests; (*c*) developing long-range (annual) goals and short-term objectives; (*d*) designing instructional methods and procedures for meeting objectives; and (*e*) determining methods for evaluating progress.

The IEP Team. Ideally the IEP team consists of all individuals who work with the student and have information to contribute to the development of a comprehensive, appropriate educational plan. Generally these individuals include the teachers (special and regular), the diagnostician, the principal, the parents, the student (if appropriate), and other specialists as needed (for example, a counselor, a music instructor, or an art teacher).

Although the team approach has been conceptualized as an ideal means for designing the IEP, practical constraints such as time and training of team members frequently prohibit team development of IEPs. Instead the special teacher generally outlines the IEP based on available information and presents the outline to the team for additional input. During the team meeting, the goals, objectives, and procedures are finalized. Members then sign the IEP to indicate that they have participated in developing the final product. Signatures do not necessarily indicate approval, and minority opinions should be noted.

Assessing Student Needs. The student's particular strengths, weaknesses, and interests, as well as predetermined curriculum goals, serve as a starting point for developing instructional objectives. Data for determining individual needs include (*a*) results of formal testing conducted during the identification/selection process; (*b*) results of informal assessment and observations by teachers; (*c*) surveys of student interests and perceived needs; (*d*) parent checklists and questionnaires; and (*e*) information from other relevant sources, such as counselors, experts in specific subject matter, and specialists in the talent area.

Developing a profile of strengths and weaknesses from the collected data can be helpful in determining the student's program. Figure 6.7 presents a sample profile. The numbers in the left column of the profile indicate chronological age equivalents. The dotted line indicates Janet's expected level of functioning given her chronological age (ten). She is functioning below age expectancy only in the leadership area; her performance in all other areas is at or above age expectancy. Team members must determine, based on the program's philosophy and goals, whether to focus on Janet's strengths or relative weaknesses in planning her educational objectives. It must be kept in mind that Janet functions in her low areas, such as spelling and reading recognition, at levels appropriate for or higher than her chronological age. Therefore, it is debatable whether these areas should be considered weaknesses requiring remediation.

Developing Long-Range Goals and Short-Term Objectives. Long-range (annual) goals derive directly from the general curriculum. Goals are stated in broad, readily understandable terms—for example, "The student will increase

Figure 6.7 Sample profile for assessing student needs

NEEDS PROFILE

Student ____*Janet*____   Date ____

Age: __*10*__ IQ __*160*__

INSTRUMENTS

Age Equivalency	Peabody and Stanford Achievement Tests						Torrance	Ross	Renzulli Scales	Expert Recommendation
	Math	Reading Recognition	Reading Comprehension	Spelling	General Information	Science	Social Studies	Creativity	Problem Solving	Leadership Motivation	Arts: *Piano*

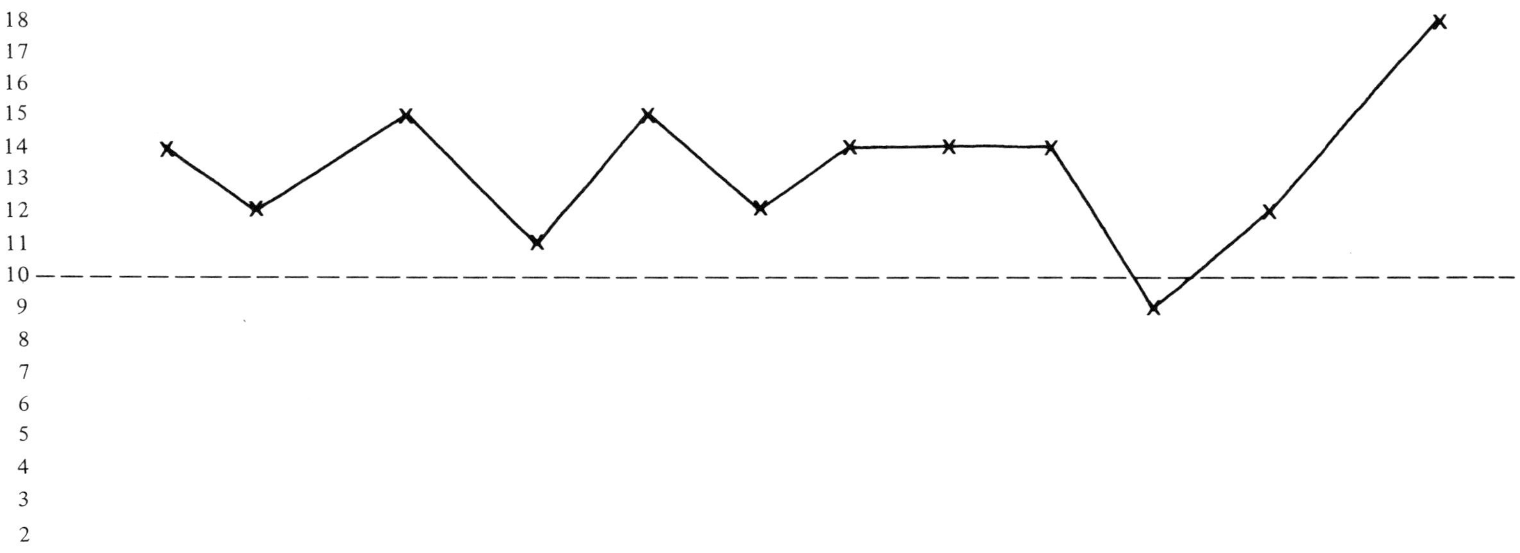

18
17
16
15
14
13
12
11
10
9
8
7
6
5
4
3
2

161

his or her knowledge of the social sciences." Objectives are more specific and should integrate curriculum (subject matter), program goals (for example, developing thinking processes or broadening interests), and student needs. Objectives for the sample goal might include the following:

1. The student will explore five social science disciplines.
2. The student will investigate the methods of inquiry of one social science discipline.
3. The student will design and implement an original study within one social science discipline, using the inquiry methods of that discipline.

Designing Instructional Methods and Procedures. The learning experiences outlined in the IEP describe how each objective will be accomplished. For example, investigating the methods of inquiry of a given social science discipline may involve guest speakers, field trips, mentorships, library research, and/or learning centers.

Determining Methods for Evaluating Progress. Evaluation methods should assess the degree to which each objective has been accomplished. When possible, observable and objective criteria should be specified. Typical evaluation methods include written or oral examination, teacher observation records, comparison of a product to predetermined criteria, peer review against predetermined standards, self-appraisal, and joint evaluation by the student and the teacher—an evaluation that considers the degree to which objectives have been accomplished, quality of work, effort applied, strengths and weaknesses of the product, and considerations for future efforts. Although some writers favor self-evaluation, others argue for teacher and/or expert appraisal because evaluation of work in the real world frequently is external.

The IEP should be continuously updated, indicating dates when objectives have been accomplished. The IEP serves as a guide that can and should be altered as the student's needs change. Major modifications should be communicated to the parents for their approval. With the exception of services provided and their duration, the IEP does not constitute a contract in the legal sense, but it should be perceived as a helpful, flexible guide for teachers, parents, and students.

Figure 6.8 offers one example of an IEP format for gifted students in pullout or part-time special programs. In the first column the teacher records the dates when instruction for each objective was begun and when each was accomplished. The "Regular Curriculum" column describes how the regular classroom addresses the objective, if applicable. Under "Special Curriculum" are listed all the methods, materials and resources, evaluation procedures, and comments for each objective that pertain to the special program. Inclusion of regular curriculum considerations promotes cooperative planning by the regular and special teachers, facilitates integrated programming, and helps avoid redundancy between programs.

Figure 6.8 Sample IEP format for a gifted student in a part-time or pullout special program

INDIVIDUALIZED EDUCATION PROGRAM

Name __Harry Noel__

Long-Range Goal __The student will improve communication skills.__

Date effective _____

Regular Teacher __Frances Kane__

Special Teacher __Richard Brian__

Date			Regular Curriculum	Method	Special Curriculum		Comments
Begun	Achieved	Objective			Materials	Evaluation	
9/15		To practice critical thinking through expository writing	To acquire rules of grammar and punctuation	Write a critique of a newspaper editorial or headline story	Newspapers; books and journals on events being investigated	Did the student consider salient facts? Offer tenable logic? Use appropriate grammar?	
10/15		To explore the creative process	To read selections by by Frost, Sandburg, Dickinson, and other American poets	Interview a local poet or writer of fiction about the creative process; begin a sketchbook including notes on the creative process and personal efforts at creative production	Resource persons; books on the creative process	Did the student ask pertinent questions? Synthesize informants' ideas? Apply these ideas in personal creative efforts?	

Figure 6.9 Sample format for developing a comprehensive IEP

INDIVIDUALIZED EDUCATION PROGRAM

Student Name ___Janet Smith___

Date established _____

Date reviewed _____

Age ___/___ yrs mos   Date of birth _____

I. Information from Parent(s):

Student Interests
Playing violin; collecting artifacts;
exploring local archeological ruins
_____

II.	Service	Initiation Date	Duration
a.	Resource room 1 day/week	9/1	6/15
b.	Advanced orchestra		
c.			
d.			
e.			

Comments/Recommendations:
Seems preoccupied with own interests;
parents would like to see more social
interaction.
_____

III. Team Comments/Recommendations:
Consider college-level coursework in
anthropology.
_____

IV.   IEP Team Participants

Signature	Title	Date

V Program Goals	Current Functioning	Objectives	Activities	Evaluation	Date Accomplished
Affective behaviors	Enthusiastic about archeology and music. Works well independently. Shows little interest in social activities, though possesses good social skills.	Support independence but encourage team interaction.	Student will make a presentation about archeology and "train" a small group of interested peers as research colleagues.	Does the student communicate effectively? Assign tasks appropriately? Motivate others? Provide good organization?	
Learning attitude					
Social interaction					
Self-esteem					
Responsibility					
Independence					
Knowledge acquisition	Superior in social studies. Needs improvement in written communication.	Expand breadth by integrating content areas. Improve written expression.	Investigate the science, literature, arts, and philosophy of ancient peoples. Write a "professional" article.	Does the student understand the importance of written communication? Of expanded interests?	
Disciplines					
Interests/Talents					
Thinking processes					
Convergent					
Divergent					
Basic skill development					
Language					
Quantitative concepts					
Reading skills					
Motor skills					
Multicultural awareness					
Appreciation					
Second-language development					

Figure 6.9 presents the IEP format developed by the New Mexico State University Preschool for Gifted Children as it may be adapted for use in other programs. In section I the teacher records information from parents and/or the student regarding the student's interests. Information concerning student interests may be incorporated into the objectives. Parent comments and recommendations are also recorded here. Section II lists the types of services to be provided, their initiation dates, and the duration of these services (determined at the EA&R meeting). In section III the teacher records general team comments and recommendations following discussion of the entire IEP. Section IV provides space for signatures to be obtained at the conclusion of the IEP meeting. In section V the teacher lists the overall curriculum and programmatic goals to ensure that the student's objectives are keyed to these goals. The student's present levels of performance are briefly noted, and objectives consistent with present performance, stated interests, and program goals are given.

Although writing an IEP takes time, the advantages of having a written document are well worth the effort. Most good teachers already know and accommodate the individual needs of their students, so putting these needs in writing does not constitute a burden. Moreover, incorporating the observations and suggestions of other key individuals, especially parents, results in a program better suited to the child considered as a total person. From surveys of special education directors and teachers and facilitators of the gifted in Kansas, Hershey (1980) found agreement that (a) IEPs are a vital part of gifted programming, (b) IEP conferences run smoothly, (c) gifted students should be involved in the IEP meeting, (d) parent involvement in IEP conferences is important, and (e) objectives should be written in an open format rather than in strictly measurable terms.

CHAPTER SUMMARY

An analysis of the state of the art in curriculum planning for gifted learners indicates that few educators have been concerned with developing comprehensive (K–12) curricula. Rather, efforts have been focused on relatively short-range programs that have been made to differ from regular offerings through modifications in content, instruction, product, or setting. Modifications have frequently been based on structured models such as the enrichment triad, the structure-of-the-intellect model, the multiple talent approach, and the taxonomy of objectives in the cognitive domain. These models serve as useful starting points and can be adapted successfully to many populations and subject areas. Care must be taken to select a model consistent with the individual district's philosophy about the gifted. The unit approach offers a vehicle for developing comprehensive curricula matched to an individual program's philosophy, goals, and target population. Increased efforts to develop comprehensive curricula specifically for gifted students would help ensure sequenced, articulated, integrated services throughout these students' educational experience—a goal yet to be attained by many existing programs.

Procedures for developing a comprehensive curriculum include establishing a districtwide committee, formulating a guiding philosophy and rationale, structuring a curriculum matrix, developing a scope and sequence, designing units, and writing lesson plans.

Individualized education programs (IEPs) adapt the comprehensive curriculum to each student by translating broad goals into specific objectives related to individual needs and interests. Use of IEPs, although not mandated in every state, encourages multidisciplinary planning and parent involvement and thus helps teachers form a picture of the student as a whole person.

ACTIVITIES FOR THOUGHT AND DISCUSSION

1. Compare and contrast the structured models in terms of their implicit assumptions about the nature of giftedness and in terms of their goals for gifted students.

2. Which subject areas of the typical K–12 curriculum lend themselves most readily to gifted education? Why?

3. Compare the benefits of (*a*) developing a comprehensive (K–12) curriculum for gifted students and (*b*) applying a structured model to a district's gifted population.

4. Develop a brief philosophy and rationale that a district might use in designing a comprehensive curriculum for gifted learners.

5. Defend a school district's decision to implement a gifted curriculum at the elementary level only or at the secondary level only.

SECTION IV

Perspectives on Instructional Methods

Chapter Seven

ENHANCING INDUCTIVE THINKING

An integral part of the renewed interest in gifted and talented learners has been and continues to be a concern about appropriate teaching methods. Recent issues of education journals are replete with suggested teaching strategies for gifted and talented students. Almost all these strategies had their origins in regular education and were not specifically developed for the intellectually superior. As Newland (1976) aptly observed, there are no instructional methods uniquely suited to gifted learners. Rather, the appropriateness of a method depends on the characteristics of the teacher, the student, and the learning situation. Newland suggested several criteria for selecting appropriate strategies for the gifted: (*a*) strategies should focus on learning how to learn, (*b*) strategies should be appropriate to the learner's level of intellectual and social development and to demands and opportunities in the learning situation, (*c*) strategies should emphasize high cognitive capacity, and (*d*) strategies should be sensitive to the learner's progression from lower to higher conceptual levels.

Methods that encourage inductive, divergent, and evaluative thinking most closely meet Newland's criteria of learning how to learn and of emphasizing progression toward higher cognitive levels. Inductive reasoning requires the learner to create a general rule from a series of examples or specific instances. Inductive thinking is contrasted with deductive thinking, wherein the learner, after being given a set of rules, applies the rules to given instances. All children need to acquire skills in both types of reasoning. Most classrooms are oriented toward deductive approaches, as in the application of grammar rules to sentence construction. For example, the child memorizes the rules for use of commas and then places the commas in given sentences according to the rules. In contrast, an inductive approach would be to present the learner with a series of sentences in which the commas are placed appropriately and a series of sentences in which the commas are inappropriately placed. From these examples the learner would attempt to derive the rules for comma placement.

Deductive reasoning is a type of *convergent* thinking wherein the learner attempts to come up with the one possible right answer. Inductive reasoning is also convergent when there is a single correct solution, as when the object of the lesson is to discover the rules for punctuation. In *divergent* thinking, on the other hand, there is no single correct response. Rather, the learner is asked to give as many solutions as he or she can. An example of a question to stimulate divergent thinking would be, "Tell me all the ways you can think of to use a sock." Note the difference between the number of possible acceptable responses to this question and to the convergent question "What is the capital of Michigan?"

A third type of thinking, *evaluative* thinking, requires the learner to weigh alternative solutions against a set of values. In this instance there is no objective right or wrong, only consistency or inconsistency with the moral, ethical, or aesthetic principles held by each individual or institution. For example, asking students to discuss whether the pardoning of Richard Nixon by Gerald Ford was good or bad would require evaluative thinking.

At least four terms appear in the literature to describe similar inductive cognitive operations: (a) inquiry, (b) problem solving, (c) discovery learning, and (d) the scientific method. Through all these processes run some threads of the central pattern in the whole inductive fabric—a situation in which the learner has considerable opportunity and responsibility for expanding his or her understanding, which, as a process, both presumes and encourages independent learning. Thus, it is natural that the inductive approach would be adapted and applied to the needs of the gifted, whose intellectual abilities permit great independence in cognitive achievement.

Interest in a formal instructional application of inductive approaches dates back at least as far as Dewey's (1933) *How We Think*, which was first published in 1910 and became the basis for Kilpatrick's (1925) "Project Method" some eight years later. Since that time there has been widespread discourse about inductive approaches.

Dewey's aim was to interpose rational thought between any perceived need for action and the resultant action. What Dewey recommended was application of the scientific method in any situation that required rational thinking. Some accounts of Dewey's early work imply that Dewey outlined five formal steps to be followed in rigid sequence: (a) define the problem, (b) gather information about significant factors inherent in the problem, (c) formulate hypotheses about the solution to the problem, (d) consider the probable value of the tentative hypotheses, and (e) test the hypotheses for the best solution. However, these processes are not five invariant steps but rather are "indispensable traits of reflective thinking" (Dewey, 1933). Since it has long been accepted that the people most capable of reflective thought are the intellectually superior, the connection between Dewey's work, inductive approaches, and education of the gifted can be easily seen.

In the recent past, much of the discourse about inductive approaches has centered on inductive methods as they relate to concept attainment. This concern regarding inductive thinking and concepts can be attributed to the influence of Jerome Bruner. According to Bruner, the structure of any discipline can be discovered by identifying the fundamental concepts. The way the fundamental concepts relate to each other is, then, the basic structure of the discipline. It is an easy logical leap to posit that if instruction is based on concepts, the attainment of those concepts can best be aided by discovery.

Presumably, students' involvement in their own learning is intrinsically motivated, although extrinsic motivation can often be a good starting point. In any case, curiosity, interest, need, and other producers of disequilibrium serve to get the inductive process under way. At whatever point the learner engages in an inductive pursuit, he or she brings to the endeavor a repertoire of skills, attitudes, and concepts either achieved or in process. The accumulated experiences of the learner can be given deeper meaning by and will influence the topic he or she investigates. During the entire process of inductive learning, the learner is developing and testing insights, extending interests, generating data, applying ideas, and generalizing conclusions.

Instructional methods that are primarily inductive in nature appear to have a strong rationale based on the following points: (*a*) inductive thinking promotes the optimum use of individual intelligence; (*b*) the learner grows in the ability to be self-directive and responsible for continued progress toward both short-range and long-range goals; (*c*) inductive thinking promotes the attainment of concepts, the formulations of generalizations, and the ability to synthesize; (*d*) inductive thinking engenders internalization and enhances transfer of learning at increasingly higher conceptual levels; (*e*) because inductive thinking is rooted in individual experience, it is equally authentic in any sociocultural context.

Gallagher (1975) observed that inductive, discovery-oriented methods generate excitement and enthusiasm in the learner but require more time for teacher preparation and student interaction with the material. However, the weight of research over the past three decades would indicate that didactic or expository teaching is not more economical than inductive approaches in terms of time (Ausubel, 1961). Gallagher (1975) also suggested that although the arguments for inductive approaches are based on solid principles of child development and learning, there is little direct empirical evidence to support the efficacy of such approaches in general. Crabtree's (1970) review of research, however, indicated that inductive approaches achieve at least as much cognitive growth as expository teaching accomplishes. Moreover, indirect evidence of the benefits of the inductive approach may be gleaned from research in cognitive psychology. For example, Osler and Fivel (1961) demonstrated that bright high school students (with IQs over 110) used higher-level strategies (hypothesis testing) to solve inductive problems than did their average and below-average peers, who tended to learn by association. It is possible, then, that inductive instructional approaches may be more appropriate for brighter than for slower students and may encourage higher-level problem-solving strategies.

Instruction for all learners, including the gifted and talented, should provide an appropriate balance of opportunities for both deductive and inductive thinking. Put another way, some necessary learning objectives are better achieved through deductive and didactic instructional methods. As Newland (1976) cautioned, children cannot be expected to *discover* all the facts accumulated since the beginnings of human existence. They need not reinvent the wheel, but ultimately they should learn to build on existing knowledge. Gifted and talented students need factual bases on which to discover and create, and in some instances rote memorization is both necessary and desirable.

This chapter presents the inductive teaching strategies of Hilda Taba and J. Richard Suchman and provides examples of applications to specific content areas. Chapter 8 will describe and apply instructional strategies for practicing divergent thinking processes. Continuing the focus on instructional methods,

Chapter 9 will examine techniques for fostering evaluative thinking and affective development. The strategies presented in each chapter can be effectively applied to almost every subject matter.

TABA'S INDUCTIVE QUESTIONING MODELS

In *A Teacher's Handbook to Elementary Social Studies,* Taba et al. (1971) presented seven teaching strategies: developing concepts, attaining concepts, developing generalizations, applying generalizations, exploring feelings, interpersonal problem solving, and analyzing values. The first three strategies are discussed in this section. The strategy of applying generalizations requires more divergent thinking and will be discussed in Chapter 8. The last three will be presented in Chapter 9 as techniques for fostering affective development and evaluative thinking. Although Taba and her associates developed and field tested these strategies for elementary social studies education, the methods have long been used in practice for children from preschool through secondary school age and with a variety of content areas.

Theoretical Foundations and Research Support

Taba et al. (1971) based their methods on the following assumptions: (*a*) thinking is learned developmentally and can be taught systematically, (*b*) thinking involves the student's acting upon the material to be learned, (*c*) all schoolchildren can think at abstract levels, (*d*) all subjects offer an appropriate context for thinking, and (*e*) specific instructional strategies can be developed to foster thinking. The authors derived support for these assumptions from the works of cognitive theorists such as Bruner, Piaget, and Vygotsky. Common to all seven strategies, for example, is the Piagetian conception of cognitive development as the result of an interaction between a child's maturational level and experience, fostered by social interaction. Such interaction promotes the expression of a diversity of ideas that may lead to conflict with one's own ideas, subsequent resolution of the conflict, and, finally, attainment of a higher level of cognition.

The efficacy of strategies for the development of transferable thinking skills and for the acquisition or modification of knowledge and attitudes was supported by research associated with the Eight-Year Study of the University of Chicago and the Taba Curriculum Development Project at San Francisco State College. The latter study, supported by a grant from the U.S. Office of Education, involved ten school districts (Taba, 1966). Results of the Taba Curriculum Development Project indicated that the basic sequences of the seven strategies should be followed for all age groups and circumstances. Taba et al. (1971) warned that unless the basic format is maintained, thinking skills may not be improved. They also found that although each sequence should be followed precisely, the time frame may vary according to the nature of the content and the child's level. The first questions of a sequence may be discussed on one day, for example, and the next questions may be raised the second day.

Other helpful suggestions emerging from the research concern the nature of the student group and the atmosphere of the learning situation. Taba et al. (1971) suggest that the strategies be employed with groups of students with heterogeneous ability levels. When students bring a variety of knowledge, experience, and conceptual levels to the discussion, some will offer concrete notions, others will offer abstract ideas, and a more complete picture of the phenomena under study will result. The authors also noted that teachers should create an accepting rather than a critical atmosphere, thus affording students an opportunity to contribute without fear of censure.

Developing Concepts

The purpose of the strategy of developing concepts is to help children enlarge and clarify key concepts critical to later formulation of generalizations.

General Method. Based on children's own experiences or a planned group experience (field trip, story, film), the teacher has the students volunteer items or ideas about the subject. When a sufficiently long and varied list has been developed, the teacher asks the students to group the items that belong together, to give reasons for their groupings, and to label the groups. Next the teacher has the children examine other possible groupings of the same items by rearranging and relabeling them. Finally, the children are asked to summarize the information in a single sentence that applies to all the groups. Table 7.1 illustrates the specific questions to be used by the teacher in the developing concepts strategy.

Application. Teachers at the Preschool for the Gifted at New Mexico State University successfully employed the developing concepts strategy within a unit on sound. Some of the twenty children, aged three to five, were not yet reading. To develop the list of ideas, the children were given a homework assignment to find a small object that made noise or sound. The next day the children shared their objects with the group. Each child gave a demonstration of how his or her object made sound. The teacher then had the children sit in a circle on the floor, their objects collected in the center. The teacher asked the children whether any of the items seemed to belong together. To clarify her question, she asked, "How can I make a good group?" She called on children whose hands were raised. A description of the interaction follows:

> Kathy raises her hand and points to the green streetcar. Teacher: "What would go with it to make a group?" John picks out the bell he has just shared. Teacher: "Why do the streetcar and the bell go together?" She makes them both ring. Mike: "Because they make the same sound." Ann: "The baby and the robot go together because they're both wind-up toys." The teacher asks what other items go together to make a group. Jill puts the harmonica and tambourine

Table 7.1 Technique for developing concepts

TEACHER	STUDENT	TEACHER FOLLOW-THROUGH

What do you see (notice, find) here?	Gives items	Makes sure items are accessible to each student—for example:
		    chalkboard
		    transparency
		    individual list
		    pictures
		    item card

Do any of these items seem to belong together?	Finds some similarity as a basis for grouping items	Communicates grouping—for example:
		    underlines in colored chalk
		    marks with symbols
		    arranges pictures or cards

Why would you group them together?[a]	Identifies and verbalizes the common characteristics of items in a group	Seeks clarification of responses when necessary
What would you call these groups you have formed?	Verbalizes a label (perhaps more than one word) that appropriately encompasses all items	Records
Could some of these belong in more than one group?	States different relationships	Records
Can we put these same items in different groups?[b] Why would you group them that way?	States additional different relationships	Communicates grouping
Can someone say in one sentence something about all these groups?[c]	Offers a suitable summary sentence	Reminds students, if necessary, to take into consideration *all* the groups before them

[a]Sometimes the teacher asks the same child "why" when he or she offers the grouping, and other times the teacher may wish to get many groups before considering "why" things are grouped together.

[b]Although this step is important because it encourages flexibility, it will not be appropriate on all occasions.

[c]This step is often omitted because as a generalizing activity it may be reserved for the next strategy.

SOURCE: Taba et al., 1971, p. 67.

together. Kathy volunteers that they both make music. Janice puts the bird and tweeter together "because they both make bird sounds." To Janice's grouping Rick adds a plastic egg which, when opened, exposes a yellow chick that chirps "because they all sound the same."

When the contributions slow down, the teacher asks the children if some of the objects can belong to more than one group. Andre suggests that the set of bells with birds perched on top could go with the birds and with the things that make music. Later in the discussion, the teacher asks if the objects can be put into different groups. Amy makes a group out of the tambourine and keys because both make clacking sounds. The children appear to have difficulty expressing verbally their reactions to the final question, "What can we say about all these groups?" One child notes that "they all make sounds."

As Taba et al. (1971) noted, the teacher's last question requires generalization and may be reserved for later activities. One generalization that could have been made in the example is that things that make sounds can be grouped according to physical similarities (for example, birds), sound similarities (for example, clacking), and function (for example, the musical instruments). Nevertheless, the children seemed able to discuss and expand on the key concepts of sound similarity, sound difference, and types of sounds. The developing concepts strategy also encourages children to engage in the processes of flexible thinking (changing mind-sets through regrouping and relabeling) and categorizing.

Attaining Concepts

The strategy of attaining concepts helps students acquire new concepts and form clear distinctions between concepts.

General Method. The teacher begins by having the students repeat the concept word and recognize its printed form. Then the teacher presents a broad range of examples of the concept and follows with nonexamples. The teacher tests the children's attainment of the concept by presenting examples and nonexamples and having the children determine which are examples of the concept. Finally the children are asked to provide a definition of the concept. The inductive attaining concepts strategy clearly contrasts with more typical deductive methods in which the teacher *begins* by presenting the definition of the concept. Table 7.2 illustrates the questioning used for this strategy.

Application. The reader will better understand the attaining concepts strategy by going through the exercise presented in Figure 7.1. The concept to be attained, *geoforms,* is a nonsense word used for illustrative purposes only.

The attaining concepts strategy has obvious applications for concept formation in virtually all content areas and at all grade levels. Consider the following examples:

— *Social studies:* propaganda, justice, sovereignty, land forms (mountain, plateau, alluvial plain)

Table 7.2 Technique for attaining concepts

TEACHER	STUDENT	TEACHER FOLLOW-THROUGH
Say this word after me . . .	Repeats word	Makes sure the word is pronounced correctly
This is an . . . (and) This is also an . . .	Looks at object, listens to description given, or reads statements that are illustrative examples of the concept	Checks for any who may not be able to see or hear
This is *not* an . . .	Looks at new object or listens to new description or reads statements that are not samples of the concept (but that may be similar, in similar form, etc.)	Checks again
Show me an . . . (or) Tell me what you think an . . . is (or) Which of these describes an . . . (or) Is this an . . .	Points to object, defines the concept, and selects from one or more descriptions	Shows additional objects or gives fresh descriptions to test and has students write down their definitions
How then would you define an . . .	Gives summary generalization (definition) of concept	Checks for accuracy

SOURCE: Taba et al., 1971, p. 71.

— *Literature:* poetic forms (sonnet, haiku), figures of speech (alliteration, simile, metaphor, onomatopoeia)
— *Grammar:* parts of speech (noun, verb, adjective), complete sentence, type of sentence (simple, compound, complex)
— *Mathematics:* geometric form (triangle, square, rectangle), equation, theorem, corollary
— *Science:* theory, hypothesis, phyla (mammal, reptile)
— *Music:* type of tempo (andante, allegro), forms (concerto, fugue, symphony), types of instruments (woodwinds, brass, percussion)
— *Art:* symmetry, perspective, chiaroscuro, style of a particular artist (Rembrandt, Pollock) or period (romantic, baroque, rococo), type of medium

Developing Generalizations

The developing generalizations strategy encourages the process of generalizing from a variety of specific instances. A generalization consists of a statement of relationships among two or more concepts. Taba et al. (1971) encouraged teach-

Figure 7.1   Sample exercise for use in the attaining concepts strategy

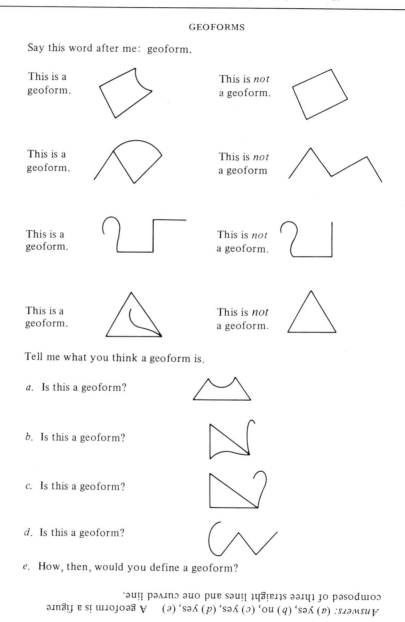

GEOFORMS

Say this word after me: geoform.

This is a geoform.

This is *not* a geoform.

This is a geoform.

This is *not* a geoform

This is a geoform.

This is *not* a geoform.

This is a geoform.

This is *not* a geoform.

Tell me what you think a geoform is.

a. Is this a geoform?

b. Is this a geoform?

c. Is this a geoform?

d. Is this a geoform?

e. How, then, would you define a geoform?

Answers: (*a*) *yes,* (*b*) *no,* (*c*) *yes,* (*d*) *yes,* (*e*)   A geoform is a figure composed of three straight lines and one curved line.

ers to help students develop generalizations that involve inference—that is, to generalize beyond the information given.

General Method. The developing generalizations strategy has three main steps. First, the teacher asks the students to examine similar aspects of given samples, such as the holidays observed in the United States, India, and Japan. Second, the teacher asks the students to describe what they have seen—for example, by noting and explaining the similarities and differences among the three nations in their cultural celebrations. Finally, the students are asked to make generalizations based on the identified similarities and differences. Continuing the example, one generalization might concern the types of events celebrated across cultures. Taba et al. emphasized that skill in reaching appropriate, meaningful generalizations supportable by data may be initially difficult for students if they have been accustomed to being asked only for facts that can be located on the printed page. Table 7.3 lists the specific elements of the developing generalizations strategy.

Application. As with the other inductive strategies discussed, the developing generalizations method can be effectively employed in many content areas. The New Mexico State University Preschool for the Gifted applied this strategy in a science unit on sound. The generalization to be derived was that sound travels through different materials at different rates. The teacher began by having the

Table 7.3 Technique for developing generalizations

TEACHER	STUDENT	TEACHER FOLLOW-THROUGH
What did you notice? See? Find? What differences did you notice (with reference to a particular question)?	Gives items	Makes sure items are accessible—for example: chalkboard transparency individual list pictures item card Chooses the items to pursue
Why do you think this happened? or How do you account for these differences?	Gives explanation, which may be based on factual information and/or inferences	Accepts explanation and seeks clarification if necessary
What does this tell you about . . . (e.g., the way people behave)?	Gives generalization	Encourages variety of generalizations, especially those of inference type, and seeks clarification where necessary

NOTE: This pattern of inviting reasons to account for observed phenomena and generalizing beyond the data is repeated and expanded to include more and more aspects of the data and to reach more abstract generalizations.
SOURCE: Taba et al., 1971, p. 75.

whole group of children suggest materials through which sound might travel. The children suggested items such as the chalkboard, air, wood, metal, carpet, glass, eggs, the body, shoes, and cloth. The children were then divided into smaller groups of six to seven, each led by a teacher. Within the small groups the children experimented to determine whether sound traveled through the material and whether the sound was loud or soft. For example, they put their ears to the chalkboard and listened and felt as someone knocked on the chalkboard with a fist. The children kept records by writing the names of the items that sound traveled through or by drawing pictures of those items, depending on their individual skill level.

The next day the children returned to the whole group and discussed their observations, comparing and contrasting the loudness of the sounds they had listened to through each material. The children responded at different levels to the final questions, rephrased for them as, "What did you learn about sound?" and "What does this tell you about the way sound travels?" Some children noted that sound vibrates through different things differently. Others suggested only that sound travels through specific items, such as the chalkboard and glass. Still others reported that sound was louder through metal than through the carpet. It should be kept in mind that this lesson, like others used as examples, was preceded and followed by other activities designed to help children acquire new insights about sound. Higher-level generalizations are to be expected as the children gain more experience and have time for their ideas to incubate.

The developing generalizations strategy has also been used with gifted students in a high school program. The content areas for this example were literature and social studies. The teachers wished to have the students derive the generalization that many societies, including our own, operate upon a class structure. The students were asked to read Aldous Huxley's *Brave New World*, which depicts a future society that determines the number of people that will be produced in each class, working class to the elite. Huxley's society no longer practices childbirth and parenthood; rather, it mass reproduces infants through carefully controlled laboratory test tubes. The students were asked to think of the differences and especially the similarities between Huxley's future society and our present American society and to explain their observations. The teachers recorded each student's response on the board. The last question, "What does this tell you about our society and societies in general?" led, among several other generalizations, to the hypothesis that societies cannot exist without a lower class.

In summary, Taba's inductive questioning models are based on a conceptual development scheme that is supported by stage-developmental psychology, especially the Piagetian tenets. Further theoretical support derives from the principles propounded by Dewey. Indeed, the Dewey proposition that some thinking processes should be taught and applied directly is one of the major bases of the Taba approach.

Suchman's Inquiry and Problem-Solving Models

J. Richard Suchman (1977) based his instructional methods on the value of heuristic learning, the active searching for new knowledge, and a concomitant concern that formal schooling may depress a child's natural motivation to explore. Suchman noted that younger, primary-grade children are eager to speculate about causes, to think of ways to test their hypotheses, and to carry out investigations. In one example children were asked to suggest possible reasons for the death of the class's pet turtle. The children relied on their previous experiences, offering the hypotheses of poisoned water or too much food. Older elementary school children, in contrast, tended to defer to authority as a source of knowledge rather than to rely on their own experiences, observations, and analyses. Suchman concluded: "Heuristic learning is a natural learning process that starts early and works well, and . . . is subject to inhibition in our educational system" (Suchman, 1977, p. 264). Suchman's inquiry and problem-solving methods attempt to foster the continuation of heuristic learning in children.

Theoretical Foundations and Research Support

To explain heuristic learning, Suchman (1977) presented the meaning model (Figure 7.2). According to this model, heuristic learning is a fundamental process by which experience is transformed into meaning. The learner derives meaning through the interaction of his or her encounters, or unorganized sensory experiences, and his or her organizers, cognitive tools that include concepts, prior encounters, and previously acquired meanings. The learner spontaneously creates meaning out of encounters based on his or her organizers. For example, children encountering a tulip for the first time may relate to it their previous concept of *flower* and thereby derive the meaningful idea that the tulip, like other flowers, should be sweet smelling and delicate to the touch. Motivation for heuristic learning is intrinsic but selective—that is, learning does not occur with every encounter. Optimal conditions for the child's engagement in the heuristic process include a low-pressure, accepting environment, which permits reflection, and discrepancy in encounters, which activates natural motivation for equilibrium and competence.

Suchman proposed that heuristic learning is pervasive and powerful and that teaching can better succeed relative to the degree that heuristic learning is

Figure 7.2   The meaning model (Suchman, 1977)

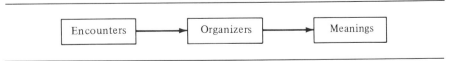

allowed to function optimally. Teachers can encourage heuristic learning by presenting encounters in such a way that children are motivated to apply their organizers to derive new meanings. In contast, traditional didactic and deductive approaches attempt to promote learning by "feeding in" meaning.

The meaning model is consistent with Piaget's cognitive development theory in that both describe motivation as intrinsic and enhanced by the presentation of an optimally discrepant event. Suchman and Piaget differ in that Piaget has described cognitive development as a stage-sequential process based on interaction between the child and the environment from infancy to adolescence. Suchman's theory describes a similar interactive process between the child and the environment (the encounter) but limits it to within a single learning incident.

Suchman compared Piaget's sensorimotor stage, where learning occurs through actions on the physical environment, with learning based on encountering, acquiring organizers, and producing new meanings. In contrast to the preoperational stage, in the operational stage organizers guide the encountering and give meaning to encounters as they occur. During the concrete operational stage, encounters are varied within a fixed framework of organizers. Formal operations do not rely on encounters, but the mind manipulates previously formed meanings to produce higher-level meanings (generalizations). This level requires a preparation of the mind through the building up of organizers and meanings and a learning environment with many opportunities for encountering.

The following general guidelines for creating a heuristic learning situation are consistent with both Suchman's and Piaget's theories. The guidelines, based on Gallagher and Quandt (1981) and Moses (1981), clearly give the learner more control over his or her learning.

1. Begin with an *encounter* or a *messing-around* stage that permits the child to interact with the materials before a problem is posed. Present concrete materials that permit children to experience and impose many kinds of change.
2. Present problems that involve *puzzling* transformations. Create situations that stimulate children to infer and reason spontaneously.
3. *Accept* children's methods of problem solving, even if they lead to failure.
4. Create a nonthreatening, *nonexternally evaluating* atmosphere. Avoid praise, criticism, or other announcements that label a child's responses; external evaluation reinforces dependence on a controlling environment.
5. Require children to anticipate—*predict* results of their actions, observe outcomes, and compare their hypothesized outcomes with results.
6. Be *responsive* to the child, who is in the driver's seat. Listen, accept all responses, and respond with appropriate feedback.
7. Permit creation of *alternative strategies*.

Little, if any, empirical research is available to support or refute the efficacy of Suchman's methods with gifted learners. One reason for the sparsity of research in this area is the lack of valid criteria for measuring change. It is important to keep in mind that Suchman's methods focus on the development of thinking processes, not on the acquisition of academic content. Second, there seems to be an antitesting sentiment among Suchman's followers to the extent that evaluation is for them analogous to pulling a plant out of the ground just to examine its roots. Nevertheless, Suchman's work provides alternative strategies that give children practice in inductive thinking and in learning how to learn.

The following subsections describe two teaching strategies suggested by Suchman for the encouragement of heuristic learning. The inquiry approach focuses primarily on children's adopting the scientific method of observing, hypothesizing, experimenting, and evaluating, at the same time posing their own questions and providing their own answers. In the second approach, problem solving, the teacher rather than the learner sets the goals.

Inquiry

General Method. The steps that follow can be used for setting up an inquiry situation.

1. The teacher provides a messing-around stage in which the child interacts freely with given materials (the encounter).
2. The teacher responds to the child's actions (child is in control and supplying the organizers).
3. The teacher poses problems to facilitate the acquisition of meaning.
4. The child poses his or her own problems.

Application. The inquiry model has been most frequently employed in the sciences. Suchman (1966) used the following example to illustrate the model. His first step (the encounter) was to present the following discrepant event to a group of children. He held a bimetallic instrument resembling a metal spatula over a flame (Figure 7.3). As the blade was heated, it bent downward; it then straightened out when immersed in water. When Suchman reapplied heat to the blade, it bent upward—a discrepant event for the children, whose current organizers, such as concepts of melting and gravity, did not account for the blade's behavior.

Steps two (teacher responds) and three (teacher poses problem) overlap and may run concurrently. In the example, step two began when Suchman told the students he would answer any question they asked about the phenomenon, with the exception of why the event occurred. He then set the ground rules and posed the problem while continuing to be responsive to the students. The problem was to explain the phenomenon by proposing a theory or hypothesis. The ground rules were that each student in succession would have the floor and would be allowed to ask questions, experiment with the materials, and/or propose a hypothesis. Suchman responded by answering the students' questions,

Figure 7.3   An example from Suchman's inquiry model (Suchman, 1966)

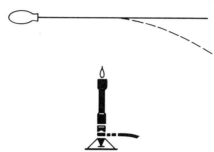

The bimetallic strip bends downward the first time it is heated; melting is
generally thought to be the cause.

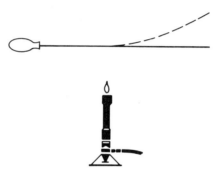

The second time the bimetallic strip is heated, the blade bends upward—a discrepant
event for most children.

inviting and helping them to experiment, and writing their names and associated
theories on the board.

Suchman was careful to capture the students' own ideas in writing; he had
the students repeat their statements, wrote them on the board, and rechecked
them with the students. He prefaced his requests for repetition by saying, "I
want to be sure I understand you" or, "Tell me again because I want to get it
right." When a student wished to relinquish the floor or did not want to speak
at turn, he or she passed. As students experimented, pondered, and listened to
each other, some changed their theories. Suchman wrote their new ideas on the
board next to their names.

Step four (child generates problems) occurred when the students began to
formulate hypotheses, determine the data needed to test the hypotheses, and
design their own experiments to collect the required data. In doing so, the
students were setting goals and posing problems to be solved within the inquiry
situation. Some students proposed new problems, such as how other metal strips
behave when heated. Because true inquiry begins when the learner pursues

answers to self-determined problems, the question of relevance is raised. "If suddenly his search veers off in a new direction, who is to say he is being irrelevant?" (Suchman, 1977, p. 270).

When the theories were exhausted, Suchman asked each student to determine which explanation he or she considered the most satisfying and to give the reason for the choice. Students were invited to continue their experiments after the session was over.

Note that Suchman, as the teacher, did not end the inquiry session by giving the correct answer. He did not volunteer the information that the implement was bimetallic (composed of two metals fused together) and therefore responded differently, depending on which side was exposed to heat. If asked, the teacher may offer his or her theory on the same basis that the students used: "Well, this is my theory . . ."

Some teachers have expressed discomfort with the idea of leaving children without the correct answer. The purpose of the inquiry method, however, is to encourage students to become involved in the inquiry *process* rather than, for example, to understand the effects of heat on a bimetallic strip. In fact, in a situation where a student offers the hypothesis of bimetallic composition, the teacher would treat the hypothesis like any other, writing it on the board with the proposer's name. If the teacher gives the correct theory, the event is no longer discrepant and the inquiry process may cease.

Suchman noted that children respond with their own level of understanding, which may be very close to what science considers the correct theory. He gave the example of a fifth-grade girl's response to a filmed encounter in which a man at a restaurant jerked the tablecloth out from under a table setting, leaving the setting in place on the table. A second man tried to repeat the act but scattered the dishes to the floor. After an inquiry session, the girl excitedly concluded: "You see, it's something like people. When you jerk the tablecloth out suddenly, you get it out before the dishes realize what is happening. But when you do it slower, the dishes have time to grab on and so they go along with the cloth" (Suchman, 1977, p. 270). The child's concept of "things grabbing on" seems an appropriate way for a fifth-grader to conceptualize friction and inertia.

Problem Solving

General Method. Problem solving in education typically refers to a sequence of steps: identifying the problem, generating alternative solutions, evaluating the alternatives, making a decision, and implementing the chosen solution. Methods for encouraging this type of problem solving will be addressed in later chapters. Suchman (1977) used the term *problem solving* to indicate a teaching method that requires (*a*) a learning objective for which the problem was designed, (*b*) a clear goal for the learner (problem solution), (*c*) materials and media that support the problem-solving activity, and (*d*) a clear set of rules. The process for facilitating problem solving is much like that for facilitating inquiry, except that in problem solving the teacher sets the goal.

Application. Suchman's inductive approach to problem solving can be illustrated in the teaching of letter recognition. In the first stage (the encounter), the child is presented with three-dimensional wooden letters that can be placed on an accompanying easel. In the second step (teacher responds), the teacher names any letter the child places on the easel. When necessary, the teacher turns the letter to its correct position (for example, if the child has placed it upside down). As he or she tries each letter, the child finds that each has a name and, with repetition, begins to associate each letter with its name. The child also discovers that he or she is in control; the child can make the teacher say something by placing a letter on the easel. The child can review forgotten letter names by repeatedly placing the letter on the easel. The child also controls the time between letter presentations and the time of letter exposure.

The third step (teacher poses problem) occurs when the teacher introduces a game: "See if you can make me say D by placing it on the easel." If the child selects the letter *A*, the teacher merely says, "A. See if you can make me say D." A typical session might produce the following interaction:

TEACHER: See if you can make me say B by putting the letter *B* on the easel.

(Child places the letter *T* on the easel but places it upside down. Teacher places the *T* in proper orientation.)

TEACHER: T. See if you can make me say B.

(Child places the letter *B* on the easel.)

TEACHER: B. You made me say B. Now see if you can make me say T.

In this third step the child attempts to match the letter with its name in the absence of external pressure to be right or wrong.

A fourth step (learner generates own problems) may occur. As the child masters the game, he or she may begin to make up problems to be solved— for example, by placing letters in combination on the easel. The teacher responds by naming all letters selected or by pronouncing the word if a word is produced. Steps one, two, and three are integral to the problem-solving approach. When learners begin step four, designing their own problems and setting their own goals, the process shifts from problem solving to inquiry.

Letter sounds, sound combinations, words, sentences, geometric figures, colors, animal names, number recognition, and basic number facts can be taught in a similar manner. Sight words and sentences can be introduced, for example, with the teacher offering to write any word a child says. Then the teacher poses the problem: "See if you can make me say ———— by placing it on the easel." Next, selecting from the new collection of word cards, the child can make the teacher say what he or she places on the easel. When the child is ready, the teacher introduces sentences based on the word cards: "See if you can make me say: The dog is black." If some words are missing (for example, *the*), the teacher writes them to form additional word cards. The teacher reads precisely what is placed on the easel.

CHAPTER SUMMARY

Most writers recommend inductive thinking processes as appropriate for gifted and talented learners. A number of specific applications of inductive processes have been used with both gifted and average learners. General conclusions based on practice and research are that (*a*) inductive methods work at least as well as expository approaches in terms of cognitive achievement gains and (*b*) inductive approaches accomplish these cognitive achievement gains in about the same amount of time as do other instructional approaches.

Taba's inductive questioning models include developing concepts, attaining concepts, and developing generalizations. The efficacy of these methods for improving thinking skills is supported by cognitive-developmental theory and applied research. The efficacy studies indicate that to maximize gains, teachers must follow precisely the described questioning sequences. Although Taba's methods were designed primarily for teaching elementary social studies, teachers can apply these strategies effectively in other content areas and with a wide range of age groups.

Suchman based his inquiry and problem-solving models on the idea that heuristic learning (children's active search for new knowledge) has value and should be fostered rather than inhibited by formal schooling. Based on the meaning model, the inquiry and problem-solving approaches represent an attempt to give more control of the learning situation to the child. The teacher serves as an acceptor of and responder to the child's initiations. Suchman's problem-solving method differs from his inquiry approach in that the teacher rather than the child determines the problem to be solved. When the learner begins to pose his or her own problems, the process becomes inquiry. The major objective of inquiry is to engage children in the scientific method rather than to promote content learning. In problem solving, both content and process goals exist. Although little empirical research is available regarding the efficacy of Suchman's methods for gifted learners, the methods are consistent with inductive approaches and hence have validity for the gifted. Like Taba's approaches, Suchman's techniques can be applied to a variety of content areas and age groups.

ACTIVITIES FOR THOUGHT AND DISCUSSION

Write a lesson plan using one of the following models:
   a. developing concepts
   b. attaining concepts
   c. developing generalizations
   d. inquiry
   e. problem solving

As was discussed in Chapter 6 ("Curriculum Development"), each lesson plan should be part of a larger, sequential unit organization rather than an isolated activity. Your lesson plan should include the following information:

a. content area or unit (for example, social studies unit on the westward movement)

b. model (for example, Taba's developing concepts)

c. objective(s): content objective (for example, "The students will further develop their knowledge of the following concepts . . .") and process objective (for example, "The students will engage in the processes of categorization and inductive reasoning")

d. rationale (why the objectives are important)

e. materials (all materials needed to conduct the lesson)

f. activity and steps to be followed

g. evaluation (how you will know that the lesson has been effective in meeting the objectives)

Chapter Eight

ENHANCING CREATIVE THINKING

An extensive theoretical and empirical literature exists on creativity. Volumes have been written to explain the phenomenon, to describe investigations of correlates, and to support various methods for training creative thinking. Despite the variety of ideas expressed, there appears to be general agreement on several important points. First, however defined, creativity is associated with both novelty and value. Creativity can be described as the ability to generate an idea or a product that is both new or original *and* socially useful, as distinguished from ideas or products that are unique but meaningless. Second, creativity is not limited to artistic production but can be found in all fields of endeavor, including science and mathematics. Third, writers agree that, at least conceptually, creativity is distinguishable from general intelligence. In other words, an individual can be extremely bright but uncreative, or highly creative but not necessarily intellectually gifted. Fourth, every individual possesses the potential for creativity when it is conceived as the associated personality qualities of spontaneity and openness to experience. However, creativity that results in major changes of far-reaching importance requires special talent or genius (Rothenberg and Hausman, 1976). Fifth, creativity can be purposely fostered. Finally, the understanding and encouragement of creativity is crucial to the survival of humankind because survival requires self-renewal when conventional means for renewal become obsolete.

The literature further indicates that distinctions must be made among creative persons, products, and processes. Numerous analyses have been conducted on creative products, such as the *Mona Lisa*, and on creative individuals, such as Thomas Edison, Sylvia Plath, and Friedrich Nietzsche, to name a few. Yet the literature has not produced consensus on what constitutes the creative *process*, the mental activities by which creative products (tangible works or intangible insights) are achieved.

Understanding the creative process is critical to teaching creative thinking so that a student's creative potential is unleashed. By knowing the conditions conducive to creative thinking, teachers can support and foster the development and realization of creative talent. Although creative abilities can be encouraged (and their use appears related to personal well-being and success), many elementary and secondary teachers do not incorporate the development of creativity into ongoing objectives, activities, assignments, and evaluation procedures (Torrance, 1963). Reluctance to emphasize creative thinking may be due to the heavily cognitive and content orientation of many teacher training programs. This chapter briefly describes the various theories that seek to explain the creative process, and then summarizes selected areas of research on creativity. It concludes by presenting several models for helping students develop their creative potential.

192

THEORIES OF CREATIVITY

In a compilation of papers on the subject of creativity, Rothenberg and Hausman (1976) presented forty-five differing conceptualizations of creativity by writers from early Greek civilization to modern times. More recently Busse and Mansfield (1980) organized the theories on the creative process that have been proposed over the last thirty years into seven categories: psychoanalytic, Gestalt, association, perceptual, humanistic, cognitive developmental, and composite. While acknowledging the multiplicity of interesting theories, we will focus our discussion on four major conceptualizations of creativity, three of which were identified by Meichenbaum (1975) as having inspired the development of teaching techniques to foster creative thinking. The categories mentioned by Meichenbaum describe creativity as (*a*) an ability to engage in controlled regression, (*b*) a product of attitudinal and personality characteristics, and (*c*) mental abilities. The fourth major theory of creativity, more recently emphasized, describes creativity in terms of hemispheric functioning.

Creativity as Controlled Regression

The concept of creativity as the ability to engage in controlled regression stems from psychoanalytic theories proposed during the period from the 1920s to the 1950s by Sigmund Freud, Carl Jung, Ernest Kris, and Lawrence Kubie. Psychoanalytic theory describes three levels of awareness: the conscious, the preconscious, and the unconscious. The preconscious contains ideas and wishes that are not presently conscious but may readily become conscious. The unconscious cannot be experienced but is only inferred from thoughts that come to the conscious—for example, through dreams that seem inexplicable to the dreamer. Psychoanalytic theory also describes personality as composed of three interacting structures: the id, the ego, and the superego. The id is unconscious, instinctual, and pleasure seeking. The ego is conscious and responsible for controlling impulses of the id. The ego, representing the realistic and rational, helps the individual interact daily as a socially responsible being. The superego acts as the conscience, representing the values and ideals of society.

Psychoanalytic theorists generally describe the creative process as a voluntary relaxing of ego controls to enable the preconscious to operate freely on ideas. When ego controls are loosened, the individual can regress to fantasy and integrate fantasy with the problem to be solved. Controlled, rational thinking inhibits the formulation of new ideas; temporarily abandoning such thinking releases the preconscious, permitting freedom in thought. During this state the ego is more receptive to drive-related impulses, and associations between the problem and other seemingly unrelated but potentially useful ideas are facilitated (Busse and Mansfield, 1980).

Psychoanalytic theorists differ with respect to their views of the actual roles of levels of consciousness. Freud emphasized fantasy in creativity as a manifestation of preconscious thoughts and feelings, but he also emphasized the role of the unconscious in creativity. The notion of regression in service of the ego as a means by which preconscious and unconscious material arises in the consciousness is primarily attributable to Kris. Kris (1952) described the shift from consciousness to preconsciousness as accounting for the feeling of clarity that occurs when, after intense concentration, the solution to a previously insoluble problem presents itself. Kubie (1958) focused on the preconscious alone in creative production. Jung (1923) described the creative artist as transforming, through mechanisms not controlled by the conscious, archetypal themes of the collective unconscious—that is, the unchanging, universal unconscious of the human race. According to Jung, it is this process that accounts for a work of art's universal appeal (Rothenberg and Hausman, 1976).

Psychoanalytic theorists also disagree on the relationship between neurosis and creativity. Some suggest that neurosis can contribute to creativity, and others (for example, Kubie) indicate that neurotic feelings of guilt and fear can inhibit the creative process. Techniques for enhancing creativity consistent with the psychoanalytic approach attempt to eliminate external and internal blocks (for example, fear of ridicule). Removal of such blocks is intended to open individuals to their own streams of thought and enable them to become more aware of their interior ideas and images (Meichenbaum, 1975).

Creativity as Personality

Theories of humanistic psychology, as represented by Carl Rogers and Abraham Maslow, describe creativity as an aspect of personality related to self-actualization, the becoming of one's potentialities. In this view every individual is born with the potential for creativity. The realization of that potential depends on the existence of supportive conditions.

Rogers (1959) emphasized creative productivity, defining the creative process as the emergence of a novel product out of an interaction between the unique individual and the materials of experience. Rogers suggested that release of creative potential requires only the following conditions: (a) openness to experience, tolerance for ambiguity, and flexibility of conceptual boundaries; (b) internal locus of evaluation (deriving satisfaction from one's own evaluation without having to rely on the praise or criticism of others); and (c) the ability to toy with concepts and elements, to play spontaneously with ideas. Based on his experience as a psychotherapist, Rogers further described ways to establish these conditions: (a) by accepting the individual as being of unconditional worth, (b) by eliminating external evaluation, (c) by understanding empathically (seeing and feeling from the subject's own viewpoint), and (d) by providing psychological freedom.

Maslow (1968) noted that self-actualizing (SA) creativeness emerges from the personality and finds expression in everyday life—for example, in doing housework or teaching. According to Maslow, each person is born with SA creativeness, but the potential frequently disappears as the individual becomes acculturated. He described SA creative individuals as less controlled and inhibited in their behavior, able to express ideas and impulses without fear of ridicule, more open to the unknown, self-accepting, self-transcending, self-integrated, and comfortably disorderly. Methods based on humanistic approaches attempt to induce a more creative self-perception or to promote conditions under which creativity will find expression.

Creativity as Mental Abilities or Processes

Several theorists have identified mental abilities or processes as underlying creative thinking. The Gestalt approach emphasizes mental processes, while the psychometric approach focuses on mental abilities.

Gestalt. Although criticized for being vague and untestable, Gestalt theories have contributed to our understanding of productive thinking by proposing the concepts of stages in thinking and rigidity in a problem-solving set (Mayer, 1977). According to Gestalt theorists, problem solving involves reorganizing or restructuring the problem situation. Mayer (1977) told the following story of Wolfgang Kohler, one of the founders of Gestalt psychology. Having been stranded on an island in the Atlantic during World War I, Kohler spent seven years studying the island's chimpanzees. One problem Kohler investigated was this: If an ape is put in a cage with several crates on the floor and a banana hanging from the ceiling, how will the ape get the banana? Kohler reported from his observations that the chimps' solution to such problems were preceded by a period of intensive thinking followed by a flash of insight.

Similarly, Wallas (1926) described human problem solving as a process occurring in four phases: (*a*) preparation (gathering information), (*b*) incubation (putting the problem aside to do other activities), (*c*) illumination (appearance of the key to the solution as a flash of insight), and (*d*) verification (checking to ensure that the solution works). Research indicates that past experience can hinder creative problem solving when such experience produces a problem-solving set, or habitual way of thinking or using objects, while the problem at hand requires thinking or using objects in a new way. Past experience, however, can be helpful when the problem situation requires simple transference of ideas from an old situation to a new one. The Gestalt idea of steps in problem solving provided a basis for information-processing theories (discussed in Chapter 3). The concept of rigidity in a problem-solving set preceded the current emphasis on the need for flexibility in creative thinking.

Psychometric Approaches. J.P. Guilford and E. Paul Torrance have emphasized mental abilities in manipulating information as underlying the creative process. Their work follows a psychometric approach—that is, operationally defining creativity in terms of performance on test items.

Guilford's work on the structure-of-intellect model (beginning in the 1950s) gave impetus to the search for creative thinking processes (Rothenberg and Hausman, 1976; Wallach, 1970). Guilford's model, described in Chapter 3, posits three bases for classifying intellectual abilities: (a) type of *operation* or thinking process, (b) type of *content* to which operations are applied, and (c) type of *product* that can result. Guilford further identified five types of operations, two of which were convergent production and divergent production. Convergent production involves generating new information from given information to produce the logical or conventionally accepted best outcome (Guilford, 1973) or, more simply, converging upon the one correct answer (Guilford, 1967). Convergent thinking is commonly associated with general intelligence and is assessed through such items as verbal comprehension, verbal reasoning, and arithmetic problem solving, for which correct responses can be objectively determined. In contrast, divergent production refers to the generation of new information from given information, leading to variety and quantity of output or alternatives. Much subsequent work on creativity as a mental ability has stemmed from Guilford's concept of divergent production.

Based on factor-analytic techniques, Guilford and his associates isolated several subprocesses of divergent thinking: four types of fluency (word, associational, ideational, and expressional), three types of flexibility (spontaneous flexibility, adaptive flexibility, and redefinition), and originality. Fluency generally relates to the ability to generate many alternatives that fulfill particular requirements, such as naming uses for bricks or writing titles for a story plot. Flexibility denotes the ability to vary one's ideas and cross familiar mental boundaries to think about something in a new way (for example, combining familiar objects, such as a hammer and string, into a new product for a new purpose). Originality refers to the ability to give unique or unusual responses, such as generating clever story endings that few other people would produce. In later studies Guilford (1967) added a fourth factor to fluency, flexibility, and originality as subprocesses of divergent production. The fourth factor was called elaboration, or the ability to provide relevant detail.

Drawing on the work of Guilford and his associates, Torrance (1966) developed new assessment procedures and suggestions for encouraging creativity in the classroom. The Torrance Tests of Creative Thinking consist of verbal and figural materials generally scored for fluency, flexibility, originality, and elaboration. An example of a verbal question would be to have the student think of many questions about a picture and suggest possible causes for the situation depicted in the picture. One figural item asks the student to sketch additions to sets of line forms to represent something unusual. The work of both Torrance and Guilford has been subject to debate, particularly with respect to the independence of their creativity measures from measures of general intelligence. Nonetheless, their contributions have given rise to many concrete methods for facilitating creativity in schools.

Creativity as Hemispheric Specialization

The theory that creative abilities have their source in specific types of hemispheric functioning has received increasing emphasis since the late 1960s. Despite its recent emergence, the hemispheric specialization theory of creativity has already spawned suggestions for enhancing creativity through methods aimed at stimulating specific parts of the brain (e.g., Wenger, 1981). Simply stated, hemispheric specialization means that the two hemispheres of the human brain are specialized for different modes of information processing (McCallum and Glynn, 1979). The left cerebral hemisphere deals primarily with verbal, analytic, abstract, logical, and sequential operations and controls the right side of the body. The right hemisphere specializes primarily in nonverbal, holistic, spatial, concrete, intuitive, and imaginal functions and controls the left side of the body. It should be kept in mind that the hemispheres are not specialized for different tasks but for how they process a given task. The same task can be approached by either hemisphere, but it will be accomplished through different processes. A bridge of nerve fiber, called the *corpus callosum*, connects the two hemispheres of the brain.

Some theorists isolate the right hemisphere as the source of creativity, suggesting that creativity can be induced by having subjects attend to right-hemisphere imagery (Gowan, 1979). Others (e.g., Bogen and Bogen, 1976) suggest that creativity depends on the coordination of the functions of the two hemispheres through the *corpus callosum*. According to this theory, the interaction between hemispheres produces creative acts, as, for example, the ongoing evaluation that occurs when a painting is being created.

Hemisphericity refers to differences in preference for right- or left-brain functioning in information processing and is established early in life (Reynolds and Torrance, 1978). Creative individuals are thought to be right-hemisphere dominant, while logical, rational thinkers are described as left-hemisphere dominant.

Investigations in hemispheric specialization began as early as 1861, when Paul Broca, a French surgeon, examined how left- or right-hemisphere-damaged patients performed identical tasks. Sperry's (1973) split brain research on animals begun in the 1950s and on epilepsy patients later brought widespread attention to hemisphere research (Myers, 1982). For example, in one study an individual whose *corpus callosum* had been surgically severed to reduce epileptic seizures was presented with a spoon in the left visual field and a knife in the right. When asked to name what he saw, he responded, "Knife"—a response consistent with the fact that language ability is located in the left cerebral hemisphere, which, in the crossing of visual pathways, received the image of the knife. When asked to select by touch the object he had seen, the patient selected the spoon, consistent with the nonverbal spatial and concrete functioning of the right hemisphere, which received the image of the spoon (McCallum and Glynn, 1979; Myers, 1982).

Recent research supporting hemispheric specialization has been conducted on subjects whose brains are intact. The findings can be summarized as follows (Katz, 1978; McCallum and Glynn, 1979).

1. *Tachistoscopic image presentation.* Visual data are presented either to the right or the left visual field and are processed in the opposite hemisphere. Results of tachistoscopic research generally suggest that verbal stimuli are processed more efficiently in the left hemisphere; spatial stimili, in the right hemisphere.

2. *Dichotic listening tasks.* Different auditory stimuli are presented simultaneously to the right and left ears. Crossover between ear and hemisphere occurs in the same way that crossover between eye and hemisphere occurs. Research indicates that linguistic stimuli (for example, words) are processed more accurately when presented to the left hemisphere via the right ear and nonverbal stimuli (for example, melodies) are processed more accurately when presented to the right hemisphere via the left ear.

3. *Electroencephalographic (EEG) responses.* EEG data are recorded while subjects engage in a task. Investigators have observed higher brain-wave activity in the left hemisphere when subjects are engaged in a math or verbal task and higher activity in the right hemisphere when subjects are engaged in spatial tasks.

4. *Conjugate lateral eye movements.* It has been hypothesized that shifting of both eyes to the left during problem solving indicates right-hemisphere activity, while eye movement to the right indicates left-hemisphere activity. Research has produced inconsistent results, suggesting that eye movements may not indicate hemispheric functioning.

5. *Self-report.* Torrance et al. (1977) have developed a forty-item paper-and-pencil self-report inventory, "Your Style of Learning and Thinking" (SOLAT), to classify adolescents and young adults as left-hemisphere dominant, right-hemisphere dominant, integrated, or mixed. One item asks subjects to indicate which of three operations—visualization and imagery, language and analysis, or no preference—best describes their problem-solving behavior. A study by Reynolds and Torrance (1978) suggested that preference for processing information through the right or the left hemisphere as indicated on the SOLAT can be modified by a brief (six- to twelve-week) training program. For example, direct and intensive instruction in creative problem solving and imaging led to changes toward greater right-hemisphere preference on the SOLAT.

6. *Single-hemisphere arousal.* Another method for testing hemispheric theory is to test creative ability, arouse one hemisphere, and then retest to determine whether arousal increased test performance. Katz (1978) reviewed research most closely using this paradigm, wherein right-hemisphere arousal was ostensibly accomplished through hypnosis or marijuana intoxication. This research, although indirect, suggested that right-hemisphere arousal may lead to improved performance on tests of creativity.

Several investigators (e.g., Katz, 1978; McCallum and Glynn, 1979; Myers, 1982) have emphasized that research supporting hemispheric specialization, as well as teaching methods based on hemispheric theory, should be interpreted with caution for several reasons. First, research using epileptic subjects may not generalize to individuals with undamaged brains. Some evidence suggests that in brain-injured patients, one hemisphere may take over the functions of the damaged portions. Second, laboratory studies (for example, tachistoscopic research) may not generalize to real life. Third, many studies have employed indirect methods, such as hypnosis or use of a creative task for inducing or measuring specific hemisphere arousal. A task used to elicit right-brain functioning may in fact have been accomplished by either or both hemispheres. Finally, when a relationship is found between right-hemispheric functioning and creativity, the relationship might be accounted for by correlates of creativity. For example, the self-confidence associated with creativity, rather than creativity itself, may be related to right-hemispheric functioning.

Writers in the field of hemispheric specialization seem to agree that because of the schools' emphasis on convergent thinking, formal education cultivates left-brain processing to the virtual exclusion of right-brain processing. As a result, the schools may fail to develop the right side of the brain and penalize students whose hemispherity, or preferred mode of processing information, is right brain (McCallum and Glynn, 1979). Myers (1982) suggested that teachers can help students strengthen right-hemisphere functioning through activities that involve suspending judgment, creating unusual or forced relationships, and stimulating incubation (the passive process of letting ideas come together to solve a particular problem). Myers suggested that these activities may be accomplished through biofeedback and meditation and relaxation techniques. In biofeedback, subjects learn to control the production of alpha waves, the presence of which implies that the brain is not engaged in complex processing. Learning to produce alpha waves in the left hemisphere may free the right hemisphere to engage in creative production. Several authors (e.g., Andrews, 1980; Gordon and Poze, 1981) have integrated hemispheric specialization theory of creativity with levels of consciousness, suggesting that right-brain processing enables subjects to tap their subconscious.

Other Theories of Creativity

Additional theories that offer insight into creative processing include association (Mednick, 1962), computer model (Crovitz, 1970), and behavioral (Skinner, 1972) approaches. Mednick's association theory defines creativity as a bringing together of remotely associated elements (for example, words) into new combinations that meet some specified requirements or are somehow useful. His work was the basis for development of the Remote Associates Test, frequently used in research on creativity. Crovitz's computer model constitutes one of several approaches attempting to provide a description of problem solving from the field of artificial intelligence. Behavioral theories generally explain creative behavior as behavior learned through the application of reinforcements from the environment (Woodman, 1981). Skinner's behavioral theory minimizes the creator's role in creative production, proposing instead that the essential elements of a creative product come from the individual's verbal and nonverbal history. The creator merely accepts or rejects these elements and combines them into the final work. The creative product emerges from random changes selected because of their positive consequences, a concept based on Darwin's theory of natural selection (Rothenberg and Hausman, 1976).

In sum, a wide variety of theories have offered divergent views on the phenomenon of creativity. Interestingly, although the various theories offer different explanations of creativity, their implications for enhancing creativity have common, or at least compatible, elements. Each theory stresses (a) providing conditions that eliminate blocks to creative thinking, such as external evaluation; (b) helping subjects value their own ideas; (c) suspending judgment; (d) practicing flexible thinking; and (e) motivating creative behavior. Each theory also holds that creativity can be enhanced.

SELECTED RESEARCH ON CREATIVITY

Areas of investigation on creativity most relevant to educators include studies of (a) relationships among intelligence, achievement, and creativity and (b) efforts to enhance creative thinking.

Intelligence, Achievement, and Creativity

Investigations that have sought to sort out relationships between intelligence and creativity and between school achievement and creativity have produced a variety of conflicting results.

Intelligence and Creativity. A number of studies have focused on the relationship between creativity and intelligence, perhaps inspired by theories (for example, Guilford's) about their independence as mental abilities and by distinctions made in early literature between the creative and intellectual capacities of famous individuals. Studies at the end of the nineteenth century and at the beginning of the twentieth (before the availability of IQ tests) reported that some decidedly "intellectual" individuals displayed poor performance on measures of imagination, such as inkblot tests (Harvey, 1982). Cox (1926), who estimated the IQs of eminent individuals based on a comparison of current developmental norms and extensive biographical material, assigned IQs of 170 or above to Goethe, John Stuart Mill, and Voltaire but assigned IQs of 140 or below to George Washington, Rembrandt, and Beethoven. Moreover, Terman and his associates were able to distinguish the highly creative from the less creative among their subjects, all of whom possessed IQs of 140 or above (Terman, 1926; Terman and Oden, 1947).

In analyzing studies of the intelligence–creativity relationship, the distinction between creativity measured by recognized achievement and creativity measured by tests of divergent or creative thinking must be emphasized. Research reviewed by Getzels and Dillon (1973) indicates that creative achievers demonstrate better-than-average intelligence, but the correlation between their intelligence scores and their creativity is low. A recent ten-year longitudinal study (Howieson, 1981) supported a low correlation between intelligence scores and real-life creative achievement. It was found that while tests of divergent thinking predicted later self-reported creative achievement in art, writing, science, and drama, IQ predicted accomplishment in only one area: leadership. In addition, IQ, but not performance on divergent-thinking tests, predicted later academic success.

Most investigations with children examine performance on tests of creativity rather than creative achievement. Several of these studies (e.g., Getzels and Jackson, 1962; Torrance, 1962, 1967) reported positive but low correlations between performance on various measures of creative thinking and performance on intelligence tests. Getzels and Jackson found a correlation of 0.26. Torrance (1967) summarized results from a number of studies that reported correlation coefficients between measures of intelligence and various versions of the Torrance Tests of Creative Thinking. Of 178 correlation coefficients between measures of intelligence and a total score of creative thinking, the median was 0.20. The median of 88 coefficients of correlation between intelligence and verbal creativity was 0.21. Torrance reported a median of 0.06 for 114 coefficients between intelligence and figural creativity. The relationship between tested creativity and intelligence appeared to be affected by students' sex, age, and range of IQ scores and by the type of creativity measured. Correlations with intelligence were higher for girls than for boys and were also higher for subjects at the lower half of the IQ range. Correlations also tended to be higher on tests of verbal as opposed to figural creativity. Finally, correlations were higher for fluency and elaboration than for originality.

Wallach (1970) reviewed research that employed Guilford's divergent-thinking concepts with children, adolescents, and young adults. Based on his analysis, Wallach concluded that of the eight subprocesses initially identified by Guilford, the literature most clearly supports ideational fluency—the ability to generate a great number of ideas within task constraints—as independent from convergent thinking and general intelligence. He found little evidence to indicate that the three types of flexibility differ from convergent-production abilities. Although research findings on originality are inconsistent, Wallach suggested that when the measurement of originality depends on uniqueness or unusualness of ideas as opposed to cleverness or facility with words, independence from general intelligence will be greater. A more recent study (Thies and Friedrich, 1977) supported Wallach's conclusions, finding that ideational fluency and originality were related, forming a cohesive dimension relatively independent of intelligence.

Wallach further argued that the scores from the Torrance tests correlate with scores on intelligence and achievement tests—that is, tests of convergent thinking—to about the same degree that the Torrance test scores correlate with one another. Wallach therefore concluded:

> No unitary dimension is defined by these measures . . . apart from that of general intelligence. Hence there is still no cause for assuming the Torrance measures reflect a cognitive disposition that could be appropriately described in terms of creativity.
>
> — Wallach, 1970, p. 1227

Wallach offered as a possible explanation for these less-than-positive findings the hypothesis that of Torrance's four criteria, two (flexibility and elaboration) measure convergent rather than divergent abilities. Moreover, both the Guilford and the Torrance measures set time limits in which subjects must respond. Emphasizing speed of response and hence implying that "correct" answers exist may depress divergent responding.

More recently, Harvey (1982) proposed another model of creativity that, he suggested, may help explain the discrepant findings regarding the intelligence–creativity relationship. Using factor analysis, Harvey examined the scores of 114 teenagers in a juvenile justice system on Wechsler IQ scales and on the Torrance Tests of Creativity. He found separate factors for general intelligence and general fluency, indicating little or no relationship between the two. However, both general intelligence and general fluency were related to a lower-order factor that Harvey called creative energy, consisting of figural elaboration, figural originality, and verbal originality. Harvey defined creative energy as the ability to produce original ideas and to extend these ideas with separate, smaller ones. He interpreted his findings as indicating that creativity and intelligence are not totally independent but are used in complex combination, as when the individual uses creative energy.

In sum, the relationship between intelligence and creativity depends on how creativity is defined by the investigator (test performance or established achievement), the type of creativity assessed (fluency, flexibility, originality, or elaboration), and the nature of the subjects examined (sex, age, IQ range). Of the four types of mental abilities subsumed under creative thinking, fluency appears to be the most distinct from general intelligence. Although findings conflict, originality and elaboration may depend on both general intelligence and fluency.

Achievement and Creativity. Getzels and Dillon concluded from their review of the literature on creativity and school performance that "many of the resolutions propounded by one study are overthrown by another" (Getzels and Dillon, 1973, p. 703). A number of researchers have found that individuals high in creativity perform as well as the intellectually advanced on standard measures of achievement, despite substantial differences in IQ. However, other investigators have failed to corroborate these findings or have found the achievement–creativity relationship to be confounded by a common dependence on intelligence. From his review of the research, Torrance (1967) reported a higher correlation between creativity and achievement when standardized tests rather than school grades or teacher ratings were used to measure achievement. Correlations ranged from negative coefficients to 0.70, depending on the type of achievement measured. For example, achievement defined as evaluation or application of knowledge produced a higher relationship to creativity than did the recognition of correct answers.

Several investigators have offered a threshold hypothesis to explain conflicting findings, suggesting that beyond some level of IQ, such as 120, creativity rather than intelligence determines achievement. However, studies investigating the threshold hypothesis have produced conflicting results. Getzels and Dillon (1973) listed additional variables suggested in the literature as affecting the achievement–creativity relationship and as accounting for discrepant findings. These variables include learning atmosphere (rigid or permissive), teacher type (convergent or divergent), grade level (elementary, secondary, or postsecondary), and subject matter (humanities, mathematics, or science). Research on these variables has also resulted in inconsistent findings.

Enhancing Creativity

The great majority of training studies conclude that creative abilities can be enhanced through instruction, especially when instruction is directly aimed at increasing creativity and provides for practice and maximum teacher and student involvement. However, critical reviews suggest that methodological weaknesses in some of these studies necessitate caution in interpretation. Moreover, although training may increase performance on tests of creative thinking, there is little direct evidence that training increases real-life creative production.

Training Studies. Parnes and Brunelle (1967) reviewed more than 40 studies that evaluated programs designed to improve fluency, flexibility, originality, elaboration, and related abilities. Taken together, these investigations included a wide range of subjects: mentally retarded to gifted, primary school to adult age groups, and individuals from a variety of fields (military, education, business). Ninety percent of the studies indicated that deliberate educational programs increased subjects' creative production. Several studies examined achievement in relation to creativity training, with some showing gains in subject matter areas, such as reading and creative writing, in addition to gains in creative abilities. Length of training appeared to influence the strength of the results. Brief practice experiences produced immediate gains in creative performance on specific tasks, but the gains tended not to transfer to later creativity tests. In contrast, investigations that involved extensive training seemed to show transfer of increased creativity to other tasks.

Torrance (1972a) reviewed 142 training studies, 103 of which employed the Torrance Tests of Creative Thinking as criteria for improved creative performance. Based on his review, Torrance concluded that children *can* be taught to think creatively, especially when teaching is deliberately focused on creative functioning, involves both cognitive and affective content, and provides structure, motivation, and opportunities for involvement, practice, and interaction with teachers and peers.

Torrance's review provided three major findings. First, studies using techniques based on the Osborn-Parnes Creative Problem-Solving Program (creative problem solving, brainstorming, and divergent questioning) and other specific, disciplined approaches evidenced the highest success rate (90 percent).

Second, Torrance found a moderate (67 to 81 percent) success rate for a variety of complex programs:

— programs using packaged materials (Purdue Creativity Program, Myers-Torrance materials, Productive Thinking Program)
— programs using arts (music, visual arts, creative writing, and movement) as the vehicle for improving creativity
— media and reading programs
— programs seeking to increase motivation (for example, through rewards and competition)
— programs seeking to improve test conditions (through warm-up activities, a gamelike atmosphere, or elimination of timing)

Programs seeking to increase motivation incorporated such tactics as competition, prizes, rewards for specific creative functions (for example, originality), and publication of the product. Torrance cautioned that external reinforcers needed to be reapplied for each event.

Torrance's third finding was that programs involving changes in curricular and administrative arrangements and programs that manipulate teacher–classroom variables have the lowest success rate (50 to 55 percent). Changes in curricular and administrative arrangements are intended to design favorable conditions for creativity and include such diverse options as independent study, enrichment, and placement in arts classes. Teacher–classroom variables may include teacher creativity, teacher control, in-service training, and grouping strategies. Torrance concluded that teacher creativity is not a significant factor in influencing student creativity, although teacher motivation is important. In-service training on specific methods also appeared to have beneficial effects.

Results of a recent meta-analysis (a statistical method for comparing findings across studies) of creativity training programs (Rose and Lin, 1984) corroborated Torrance's findings. Based on data from 46 studies, Rose and Lin concluded that training does appear to affect creativity as measured by changes in performance on the Torrance Tests of Creativity and that Parnes's Creative Problem-Solving Program produced the greatest changes. The authors also reported that creativity training had greater impact on verbal than on figural creativity, as would be expected from most training programs' emphasis on verbal expression. Finally, training had the greatest effect on originality and fluency.

In their critical review of training studies, Mansfield, Busse, and Krepelka (1978) pointed out three major limitations. First, investigators frequently assume that creativity is equivalent to divergent thinking and can be measured by divergent-thinking tests. The great majority of training studies use as the criterion for effectiveness improved performance on divergent-thinking tests, but improved performance on tests may not be related to real-life creative accomplishments. Second, success on divergent-thinking tests after creativity training may be due to increased persistence or to greater knowledge about the types of answers expected rather than to real changes in creative abilities. Third, many training studies evidence common methodological problems—for example, small sample size, failure to control for the teacher variable, use of intact classrooms but individual scores, nonrandom assignment, and use of training tasks that teach to the criterion measure.

Mansfield, Busse, and Krepelka concluded that the complex programs involving packaged materials (reviewed by Torrance as moderately successful) lead to increased creative performance only on tests whose items are similar to training tasks. Hence, making generalizations from training that uses these programs to real-life situations is questionable. For the Productive Thinking Program (Covington et al., 1974) and the Purdue Creative Thinking Program (Feldhusen, Treffinger, and Bahlke, 1970; Treffinger, Speedie, and Brunner, 1974), the largest training effects were produced by studies with the most serious methodological flaws. Like Torrance (1972a) and Rose and Lin (1984), the authors found that Parnes's Creative Problem-Solving Program appeared to be more successful than others in training divergent thinking. This program will be reviewed later in the chapter. Tangential evidence from longitudinal studies suggests that improved performance on divergent-thinking tests may be reflected in real-life creative production.

Longitudinal Studies Relating Divergent Thinking to Creative Production.

Almost no literature is available on long-term, real-life effects of training in divergent thinking. However, a few longitudinal studies have been reported regarding the validity of divergent-thinking tests as predictors of later creative performance in real life. Kogan and Pankove (1974) tested fifth-grade students on the Wallach-Kogan tests of divergent thinking and examined their creative accomplishments in high school as measured on a biographical self-report inventory of nonacademic talent attainment. The authors concluded that fifth-grade divergent-thinking performance has little predictive value for nonacademic talent in high school. They suggested, however, that there may be a sleeper effect—that is, the tests may lack predictive validity for intermediate years but may be accurate predictors of accomplishment in later adulthood.

Torrance (1972c) reviewed five long-range studies that supported the utility of the Torrance Tests of Creativity for predicting later creative behavior, such as creative teaching, awards in the arts, and self-reported creative achievements (for example, patents held or poems, stories, songs, books, and scientific papers written or published). One study identified sixteen creative elementary students based on their performance on the Torrance Tests of Creative Thinking. Twelve of the students continued in an out-of-school program designed to help develop their creative abilities. Ten of the twelve revealed superior talent as evidenced by awards and scholarships in the arts and sciences. Torrance also reported from his twelve-year follow-up of high school students that creativity tests administered in grades seven through twelve can predict real-life adult creative achievement. Adult achievement was measured by quantity of self-reported accomplishments and quality of accomplishments as assessed by expert judges.

More recently Howieson (1981) conducted a ten-year follow-up of 130 of 394 subjects in western Australia who had been initially tested on subtests of the Torrance Tests of Creative Thinking at age twelve. Based on the Torrance subtests, a group of creative students (top 20 percent) and a less creative control group were established. At the time of follow-up, the subjects were twenty-two years old. The criterion measure of creative accomplishment was adapted for Australia from the biographical self-report inventory used by Kogan and Pankove (1974) and was designed to measure nonacademic talent accomplishment in leadership, art, writing, drama, music, and science. By examining biographical data, Howieson found that over the ten-year period, members of the creative group had accomplished significantly more than had members of the noncreative group on general achievement, science, art, writing, and drama. Closer examination of the data, however, revealed greater predictive accuracy for males than for females. The initial creativity tests correlated with later general achievement, art, writing, and science for males, but they correlated with only drama and music for females. These data suggest that male performance and female performance on tests of divergent thinking do not have the same implications for real-life behavior. Howieson cautioned that the correlations were significant but low (0.21 to 0.44) and account for a small portion of the variance in later life performance. He also suggested that his findings may support the sleeper effect since predictive validity was established for creative performance in adults who had been out of high school for four years.

In sum, it appears that direct training in creativity leads to improved performance on divergent-thinking tests, especially when training and test items are highly similar. Some evidence suggests that test performance may predict creative behavior in later life. However, the evidence is highly indirect since the longitudinal studies reported do not examine test performance and real-life creativity in relation to creativity *training*.

METHODS FOR DEVELOPING CREATIVE POTENTIAL

The literature provides a variety of theories on creativity and a host of research studies examining different methods for enhancing creative production. Despite the seeming variety of theories and instructional programs, a set of common techniques emerges. This section describes the research-supported methods for encouraging creativity that can be applied in regular or special classrooms with a variety of age groups and with minimal training. For readers who may be interested in investigating and applying packaged programs, two well-supported packaged programs are also described briefly.

Specific Techniques

One of the major obstacles to creative thinking at all age levels is the need to be "correct"—to have the right answer. This need stems from societal values that reinforce achievement in terms of school grades and acquisition of factual knowledge derived from authorities. Although formal education plays a major role in promoting such values, many middle-class parents enforce similar values in their children, beginning when the children are quite young. Children three and four years old, with no previous school experience, frequently enter pre-school already evidencing discomfort with ambiguity and a need to be able to respond correctly. For example, when asked to make something no one else will think of, many young children look for models to copy and ask, "Is this right?"

Because the need to be correct is often established prior to school entrance and is reinforced in school, children of all ages may have difficulty responding to initial attempts to encourage creative thinking. Teachers should not be discouraged by low creative responses when beginning to incorporate into the regular classroom structure methods designed to enhance creativity. With patience, motivation, and enthusiasm on the part of the teacher and with provision of opportunities for practice, all students (kindergarteners through adults) can learn to think more creatively. Specific techniques include establishing conditions favorable to creative production, employing divergent-questioning models, and teaching students to increase creativity through self-instruction.

Establishing Favorable Conditions. Torrance (1963, 1965) summarized approximately thirty studies conducted by himself and his associates that investigated factors affecting creative growth. The results of these investigations provide helpful suggestions for establishing conditions conducive to increased creativity.

1. *Offer many opportunities for creative behavior.* Make assignments that require original work, independent learning, and experimentation. Ask questions that require creative thinking. Use strategies specifically designed to enhance creativity. Examples are brainstorming and synectics (the conscious application of metaphors in problem solving), discussed in detail later in this chapter.

2. *Show respect for unusual questions, unusual ideas, and unusual solutions.* Creative children will discern relationships that teachers miss; their responses should be accepted and worked with rather than summarily dismissed.

3. *Show students that their ideas have value.* Listen to, consider, test, and apply students' ideas. Have the students communicate their ideas to others.

4. *Construct a nonevaluative, nonthreatening atmosphere.* Constant evaluation by the teacher inhibits children's creativity by making them afraid to take risks in responding.

5. *Avoid critical peer evaluation.* Encourage creative or constructive peer evaluation by having students point out other possibilities rather than pointing out defects.

6. *Provide experiences that encourage sensitivity to environmental stimuli.* Have students describe sensations experienced through sight, smell, touch, taste, and hearing.

7. *Avoid giving examples or models that shape thinking.* When the objective is to encourage originality, such as by making a unique sculpture out of throw-aways, provision of a model often creates a mind-set that children have difficulty breaking; they may view the model as the "correct" product.

8. *Occasionally organize small groups according to ability.* Small groups that are homogeneous in ability tend to exhibit less disruption and more cooperative interaction than do heterogeneous groups.

9. *Permit flexibility in schedule and curriculum.* Overreliance on a prescribed curriculum to be covered in a prescribed time period precludes the teacher's taking advantage of children's spontaneous ideas.

Divergent-Questioning Models. Teachers can give students practice in abilities related to creative thinking by incorporating techniques of divergent questioning into ongoing units. Divergent questioning can be conceptualized according to the four factors described by Guilford and Torrance: fluency, originality, elaboration, and flexibility. Ideational fluency has been most supported by research as a factor in creative production. Originality and elaboration appear to rely on elements of both convergent and divergent abilities. Again, divergent questioning permits a variety of acceptable alternative responses, as opposed to questioning for which there is only one correct answer.

Fluency is the ability to give many different responses. Questions that encourage fluency generally ask students to "describe all the ways you can think of" to solve a particular problem or "list all the things you can think of" that meet a given set of conditions. Fluency questions can be used to deal with problems that arise spontaneously (How can we raise money for a new telescope?), or they can be planned as part of subject matter activities. The following are examples of fluency questions:

— How many ways can you think of to end this story?
— What are all the factors that might affect a country's agricultural production?
— How many invertebrates can you think of?

— What are all the things this music makes you think of?
— How many techniques can you think of to express emotion in painting?
— How many situations can you think of that require a knowledge of geometry?

Brainstorming is one common method of structuring fluency questions. Brainstorming generally requires the inhibiting of evaluative responses to enable the free flow of a large quantity of ideas. The objective is to gather as many ideas as possible, without self-criticism or peer or teacher criticism. With a large quantity of ideas, chances improve that a valuable idea will be among them. The steps involved in brainstorming are described in the following list.

1. *Establish ground rules.* For example, "Everyone's contributions are important and will be accepted without critical comment. There will be no snickering, rolling of eyes, and so forth."

2. *Pose the question or problem.* For example, "What are all the ways you can think of that would enable a small, developing country to cope with famine related to rapid population growth?"

3. *Record each response.* Permit and encourage piggybacking, or integrating of ideas. For the famine question, possible responses might be the following:

a. Request foreign aid.
b. Exterminate everyone over or under a certain age.
c. Mandate birth control.
d. Train the people in food production.
e. Redistribute the nation's wealth.
f. Legislate land reform to redistribute the nation's wealth.

4. *Establish criteria.* If the intent of brainstorming is to find a workable solution to a problem, criteria for determining the best solutions should be established after all responses have been exhausted. For example, the students might set the following criteria for solutions to the famine problem: (*a*) respect for the sanctity of life, (*b*) use of democratic as opposed to totalitarian means, and (*c*) conformity to the logic of economics.

5. *Evaluate recorded responses against the criteria.* Refrain from attributing responses to individual children (for example, "George's idea does not meet the first criterion").

Brainstorming can be useful in many instances where the objective is not to find a best solution but rather to establish a foundation for subsequent activities. As part of a lesson on holidays, we asked young children to name all the ideas they had related to valentines and Valentine's Day (for example, Saint Valentine, cards, lace, love, hearts). The children's responses were written on the chalkboard and left there for several days. Their list served as a basis for discussing the history, meaning, customs, and events associated with Valentine's

Day. Later the list provided a starting point for composing group-authored poems about the holiday. One poem read:

valentines

give, receive,

bumpy, lacey, complicated

great, excited, happy, loved

valentines

Having students brainstorm ideas about a new topic also helps the teacher assess their beginning level of concept knowledge related to the topic.

As with all divergent-questioning models, brainstorming should be used within the context of established curriculum objectives. Brainstorming activities unrelated to content objectives may be perceived as frivolous exercises. When brainstorming is used in context, students develop a better understanding of how the technique can be generalized to other situations that require the generation and manipulation of ideas.

Taba's "applying generalizations" technique (Taba et al., 1971) offers another structure for giving students practice in fluent production (see Table 8.1). The aim of the strategy is for students to demonstrate transferability of new knowledge by applying newly acquired generalizations to different situations. The teacher begins by encouraging students to predict and hypothesize what will occur if a situation similar to the one under study happens in another location, or if there occurs a variation in the situation under study. For example, after the class has studied the history and social consequences of slavery in the United States, the teacher might ask, "Suppose China defeated the United States in a third world war in which many young adults serving in the Chinese army were killed. With China's tremendous postwar need for manpower to increase production of food and manufactured products, what would happen?"

In the second step of learning to apply generalizations, students are asked to explain or support their predictions by reasoning out the causal links. Finally, students verify their predictions through logical reasoning or, if the event has actually occurred, against the facts. In the preceding example, John Hersey's novel *White Lotus*, whose subject is American slaves in China, might be consulted. Taba et al. noted that the processes of hypothesizing and predicting consequences involved in the application of generalizations require divergent thinking and challenge students to produce logical, factual support and to discriminate between tenable and untenable hypotheses. Supportive strategies recommended by Taba et al. include repeating student responses and asking for more information, rephrasing the responses without altering their meaning, asking for additional predictions, and asking for explanations of predictions. The authors' research suggested that appropriate use of these minor strategies leads to higher-level generalizations.

Table 8.1 Technique for applying generalizations

TEACHER	STUDENT	TEACHER FOLLOW-THROUGH
Suppose that . . . (a particular event occurred given certain conditions), what would happen?	Makes inferences	Encourages additional inference; selects inference(s) to develop
What makes you think that would happen?	States explanation, identifies relationships	Accepts explanation; seeks clarification if necessary
What would be needed for that to happen?	Identifies facts necessary to a particular inference	Decides whether these facts are sufficient and could be assumed to be present in the given situation
Can someone give a different idea about what would happen?	States new inferences that differ in some respects from preceding ones	Encourages alternative inferences; requests explanations and necessary conditions; seeks clarification where necessary
If, as one of you predicted, such-and-such happened, what do you think would happen after that?	Makes inferences related to the given inference	Encourages additional inferences; selects those to pursue further

NOTE: This pattern of inviting inferences, requiring explanations, identifying necessary conditions, and encouraging divergent views is continued until the teacher decides to terminate the activity.
SOURCE: Taba et al., 1971, p. 85.

Robert Crawford's "attribute listing" constitutes a third model for encouraging fluency (Davis, 1976). Crawford proposed that all instances of creativity consist of (*a*) modifying important attributes of a problem or (*b*) transferring attributes from a given situation to a new one. For instance, suppose the problem is to develop a new fast food. An example of modifying attributes would be to have students identify the important attributes or characteristics of fast foods: speedy preparation, take-out convenience, good flavor, inexpensive packaging, and so forth. The teacher first lists the attributes on the board. After all the important attributes have been identified, students are asked to generate specific ideas for each, as well as combinations and elaborations, leading ultimately to suggestions for new fast foods.

The technique of transferring attributes could also be used in designing the physical premises for a fast-food establishment. Students borrow attributes from an unrelated setting, such as a different time period (for example, prehistoric times), from a different geographical location (for example, Greece), or from a specific theme (for example, church, jail, or circus). Attribute listing can also be used to stimulate student development of other products, such as short stories and poems. Modifying and transferring attributes give students practice in original, elaborative, and flexible thinking.

Besides fluency, the abilities related to creative thinking are originality, elaboration, and flexibility. Originality concerns uniqueness of responses and can be encouraged by asking students to give a response that no one else would think of or by presenting unfamiliar situations that require unique solutions. Instead of following a model to create a puppet, the teacher might supply a variety of materials and have the students develop novel products that still meet the criteria for being a puppet. Children may have difficulty getting started without an example to follow and may look to other children's ideas. The teacher can provide encouragement by praising each original effort, no matter how small ("I like how you used drinking straws for hair; I would never have thought of that"). In one example of using unfamiliar situations to elicit unique responses, a high school teacher had her students read about the everyday problems of weightlessness in space. She then asked students to find a solution to the problem of collecting and disposing of human waste, as differentially experienced by male and by female astronauts. Another unique situation might concern the disposal of toxic wastes.

Elaboration refers to the embellishment of an idea, the adding of detail. Elaboration can be encouraged by asking children to add detail to a figure to create something new. Young children learning the letter K might be given a series of Ks on a sheet of paper and asked to add details to make designs or pictures. The teacher might ask older students to describe or draw something novel in detail, such as a thing seen from another perspective: How did Gulliver's feet look to a Lilliputian? How might an electron appear to a neutron? How might a Communist feel about capitalism? This activity can be aided by imaging—that is, fantasizing how something will occur by producing mental images that depict in detail the sights, sounds, and sequencing of events.

Flexibility refers to facility in changing one's mind-set or seeing things in a different light. Being able to redefine a problem logically requires flexible thinking and can be crucial to effective problem solving. Getzels (1975) gave the example of a driver who has a blowout on a deserted road and has no jack. The driver defines the problem as "Where do I find a jack?" and walks several miles to a gas station. A second driver, also with a blowout and no jack, defines the problem as "How can the car be raised?" and finds a pulley at a nearby farm. Teachers can help students redefine problems by asking them to think about the basic objective behind the problem (what really needs to be accomplished) and by trying several paraphrasings of the question. Forced-association questions, which require students to find similarities in seemingly dissimilar objects, also give students practice in flexible thinking: How are a cat and a guitar alike? How are a horse, a plane, and a boat like a book? Khatena (1978) suggested additional strategies for breaking away from the mind-set, including recording familiar sounds and having students guess what they might be. Students are encouraged to think of ideas or images other than the familiar. For example, the sound of light rain against a window might be the firing of tin soldiers.

Increasing Creativity through Self-Instruction. Meichenbaum (1975) developed and tested a cognitive behavior modification method for increasing creative production. Subjects were taught to talk to themselves explicitly to change behavior. Training involved having subjects (*a*) become aware of their negative self-statements and (*b*) emit incompatible self-statements that would foster self-control and behavior change. The self-statements incorporated concepts from psychodynamic, personality, and mental ability conceptualizations of creativity. In the course of six sessions, subjects became aware of their negative self-statements (for example, "I am not very original"), developed positive self-statements from their own and others' experiences, and learned to instruct themselves to be more creative. Meichenbaum's data indicated that subjects using this method made improvements both in self-perceptions about creative ability and in performance on measures of divergent thinking.

Although Meichenbaum's study was limited to young adults, his findings suggest that the method had potential for increasing creative production. Cognitive behavior modification strategies have also been demonstrated as useful for improving other aspects of behavior in children (e.g., Finch and Spirito, 1980). Based on the work of Meichenbaum and of Finch and Spirito, specific steps for applying a cognitive behavior modification approach for enhancing creativity may be outlined as follows:

1. While the children observe, the teacher performs the creativity task and models the self-instructional statements by talking out loud. (The initial tasks might be similar to those on divergent-thinking tests, such as making unique designs from a series of circles. Later, self-instruction might be applied to real-life projects, such as sketches, essays, or sculptures.)
2. The children perform the task, instructing themselves out loud—first with help from the teacher and then without assistance.
3. The children perform the task, talking to themselves first in a whisper and then covertly.

Content of the verbalizations modeled by the teacher and rehearsed by the children includes (*a*) problem definition ("What do I need to do?"), (*b*) focusing of attention ("I have to concentrate"), (*c*) coping statements ("If I make a mistake, I can start again"), and (*d*) self-reinforcement ("Good! I did it!"). A sample set of self-instructional statements (derived from Meichenbaum, 1975) is as follows:

> Okay, what is it I have to do? I have to add detail to these circles to make something unique. Don't worry what others think; just be freewheeling. Think of something no one else would think of. Release the controls; relax and let it happen. I'm in a rut. That's okay; just try something new. Go slow; no need to hurry. Good! I'm getting it!

Established Programs

Two programs that have demonstrated effectiveness in helping people in a variety of fields (business, industry, government, education) increase their creative production are Gordon's synectics and Parnes's creative problem solving.

Synectics. Developed by William Gordon (1961, 1972; Gordon and Poze, 1971, 1980), synectics is a technique that can be useful for helping students see things in innovative ways. In synectics training, students learn to consciously apply metaphors in solving problems. Gordon's research with synectics supports the idea that everyone has the capacity for creativity and that this capacity can be nurtured.

Gordon (1972) described two interdependent problem-solving processes: the innovative process and the learning process. The innovative process occurs through making the familiar strange—that is, viewing a familiar problem from a new viewpoint. For example, Gordon suggested that Harvey discovered how blood circulates by observing a fish's heart (familiar) and making the (strange) connection to a pump he had seen. This situation is contrasted with the learning process, in which one gains understanding of a new concept by making the strange familiar—that is, making a personal connection between already acquired knowledge and new information. Gordon gave the example of a student observing a fish's heart (strange) after his professor had explained how a heart functions like a pump. The student remembered from past experience (familiar) that in a swimming pool dirty water is pumped through a filter and back into the pool. Thus, the student realized the connection between a heart and a water pump. The student also made other connections, observing how the lungs and the liver act as filters to cleanse the blood. Gordon suggested that both the innovative and the learning processes involve the use of creative comparisons and highly personal connection making between two seemingly unlike objects or systems. Gordon concluded that the creative process depends on using new contexts for viewing familiar phenomena and that the new context can be derived from metaphors.

Gordon identified three basic metaphorical mechanisms for creative innovation and learning. The first—direct analogy—refers to a comparison of one thing with another. He suggested, for example, that the Wright brothers based some of their concepts for the airplane on observations of buzzards in flight. The second mechanism, personal analogy, involves empathic identification with something external, as when a physicist imagines himself or herself as a beam of light while attempting to solve a problem related to solar energy. The third mechanism is symbolic analogy, or compressed conflict, and consists of yoking words that fight each other into a phrase. For example, Gordon suggested that Pasteur based his antitoxin work on the idea of "safe attack."

The teacher can help students make the familiar strange and the strange familiar by discussing the concepts of metaphor, analogy, and empathy and then having the students apply these concepts to problem situations. For example, if the situation concerns competition among cliques in school, the teacher could ask the students to consider what other structures outside school could be used to think about the social processes of school in a different way. The teacher could suggest: "Think, for example, of a beehive or a demilitarized zone. How could we conceptualize the problem of small, competing social groups within these strange contexts? What solutions are suggested by each? Try being something or someone else in the problem situation, seeing and feeling in detail what that thing or person feels."

Creative Problem Solving. Based on Alex Osborn's work on applying imagination to practical situations, the Creative Problem-Solving Model was developed by Sidney Parnes as a structured, comprehensive process for stimulating the use of imagination in problem solving (Parnes, 1977, 1981; Parnes, Noller, and Biondi, 1977). Like Gordon's synectics approach, Parnes's model assumes that some level of creativity exists in all individuals and that creative behaviors can be learned. The model consists of six steps and incorporates a variety of research-supported techniques for stimulating creativity, including brainstorming, synectics, incubation, imaging, deferred judgment, forced relationships, and practice. The steps are briefly described in the following list (Parnes, 1977).

1. *Objective finding.* The student brainstorms to come up with a problem, idea, or situation to be handled. The teacher instructs: "List any thoughts you have in mind, some challenge or problem, goals or aspirations; then select from the list the idea most important to you." (This step is required when the student does not begin with a specific problem. If the problem is given, the student begins with step 2.)

2. *Fact finding.* The student explores what is known about the situation. The teacher instructs: "List all you know about the problem. What is and what is not happening? Who is and who is not concerned? Why and when does the problem occur?"

3. *Problem finding.* The student examines the situation from different viewpoints. The teacher instructs: "List as many questions as you can think of about the situation. Redefine the problem by reviewing objectives and paraphrasing. Ask questions beginning with 'In what ways might I . . .'."

4. *Idea finding.* The student generates many alternative solutions. The teacher instructs: "Defer judgment and evaluation; allow the ideas to flow freely. List as many ideas as you can to solve the problem. Play music to aid incubation; look for strange metaphors; try to force relationships with other objects or situations to stimulate ideas."

5. *Solution finding.* The student selects the best solutions for solving the problem. The teacher instructs: "List the evaluative criteria that will determine the most useful solutions. Become something or someone in the situation and empathize fully with that thing or person to bring more connections or ideas into focus. Change the criteria as new ideas evolve."

6. *Acceptance finding.* The student develops a plan for implementing the solution and gaining acceptance for it. The teacher instructs: "Apply the criteria to the listed solutions to determine the best alternatives. Brainstorm ideas for gaining acceptance and for implementing the solutions. What will aid implementation? What will help ensure success? What objections might be anticipated, and how might the objections be overcome? Physically relax each muscle to incubate the ideas. List specific steps for implementing the plan. Fantasize in detail; put the plan into action and determine consequences thereof; adjust the plan accordingly."

CHAPTER SUMMARY

Creativity can be defined as the ability to generate an idea or a product that is new and useful. Fostering creativity is important to the betterment of human life. Many theories have been proposed to explain creative functioning. The psychoanalytic theory views the creative process as controlling regression to permit the preconscious mind to operate freely. Humanistic theorists suggest that creativity is founded in attitudinal and personality factors that can emerge given supportive conditions. Mental ability theories describe creativity in terms of divergent-thinking processes, such as fluency, flexibility, originality, and elaboration. The research supports fluency, and to some extent, flexibility and originality, as independent of general intelligence. Most recently, creativity has been conceptualized as a process associated with right-hemisphere functioning, although both hemispheres interact in creative production.

In addition to the theoretical literature, an abundance of research exists on creativity. Studies on intelligence and creativity indicate that the relationship between these traits is complex, with correlations affected by such factors as IQ range, sex, and age of subjects and type of creativity assessed. Some longitudinal evidence suggests that divergent-thinking tests better predict later self-reported real-life creative achievement than do IQ measures. Most investigators agree that creativity, as measured by divergent-thinking tests, can be purposely enhanced. However, few data have been collected to determine whether training leads to later real-life creative production.

The literature also provides an abundance of suggested techniques, programs, and packaged materials for enhancing creativity in the classroom. Although derived from different theoretical perspectives, many of the techniques and programs are highly compatible and can be used effectively in combination. Techniques for fostering creativity include eliminating fear of ridicule, suspending judgment, providing practice, brainstorming, redefining, and employing synectics and creative problem solving. Brainstorming itself incorporates the techniques of eliminating fear from evaluation and suspending judgment.

Teacher reluctance to employ open-ended questions and student socialization toward being "right" present barriers to implementing techniques designed to improve creative production. With practice, however, teachers and students find that activities that focus on creative production can be enjoyable, rewarding, and helpful in the realization of creative potential.

ACTIVITIES FOR THOUGHT AND DISCUSSION

1. Which theory of creativity is most appealing to you? Why? Do some further reading on the theory you have chosen. What specific techniques does the theory suggest for enhancing creativity? What research supports these techniques?

2. Brainstorm the following:

a. What else do I want to know about creativity?

b. What additional topics would I suggest to researchers in the field?

3. Use Parnes's Creative Problem-Solving Model to select a personal problem or situation to be analyzed and solved.

4. Using the lesson plan format given at the end of the preceding chapter, develop a lesson plan in a content area, incorporating one or more of the techniques for enhancing creativity.

Chapter Nine

ENHANCING EVALUATIVE
THINKING AND
AFFECTIVE DEVELOPMENT

When the teacher presented a cow brain during a unit on anatomy, four-year-old Bud demanded to know if the cow had been killed just so that the children could view its brain. After a discussion on international policy, fifteen-year-old Crystal agonized over Congress's vote to give foreign aid to a developing country that had a history of abridging human rights but whose support was imperative for national security. Christopher, age ten, had always sensed that he was somehow different from other children. But when he sought to share his interest in the parasitic nature of the mistletoe his classmates were collecting for the holidays, they pronounced him a freak and an egghead.

The dilemmas faced by Bud, Crystal, and Christopher serve to illustrate the importance of evaluative thinking and affective concerns in the education of gifted students. Evaluative thinking can be defined as conscious decision making against a set of standards, or the ability to make sound judgments regarding moral and ethical (values) issues. Evaluative thinking is crucial in a world where many questions cannot be resolved on the basis of empirical data but require value judgments.

Affective development refers primarily to the noncognitive domain of feelings, emotions, motivations, and self-perceptions. Goals for affective development in gifted education focus on fostering mature emotional reactions in students as individuals and as members of society. Goals for individual development include fostering a sense of responsibility and independence, a realistic self-concept, and positive self-esteem. Goals for the individual as a member of society include developing empathy, compassion, willingness to help others, respect for humanity, and a sense of the interrelatedness and interdependence of people. This chapter describes the theoretical bases underlying development of evaluative thinking and affective behavior and presents corresponding instructional activities.

EVALUATIVE THINKING PROCESSES

Although there are several theories of moral development—for example, social learning, psychoanalytic, and cognitive developmental—the approaches that have had the greatest impact on education related to evaluative thinking are the values education movement and Lawrence Kohlberg's theory of moral judgment development. Both were developed for the general population but have significant implications for the gifted.

Importance of Values Education

Over the past two decades a great deal has been written about values education. One factor contributing to this concern is society's attempt to rediscover worthy goals and a sense of purpose following the social traumas of the fifties, sixties, and seventies resulting from two wars, the continuing cold war with the Communist world, the Watergate affair, and the danger of nuclear holocaust. A natural reaction to unsettling social conditions and events is to question the social institutions and the people who are responsible for them. One point of view in this country suggests that if a social ill exists, public schools should seek the remedy. Since the most casual observer of American society over the past thirty years would conclude that the country is suffering through a crisis of values, it seems reasonable that values education will help improve the situation.

More basic than this rationale is the view, implicit but nonetheless powerful, that collective decision making requires of every voting citizen a set of values congruent with the presumed ideals of society. In other words, societies are founded and survive on shared values. Members of a democratic society must have a moral consciousness if the society is to develop the social conscience necessary for national purpose in an interdependent world. The so-called American dream as reflected in the education system appears to be based on a balance of competence and compassion.

For these reasons the literature on values education has been growing. Unfortunately, values education suffers from a lack of standard definition. The problem stems partly from the existence of numerous definitions, each with varying shades of meaning. Our definition is a consensual one: Values education is that aspect of education that focuses on the processes of clarifying and understanding personal–social values for the purposes of self-fulfillment and socially responsible behavior.

The literature also reflects disagreement concerning how values education should be taught. For example, Superka (1974) identified eight different approaches to values education. Despite the lack of consensus regarding definitions and methods, values education for the gifted constitutes an educational imperative for several reasons. First, gifted students are a valuable social resource and are likely to achieve positions of influence; therefore, they must possess a standard of ethics and values compatible with social ideals. Second, conflict resolution will continue as a priority in our society and in the world at large. The cognitive attributes of the gifted represent a valuable means of clarifying issues and formulating solutions to complex problems. However, the abilities of the gifted would have negative consequences if the problem solvers had no defensible value orientations. Third, the analytical/critical thinking required in the process of identifying and clarifying values is suited to the gifted.

Values Education in the Curriculum

The content of values education does not derive from any discipline per se. The content is, in essence, the process of applying inquiry and inductive methods to issues that permit various viewpoints. Subject areas most often used in values education are social studies and language arts, although there are applications in every subject area. Social imperative issues occur in science, literature, mathematics, and athletics, as indicated by the following examples:

1. What are the social responsibilities of research scientists who deal with nucleonics, nerve gas, and the like?

2. Who is instrumental in determining standards of excellence in art and literature? Who are the arbiters of the public taste?
3. What should be the social values of engineers and technicians in a high-technology society?
4. Is the emphasis on winning in junior high interscholastic athletics justified? Should competition be emphasized since it constitutes one of the cornerstones of American culture?

Although these examples relate primarily to secondary school students, values education must form a part of the curriculum for gifted students at every level. Gifted children at the first-grade level can (a) choose alternatives on a rational basis and consider the consequences of each alternative and (b) articulate priorities in personal–social values. For example, in a first-grade classroom the teacher introduces a social studies unit on rules and regulations by asking the class, "Should you help make school rules? Why or why not? Should you help make rules at home? What should you do about school and home rules that you don't agree with?" At the fifth-grade level in science, the teacher asks, "Should we conduct experiments on live animals? Why? What is important about the lives of laboratory animals? Should we experiment on live plants? Is it acceptable to kill plants?"

Additional methods for values education, such as use of thought-provoking stories, ranking of priorities and preferences, and demonstration of various views through a values continuum are discussed by Fraenkel (1977); Raths, Harmin, and Simon (1966); and Volkmor, Pasanella, and Raths (1977).

The schools should not coerce values or force choices with regard to students' beliefs or value systems. However, the schools are responsible for providing opportunities for all students, especially the gifted, to select and evaluate alternatives in controversial situations, to clarify their values, and to accept and understand the values and beliefs of others. These opportunities should be structured as part of the comprehensive curriculum. Teachers inexperienced in values education require appropriate in-service training, and districts must make available instructional materials adequate to the task.

Despite the volumes of professional literature supporting values education on cognitive bases and on the grounds of citizenship education, some writers emphatically reject the claims of values education proponents. Fraenkel (1977) has articulated a number of weaknesses in the general values clarification process as commonly practiced, including (a) lack of a theoretical base for values education and (b) the possibility that students may come to accept uncritically both their own and society's values.

Development of Moral Judgment

Theory. The cognitive developmental theory advanced by Kohlberg (1964, 1967, 1968, 1969, 1976; see also Colby et al., 1983) describes moral judgment, or the capacity to reason about moral issues, as developing through an invariant sequence of six stages. Progress through the stages is characterized by increased integration, with each step incorporating elements of the previous state but organizing them into higher-order structures.

Kohlberg groups the six moral stages into three levels: preconventional, conventional, and postconventional. The preconventional level describes the moral level of most children under the age of nine, some adolescents, and many criminal offenders. Preconventional individuals do not yet understand or uphold conventional societal rules. Most adolescents and adults are at the conventional level, where individuals conform to societal rules and expectations because society has established those rules and expectations. Only a small portion of adults achieve the postconventional level, and usually only after the age of twenty. At this level individuals understand and accept society's rules but are more concerned with the general moral principles that underlie the rules. When a society's rules conflict with these moral principles, postconventional individuals abide by the moral principles (Kohlberg, 1976). The six stages can be described as follows in terms of what constitutes "good" behavior:

Level I: Preconventional

> *Stage 1: Punishment/obedience orientation.* A person behaves correctly to avoid punishment or in obedience to the superior power of authorities.
>
> *Stage 2: Instrumentalism.* Correct behavior is that which satisfies one's own needs and lets others do the same. Fairness in the sense of equal exchange is also important.

Level II: Conventional

> *Stage 3: Mutual interpersonal expectations.* Good behavior is conformity to roles and expectations; it means having good motives, showing concern for others, being trustworthy, loyal, and respectful.
>
> *Stage 4: Social consciousness.* Good behavior is oriented toward fixed rules and maintenance of social order; right is contributing to society to keep it going.

Level III: Postconventional

> *Stage 5: Social contract.* Right action is defined in terms of standards agreed upon by society as a whole. These standards, although relative to specific groups, should be upheld as part of the social contract. One abides by laws and family, friendship, and work obligations because these support the greater good.
>
> *Stage 6: Universal ethical principles.* Good behavior is following self-chosen ethical principles—universal principles of justice, equality, and respect for human dignity. When laws violate these principles, one acts in accord with the principles.

Consistent with Piaget's theory of cognitive development (discussed in Chapter 3), Kohlberg posits that progression from stage to stage involves resolution of conflict and disequilibrium that arise from being faced with arguments from a higher moral level than one's own. Development also depends on the individual's interactions with the social environment and is influenced by the ability and opportunity to take different roles or perspectives. Role-taking opportunities are supported by participation in the family, the peer group, and secondary social institutions of law, government, and work. A recent report of a twenty-year longitudinal study of moral judgment development (Colby et al., 1983) found moral level positively correlated with age, socioeconomic status, and education. The rate of moral development in childhood and adolescence was not significantly related to IQ. However, the final level of moral reasoning achieved in adulthood showed moderate correlations (0.37–0.60) with intelligence. Generalizations from this study with respect to the relationship between moral judgment level and intelligence may be limited because the study included only males with IQs ranging from 100 to 120. Although the evidence is contradictory, other writers have found a relationship between moral reasoning and intellectual ability (Diessner, 1983; Karnes and Brown, 1981). There is general agreement that intelligence accounts for only a small portion of the variance in capacity for moral reasoning.

An individual's level of moral judgment development is assessed by a moral judgment interview, which consists of hypothetical moral dilemmas followed by questions designed to elicit moral judgments and justifications. A sample dilemma from a moral judgment interview follows:

> Judy was a 12-year-old girl. Her mother promised her that she could go to a special rock concert coming to their town if she saved up from babysitting and lunch money for a long time so she would have enough money to buy a ticket to the concert. She managed to save up the $15.00 the ticket cost plus another $3.00. But then her mother changed her mind and told Judy that she had to spend the money on new clothes for school. Judy was disappointed and decided to go to the concert anyway. She bought the ticket and told her mother that she had only been able to save $3.00. That Saturday she went to the performance and told her mother that she was spending the day with a friend. A week passed without her mother finding out. Judy then told her older sister, Louise, that she had gone to the performance and had lied to her mother about it. Louise wonders whether to tell their mother what Judy did.
>
> 1. Should Louise, the older sister, tell their mother that Judy had lied about the money or should she keep quiet?
> 1a. Why?
>
> — Colby et al., 1983, p. 81

Scoring is based on moral reasoning, or the justification for the decision, not on the individual's specific decision.

Educational Implications. Kohlberg has suggested that the aim of moral education is to stimulate students to the next stage of moral judgment development. Sisk (1982) has argued that moral education is particularly important for gifted students because of their uniquely high concern with values and morals, their advanced capabilities for abstract reasoning, their extreme sensitivity, and their need to realize their roles in shaping the future. Gifted students should be encouraged to develop moral judgment maturity, or the general ability to make decisions based on universal principles, because teachers and parents cannot educate them on every specific issue that may arise. Because an individual's level of moral maturity is determined not by what decision is made but by the reason for making it, moral judgment education does not require a student to agree with the teacher's own decision or with the values of any particular culture. The general instructional method is to present issues involving moral judgments and to encourage students to reason and resolve inconsistencies in their own thinking. Weber (1981) has developed a curriculum guide for moral education that includes activities asking students to resolve moral dilemmas according to their own values.

Some evidence exists that applications of Kohlberg's theory with secondary school students and adults can increase the level of moral reasoning. However, the increase does not appear to affect moral *behavior*. Power and Reimer (1978) have hypothesized that membership in a group affects the relationship between moral judgment and action—for example, when individuals facing a common moral conflict join to create a support group. Group members then jointly discuss the moral issues and arrive at a decision to be carried out. Power and Reimer suggest that a positive effect occurs when the moral atmosphere of the group (indicated by normative values) is at a stage as high as or higher than that of its members.

Consistent with Kohlberg's theory, teachers can challenge gifted students to develop increasingly higher levels of moral reasoning by presenting moral dilemmas and having students make judgments and discuss their reasons for making these judgments. The teacher should ensure that students are confronted with reasoning at a level higher than their current one. In addition, the teacher should focus on the student's rationale for his or her decision, not on the decision itself. Moral dilemma activities should not be used in isolation but should be integrated into ongoing content units. Many historical and current events readily lend themselves to discussion of dilemmas: German military personnel and civilians following Hitler's commands to exterminate Jews; President Ford's pardon of former President Nixon; a journalist's refusal to divulge confidential sources.

The following story, based on a recent news item, can be used to illustrate how moral judgment advances through six stages:

> John's wife, Mary, has just given birth to a handicapped child. John is currently unemployed and on disability. Mary's doctor has determined that the child will be severely mentally retarded. The child has a respiratory problem that requires an oxygen support system for survival. Alone, trying to cope with his tremendous disappointment, John observes his child in the respirator. John wonders how he will be able to support this child and whether the child will ever enjoy life. Suddenly the respirator malfunctions, and the oxygen indicator

moves toward zero. John considers whether to summon help or to let the child suffocate. Should John summon help?

Stage 1:   *Yes.* If John lets the child die, he could be charged with child neglect or murder.
           No. If John lets the child live, he will be blamed for burdening his family and society.
Stage 2:   *Yes.* The child may die anyway or can be kept in an institution.
           No. The child may die anyway and no one would blame John.
Stage 3:   *Yes.* A good father protects his child and would fight to keep the child alive.
           No. A good father would not want his child to suffer through life.
Stage 4:   *Yes.* If everyone were permitted to allow others to die, society would not survive.
           No. Keeping the child alive would be unfair to the public, which must support the child.
Stage 5:   *Yes.* John's obligations to his family require that he help the child live.
           No. A defective child can contribute to the general deterioration of the intellectual gene pool in society.
Stage 6:   *Yes.* Respect for life is a universal value that must be upheld at all costs.
           No. Quality of life is the most important principle.

Fraenkel (1977) has suggested that (*a*) dilemmas presented as examples focus on general principles relevant to many students rather than on specific instances, (*b*) teachers present dilemma situations through a variety of media, and (*c*) teachers present and systematically consider a range of alternative solutions and encourage student ideas to ensure that students are exposed to higher-level alternatives.

Moral dilemma activities are also appropriate as a vehicle for resolving everyday problems encountered by students in the classroom and for making decisions for group action or for individual action supported by the peer group. Students can discuss problems of stealing, cheating, or lying as dilemmas. Gifted students, who are usually sensitive to inequities in the system, may present dilemmas from their own experience or their own readings. For example, students have raised issues concerning parents justifying minor distortions on income tax returns, city administrators passing regulations to benefit their own private businesses, and store employees supplying friends with free goods in the name of friendship and loyalty. Peer group support for the individual who must resolve a personal moral or ethical conflict, as well as high standards of behavior demanded by the group, may increase the probability that higher levels of moral *reasoning* will result in higher levels of moral *behavior*.

Despite the support for moral education of future leaders, little empirical evidence exists that moral education of the gifted improves their judgment or behavior. Smith (1983) has argued that moral education for the gifted is based on a set of unvalidated assumptions: (*a*) gifted students' moral development differs from that of their nongifted peers, (*b*) moral development in gifted students is precocious compared with age mates, (*c*) teachers of the gifted are cognitively and morally able to deal with principled moral judgments, and (*d*) moral development will occur as a result of occasional short teaching sessions. Smith noted that the most critical consideration is the ability of teachers of the gifted, if not gifted themselves, to provide an appropriate model of moral reasoning and to respond effectively when working with gifted students on moral dilemmas.

AFFECTIVE DEVELOPMENT

Terman's longitudinal studies (Terman, 1926; Terman and Oden, 1947) early on dispelled the myth that intellectually gifted individuals are prone to mental illness. In fact, Terman and his colleagues reported that their intellectually gifted subjects evidenced superiority in physical, social, and emotional adjustment. A trend has emerged recently that questions the "Terman myth" and asserts that gifted individuals experience social–emotional stresses because of their uniquely high abilities and sensitivities (Altman, 1983; Whitmore, 1980). However, several recent investigations have indicated that gifted students evidence average to better-than-average adjustment and behavior (Ludwig and Cullinan, 1984).

Educators of the gifted emphasize the interpretive error in assuming that gifted students do not experience social and emotional difficulties. Rather, gifted students' advanced cognitive functioning, ability to comprehend adult problems, mature thinking on values issues, rapid development ahead of peers, and awareness of being different can result in perfectionism, self-criticism, social isolation, and other stresses (Altman, 1983). Manaster and Powell (1983) have suggested that gifted adolescents are particularly prone to social–emotional problems related to such characteristics as boredom, pressure to achieve success, uneven development, alienation from peers, sensitivity to concerns not shared by peers, and tendency to challenge adult authority.

Although gifted students appear to be at least average in terms of social–emotional adjustment and self-concept, affective education is important as a means of encouraging feelings of confidence, positive attitudes toward learning, positive self-esteem, and sensitivity to the needs and feelings of others. Teachers of the gifted can encourage development of positive self-attitudes and positive attitudes toward school by providing a supportive environment. For example, a friendly, responsive, student-centered atmosphere helps students feel accepted, secure, and willing to take risks. Teachers can help establish such an atmosphere by providing opportunities for students to (*a*) pursue their own interests, (*b*) make choices about their learning, (*c*) display their creations, (*d*) communicate their ideas to others, (*e*) share responsibility and decision making, (*f*) encounter challenging ideas, and (*g*) engage in self-evaluation.

Teachers can demonstrate their sincere interest in students by making time for both casual and formal interactions on an individual basis, by listening attentively to students' concerns, and by reflecting rather than criticizing feelings expressed. Whitmore (1980) suggested that developing a cohesive group identity generates pride and a sense of belonging. To foster cohesive group interaction, teachers should emphasize cooperation and encourage intraindividual competition, as in striving to exceed one's own goals. Class meetings for sharing and solving mutual problems, as well as the use of the interpersonal problem-solving techniques described in the following sections, may also facilitate group cohesion.

Specific models for building activities supportive of social–affective development include cognitive developmental approaches to role-taking development; Krathwohl, Bloom, and Masia's (1964) taxonomy of educational objectives for the affective domain; the inductive strategies of Taba et al. (1971); and bibliotherapy.

Cognitive Developmental Approaches to Role-Taking Development

Developmental theories of social cognition suggest that a variety of prosocial behaviors (cooperation, helping, friendliness, and so forth) may require role- or perspective-taking ability—that is, the cognitive capacity to know how others feel or the ability to understand another person's viewpoint. Reviews of research on social cognition (Grusec and Arnason, 1982; Rubin and Everett, 1982; Shantz, 1975) report inconsistent findings regarding the relationship between role-taking ability and positive social behavior. Grusec and Arnason (1982) have suggested that empathy and role-taking ability are related to prosocial behavior only in children below the age of ten. After age ten most children have developed empathy and role-taking ability, and individual differences in prosocial behavior depend more on knowledge of social norms and on self-concept.

Strategies for helping children of primary school age develop empathy, role-taking ability, and positive social behavior consistent with theory and research on social cognition include role playing and exchanging roles to understand different perspectives. Specifically, the teacher presents a problem or a dilemma. For example, in one situation a child needs help and must ask another to provide that help. In another situation several children who need money find a purse that contains money. The teacher selects individual students to play the various roles and explains that the purpose of the role playing is to help the children understand individuals' feelings and to find alternative ways to solve the problems. Students trade roles to understand the situation from all perspectives. The teacher encourages other students to demonstrate, through role playing, alternative ways of resolving the situation. After each alternative is played, the students share their feelings as the characters, discuss causal relationships, and evaluate the alternative.

For very young children role playing can be done with puppets. We found (DeLeon, 1983a) a cognitive developmental method first proposed by Chittenden (1942) that is useful for improving social behavior in young children. The method requires individual instruction. First the teacher acquaints the child with two dolls (or puppets), who will serve as the interactants for all role-playing situations. Then situations are presented in which the child is asked to discriminate between unsatisfactory and satisfactory solutions to problems confronting the dolls (for example, when both dolls want the same toy, the result is a fight in one instance and taking turns in another instance). After the child demonstrates clearly the ability to discriminate between satisfactory and unsatisfactory outcomes, the dolls are used to play out situations that model, in different instances, positive behaviors such as taking turns, sharing materials, and playing together. Finally, the dolls act out problems, and the child is asked to tell and show the dolls how to resolve the problems in a positive manner.

Using positive peer and adult models, coaching in desired social behaviors, explaining consequences of misbehavior for others, making demands for altruistic behavior, and reinforcing positive behavior can also encourage empathy and perspective taking in young children.

Educational Objectives for the Affective Domain

In attempting to provide structure in the affective domain, Krathwohl, Bloom, and Masias (1964) developed a taxonomy of educational objectives for the affective domain. Their taxonomy consists of the five categories shown in Table 9.1. The taxonomy is a sequence of attitudes presumed to reflect the kinds of objectives desired and needed for school learning in our society. The taxonomy includes receiving (simple awareness), responding, valuing, organization, and characterization of a value (the highest level of commitment to a value). The taxonomy resembles the stages of moral development described by Piaget and Kohlberg.

Table 9.1 Taxonomy of educational objectives for the affective domain

CATEGORY	SUBDIVISIONS	STUDENT BEHAVIOR TO BE ATTAINED (EDUCATIONAL OBJECTIVES)
1.0 Receiving	1.1 Awareness	Observes: recognizes, is aware of; develops sensitivity to
Attending	1.2 Willingness to	Accepts others; develops a tolerance for; listens carefully: recognizes persons as individuals
	1.3 Controlled and selected attention	Discriminates; appreciates alertness to values; selects reading materials
2.0 Responding	2.1 Acquiescence in responding	Willing to comply, observes rules and regulations

Table 9.1 (continued)

CATEGORY	SUBDIVISIONS	STUDENT BEHAVIOR TO BE ATTAINED (EDUCATIONAL OBJECTIVES)
	2.2 Willingness to respond	Voluntarily seeks information, engages in variety of activities. Responds to intellectual stimuli; engages in research
	2.3 Satisfaction in response	Finds pleasure in reading, listening, conversing, art, participation in groups
3.0 Valuing	3.1 Accepting a value	Develops a sense of responsibility, of kinship, of need for worship
	3.2 Preference for a value	Interest in enabling others; examines a variety of viewpoints; assumes active role in politics, literary organizations
	3.3 Commitment	Displays a high degree of certainty, loyalty, faith in the power of reason
4.0 Organization	4.1 Conceptualization of a value	Establishes a conscious base for making choices; identifies admired characteristics; analyzes basic assumptions underlying codes of ethics and faith; forms judgment as to responsibility of society to the individual and environment; develops personal goals
	4.2 Organization of a value system According to Edward Spranger, values may be organized around the following: 1. Theoretical 2. Economic 3. Aesthetic 4. Social 5. Political 6. Religious	Examines role of democracy in conserving human and natural resources; accepts own potentialities and limitations realistically; views people as individuals, without prejudice; develops techniques for conflict management; accepts responsibility for the future
5.0 Characterization of a value	5.1 Generalized set: the basic orientation that enables the individual to act consistently and effectively in a complex world	Readiness to reverse judgments or change behavior in light of evidence; to change one's mind and face facts; confidence in ability to succeed; solves problems in terms of what is rather than wishful thinking
	5.2 Characterization: one's personal philosophy of life demonstrated in behavior	Develops a code of behavior based on the ethical principles consistent with democratic ideals: behavior that is consistent with beliefs

SOURCE: Krathwohl, Bloom, and Masias, 1964.

Teachers can use the affective domain taxonomy by reading across each category and its subdivisions to the student behavior to be attained (the educational objective) and then asking, "What kinds of instructional activities will help meet the objective?" Using the social studies curriculum outlined in Chapter 6, the teacher begins by identifying the affective objectives as they relate to the topic of environmental deterioration—specifically, pollution. The ultimate aim (objective) will be to have students reach the level of characterization, which can occur at a cognitive level at any time. Given the complexity of the objective and the maturity required, it may take several years to incorporate the objective into actual behavior. The following sequence of activities is suggested.

1. *Receiving*. Awareness activity: Have students bring in magazine pictures depicting some kind of pollution. Attending activity: Have students listen as others briefly describe their pictured examples of pollution.

2. *Responding*. Willingness activity: Ask how many of the students will look for examples of pollution in the neighborhood or community.

3. *Valuing*. Accepting activity: Ask open-minded questions about whether the children feel that pollution is a major problem (for example, "Won't the wind just blow air pollution away?").

4. *Organization*. Conceptualizing activity: Have students work in groups to identify the kind(s) of pollution most prevalent in their environment. Then have the groups decide on some role playing that reflects how they wish adults in the community would act to reduce or eliminate pollution.

5. *Characterization*. Readiness activity: Present value-clarifying information. Have students (*a*) tell how they think they would act if given choices about polluting, (*b*) rank order a set of prepared scenes depicting various levels of severity of pollution, (*c*) read a scenario of a community with serious pollution problems and extend the scenario by telling what they would do if they lived in that community.

Inductive Strategies for the Affective Domain

Taba et al. (1971) proposed three inductive strategies that integrate the affective and cognitive domains: analyzing values, exploring feelings, and interpersonal problem solving.

Analyzing Values. The intent of this technique is to encourage recognition and acceptance of individual and cultural differences through inferring of values from other people's behavior and through consideration of one's own behavior and values. The instructional steps (Table 9.2) begin with a presentation (a film, readings about another culture or subculture, a description of a local or personal encounter, a biography) that describes the behavior of an individual or group. The teacher asks students to describe specific behaviors of the individual or group, to hypothesize about why these behaviors occur, and to induce the values

Table 9.2 Technique for analyzing values

TEACHER	STUDENT	TEACHER FOLLOW-THROUGH
What did they do . . . (e.g., to take care of their tools)?	Describes behavior	Sees that description is complete and accurate
What do you think were their reasons for doing/ saying what they did?	States inferences	Accepts; seeks clarification if necessary
What do these reasons tell you about what is important to them?[a]	States inferences regarding values	Restates or asks additional questions to ensure focus on values
If you . . . (teacher specifies similar situations directly related to student— e.g., "If you accidentally tore a page in someone else's book") what would you do? Why?[b]	States behavior; gives explanation	Accepts; may seek clarification
What does this show about what *you* think is important?	States inferences about his own values	Accepts; seeks clarification if necessary
What differences do you see in what all these people think is important?	Makes comparisons	Ensures that all values identified are compared

NOTE: Sometimes all questions are not asked. However, the question exploring the students' own values should *not* be omitted.

[a]This sequence is repeated for each group or person whose values are to be analyzed. Each group is specified by the teacher and has been previously studied.

[b]This sequence is repeated in order to get reactions from several students.

SOURCE: Taba et al., 1971, p. 81.

that underlie these behaviors. The steps are repeated for analyzing the behaviors of other individuals or groups. The teacher then asks students to predict their own reactions and behaviors in similar situations and to analyze what their projected behaviors imply about their own values. Finally the teacher asks students to compare the various value systems discussed to encourage understanding of differences among people.

Exploring Feelings. The objectives of this strategy (summarized in Table 9.3) are to encourage students to explore their own feelings, to consider the feelings of others, and to make generalizations about differences among individuals in the feelings they might have under similar circumstances. The teacher presents a situation that involves emotional reactions—for example, a current event or a recent occurrence in the school playground. Students summarize the incident or events and hypothesize about how each of the central figures felt.

Table 9.3 Technique for exploring feelings

TEACHER	STUDENT	TEACHER FOLLOW-THROUGH
What happened?	Restates facts	Sees that all facts are given and agreed upon; if students make inferences, asks that they be set aside temporarily
How do you think . . . felt?[a]	Makes inference as to feelings	Accepts inference
Why do you think he or she would feel that way?	Explains	Seeks clarification if necessary
Who has a different idea about how this person felt?	Makes alternative inferences and explanations	Seeks variety if necessary; asks for reasons if necessary
How did . . . (other persons in the situation) feel?	States inference about the feelings of additional persons	Seeks clarification if necessary; encourages students to consider how other people in the situation felt
Have you ever had something like this happen to you?[b]	Describes similar event in own life	Ensures description of event
How did you feel?[a]	Describes feelings; may reexperience emotions	Seeks clarification if necessary; provides support if necessary
Why do you think you felt that way?	Offers explanation; attempts to relate feelings to events recalled	Asks additional questions, if necessary, to get beyond stereotyped or superficial explanation

NOTE: The teaching strategy consists of asking the questions, usually in the order given. Sometimes only certain of the questions are asked. The teacher should omit questions if students have answered them spontaneously.

[a]This question is repeated in sequence several times in order to obtain a variety of inferences and fewer personal experiences.

[b]If students have difficulty responding, the teacher may wish to ask, "If this should happen to you, how do you think you would feel?" or "Has something like this happened to someone you know?" Another useful device is for the teacher to describe such an event in his or her own life.

SOURCE: Taba et al., 1971, p. 78.

The teacher then asks students to recall similar personal experiences and describe their feelings at the time, as well as reasons for those feelings.

Interpersonal Problem Solving. This strategy (summarized in Table 9.4) encourages students to generate and evaluate alternative methods for solving interpersonal problems and to evaluate their own interpersonal behaviors. The teacher begins by presenting a problem situation involving interpersonal conflict, such as an actual disagreement among classmates or an incomplete story. Students

Table 9.4 Technique for interpersonal problem solving

TEACHER	STUDENT	TEACHER FOLLOW-THROUGH
What happened? or What did . . . do?	Describes events	Sees that all events are given; tries to get agreement or, if not possible, a clear statement of differences in perception of what occurred
What do you think . . . (a protagonist) should do? Why?	Gives response	Accepts response; seeks clarification where necessary
How do you think . . . (others) would react if he or she did that? Why?	Makes inference; explains	Accepts; seeks clarification if necessary
Has something like that ever happened to you?[a]	Relates similar event in his or her life	Provides support if necessary
What did you do?[b]	Relates recalled behavior	Seeks clarification if necessary
As you think back now, do you think that was a good or a bad thing to do?	Judges past actions	Encourages student to judge his or her *own* past actions[c]
Why do you think so?	States reasons	Accepts reasons; if necessary, asks additional questions to make clear the criteria or values that the student is using in judging his or her actions
Is there anything you could have done differently?	Offers alternative behavior	Accepts; asks additional questions to point up inconsistencies where they occur (e.g., "How does that agree with reasons you gave earlier?")

[a]If students have difficulty responding, the teacher may wish to ask, "If this should happen to you, how do you think you would feel?" Or "Has something like this happened to someone you know?" Another useful device is for the teacher to describe such an event in his own life.

[b]This question is repeated in sequence several times in order to obtain a variety of responses.

[c]The teacher may need to prevent others from entering the discussion at this point.

SOURCE: Taba et al., 1971, p. 79.

describe the events, suggest alternative approaches to solving the problem, infer possible consequences, describe their own responses to similar situations, and evaluate their own responses. Teachers using this method are urged to refrain from judging students' answers and to discourage peer judgments. To protect honest responses and encourage self-assessment, students need an accepting, nonevaluative atmosphere.

Bibliotherapy

Bibliotherapy refers to the reading and discussion of literature as a means of understanding and solving personal problems. Supporters of this approach suggest that by reading novels, biographies, plays, and poetry about how people deal with problems similar to their own, students experience vicariously various ways of solving problems and the consequences of these solutions. It has also been suggested that bibliotherapy can promote affective development, including empathy, positive attitudes, improved adjustment, better self-esteem, new interests, and appreciation of individual differences (Sisk, 1982). Like most techniques for the gifted, bibliotherapy was developed as a tool for general education. However, gifted students' generally high reading ability, interest in literature, and capacity for analysis, generalization, and application make the method particularly suited to their needs.

Frasier and McCannon (1981) have outlined specific steps a teacher can follow to establish a bibliotherapy program for gifted children:

1. Determine the specific problems faced by gifted students in the classroom (for example, through observation, interview, group discussion, and responses to open-ended sentences).
2. Consult librarians for help in selecting books appropriate to the identified problems.
3. Make arrangements with the librarians to ensure long-term availability of the selected books.
4. As appropriate readings are located, record on file cards the bibliographic information, a summary that highlights the problem addressed, and reading level. Cards can be filed according to problem area.
5. Invite students to read the selections as appropriate. Some selections may be appropriate only to one individual or to a small group; the entire class may read the book if the problem is common to all.
6. Provide meaningful follow-up activities, including peer-centered discussion, role-playing, creative problem solving, journal writing, diaries, dramatizations, and bulletin boards.

Frasier and McCannon provide a list of sample readings for gifted students keyed to problem areas (personal, social, and educational/vocational) and grade levels. Problems faced by the characters in these readings include parent opposition to artistic career aspirations, conflict with teachers, hiding of talents and abilities, peer rejection, and effects on social and family life of preoccupation with an intense interest.

Although bibliotherapy provides a pragmatic, motivating, academically oriented method for dealing with a range of feelings and challenges, additional research is needed to support its efficacy in meeting the affective needs of gifted students.

CHAPTER SUMMARY

Instruction in evaluative thinking processes and affective development is important for all students but has special significance for the gifted. Gifted individuals who assume positions of influence through political leadership, creative production in literature and the arts, or technological innovation require sound values and humanistic compassion as a basis for decision making.

The literature on evaluative thinking and affective development offers both general and specific methods for practice, including values education, discussion of moral dilemmas, creation of a positive atmosphere, practice in role taking, use of the taxonomy of educational objectives in the affective domain and Taba's inductive strategies, and bibliotherapy. Despite the logic of these approaches, little research is available to indicate whether they are effective in changing behavior. Evaluating the use of such strategies is difficult because attitudinal and behavioral changes may not appear for several years.

Despite a lack of direct evidence indicating the efficacy of training in evaluative thinking, a strong rationale exists for working with gifted students in the areas of values and affective development. Instructional activities should receive the same careful, articulated planning afforded in any other subject area and should be incorporated into the comprehensive curriculum. Teachers who model high values and humanistic concern and who can challenge students to higher levels of thought and action are requisite to an effective values education program for gifted students.

ACTIVITIES FOR THOUGHT AND DISCUSSION

1. Describe how you received education in values (for example, through school or family). Was your education in values effective? What suggestions would you make for improvement?

2. What situations have arisen in your own experience that could serve as the basis for moral dilemma scenarios? Take one scenario and describe yes and no responses for each of Kohlberg's six levels of moral judgment development.

3. Mr. Thompson's gifted students demonstrate mastery of social skills as long as they are being observed. However, when they think Mr. Thompson is not watching, they engage in some socially unacceptable behaviors, such as taking objects from other students and name calling. What activities might you suggest to help resolve this situation?

4. Develop three lesson plans based on the inductive strategies suggested by Taba et al. (1971).

5. Using your knowledge of characteristics of the gifted, develop a file of literature appropriate for bibliotherapy. Cross-reference each selection by age, topic, and any other factors you deem appropriate.

SECTION V

Perspectives on Educational Content

Chapter Ten

THE ARTS AND
LEADERSHIP

The three preceding chapters focused on instructional methods that encourage inductive, creative, and evaluative thinking while communicating subject matter. However, it must not be assumed that programs for the gifted should emphasize training in thinking processes to the exclusion of content acquisition. In fact, attainment of knowledge should be a major goal, if not *the* major goal, of programs for gifted students. Discovering a new planet, developing a medical cure, or refining an artistic technique require productive thinking, but discoveries and developments cannot occur without a foundation of accumulated knowledge and facts. Most scientific and technological advances were accomplished not by men and women who had received specific instruction in how to think, but by people who had mastered the knowledge and methods of their fields. Moreover, not all content is most efficiently acquired through inductive learning; some things—for example, multiplication facts—may require rote memorization or deductive application of given rules.

It is beyond the scope of this text to provide readers with thorough foundations in academic content. Rather, the intent is to help teachers communicate their already acquired content through instructional techniques appropriate to gifted learners. Nonetheless, two areas—the arts and leadership—deserve further discussion because of their specific association with gifted education. This chapter describes issues and programs related to the arts and leadership. The following chapter outlines major considerations in social studies, language arts, science, and mathematics for gifted students.

The Visual and Performing Arts

The visual arts include drawing, painting, sculpture, and other means of artistic expression directed at the eye. The performing arts refer to music (instrumental and vocal), theater, and dance. The arts constitute an essential part of education because they help individuals develop and express sensitivity, provide alternative modes of communication, serve as sources of recreation and enjoyment, encourage problem solving, and demonstrate the universality of human creativity. This section describes problems, issues, and curricular considerations related to visual and performing arts education for gifted and talented students.

Obstacles to the Development of Arts Education Programs

Larsh (1979a) listed seven major federally supported arts programs that emerged during the 1960s and the 1970s. These included Titles I and III of the Elementary and Secondary Act of 1965, the Office of Education's Art and Humanities Program, the Artist-in-Schools Program, the National Institute of Education program in arts research, and the Alliance for Arts Education. Kreuger and Newman (1974) have described several additional federally funded programs and private foundations that support development of the arts and humanities in the public schools.

Despite federal support for programs in the visual and performing arts, substantial efforts continue to be needed. According to Larsh (1979a), an estimated 11 million of 14 million secondary students in the United States have had no exposure to art opportunities within the secondary school system. Larsh also points out that in 1976 there were 3,055 two- and four-year colleges and universities in this country; 63 percent did not offer a major in art, and only 1,214 institutions offered even a single art course. Only 233 institutions offered a bachelor of fine arts degree, and only 130 bestowed a master of fine arts degree. Hurwitz (1976) has argued that many students attending art classes in junior and senior high are not gifted; they take these courses for an easy workload or for other reasons. Petzold (1979) reported more positive statistics in regard to music education: 91.7 percent of 22,737 surveyed secondary schools (grades seven through twelve) offered choir or chorus, 83 percent offered band, and 25 percent offered orchestra.

Provisions for articulated programs in the visual and performing arts in elementary schools are frequently left to regular classroom teachers or, in more affluent schools, to specialists who meet with classes on a regular basis. Some school systems provide itinerant art and music teachers whose responsibilities extend to several buildings. Choir and band classes are frequently offered at upper-elementary levels (grades five and six). Although few data are available on the extent of specific instruction in the arts and music at the primary levels, we suspect that many public schools provide little beyond crafts, rhythm and song, and play-acting activities. Special arts and music programs also tend to be the first victims when financial difficulties require retrenchment.

Yet there is evidence that many Americans do value arts education. Larsh (1979b) cited findings from a Harris poll, "Americans and the Arts," which indicated that the American public places a high priority on arts opportunities in schools and feels that arts contribute to the quality of life. Why, then, do we still have so far to go in providing educational opportunities in the visual and performing arts?

Four obstacles stand in the way of developing quality arts programs in public schools. The first obstacle concerns priorities. Although both the federal government and the state governments recognize the need for arts education, the focus since *Sputnik* has been on strengthening academic programs. In the recent upsurge of interest in education, spurred by the report of the National Commission on Excellence in Education (1983) entitled *A Nation at Risk*, the emphasis continues to be on academics. The report's indicators of risk include international comparisons of student achievement on academic tests and a decline in science, math, and verbal achievement scores over time. The commission's report makes no mention of comparative opportunities for immersion in culture and the arts. The report's recommendations are directed at improving academic achievement by upgrading high school graduation requirements in English, math, science, social studies, computer science, and foreign language and by allotting more time to "basics." Ironically, the artistic expression of human emotion is not considered a basic.

While academics, especially the hard sciences, will continue to be a national priority in the race for technological superiority, it is important to question whether the development of increasingly powerful nuclear weapons is more valuable to the quality of life than is the creation of a new symphony. One positive effort being made is the Arts Recognition and Talent Search (ARTS), sponsored by the National Foundation for Advancement in the Arts, which supports high school students who demonstrate exceptional potential in dance, music, theater, writing, and the visual and performing arts (Hurwitz, 1981; Wenner, 1985).

The second obstacle to developing comprehensive arts programs is the perception on the part of many taxpayers and public school personnel that training in specific arts is the responsibility of parents. Findings from descriptive studies emphasize the division between public school education and talent development and suggest that much needs to to be done to make public schools a home for the arts and humanities. Bloom and Sosniak (1981) found from their research on individuals gifted in specific talent areas, including piano and sculpture, that factors that foster talent development are not generally characteristic of typical school settings. For example, public schools generally focus on group rather than individual instruction, on generalization rather than specialization, on sequencing of learning objectives by grade level rather than by individual needs, and on recognition of achievement by classroom rather than by the larger society.

Bloom and Sosniak's (1981) data indicated that in some cases school personnel supported and encouraged talent development by making the talented individual feel valuable and important, by sharing the student's enthusiasm and commitment to high standards, and by arranging for the student to perform within school programs. In other schools, however, talent development and schooling constituted completely separate spheres. School personnel did not interfere with a talented student's artistic training, but neither did they assist or even discuss the student's artistic efforts. For yet another group of talented individuals, school experiences had a negative effect on talent development. Teachers and administrators admonished the students to spend less time on their nonacademic pursuits, and in some cases talented students were isolated by their peers.

Because schools have a commitment to developing the total person, the arts and humanities must constitute a substantial portion of the elementary and secondary curriculum. A major problem with separating the arts from general education and delegating arts instruction to special teachers hired by parents is that opportunities for talent development in the arts are limited to students whose parents recognize the need for arts development and can afford lessons, equipment, and supervision time. Art development opportunities, unless provided by public schools that serve *all* children, will be denied to those who have no access to artistic expression and development in the home. Furthermore, it is not sufficient merely to provide materials and expect even talented children to improve without direction. Specific instruction is essential to the development of artistic talent for students of all ability levels (Clark and Zimmerman, 1984).

Absence of a national policy on arts education and a concomitant lack of national arts curricula constitute a third obstacle to the development of comprehensive arts programs. The burden of responsibility for developing programs in arts education falls on state and local education agencies. Individual cities and states—for example, New York City, Washington, D.C., and North Carolina—support some exemplary programs, but these programs tend to be isolated efforts that do not reflect the national picture. On the positive side, all the states have state art councils, and many community art councils have also been established (Larsh, 1979b). Some of these councils are working with local school districts to develop and implement arts programs using community resources and local artists.

A fourth obstacle to developing arts programs in the schools is the failure of many teacher education institutions to prepare regular elementary teachers and teachers of the gifted for developing and implementing instructional programs in the arts. One finding of the National Forum on the Arts and Gifted, held in 1978 by the Office of Education, was that teacher certification requirements at elementary and secondary levels have made it difficult, if not impossible, to make effective use of arts professionals in the education of gifted children within the schools (Larsh, 1979b). A subgroup of the forum supported radical reform of teacher education programs to provide student teachers and in-service teachers with opportunities for practicing arts as an integral part of teacher preparation. The forum recommended that policies be established in cooperation with arts education associations and certification agencies to make more effective use of arts professionals in programs for the gifted and talented.

Issues in the Development of Arts Education

Two philosophical issues require resolution before school districts can initiate comprehensive programs in the visual and performing arts for gifted and talented students. The first issue is the nature of the population that will participate in the arts program; the second is selection of program goals.

Selection of Participants. Who should benefit from comprehensive programs in arts education—all students, all gifted and talented students, or only those students who are talented in the arts? Ideally arts programs should be available to all students, just as academic instruction is provided to all. However, as is the case for academic programs, arts programs for gifted and talented students should be differentiated from those for nongifted students. Programs for gifted students should be based on the students' unique abilities and needs. Buttermore (1979) emphasized the need for gifted and talented arts curricula differentiated from the core arts curriculum because many gifted students, given appropriate guidance, demonstrate higher aptitude for creativity and quality performance in art than do nongifted children. Both the Forum on the Arts and the Gifted

(Larsh, 1979b) and the National Conference on Arts and Humanities/Gifted and Talented (Kreuger and Newman, 1974) argued the need for arts programs for all children and special programs for developing the special artistic potential of the gifted and talented. Few empirical data are available to support the theory that academically gifted children have special needs in regard to arts education; we must rely on the subjective impressions of experts.

Petzold (1979) has reported a positive but low correlation between general intelligence and musical aptitude (potential for musical achievement) and a somewhat higher correlation between general intelligence and musical achievement (learned skills). Clark and Zimmerman (1984) have suggested that although not all highly intelligent children possess artistic talent, all children with superior artistic talent demonstrate higher-than-average IQ scores. One-third of the intellectually gifted children in Terman's (1926) studies were reported by their parents to possess superior ability in music; somewhat fewer were reported to have superior ability in dramatics, drawing, or painting. More than half the group received private lessons in subjects such as music, drawing, painting, dance, and language. McKay (1983) has observed that academically gifted students with less-than-outstanding musical talent often excel in secondary-level music programs because of their intelligence, motivation, and speed of learning. He warned, however, that when such students enter college, they find that increasing amounts of practice time are necessary if they are to excel, and they are often unable to meet the program's standards. Other writers have cautioned that some gifted students may become frustrated if they are unable to perform at a level commensurate with their own expectations; moreover, they may not be willing to make the high level of personal commitment required by arts disciplines. The Assembly of National Arts Education Organizations (1979) therefore concluded that realistic interest must be one criterion for selecting gifted students to participate in special arts programs.

Selection of Program Goals. The major issue with respect to program goals concerns relative emphases on arts appreciation (being a consumer of arts) and on development of performance mastery. The Assembly of National Arts Education Organizations (1979) has compared loving of music without being able to sing or play an instrument with loving of literature without being able to read. The assembly argues that performance skills are necessary for full understanding of the arts. Yet one of the major goals of any worthwhile music program should certainly be the development of creative and critical listening skills. Extending the analogy that playing a musical instrument is to music what reading is to literature means ignoring most of the essential differences between reading and music. To do so certainly eliminates achievement of the goal just articulated. The musically talented composer, even if an incipient Charles Ives, must learn both the state of the musical world and the use of the tools necessary to enter that world. Undeveloped talent, like any undeveloped resource, is hardly in demand.

Curricular Considerations in Arts Education

A school district's commitment to arts education for gifted and talented students depends on many factors, including the attitudes of the school board, the administrators, and the teachers; the availability of funds; the availability of specialized arts educators; and the variety and quality of community resources. Development of arts programs too frequently awaits the fortuitous appearance of a uniquely qualified and motivated individual (teacher, administrator, parent, or community leader) who works toward establishing an arts program as a personal goal. To help teachers and administrators begin thinking about developing an arts program or improving an existing one, this section describes (*a*) program models, (*b*) elements of outstanding arts programs, and (*c*) instructional goals and methods.

Program Models for Arts Education. Alternative program models for providing differentiated arts education for gifted and talented students parallel the administrative arrangement for general gifted programs described in Chapter 5. Currently existing models include programs outside the regular school, programs within the regular school, and programs for parents.

Special schools for students gifted in the visual and performing arts generally occupy buildings physically separate from conventional elementary and high schools. The special schools offer full-day programs and provide both academic instruction and training in the arts. For example, North Carolina's School of Arts offers ten years of arts and academic instruction for seventh grade through college (Stone, 1976). The school grants a high school diploma as well as a bachelor of fine arts and bachelor of music degrees. Admission is based on talent and career promise, assessed primarily through audition. Students select programs in dance, design and production, visual arts, drama, and music. The department of academic studies offers a curriculum for completing high school graduation requirements and college-level course work for the bachelor's degree. There are approximately sixty to seventy-five arts high schools in the United States, most of which are public schools (Galbraith, 1985). Examples of special schools at the elementary level include the Chula Vista Academy of the Fine Arts of the Corpus Christi, Texas, Independent School District and the several music academies of the Houston, Texas, Independent School District (Tatarunis, 1981).

Program models that include arts centers permit students to attend the regular elementary or high school program for half the day and then travel to the arts center for specialized instruction (Carroll, 1976). For example, the New Orleans Center for Creative Arts provides in-depth training in dance, music, theater, visual arts, and writing for elementary and secondary students on a half-day basis (Kaufmann, Tews, and Milam, 1985; Tews, 1981). Several universities and arts centers offer summer residential programs for young artists. Some programs that have no physical facilities for arts instruction place talented students as apprentices with artists and arts institutions (for example, orchestras, opera companies, or professional artists). Cohen (1981) has described an arts program in which gifted elementary students apprentice with a professional to design and build scenery or to work as stage managers, directors, singers, conductors, writers, and dancers. Another out-of-school model is the Saturday workshop. For example, the Gifted Child Society offers a Saturday workshop for musically talented elementary children. A Saturday program held on the campus of Purdue University provides enrichment outside the regular school program for gifted students in grades two through nine; the program includes special courses in listening and music (Tatarunis, 1981).

Arts programs can also be provided to gifted and talented students within the regular school setting by making arts educators and community artists part of the instructional team. The Artist-in-Schools Program began as a cooperative effort by the Arts Endowment and the U.S. Office of Education to bring professional artists into elementary and secondary schools, where they demonstrate their skills and familiarize students with various media. Rosenberg (1974) suggested an actor/teacher model based on the Theatre in Education begun in 1964 by the Belgrade Theatre in Coventry, England. Actor/teachers receive training in both theater and education and work closely with classroom teachers. The actor/teachers tour schools, performing plays aimed at children's cognitive and interest levels and conducting drama workshops for children and courses for teachers.

On the theory that the teacher or mentor constitutes the most important outside factor in an artist's development, Szekely (1981, 1982) established a network of artists and children. The Art Partnership Network, developed at the University of Kentucky, matches college art students with gifted elementary students. The college students serve as friends, mentors, and art instructors; their aims are to expand the children's awareness of the world of art, develop the children's artistic gifts, help the children deal with the sense of isolation common to artists, and develop the children's confidence and creativity and encourage them to produce independent work.

Gilbert and Beal (1982) have suggested that Renzulli's (1977) enrichment triad model can be an appropriate vehicle for providing gifted and talented students with music experience within the regular school setting. For example, a unit on American folk music can combine activities aimed at both appreciation and mastery. Students explore folk songs through albums, books, collections, and speakers; write a ballad or make a dulcimer; and arrange a performance in which they use the final product before a live audience. Gregory (1982) described an arts education program for children and adolescents based on Feldhusen's three-stage enrichment model for gifted education developed at Purdue.

Most arts educators agree that parents play a major role in their children's artistic development. In addition to special arts programs for gifted students, special programs can also be offered to parents as a means of enlisting their support and helping them work effectively with artistically gifted children at home. Malone (1976) has described several ways in which parents affect children's artistic development. For example, children learn to value art when they observe adults' involvement as demonstrated through discussions about art and participation in art activities. Parents can discourage their children's development in art by demanding skill acquisition before children become interested in learning the skills. Malone points out that to encourage children's interest in the arts, parents need not be artists or even be knowledgeable in the arts. They can, for example, direct their children's attention to details in televised art productions, noting graceful versus bold movements. Parents can also take their children to visit art centers, studios, art classes, marching bands, demonstrations, and festivals. Finally, parents can establish practice schedules, serve as supportive critics, provide interesting experiences and materials as subjects for art expression, invite artists to their homes, and have their children participate in activities, such as room redecorating and selecting art objects for the home, that require artistic judgment (Szekely, 1981).

Elements of Outstanding Arts Programs. Larsh (1979b) has recommended that every medium-sized or larger city have at least one school of arts that offers talented students regular academic studies plus specialized curricula in the visual and performing arts. Readers interested in goals and objectives for dance, music, theater, visual arts, and writing within a special arts school should consult Tews (1981).

However, having a separate school for the arts is not practical for many school districts. Moreover, while segregated arts schools provide the most appropriate instruction for some artistically gifted students, other gifted and talented students are better served by differentiated arts programs integrated within the regular school setting. This section and the following one focus on arts programs within the regular school setting. Whatever plan or model best meets the needs of a school district's gifted population, the elements listed in the following paragraphs are described by arts specialists as characteristic of superior programs (Kreuger and Newman, 1974; Larsh, 1979b).

1. *Cooperative development of arts programs by gifted program personnel and arts personnel (arts educators and professional artists).* Team efforts not only help ensure quality and appropriateness in the design of programs but also encourage cooperation in implementing arts instruction. Mutual support is critical for the success of arts programs. Arts experts will need flexibility in scheduling and consistent support of arts objectives during the regular program. In turn, teachers will also have schedule requirements and academic objectives that can be supported through the arts program.

2. *Direct involvement of community resources.* Community resources, such as local and state arts councils, professional artists, and arts organizations can function as mentors, teachers, judges, curriculum consultants, and sponsors of competitions, recitals, and exhibits.

3. *Inclusion of qualified arts and music instructors as program implementors.* Arts experts agree that those who instruct students in the arts should be qualified arts educators or professional artists who have demonstrated abilities in teaching their skills to children. The instructors must be accessible to interested and potentially talented students who cannot afford to study with private teachers.

4. *Planned articulation of curricula from kindergarten through high school.* Too frequently arts programs are implemented as a series of unrelated events or field trips. Also, schools commonly schedule an "artist series" more as entertainment than education. Through districtwide planning committees composed of teachers and art specialists representing all educational levels, articulated curricula can be successfully developed.

5. *Availability and utilization of physical facilities, materials, and equipment that correspond with the articulated curriculum.* Unfortunately, there is a notable absence of national arts curricula and instructional materials available for gifted and talented students. Schools need to ensure availability of basic equipment (for example, musical instruments, canvas, easels, brushes, kilns) and basic facilities (for example, work areas with adequate lighting and acoustics; storage and display areas). Parent groups (for example, "band parents") frequently organize to raise funds for needed equipment and space.

6. *Special provisions to challenge students who demonstrate special potential or talent.* In all areas of gifted education, a few students will stand out from their peers in terms of talent and achievement. To prevent boredom and promote realization of extraordinary potential, educators must offer these students additional help—for example, special tutoring from a community mentor or accelerated program options. Chetelat (1981) has suggested a station learning model to accommodate gifted students within a regular elementary art education class. The teacher sets up a learning station where gifted students can investigate the same visual arts concepts as their classmates, but in a more discovery-oriented, independent, and accelerated manner. *School Arts*, an art education magazine for teachers, contains a monthly newsletter called "The Gifted and Talented Times" that provides a vehicle for exchanging information about school and community programs, publications, materials, and legislation that pertains to the education of students talented in the visual arts.

7. *Integration of the arts with the academic curriculum.* Integrating the arts in academic subject areas can help students understand that the arts have always been an integral part of the human experience. For example, introducing paintings and musical pieces composed during the period under study in a history unit can help illustrate the emotional responses of people to historical events.

8. *Provision of in-service training in the arts for cooperating teachers and training in the characteristics of gifted students for cooperating artists.* In-service training can facilitate cooperative program planning and implementation by helping professionals from diverse disciplines appreciate the objectives, methods, problems, and prospects of each field and the ways in which these apply to the gifted population.

9. *Opportunities for parent involvement.* To enlist the aid of parents in supporting arts objectives, many quality arts programs for gifted and talented students have established parent programs. Parents are encouraged to share information on community resources and maintain communication between home and school regarding students' artistic endeavors.

10. *Career education.* Arts programs should offer students information on careers in the arts. Career education units can provide talented students with a realistic appraisal of their chances for success in an arts vocation, where jobs are extremely scarce and highly competitive. Career education can also emphasize development of artistic ability as a fulfilling avocation.

11. *Provision of lifelong learning opportunities to help individuals beyond school age to develop their artistic talents.* Many adults would enjoy developing artistic skills that have previously lain dormant because of lack of opportunity, money, time, or encouragement. Ideally, schools and community organizations would provide programs for adults who wish to continue learning in the arts.

Instructional Goals and Methods in Arts Education. Although specific instructional goals will depend on the established philosophy of the arts program, the characteristics of program participants, and the desires of the community, a three-part goal can be offered as a general guideline: understanding and utilization of (*a*) the affective, (*b*) the technical, and (*c*) the cognitive aspects of the arts. Affective understanding includes perceiving and using art as a means of emotional expression and developing creative responses to experiences that can be translated through artistic media. The technical aspects of arts education concern the development of artistic skill in using different media and methods. Cognitive components of arts education include an understanding of art history, the philosophy of art, and the role of the arts in the human experience. Objectives of an arts program can be arranged taxonomically as affective, technical, and cognitive, and goal development can and should be initiated at the primary level. Taking the visual arts as an example, the three-part general goal can be broken down into specific objectives. Affective understanding includes the objectives listed in the following paragraphs.

1. *Understanding that a work of art can express the artist's feelings about the subject.* For example, the teacher can present young children with selected paintings or sculpture and ask the children to interpret the artist's feelings. Older students can compare paintings that express different emotions and describe the artistic techniques used to convey those feelings.

2. *Using artistic elements (for example, color, line, movement) to convey emotion.* Students of all ages can be asked to express their feelings through art. With increasing maturity, students can learn to manipulate artistic elements to express specific emotions.

Technical understanding includes the objectives listed in the following paragraphs.

1. *Understanding and using the elements of design: line, color, texture, shape, mass, light, movement, and space.* For example, two objectives for artistically gifted upper-elementary children would be to understand that lines may be used to create textures and that texture and pattern can describe surfaces and objects (Chetelat, 1981). These objectives can be taught by having students (*a*) study works of famous painters who have used lines in these ways; (*b*) describe the painters' techniques from their own observations; and (*c*) practice these techniques in their own drawings.

2. *Understanding and using qualitative relationships that arise when the elements of design are juxtaposed in composition.* Elements of design include balance, contrast, gradation, variety, unity, direction, pattern, and rhythm (Luca and Allen, 1973).

3. *Experimenting with and mastering media and associated tools.* Drawing tools include pencils, charcoal, and pastels; painting tools include watercolors and acrylics; collage and construction tools include paper and wire; printmaking tools include stamps and rubbing materials; ceramics tools include clay; weaving and stitchery tools include thread and yarn; sculpture and model-building tools include plaster, wax, and wood (Luca and Allen, 1973). Upper-elementary and secondary curricula may focus on in-depth work in two selected media.

Cognitive understanding includes the objectives listed in the following paragraphs.

1. *Understanding the cultural role of art.* For example, Luca and Allen (1974) suggest as a concept for primary children the idea that art is a universal language. One activity to develop the concept is to have children compare their art themes with those of children from other nations.

2. *Developing artistic judgment and standards.* For example, teachers can present young children with two paintings or sculptures, have them determine which of the two they prefer, and provide a rationale for their preference.

3. *Understanding the philosophy and history of art.* Students of all ages can learn to recognize and evaluate the various types of art and the philosophy underlying their expression—for example, classical, cubist, or surrealist (Brown, 1973). Through integration of art with history, social studies, and literature, students can learn how artistic styles have changed over time and how particular forms can be associated with historical events, beliefs, and periods (for example, the Renaissance).

Like an art curriculum, a music curriculum can be conceptualized in terms of affective, technical, and cognitive themes. The technical aspects of music would include (*a*) music literacy (reading and writing music), (*b*) elements of music (tone, pitch, rhythm, loudness, timbre), (*c*) forms of composition (symphony, sonata, concerto, fugue), (*d*) recognition and playing of instruments, (*e*) recognition and mastery of musical techniques, and (*f*) composition and arrangement.

Regular classroom teachers can contribute immensely to gifted children's arts education by providing time for children to work on arts projects; by recognizing, discussing, and encouraging artistic efforts; by providing space for working on, exhibiting, and storing art products; by organizing field trips related to the arts as well as to academic subjects; and by making available books, journals, and materials that deal with art and music.

LEADERSHIP

Although the concept of leadership education is not new, recent years have witnessed a resurgence of interest in this area due to inclusion of leadership as a talent category and to widespread perceptions of a need for leaders with a vision. At no time in world history has effective leadership been more crucial as we face a future rendered uncertain by increasing international tensions, continuing poverty and oppression, and nuclear arms buildup. This section examines definitions of leadership, issues related to leadership education, and strategies for developing leadership among the gifted and talented.

Defining Leadership

Definitions and conceptualizations of leadership vary depending on the context in which leadership is being discussed. We will begin with an examination of leadership in general and then discuss leadership with respect to gifted and talented students.

General Views on Leadership. In his comprehensive survey of research on leadership, Stogdill best summarized the state of the art: "The endless accumulation of empirical data has not produced an integrated understanding of leadership" (Stogdill, 1974, p. vii). Despite thousands of studies conducted over four decades, Stogdill found no unifying theory and little agreement concerning the meaning of the concept. Bass (1981), who updated and expanded on Stogdill's work, identified eleven conceptualizations (for example, leadership as inducing compliance, as an instrument of goal achievement, and as an effect of interaction) and ten theories (for example, the great man theory, the environmental theory, and the personal–situational theory). Bass's review also described a number of leader types and typologies. Crowd leaders might be crowd representative or crowd compelling; institutional leaders include autocratic, democratic, executive, or reflective–intellectual types. Further complicating the issue, Pfeffer (1978) questioned whether leaders even matter, given their lack of control over outcomes within the organizational context.

Foster (1981) has provided a taxonomy of four approaches to leadership that brings order to the many competing theories. The first approach is the great person model, which asserts that leadership is a matter of personality. According to this view, leaders are born rather than trained. The second approach, the small-group-dynamic model, describes leadership as a skill-based process produced by the demands of the small group. The implication is that leadership can be taught as a series of skills. The third, or attribution, approach suggests that leadership is a construct created by the attributions of group members. Thus, leadership is defined by the expectations of followers and possesses no authority in and of itself. The final approach is the social role model, which proposes that leadership is primarily situational, a formalized social role sanctioned by the organization. In this view personality, skills, and attributions of others play a relatively minor part. Considered together, the four approaches in Foster's taxonomy offer a more comprehensive description of leadership than any one taken alone.

Gifted and Talented Leadership. Despite the lack of agreement in the general literature, at least a tacit consensus exists in the gifted and talented field regarding the desired type of leader and the accepted conceptual approach. Foster (1981) has noted that the focus of gifted and talented programs is on active leaders—that is, individuals responsible for maintaining and changing social processes. His review of current leadership training efforts for the gifted indicated a skills orientation reflective of the small-group-dynamic model. The selection of this particular model is logical since it is the only model that assumes that leadership skills can be taught. Passow's (1978) analysis of leadership training for the gifted and talented also points to leadership as a social process defined by group members, with the implication that individuals can acquire the means to lead, can learn to lead more effectively, and need not be born with certain traits.

Issues in Leadership Education

The major controversies surrounding leadership education concern (*a*) who should receive leadership training, (*b*) what should be the goals and content of the training, and (*c*) how effective are identification and training programs.

Recipients of Leadership Training. The literature describes leadership education programs designed for gifted children, children who evidence leadership talent, children in general, and children who evidence deficiencies in social skills. Stacey and Mitchell (1979), for example, presented leadership training techniques designed for intellectually gifted elementary and junior high students. Activities suggested by Karnes and Strong (1978) were targeted at preschoolers who evidence leadership potential. Magoon (1980) described methods to help children with leadership talent and children whose potential is less obvious. Stark (1978) offered training techniques to foster leadership in virtually all kindergarten and first-grade children. Judkins (undated) recommended that teachers expect all children to be leaders, with the understanding that those who are not may become better followers as a result. Social skills similar to those proposed as components of leadership—responding positively, communicating accurately, being expert, and initiating a relationship—are also considered important in helping children who are social isolates (see Asher, Oden, and Gottman, 1981; Furman, Rahe, and Hartup, 1979). Hollingworth (1939) early on raised another "who" issue: the right of the potential leader to refuse leadership and leadership training.

Purpose and Content of Leadership Training. Goals and content are necessarily interrelated. As noted earlier, Foster focused on the development of active leaders through skills training:

> Engaging young children and youth in educational activities for the purpose of enhancing the possibility of their attaining eminence as action leaders in later life is certainly a worthy goal. Those of us interested in the field of gifted and talented have established programs intended to achieve that end. Gifted youngsters are exposed to special educational experiences designed to introduce them to the process skills involved in leading small groups.
>
> — Foster, 1983, p. 23

Most leadership training programs appear to support Foster's observation. For young children, Magoon (1980) suggested building on social skills such as sharing, cooperating, and taking responsibility. Stark (1978) described specific activities aimed at moral education, leadership style, communication, creative problem solving, and organization.

In addition to active leaders trained in the small-group-dynamic tradition, other types and models of leadership might be equally appropriate for the education of all gifted students (Kitano and Tafoya, 1982). While the development of active leaders appears to be a worthy goal, reflective leadership is also a critical societal need. In contrast to active leaders, reflective leaders achieve eminence through thoughtful production rather than through social action. Reflective leaders may be less visible. Former HEW secretary John Gardner gave some examples of reflective leaders: value shapers, clarifiers, codifiers, teachers, inspirers, and role models (Hubert H. Humphrey Institute of Public Affairs, 1981). These types of leaders may be found in any field—government, industry, the arts, the sciences, or the media.

Reflective leadership is most consistent with the great person model, wherein authority is vested in the individual by virtue of personal characteristics. Harland Cleveland (1980), director of the Hubert H. Humphrey Institute of Public Affairs, described reflective leaders as more inclined than followers to integrate information, to perceive a situation in its entire context, to be unusually curious about issues and methods outside their initial disciplines, and to be concerned with values.

While the great person model does not support the trainability of leadership, experiences can be selected that provide optimum conditions for the realization of reflective leadership potential in individuals already identified as having personal characteristics consistent with reflective leadership (for example, high intelligence or broad vision). The educational implications of the great person approach to reflective leadership stand in contrast to those of the small-group-dynamic model of active leadership. The latter approach reduces leadership to a set of discrete, trainable skills—for example, communication, problem solving, decision making, and conflict management. Education for reflective leadership, on the other hand, promotes academic and experiential breadth for individuals identified as potential leaders. Considering the characteristics of effective leaders and the multidisciplinary nature of all real-world problems, Cleveland asserted that "the critical dimension of leadership, and the centerpiece of education for leadership, is not the technology of committee sitting. It is organizing your mind for the analysis and projection of breadth" (Cleveland, 1980, p. 2). The Humphrey Institute's Education for Reflective Leadership Program, a mid-career program for adults, proposes that the foremost factor with which leaders must cope is uncertainty:

> A program of education for leadership therefore cannot be focused mainly on how-to-do-it skills, nor can it offer what-to-do prescriptions. Rather, it has to concentrate on helping each leader get used to the assessment of uncertainty, clarify his/her ethical values, and develop for his/her own personal use a comprehensive view appropriate for an ambiguous future.
>
> — Hubert H. Humphrey Institute of Public Affairs, 1981, p. 14

McCall and Lombardo, in their innovative examination of leadership, called attention to what might be considered reflective leadership: "What are the criteria for leadership when there are no readily identifiable followers? Leaders in ideas are one example—who is in Aristotle's work group?" (McCall and Lombardo, 1978, p. 154).

Effectiveness of Early Identification and Training. Literature describing methods for identifying leadership potential and for leadership training appears in relative abundance. However, the long-term predictive validity of early identification methods has not been established. Buhler (1931) has suggested that leadership characteristics can be identified as early as the first year of life. Leadership behaviors at this age include self-assuredness in the presence of other infants and acting as the initiator and model for others' activities. Buhler further asserted that even at preschool ages "the leader is characterized by the same qualities which we shall also find to be decisive for leadership in later years, *initiative, organizing ability,* and *conformity* with the substantial tendencies of the group" (Buhler, 1931, p. 401). Yet Buhler cited other evidence to show that during different periods of adolescence, different types of leaders are preferred. More recently, Hillman and Smith (1981) noted that while dominance, initiative, and self-confidence continue to characterize leaders from the preschool through the elementary school years, leadership among adolescents is determined by additional factors: the group's gender, degree of homogeneity, values, and traditions. The inference is that the same individual may not function as a leader at different times during his or her development. For adults, however, leadership appears to be transferable from situation to situation; research supports the theory that the leader in one group will emerge as leader when placed in other groups, especially when tasks are similar (Bass, 1981).

Stogdill (1974) reviewed early studies that suggested that leadership in elementary school, high school, and college was predictive of adult leadership in business and social activities. He found that leadership in extracurricular activities was more highly related to later leadership than was academic achievement. However, he concluded only that behavior at the secondary and post-secondary levels tended to predict adult leadership; he left unanswered questions about the stability of early leadership behavior. Answers to these questions require longitudinal studies that provide follow-up information about students identified as leaders in the elementary years.

In addition to longitudinal approaches, one promising avenue for research concerns investigation of the developmental correlates and precursors of leadership ability. For example, Jennings (1975) found social knowledge of preschool children to be significantly correlated with observed peer leadership ($r = 0.44$), ability to get along with others ($r = 0.34$), forceful pursuit of what one wants ($r = 0.34$), and ability to self-start ($r = 0.40$). Social knowledge was measured primarily through tests of role taking and moral judgment abilities. As will be recalled from Chapter 3, such tests are frequently used to assess children's social–cognitive level within the framework of cognitive developmental theory. These findings do not suggest a causal relationship or a direction of causality. They are interesting, however, because of their theoretical significance. The inference to be pursued is that there exist developmental prerequisites or precursors to leadership behavior—for example, a minimum level of role taking or moral reasoning ability. Such an approach would question the efficacy of specific leadership skill training and focus on the development of more general social–cognitive structures.

Training methods that have been researched (primarily with adults) include lecture/discussion about effective leadership, role-playing leadership–followership situations, problem solving (establishing goals and solutions for specific problems), simulation games (for example, setting priorities), and sensitivity training (aimed at increasing leaders' openness, sharing, and sensitivity to followers' needs). Stogdill (1974) concluded from his review of the research conducted through the 1960s that while problem solving appears to be a more effective training method than role playing or sensitivity training, the research is generally inadequate in design. Researchers failed to address significant questions concerning the effects of training on maintenance of leadership and on group performance and member satisfaction.

Updating Stogdill's review, Bass (1981) also cited evidence that, compared to role playing, task-oriented problem solving permits followers to take a more active role. Effectiveness of role playing in terms of learning retention is increased when players receive feedback on their performance—for example, through videotaped playback. The research on sensitivity training suggests that while sensitivity training may induce attitude change, negative consequences may also result. Moreover, few data are available to support the transfer of such training to the real world. Newer, more highly structured methods such as behavior modeling—that is, viewing a model appropriately handling a situation, discussing the model's behavior, practicing the behavior through role playing, and receiving feedback—have shown positive results. A number of programs use on-the-job leadership training (for example, coaching), although few efficacy studies have been conducted on this method. Effectiveness of training is influenced by the trainee's personal attributes (for example, authoritarianism), the trainer's characteristics (for example, attitude or attractiveness), group composition, follow-up strategies (feedback and reinforcement), and congruence between training and real-world environment.

In sum, longitudinal studies are needed to determine whether children identified as leaders during the preschool and elementary years maintain their leadership status as adults. Research on training in leadership skills indicates that the most effective programs (a) focus on task-oriented problem solving—that is, provide opportunities for problem solving aimed at specific goals; (b) provide appropriate models of leadership behavior and opportunities for discussing the model's behavior; (c) provide opportunities for practicing leadership skills; (d) provide constant feedback; (e) create training situations that simulate actual situations in which trainees will apply their leadership skills; (f) provide opportunities for real-life implementation (for example, student government).

Strategies for Fostering Leadership Development

Several assumptions underlie the following suggestions for creating a curriculum that will enhance leadership development of gifted students. First, all gifted and talented students, not just those with obvious leadership potential, should receive leadership training because all fields of human endeavor require effective leaders. Second, leadership curricula should be matched to individual behavioral style and preference. Students whose behavioral style indicates potential for active leadership, such as those adept at persuading and motivating others to achieve common goals, should focus on skills training. Students who prefer reflective leadership, such as in providing ideas for thought and social change, might be prepared best through a broad academic curriculum. Third, although the long-term efficacy of strategies for training active and reflective leaders has not been demonstrated, the suggested methods have theoretical support; methods for training active leaders may be helpful in improving interaction skills, and methods for training reflective leaders may help increase students' knowledge of social problems. Fourth, as emphasized by Maccoby (1981), the goals of leadership in today's society are human and social: (a) to effect institutional change and (b) to promote self-development in others.

Goals and Methods for Active Leadership.

The literature suggests that effective leaders possess a core of traits and skills (Bass, 1981). Personality traits of leaders include persistence, task orientation, personal autonomy, integrity, self-confidence, and self-actualization. Although such characteristics are difficult to teach, educators can promote their development by providing opportunities for manifestation of these characteristics and by reinforcing them when they appear. For example, preschool-age children can be helped to develop personal autonomy and independence by learning to solve their own problems. In the New Mexico State University Preschool for the Gifted, children who report, "Teacher, I don't have a chair" or "John won't give me the ball" are asked, "What do you think you can do about it?" The teachers then support the children for generating, selecting, and carrying out constructive responses. Teachers can help promote task persistence by providing opportunities for individual and small-group work with specific objectives (for example, building a model or composing a thank-you letter) and by reinforcing task completion. Hillman and Smith (1981) recommend that teachers provide preschool and elementary school children with opportunities for making choices and permit children to solve their own conflicts. Parents can encourage development of leadership at home by being clear and consistent, explaining decisions, offering opportunities for children to participate in decision making, and modeling leadership behaviors. Leadership skills, which are the purpose of a leadership skills training program, are listed in the following paragraphs, together with suggestions for enabling activities.

1. *Active participation in group activities.* The active participants in group situations generally tend to emerge as the leaders. Teachers can encourage a reserved child to voice ideas and opinions by (*a*) providing opportunities to observe an effective leader who serves as a model; (*b*) placing the child in a small group of three students, none of whom is dominant, and assigning the group a clear task to be accomplished; (*c*) reinforcing participation; (*d*) gradually increasing group size; and (*e*) changing the composition of groups so that children have the opportunity to try their skills with a variety of individuals. Specific interaction skills—for example, meeting others, keeping conversations going, asking questions to draw others out, relating one's comments to those of other individuals, and indicating that one is listening attentively—can also be modeled, discussed, role played, and evaluated.

2. *Effective problem solving.* Students at all age levels can benefit from practice in identifying the critical features of a problem situation, generating alternative solutions, weighing alternatives and their possible consequences, selecting the most appropriate alternative, implementing the solution, and evaluating the outcome.

3. *Anticipating future events.* Forecasting and predicting activities can be incorporated into any content area at any grade level. Young children can be asked to predict endings to stories and justify their predictions with facts from the stories. Older students can be asked to predict the outcome of science experiments, current events (for example, a terrorist bombing or an airplane hijacking), and political campaigns. "What if" questions can stimulate discus-

sion of hypothetical changes in history (What would life be like now if America were still a British colony?), of imaginary events (What would happen if all children were born blind?), and of possible events (What would happen if the dollar were suddenly deflated?). In each discussion students should be required to provide logical support for their predictions based on available data and, if feasible, to compare their predictions with actual outcomes.

4. *Planning.* Planning requires that students set objectives, anticipate problems in meeting objectives, and organize the resources (materials, time, and energy) necessary to meet the objectives. Young children can begin by helping the teacher plan snacks—for example, they can help decide what nutritious snack the class would like, and determine the ingredients, implements, time, and number of classmates needed for preparation. Older students can plan major projects, such as independent study activities, school assemblies, fund raisers, and arts exhibits.

5. *Decision making.* Good decision making requires students to exercise appropriate judgment in choosing among alternatives, frequently based on previously established criteria, and to provide firm support for the decision. Given information on the duration of a field trip, amount of space available, temperature, and physical environment, young children can be asked to decide what items they will take on the trip. Secondary students can simulate administrative decision making in job roles by examining a list of tasks that must be accomplished within a week and giving the tasks priority according to "company" objectives, personal values, consumer demands, cost effectiveness, and other variables.

6. *Communicating.* Effective communication requires several different skills: articulating orally and in writing one's feelings and ideas, recognizing and interpreting the feelings and expressions of others, and understanding visual cues. Students of all ages can be presented with stimulating situations and asked to describe on tape, before an audience, or in written form their feelings and thoughts about the situation. For example, history students can articulate the impressions of a Civil War soldier anticipating a battle. Science students might be asked to describe the circulatory system of a frog in terms that a younger child can understand. In each case students must understand the perspective of others and consider the nature of their intended audience. They should be encouraged to use vivid and precise rather than vague terms and to provide concrete examples of their main ideas. With regard to receptive communication skills, students can practice reading visual cues by identifying and interpreting mimed emotions or soundless videotapes of human interaction sequences. Students can learn to attend carefully to both auditory and visual signals by observing role playing or videotaped interaction sequences and simultaneously using a checklist to pinpoint types of behavioral cues emitted by the participants. Friedman (1980) provides additional activities for developing communication skills for leadership.

7. *Promoting teamwork.* To develop an effective working team, leaders must learn to recognize and capitalize on the strengths of group members, reinforce members for teamwork, and share power by encouraging member participation in decision making. Even young children can work on these objectives by learning to invite others to join a play group and assigning the newcomers with roles that permit active participation (for example, "We're playing barber shop. Would you like to play? You can be the shampoo seller"). Gifted elementary students in one school designed and promoted a play by (*a*) having each student list his or her own strengths and interests on the board, (*b*) making group decisions about assigned roles based on these strengths and interests, and (*c*) working out specific job responsibilities. Finally, students need to practice the art of seeking out and complimenting the strengths and efforts of others.

8. *Promoting self-development in others.* Using simulation, students can take turns playing corporate executive and interviewing subordinates about their professional and personal aspirations. The executive must design feasible individualized plans to help subordinates achieve their goals.

9. *Recognizing and implementing creative ideas.* While some successful leaders are highly creative, others are not themselves creative but have the ability to recognize the creative ideas of others and to put these ideas in motion. Leaders in training can learn to enhance creative thinking in group members by using the techniques described in Chapter 8. Problem-solving techniques can help students determine ways to implement selected ideas.

10. *Recognizing and seeking out opportunities.* A major factor in actual achievement of leadership positions is chance, or being in the right place at the right time. Potential leaders need to maximize the probability of advancement into positions of leadership by scanning the environment for opportunities to display their leadership and by creating additional opportunities. Recognizing and using opportunities is also important for established leaders in striving to promote the goals of the group (for example, finding new markets and buyers or taking advantage of new technology).

Additional skills that might be taught in a program for active leadership include social skills (manners, tact, diplomacy, and protocol), rational thinking, and parliamentary procedure (Magoon, 1980). Teachers can encourage students to practice these skills in real-life leadership situations that require responsibility and judicious use of power—for example, class and student government, athletic management, service organizations, in-school and community improvement projects, classroom panels, debates, and other group activities.

Types of leadership programs that have been developed for the gifted and talented include intensive skills training workshops, mentorship and internship programs, and programs with specialized curricula. Foster (1981) has described a four-day intensive training workshop in Illinois for high school students with leadership potential. The students acquire knowledge of and practice in leadership theory and learn procedures for leading meetings, for conflict management, and for interpersonal communication. The Center for Creative Leadership in Greensboro, North Carolina, promotes research on the development of creative leadership and the application of research to practice. The center offers intensive programs open to individuals in leadership positions (for example, business and government executives and school administrators), as well as individuals who want to improve their creative leadership skills. The center maintains that leadership can be acquired in three ways: (*a*) practice (in making decisions, learning from mistakes, and trying out new skills), (*b*) feedback (counseling regarding personality, skills, behavior), and (*c*) learning to change (through self-analysis, behavior assessment, ratings on training, psychological test results, and staff and peer observations) (Cavedon, undated).

Mentorship programs for gifted students match leaders from the community to program participants. The mentors introduce their charges to the daily activities and responsibilities of the leadership positions the mentors hold. Mentorship programs recruit leaders from politics, business, social services, and other community agencies. Hirsch (1976) described the Executive High School Internship program sponsored by New York City and several major foundations. This program has served thousands of juniors and seniors in seventeen states. The students learn about organizational leadership as one-semester interns to business and government executives, hospital directors, and judges. One day each week, participants attend seminars on management, administration, and decision making, using a case study approach adapted from the Harvard Business School.

Specialized instructional activities and materials have been developed for leadership education. Feldhusen (1978) has developed leadership training materials based on the small-group-dynamic approach. Stacey and Mitchell (1979) have provided examples of activities designed to develop leadership through future-directed instruction. The Future Problem-Solving Program developed by Torrance (Crabbe, 1982) trains problem-solving teams of four to (*a*) develop images of the future, (*b*) enhance creativity, (*c*) improve communication skills, (*d*) increase teamwork, (*e*) use a problem-solving model, and (*f*) develop research skills. Teams compete in state bowls in preparation for the final bowl in Cedar Rapids, Iowa. Sisk (1977) has presented specific activities for leadership training based on a humanistic model of creativity that emphasizes self-understanding and self-actualization through trusting, listening and responding, resolving interpersonal conflict, and encouraging independence. Parker (1983) has proposed a model that combines development of cognitive and affective skills through four major components: cognition, problem solving, interpersonal communication, and decision making.

Goals and Methods for Reflective Leadership. The general purpose of programs for reflective leadership is to encourage development of humanistic, socially oriented leaders who are motivated to solve human problems and who recognize the interdisciplinary nature of such problems. Reflective leaders tend to possess the following characteristics, which influence the formation of the curriculum goals: intellectual abilities of analysis, synthesis, and evaluation; competence in several fields; interdisciplinary perspective; high standards of excellence; moral and ethical integrity; and a keen sense of humanity. Programs that help build these characteristics provide a broad education aimed at the humanities (arts, literature, and history), the social sciences (psychology, sociology, anthropology, economics, and political science), and foreign languages. Human issues—that is, the causes and consequences of human problems over time and place—should constitute the theme for this curriculum, and instructional methods should aim to foster increasingly higher levels of inductive, analytic, and evaluative thinking. Specific activities for encouraging a sense of humanity and an interdisciplinary perspective include those listed in the following paragraphs.

1. *Using world history and literature as a vehicle for identifying universal problems that have plagued humanity.* For example, what similar problems have people faced in diverse times and places—for example, the post–Civil War American South, Nazi Germany, or contemporary South Africa? What factors—economic, psychological, sociological, or political—contributed to the problems? What did it take to solve the problems? Where did people start to work on solutions?

2. *Researching and experiencing worldwide human problems.* Students begin by reading literature that depicts in human and statistical terms the dimensions of a problem—hunger, lack of health care, malnutrition, pollution, energy depletion, nuclear warfare, crime, or oppression of human rights. In regard to the problem of crime, students might read articles that describe the number and types of crimes committed, the probabilities of one's becoming a victim of crime, the effects of crime on victims, the resources needed to bring perpetrators to justice, and the effectiveness of the legal system. As a next step teachers would arrange small-group field trips that give students a feeling for the consequences of the problem. For example, students might visit with and interview crime victims, who would tell how their lives have been affected. Students then determine what kind of information they must have to understand the problem and begin to formulate solutions. Fact-finding activities for small groups might include setting up interviews, bringing in guest speakers, or reviewing public documents. People contacted might include law enforcement officials, victims, criminals, probation officers, sociologists, and psychologists.

3. *Solving problems through interdisciplinary teamwork.* Each student in a small group approaches the given problem as a specialist—for example, an economist, a sociologist, an agronomist, a political scientist, an educator, or an anthropologist. Team members exchange views on how they conceptualize the problem, the types of questions to be posed, the types of data to be collected, possible solutions, and consequences of solutions. Members work toward interdisciplinary understanding of the problem and toward an integrated solution.

4. *Learning how social policy is developed and implemented.* Students will want to know how their ideas and suggestions can be implemented. Thus, the curriculum should include local, state, and federal policymaking processes— that is, information on how social policy is developed and implemented and how these processes can be influenced. Specific activities include visiting seats of government and interviewing policymakers (for example, legislators, legislative staff, and lobbyists).

The activities we have described are most appropriate for upper-elementary and secondary-level gifted students. Teachers can help foster the development of reflective leadership in young gifted children by introducing them to the different disciplines through guest speakers and field trips. Even preschool-age children will understand the major function of an anthropologist, for example, and the general problems and methods of the field. Young children can also empathize with the problems of other children and adults (for example, hunger and malnutrition) and feel gratified that health-care workers and nutritionists contribute their expertise around the world to help alleviate the situation.

In her treatise on early selection and training of leaders, Hollingworth (1939) presented a children's model consistent with the idea of education for reflective leadership. Her program focused not on specific skill training but on providing an educational climate conducive to the fruition of leadership potential. The basic curriculum was designed to broaden children's horizons and instill in them an understanding of the nonstatic nature of human affairs. The component called intellectual education included the study of the evolution of common things to create a sense of past, present, and future; the study of biographies of people who guided the development of civilization; the study of foreign language; and for some, the study of forensics. A second component, emotional education, taught children to make constructive use of time, to "suffer fools gladly," to avoid a negative attitude toward authority, to keep from becoming isolated, and to avoid "extreme chicanery."

Maccoby (1981) emphasized that to realize their human potential, leaders need education in the humanities to develop a sense of the centuries-old struggle against ignorance and injustice. In addition to skills in writing and speaking, Maccoby prescribed the need for a clear sense of history and a knowledge of religion, psychology, ethical philosophy (derived from the works of Heraclitus, Aristotle, Aquinas, Spinoza, and Kierkegaard), and literature that probes the human character (for example, the works of Shakespeare, Tolstoy, and Ibsen).

Whether one chooses to focus on active leadership, on reflective leadership, or on both, a final consideration in identifying and training leaders concerns cultural diversity in leadership style. Bass (1981) noted that clear anthropological evidence exists for variations across cultures in respect to characteristics of effective leaders. Cultures whose values differ are likely to prefer different types of leaders and to reinforce different leadership styles. For example, one culture may emphasize traditionalism over modernism, the obligations of friendship over the obligations to society, or competition over cooperation. Research on subcultural groups in the United States also points to possible differences in leadership styles. Bernal (1978) has suggested that the leadership style of Mexican-American children may be less obtrusive than in the case of Anglo children. Fu (1979) compared leadership characteristics among middle- and lower-income preschool children and found no significant differences in quantity of leadership behavior. However, her data indicated that the middle-income children exhibited more behavior characteristic of followers than did lower-income children, while the latter demonstrated more nonconformity (ignoring of another's suggestions). Fu interpreted these results to indicate that while both groups value leadership, differences may exist in types of leader behaviors preferred. She suggested that social class differences in child-rearing practices and values—for example, cooperation and respect for authority as opposed to independence and assertiveness, as well as emphasis on verbal persuasion as opposed to nonverbal communication—may help explain class differences in leadership behavior.

CHAPTER SUMMARY

Although current definitions of giftedness specifically include students with high performance capability in the arts and in leadership, both areas generally have received less attention than traditional academic fields. Obstacles to greater emphasis on arts and leadership include competing priorities, limited funding, and difficulties in coordinating available resources. Yet the visual and performing arts constitute an essential part of gifted education because they help students develop and express sensitivity, they provide enjoyment, and they demonstrate the universality of human feelings. Leadership education programs can promote development of active or reflective leaders. The importance of leadership training derives from the fact that many gifted students will become leaders in their chosen fields.

ACTIVITIES FOR THOUGHT AND DISCUSSION

1. Investigate potential resources in your community that could support an arts program for gifted students.

2. Develop and conduct a survey of local citizens to determine whether they would support a tax-based differentiated arts program for gifted students.

3. Should leadership programs focus on developing active or reflective leaders? Why?

4. Develop a list of leaders from several different fields. What characteristics and behaviors do they have in common? Can a person be trained in these qualities?

5. Selecting either the arts or leadership, develop a list of objectives appropriate for gifted and talented students. First you may need to determine whether the target students are intellectually gifted and/or gifted in the specific area (arts or leadership).

Chapter Eleven

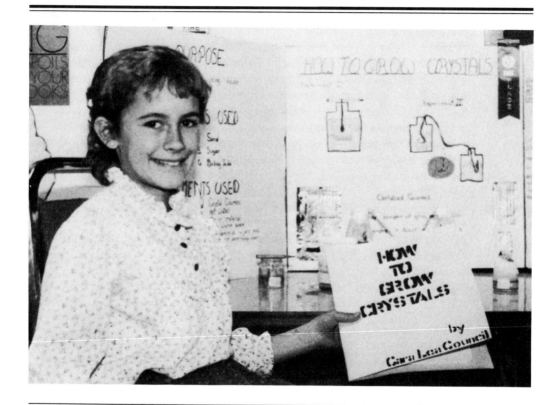

SELECTED ACADEMIC CONTENT AREAS

Continuing from the preceding chapter the idea that content acquisition is a major goal of programs for the gifted, this chapter describes major considerations in four academic content areas: social studies, language arts, science, and mathematics.

SOCIAL STUDIES

Social studies constitutes a core area of investigation for gifted students of every age. No matter what fields a gifted individual ultimately elects, his or her activities will affect and be affected by the human interactions and institutions that form the bases of social studies. One issue in American social studies education for the gifted concerns the concept of social studies as the "democratizing" subject matter based on principles of equality among people from all cultures, regions, and economic backgrounds. However, our view is that the social science disciplines that constitute the bases for social studies should be differentiated for the gifted, just as are other disciplines such as science and mathematics. Two major approaches to social studies education for the gifted appear in the literature: the social science approach and the social studies approach.

The Social Science Approach

In the social science approach, the social science disciplines—anthropology, economics, geography, history, political science, sociology, and psychology—make up the bulk of the social studies curriculum. A social studies program for the gifted with a disciplines focus might present material selected from the social science disciplines as separate units, with students learning both content and corresponding methods of investigation—for example, history and historiography; anthropology and ethnography. In this approach, each discipline is treated like a natural science; it contains both accumulated knowledge and a method of inquiry for the creation of new knowledge. Hence, a main objective at the secondary level might be the undertaking of original research that might yield new information on human interactions and institutions. Supporters of the social science approach argue that gifted students are capable of acquiring sophisticated content *and* the high-level thinking skills and inquiry methods employed by social scientists.

The major goals of a social studies curriculum based on a social science approach for gifted students include (*a*) acquisition of knowledge from social science content, (*b*) development of inquiry skills, and (*c*) production of new knowledge or new applications of existing knowledge in the social science disciplines. In general, the same disciplines can be incorporated into the curriculum at every age level; the complexity of concepts and generalizations is simply increased as students mature and master enabling concepts. Exceptions occur for those disciplines whose concepts depend on children's developing cognitive abilities, such as time concepts in history and the complex interrelationships involved in political science.

Concepts and generalizations from other social sciences can be used effectively across all grade levels. For example, teachers at all grade levels can incorporate anthropology into the social studies curriculum. At the preschool level, children can encounter the concept of cultural universals. In one activity at the New Mexico State University Preschool for Gifted Children, the children examined clothing, cooking and eating utensils, games, music, and writing from the People's Republic of China. Children were asked to name things that were the same and things that were different about China and the United States. Later they were asked to make generalizations about the things every culture has—for example, language, festivals, modes of dress, and games. A visiting anthropologist then discussed how people learn about other cultures—that is, through observation, participation, and interview.

For gifted elementary students, one goal of studying anthropology would be to understand the concepts of ethnocentrism, acculturation, enculturation, and socialization. The teacher might discuss problems of border communities and ports of entry, such as Miami, which receive large numbers of immigrants from other cultures. Students would then engage in problem-solving activities, observations, and interviews, based on anthropological methods of investigation and would be asked to propose possible solutions.

At the secondary level the complexity of anthropology concepts increases. For example, students might study the implications of international competition and interdependence and might engage in problem finding as well as problem solving. They might also be asked to design and conduct independent research using anthropological modes of inquiry. Thus, as students develop and become more sophisticated, teaching moves from guided discovery and inquiry to more heuristic, scientific methods.

The Social Studies Approach

The social studies approach (Kaplan, 1979b) integrates the social science disciplines by focusing on social problems or broad themes, such as human rights or people's dependence on the environment. Proponents argue that this approach is more relevant to student interests, more useful to society (Ponder and Hirsh, 1981), and more realistic in terms of the interdisciplinary nature of all human problems. Goals of the social studies approach include citizenship education, understanding of society and social issues, informed decision making, and appreciation of democratic principles. Supporters of the disciplinary perspective criticize the integrative social studies viewpoint for diluting disciplinary knowledge and methods, eroding the boundaries of the disciplines, and preparing consumers of social studies knowledge rather than producers of new knowledge.

Kaplan (1979b) has suggested a framework for developing social studies curricula for gifted elementary students that incorporates horizontal, vertical, and supplementary enrichment into a single structure centered on a given theme, such as people's need to communicate. Horizontal activities provide further practice of learned skills, concepts, and generalizations and the application of acquired knowledge. For example, students might study the effects of news releases on the family. Vertical enrichment provides opportunities for learning beyond the core curriculum and encourages transfer of acquired knowledge. Within the communications theme, for example, students could assess the effects of linguistic style within the black culture. Supplementary activities permit students to investigate areas usually omitted from the regular curriculum and encourage integration and previous learnings with new ones. For example, within the same broad theme a student might conduct an independent study on electronics.

Jones (1983) proposed a ten-step model for developing social studies units for the gifted around broad themes. The model is intended to permit many alternatives for accomplishing unit goals and to foster the formation of generalizations.

Social Studies for the Gifted in the Regular Classroom

From their historical analysis of social studies education for the gifted, Ponder and Hirsh (1981) concluded that neither the social science nor the social studies approach is widely used in today's schools. During the 1960s, the social science approach gained impetus from the New Social Studies, which was organized around the structure of the disciplines. After the launching of *Sputnik*, federal funds were allotted to a number of social studies curriculum projects that promoted a hard sciences approach by organizing social studies around the major concepts and modes of inquiry of the social science disciplines. Bruner's *Man: A Course of Study* resulted from one such project. However, recent investigations indicate that schools have not incorporated the inquiry-based reforms of the New Social Studies. Rather, social studies practice continues to consist largely of lecture, recitation, and worksheets based on traditional textbooks (Ponder and Hirsh, 1981). History continues to dominate the social studies curriculum. Moreover, analysis of a small sample of history textbooks suggests that history texts do not reflect the inquiry goals of the social sciences and do not encourage high-level thinking skills (Shermis and Clinkenbeard, 1981).

Efforts to enrich social studies curricula through interdisciplinary emphases on social problems and broad themes have been largely unsuccessful. Current social studies curricula include few interdisciplinary programs, and those that are initiated appear to be short-lived (Ponder and Hirsh, 1981). One reason may be that interdisciplinary programs depart from the familiar structure of the textbook.

Ponder and Hirsh (1981) have suggested that the structure of the regular classroom may not support either inquiry or interdisciplinary approaches; these methods may be more successful in homogeneous classes for the gifted, where students are more independent and task oriented. However, some experts argue against grouping students of homogeneous ability levels for social studies education. The question of whether to place gifted youngsters in homogeneous classes is more than a question relating to academic achievement. It is a question of fundamental philosophy: Should students who are not gifted be arbitrarily deprived of academic and social interactions with their gifted classmates so that the gifted students may achieve more efficiently? Little evidence exists to show that even a basic rationale has been developed for structuring a comprehensive social studies curriculum for the gifted. (However, neither has a rigorous rationale been developed for a comprehensive curriculum to accommodate *both* gifted and nongifted.) The fundamental argument of those who would place gifted social studies students in homogeneous classes is that the gifted can achieve better and more quickly if they do not have interference from the nongifted.

One argument for keeping gifted students in the regular classroom for social studies is the nature of the subject matter. Many modern writers in social studies education, like proponents of the social studies approach, favor inclusion of certain humanities—music, art, drama, architecture, history—in social studies curricula. Placing gifted students in a special social studies class may hinder presentation of an integrated curriculum. Moreover, by definition the content of social studies focuses on human interaction. Taking gifted students from the regular classroom removes them from a real-life social situation and establishes artificial environments in which the gifted study social life without interacting with their nongifted peers. Individuals of all ability levels make up the social fabric. If the schools are to reflect the society in which they exist, it follows that confronting social problems in the company of individuals representative of the larger adult population would be a necessary element of social studies education.

Because social studies differs from other subject areas in its social implications as well as in some academic premises, a rationale can be built for delivering social studies instruction to gifted students within the regular classroom, provided that the special needs of the gifted are met. Organizing social studies instruction around learning centers and utilizing inquiry approaches can satisfy the wide range of abilities, backgrounds, and interests to be found in the typical classroom.

LANGUAGE ARTS

Language arts curricula generally include reading, literature, composition, and oral communication. Students gifted in language arts frequently exhibit such characteristics as early facility in language development and reading; avid interest in reading; frequent and fluent writing, often for pleasure; ability to organize and relate experiences; desire for clarifying and exchanging ideas; a questioning attitude; enjoyment of speech activities such as discussions and conversations; and ability to perceive and produce humor (Miller, 1982; West, 1980). A recent study of intellectually gifted fifth-grade students (IQ 125 or above) indicated that gifted children are superior to their peers of average ability in reading comprehension, especially in answering factual recall questions (Devall, 1982). The gifted children were less adept at questions requiring inference and evaluation than at factual questions. Gifted subjects were also more field-independent than the controls. Drawing from these findings, Devall suggested that gifted students need opportunities for independent investigation, hypothesis testing, evaluation of conclusions, and reporting of results. Dawkins (1978) reported similar results for gifted junior high students, who exhibited weaknesses in figurative language, judgments, inference, and cause–effect relationships.

The characteristics of intellectually gifted students and students gifted in language arts suggest that language arts curricula for the gifted can be differentiated from the standard curriculum through (*a*) telescoping of basic skills (for example, rules of grammar and punctuation), (*b*) emphasis on higher thinking processes (critical thinking, inference, analysis, synthesis, evaluation), (*c*) selection of mature themes (for examples, human foibles, ethics), (*d*) emphasis on creativity (creative reading and creative expression), (*e*) emphasis on mastery of literary classics (content and form), and (*f*) emphasis on oral and written production for wide audiences. Language arts should be treated as an integral part of the total curriculum rather than as a separate subject (Kaplan, 1979b). Integration promotes transfer of skills and knowledge from one discipline to another. The language arts curriculum should include both receptive skills (reading, listening) and expressive skills (speaking, writing) as well as specific content. The following discussion focuses on reading skills and written expression for gifted students.

Reading

Several authors have argued the need for special accommodations in reading and literature for the gifted at the elementary level (e.g., Stank, 1983) and at the secondary level (e.g., Dawkins, 1978; Jensen, 1979). Journals for reading teachers and teachers of the gifted offer practical suggestions for teaching reading to gifted and talented learners (Boothby, 1979, 1980; Cassidy, 1981a; Jensen, 1979; Sakiey, 1980; Switzer and Nourse, 1979; Trezise, 1977, 1978; Vida, 1979). Several books on the subject are also available (e.g., Labuda, 1974; Witty, 1971). However, reading components suggested for gifted readers often differ little from those prescribed for normal readers (Dole and Adams, 1983). Several recent studies have attempted to determine how the teaching of reading for gifted and talented students should differ from the teaching of reading for nongifted learners and whether schools currently provide differentiated programs for the gifted.

To determine how the reading curriculum should be differentiated for gifted learners, Dole and Adams (1983) conducted a national survey whose respondents included forty-three experts in gifted education, thirty-nine experts in reading education, and seventeen experts in both areas. Results indicated that components of a reading curriculum for gifted readers do not differ greatly from components suggested for typical developmental reading curricula. However, experts in gifted education and reading educators tended to agree that for gifted students, emphasis should be given to independent and long-term research projects, research skills, higher-level questioning, individual work with mentors, self-selected reading experiences, involvement with Great Books programs, and guided study of literature genre. Additional research is required to determine whether program differentiation of these components will result in greater reading achievement and more positive attitudes toward reading among gifted students (Dole and Adams, 1983).

McCormick and Swassing (1982) conducted a nationwide survey of school systems to investigate the approaches being used to provide reading instruction to gifted students. Responses from 149 school districts in forty-four states yielded several interesting findings. First, over three-fourths of the districts reported making some type of special reading provisions for gifted learners, most commonly within the regular classroom. Programs outside the regular classroom were under the direction of various individuals—for example, special education teachers and reading specialists. Second, only 17 percent of the districts provided special programs in reading at the kindergarten level. This finding is of particular concern because according to Terman's (1926) study, 44.3 percent of the boys and 46.4 of the girls learned to read before they started school (that is, by age five). Although Cassidy and Vukelich's (1980) study of a small sample of gifted children suggested that a lower percentage of children (17 to 23 percent) are early readers, there is no doubt that a substantial number of gifted children do know how to read before they enter kindergarten. Furthermore, many kindergarten teachers are not aware of a gifted child's reading abilities because the child may not have opportunities to display reading skills in the classroom.

A third finding by McCormick and Swassing was that provisions for reading in the regular classroom included use of higher-level reading materials, placement in a higher grade just for reading, self-paced reading, access to special resource materials libraries, individually planned reading lists, reading-related research projects, and critical reading programs. Finally, while the most frequently reported extraclass reading program was the Junior Great Books program, other programs included critical reading, problem solving, the study of literature, and production of a literary magazine.

In sum, the literature suggests that reading programs for the gifted focus on (*a*) pursuit of student interests, (*b*) development of research skills and the ability to conduct independent investigations, (*c*) instruction in critical and creative reading, and (*d*) understanding and appreciation of the classics and literary genres. (Programs for developing research skills related to reading integrate reading and composition skills and are discussed in the section dealing with writing.) The following subsections describe three elements of reading programs from which gifted students can benefit: critical reading, creative reading, and the study of literature.

Critical Reading Programs. Critical reading emphasizes the ability to discriminate fact from opinion and to evaluate the logic and credibility of written analyses. Boothby (1979) has suggested teaching (*a*) the distinction between connotation and denotation and how connotation can be used to create images, (*b*) an awareness of how language is used in advertising, and (*c*) analysis of editorials. Miller (1982) provides practical suggestions for using the newspaper to promote awareness of propaganda techniques (transfer, testimonial, bandwagon, name calling) and to show how language can be manipulated through analogy and euphemism. One technique is to have students collect political cartoons and discuss why the cartoons appear in the editorial sections, what events inspired the cartoons, how the cartoonist represents fact and opinion, and what historical events or situations are used to make the point.

Creative Reading Programs. The purpose of creative reading is to integrate what is read with previous knowledge and to apply information thus gleaned in new ways. Torrance and Myers (1970) provide a number of guidelines for fostering creative reading. For example, prior to reading, activities should be assigned to stimulate curiosity by confronting students with ambiguities and uncertainties, a problem to be solved, or a gap to be filled. The story itself can have characters who model creative problem solving. The reading material may explore mysteries, require predictions based on limited information, encourage visualization, heighten surprise and suspense, or have an unpredictable outcome. After the reading has been completed, activities should include elaborating on what was read (for example, filling in the details of one character's life); projecting the future, going beyond what was read (for example, anticipating how a character might change or mature if the story were continued); hypothesizing, transforming, or rearranging what was read (for example, retelling the story with a change in one of its elements—time, place, or characterization); returning to previously acquired information to see a new relationship, or returning to an unsolved problem. Martin and Cramond (1983) surveyed fifty-three gifted junior high students in a large southern city to determine how frequently they had experienced creative reading activities in elementary school. Though based on a small sample, their data suggest that creative reading techniques are not widely used in the schools, or at least that students do not recall their being used.

The Study of Literature. For gifted students the study of literature includes analysis, criticism, and appreciation of great works in a variety of genres. Rindfleisch (1981) has suggested that teachers organize literary study for able students around four approaches. The first, *history and chronology*, provides students with a historical perspective that enables them to see how literature is integrated in all aspects of life. The second approach, *genre*, gives students knowledge of the various forms of literature—poetry, novel, short story, fiction, nonfiction— and of how form relates to content, theme, and the times. The third approach, *textual analysis*, involves students in evaluative thinking through the study of structure, style, language usage, and meaning. The fourth approach, *organizing around themes*, helps students understand literature as an attempt to imitate life. Vida (1979) has suggested for elementary-age gifted children several literary genres—biography, realistic fiction, tragedy, and poetry—with themes such as hero identification and the ability to shape one's own destiny.

As a guide for teachers of academically gifted high school English students, Brown (1982) has provided a list of supplementary periodicals in the following categories: literary anthology; cultural and historical heritage; humor; literary criticism; literary, political, and social review; and news. A series of half-hour videotapes called Profiles in Literature was initiated in 1969 by Jaqueline Shachter and Carolyn Field, coordinator of the Office on Work with Children of the Free Public Library of Philadelphia (Shachter, 1979). The videotapes present interviews of outstanding children's authors, artists, and editors and are designed to help motivate students to read literature and improve their writing. Among the award-winning subjects are author-illustrator Jean Craighead George, artist Lynd Ward, and authors Virginia Hamilton and Maurice Sendak.

Writing

Students who evidence high abilities in reading do not necessarily evidence similar talents in written expression. Therefore, language arts curricula for the gifted must emphasize improved writing skills. Newcomer and Goldberg's (1982) study of 107 gifted seventh-grade students suggested that their reading and writing abilities were not highly interrelated. Moreover, while the students tended to be especially efficient in the technical aspects of writing (spelling, handwriting, punctuation, and capitalization), their ability to convey ideas creatively was described as only adequate. The authors blamed the gifted students' relatively weak expressive writing skills on failure of the schools to emphasize creative expression in instruction. Composition objectives for gifted students include (*a*) effective use of the mechanics of language: syntax, word precision, selection of details for support; (*b*) creative expression; and (*c*) effective problem solving, critical thinking, reasoning, and articulation. The approaches described in the following subsections can be used to give gifted students a solid base of writing skills.

Improving Technical Skills and Creative Expression. Stoddard and Renzulli (1983) found that the writing abilities of above-average fifth- and sixth-grade students could be improved through the addition of sentence-combining and creative-thinking activities either within the regular classroom or in a special pullout program. Sentence combining led to improved syntactic maturity. Lessons included such activities as presenting a series of base sentences and having students combine them to form a longer sentence. Use of *New Directions in Creativity* (Renzulli and Callahan, 1976), a five-book series of reproducible worksheets aimed at fluency, flexibility, originality, and elaboration, produced improvements in creativity of written expression. Exercises encouraged use of colorful words and vivid descriptors.

Improving Written Expression through an Integrated Curriculum. It has been argued that ready-made kits and "creativity boosters" provide initial stimulation but are only short-term, gamelike, provisional activities (Master, 1983). Gifted students require something more—namely, a solid, well-integrated, appropriately sequenced curriculum. Kaplan (1979b) has suggested that teachers include three processes in language arts instruction: (*a*) exposure, or introducing of the topic to be learned; (*b*) analysis—for example, dissecting a story's characters; and (*c*) expression, or the "doing" part of the language arts curriculum. For example, in covering science fiction, a unit might integrate literature, science, values, history, and futuristics. The teacher exposes students to science fiction through films, recorded radio broadcasts, short stories, and novels. Students analyze the defining features of the genre and then express their own ideas in an original science fiction story. Alternatively, students might write a composition comparing the new frontier of space with the American frontier of the 1800s.

Master (1983) applied Kaplan's three processes—exposure, analysis, and expression—to writing programs for gifted elementary students. Master argued that programs for the gifted often neglect the first two processes, and instead require students to write without the background, stimulation, and skills provided through exposure and analysis activities.

Improving Written Expression through Problem Solving. Several authors have described writing programs that use individual or small-group research projects as a vehicle for developing writing skills at the elementary and secondary levels (e.g., Cassidy, 1981a; Reynolds, 1981; West, 1980). The Johns Hopkins University Program for Verbally Gifted Youth (PVGY) provides writing skills workshops that follow a problem-posing and problem-solving approach (Reynolds, 1981; Reynolds, Kopelke, and Durden, 1984). The first-year program focuses on the development of accurate and imaginative expository style. The second-year program emphasizes effective analytic writing based on knowledge of the semantic, structural, and rhetorical powers of language. The workshops involve groups of students in resolving problems and discovering writing techniques through the problem-solving process.

Royer (1982) has suggested that students write about a current problem and that specific writing assignments be matched to the level of Bloom's taxonomy appropriate to the student. For example, the teacher might begin with a local problem, such as the anticipated overcrowding of a neighborhood on account of a proposed housing code that would permit private homes to be converted to apartments. A knowledge-level activity would be to have students write a news article that a journalist might write about the situation. Students at the analysis level would write an argument that attacks or defends the proposed housing code. A synthesis activity would be to write an essay explaining how the proposed code should be revised. West (1980) has advocated the following lesson sequence for sixth- through twelfth-grade gifted students.

1. *Interest arousal.* The teacher provides a stimulating experience, such as a film, speaker, recording, or field trip, and guides students in a discussion of concepts, history, and vocabulary. The students relate the new information to previous experience.

2. *Oral language experience.* Students discuss, respond, relate, compare, and analyze. For example, if the stimulus was an artistic film, discussion might center on determining the author's major point, the methods the author uses to convey ideas, and the significance of the ideas projected.

3. *Group planning.* To extend the unit theme, students brainstorm ideas for individual or small-group projects, such as research investigations, creative writing, or film production. Students determine sources of information they will need and procedures for completing the project.

4. *Individual and group creative activities.* Students work on their projects; the teacher provides additional resources. During this time the teacher also arranges whole-group activities related to the unit theme.

5. *Presentation.* Students share their projects in the form of a product, such as a performance, publication, or research report. The whole group helps determine whether a wider audience would be appropriate.

6. *Discussion and critique.* Students critique their own projects with input from the teacher and their peers. Considerations might include time and energy spent, problems encountered, judgments about the product's value, and worth of the experience.

SCIENCE

A prominent feature of modern society is its reliance on technology for both comfort and survival. We rely on technology for transportation, food preparation, heating, medical attention, entertainment, communication, commerce, exploration, and defense. Yet evidence indicates that American schools are not developing a scientifically literate population or fostering achievement of the scientifically gifted students who will carry technology forward.

The National Commission on Excellence in Education (1983) reported that in many industrialized countries, students begin mathematics, biology, chemistry, physics, and geography in grade six and that these subjects are required of all students. Moreover, students in these nations spend three times as many classroom hours on mathematics and science as do scientifically oriented American students (those who select four years of mathematics and science in secondary schools).

Writers in the field of science education for the gifted agree that scientifically gifted students require experience with the unknown as the real subject matter of science (Brandwein, 1981; Scobee and Nash, 1983; Sternberg, 1982; Yager, 1982). Yet a National Assessment of Educational Progress survey indicated that

American adolescents perceive science courses as characterized by facts to be memorized and as allowing few opportunities for student selection of projects. Furthermore, the National Science Foundation has reported that school science programs tend to be characterized by textbooks (Yager, 1982). Teachers use textbooks to determine content, sequence, examples, and applications in science courses; they train students to seek the correct answers as contained in the textbook. Experiments from texts and laboratory manuals, which have predetermined solutions, give students a false impression of the actual process of scientific investigation. Prospective scientists need opportunities to do what scientists really do: original research through problem finding, problem solving, problem reevaluation, and communication of results (Sternberg, 1982). Problem finding, the process of deriving problems of significance, distinguishes between gifted and ordinary scientists (Sternberg, 1982) and cannot be experienced through a textbook. Science programs for gifted students require appropriate goals, identification procedures, instructional strategies, and delivery models.

Goals of Science Education

The education of future scientists has three broad goals: (*a*) mastery of the content of the scientific discipline, (*b*) understanding and application of the actual process of scientific inquiry to produce new knowledge, and (*c*) integration of scientific knowledge with a thorough understanding of the needs of humankind. This last goal requires that future scientists receive a strong education in the humanities and social sciences. Values clarification may facilitate responsible decision making regarding value-laden research areas such as genetic engineering and nuclear energy (Pyryt, 1979) and aim scientific endeavors toward accomplishment of the nation's humanistic goals (Daddario, 1977).

Identification of the Scientifically Gifted

As with other specific talent areas, identification of the scientifically gifted depends substantially on opportunities and encouragement for the development and pursuit of scientific interests. Children whose families have vocational or avocational interests in the sciences and encourage such interests in family members may demonstrate potential for scientific achievement at an early age. However, children who are members of non-science-oriented families and whose elementary education does not emphasize science may not indicate their interest or ability until the secondary years, when science courses are offered. Busse and Mansfield (1981) have pointed out that some late-blooming but highly accomplished scientists did not enter the field until their twenties, showed little interest in science during their school years, and/or demonstrated little excellence in academic pursuits during their school years. When schools have extensive science curricula incorporating instructional methods that encourage independent inquiry, the scientifically gifted identify themselves through their motivation and original research (Brandwein, 1981).

A general IQ score does not predict achievement in a specific academic area such as science (Brandwein, 1981; Pyryt, 1979). Creative production in science seems to require a combination of intellectual, personality, and opportunity factors (Brandwein, 1981). For example, based on their work at the Bronx High School of Science, Kopelman, Galasso, and Strom (1977) found that the creatively gifted in science possess strong motivation toward learning and achieving in science; ability to work independently in laboratory and classroom; curiosity about phenomena; tendency to be stimulated by problem-solving approaches to learning; ability to identify significant problems within a mass of information; ability to induce, deduce, and make connections among ideas; ability to perceive different approaches; creativity and achievement in other areas; skills in relating to peers and elders; and an established set of long-term goals.

Methods and Programs for Science Education

Appropriate methods for teaching content and process objectives in the sciences include inquiry, problem solving, divergent questioning, independent study, and mentoring, all of which have been described in earlier chapters. Cooke (1980), Knutsen (1979), Parker and Kreamer (1983), and Romey (1980) describe applications of these approaches to specific science activities.

Most programs for students gifted in science begin at the secondary level, when students have the opportunity to take science courses and identify themselves as possessing interest and ability in the field. However, gifted children in general also benefit from science education during the preschool, primary, and upper-elementary years.

Preschool and Primary Programs. Science programs for young children focus on (*a*) explorations of a variety of science fields and (*b*) participation in the fundamental processes of scientific study, such as the observation of phenomena. Examples of unit topics in science appropriate for young gifted children include the following:

FIELD	UNIT	SAMPLE CONCEPT
Geology	Rocks and minerals	Rocks have identifiable characteristics.
Meteorology	Weather and seasons	Climatic conditions are related to geographic location.
Biology	Plants and animals	Plants and animals require certain environments.
Ecology	Conservation	Population size is related to availability of natural resources.
Physics	Sound	Some materials are better conductors of sound than others.
Technology	Communication	Forms of communication have changed over time.

One preschool unit on animals included a visit to the zoo, where children observed animals that naturally inhabit arctic regions. Back in class, the children described characteristics that help tundra denizens adapt to and survive in their frozen habitat. Later, children "designed" animals for a newly discovered planet with given climatic and topographical features. For example, given a frozen planet, a five-year-old drew a picture of a spherical animal that was totally covered with fur and moved about by rolling. Lacking appendages, the "roller bear" could not suffer frostbite!

Teachers of preschool and primary school gifted children can introduce basic processes of science—for example, observing, recording, comparing, and predicting—through mini-field trips. For example, in a unit on sound, small groups of preschool students could take a short walk, observing and recording (through words or drawings) things in the environment (playground or park) that produce sound. They might then compare the various sounds in terms of loudness. Later they could attempt to predict the sounds new objects would make.

Upper-Elementary Programs. Gifted students in the fourth, fifth, and sixth grades can continue their explorations of various content areas and participate in more complex processes. Riner (1983) has described steps for developing gifted elementary children's problem-solving skills in science. Examples of observation activities include describing the flying motions of birds, comparing two plants, and explaining why ducks bob their heads. In problem finding, children select a project, such as raising insects, share their experiences, and respond to questions. Children learn note taking through maintenance of a written or tape-recorded log. One activity to stimulate hypothesizing is to mark off an area with a hula hoop, study the area's ecology, explain changes over time, and suggest causes for changes. Students can also compare two areas and hypothesize reasons for the similarities and differences they find.

As students progress, they can begin to focus on one or two science disciplines and their respective methodologies. Formulations of original questions and problems should be encouraged.

Secondary School Programs. At the secondary level, students who possess the ability and interest can complete independent research projects that add knowledge to the chosen field. Gifted students whose interest in science is more general can pursue enrichment activities that provide breadth but permit in-depth follow-up investigations as desired.

One model that provides both enrichment and independent investigation is the University of Iowa's science program for secondary students (Pizzini, 1982). This program offers a variety of experiences designed to supplement the regular science curriculum through exploration or in-depth investigation in a range of science areas, following Renzulli's enrichment triad model described in Chapter 6. Activities include enrichment experiences, field studies, accelerated courses, and research participation programs. Enrichment experiences, such as a canoe trip or a museum visit, begin with planning sessions and conclude with follow-up interviews to determine next steps according to student interest. Field studies involve a weekend to six weeks of study in a "living laboratory," such as a state park. Students take diagnostic tests in science to determine eligibility for accelerated courses that attempt to increase knowledge while developing thinking processes. These courses also permit independent study. Research participation programs permit students to work as team members in research laboratories. The students also participate in a communication course to improve their written and oral skills in scientific reporting.

The Bronx High School of Science specifically prepares students to carry out independent research projects (Galasso and Simon, 1981; Kopelman, Galasso, and Strom, 1977). Among its graduates are several Nobel Prize winners and political leaders, including a cabinet secretary. Although the school emphasizes science and mathematics, students pursue a well-rounded curriculum that includes four years each of English, social studies, and health education; three years of a foreign language; and one year of music and art (Galasso and Simon, 1981).

General Programs. Science programs for the gifted can follow the general models of enrichment, grouping, and acceleration. Abeles (1977) has supported acceleration of science courses at the secondary level. For example, if gifted students take biology in the seventh or eighth grade while the regular sequence places biology in the ninth grade, these students can take advanced courses or explore additional science fields during the eleventh and twelfth grades. In programs for the gifted that provide accelerated sequencing, each science course must be structured to encourage opportunities for problem finding and independent investigation.

Grouping can occur at the regular school or in special schools, such as the Bronx High School of Science. The science center concept provides another grouping alternative. For example, Atamian and Danielson (1977) have described a regional center for science education founded at an abandoned Nike radar site. The center offers weekday courses, Saturday research courses, and a summer research program for gifted students in grades four through twelve. One student's study of the granulation characteristics of a glacial deposit indicated that the deposit had been incorrectly identified on geological maps, and her research paper resulted in the deposit's reidentification.

Museums also serve as science centers for the gifted at both elementary and secondary levels. For example, Ryder (1972) described a docent program conducted at a science museum where gifted elementary students met for half a day per week. They spent one semester on biology and a second on physical science and taught science to museum visitors. Program goals were academic learning, leadership, and improved self-concepts.

The Chicago public schools' cooperative programs at the Field Museum of Natural History, the Shedd Aquarium, the Adler Planetarium, and the Lincoln Park Zoo provide gifted students access to extensive learning laboratories, libraries, collections, documents, and science experts (Maxwell, 1980). At the Field Museum of Natural History, students learn the history and function of museums and conduct special projects that focus on geology, botany, zoology, and anthropology. The Shedd Aquarium program provides first-hand experience in freshwater biology and methods of collecting and processing information. Students compare local rivers and lakes, study food chains, master plankton-sampling techniques, and investigate the impact of industry on fisheries and water quality. Students at the Adler Planetarium study the solar system, space exploration, and the evolution of stars and galaxies. The program culminates in a student-designed sky show. The Lincoln Park Zoo programs permit gifted students to explore a major urban zoo and engage in in-depth study of the behavior, structure, adaptations, locomotion, and diet of reptiles, birds, and mammals.

MATHEMATICS

The type of differentiated program prescribed in mathematics depends on whether the target group consists of children identified as gifted in general intellectual ability or children specifically gifted in mathematics. Enrichment activities in mathematics are frequently aimed at (*a*) broadening applications of mathematics or (*b*) practicing creative thinking through use of numbers. Examples of broadening activities include studying the use of numbers throughout history, reading about the lives of famous mathematicians, writing essays on the aesthetics of numbers, and investigating careers in mathematics. Creative-thinking activities often focus on brain teasers and games, such as a calculator game that requires that students produce a story involving several numbers (for example, 142 barrels and 5 Texans) that, when manipulated, produce an appropriate answer (in this case, multiplying 142 by 5 and holding the calculator upside down yields the word *oil*). While such activities provide time-filling diversions, they do not meet the needs of students specifically gifted in mathematics. Such students are better served through carefully planned, well-articulated accelerated programs.

Accelerated Mathematics Programs

The most well researched and empirically supported model for accelerating mathematically talented students is the Study of Mathematically Precocious Youth (SMPY) developed by Julian Stanley and his associates at Johns Hopkins University (Stanley, 1977, 1985; Stanley and Benbow, 1983). Mathematically gifted students were defined in the study as those having extremely high mathematical aptitude as indicated by their standing in the top 1.0 percent or 0.5 percent of their age group on a nationally normed test such as the Scholastic Achievement Test. Such students master mathematics concepts at a significantly faster rate than do typical above-average and honors students. Mathematically gifted students may not demonstrate outstanding potential in other academic areas, although some do.

The SMPY program assumes that because mathematics learning is sequential and not dependent on the learner's chronological age or life experience, acceleration constitutes the most appropriate instructional approach for the mathematically talented. A second assumption is that because math giftedness is related to math reasoning rather than to computation, the identification process should occur after the school grades in which computation (arithmetic) is mastered but before the grades in which arithmetic reasoning (beginning with algebra) is emphasized. Acceleration therefore generally begins at the end of the sixth grade or during grades seven and eight. Exceptions can be made when younger gifted children demonstrate readiness to learn algebra. SMPY researchers caution that academic acceleration is an appropriate approach only when (a) long-range planning permits continuation of acceleration opportunities, (b) students receive credit for what they learn, and (c) students are strongly motivated to participate in the accelerated program.

Bartkovich and George (1980) have described the two major teaching strategies of the SMPY program as (a) the fast-paced mathematics class and (b) diagnostic testing followed by prescriptive instruction (DT–PI). Distinguishing features of the fast-paced mathematics class are homogeneous grouping, elimination of repetition, and teacher pacing rather than student pacing. The teacher presents concepts and moves ahead when the top one-fourth to one-third of the class understands the concept. Students who have not mastered the topic in class learn the topic through homework. The teacher maximizes student participation by using inquiry approaches—for example, by asking students how to proceed on a problem requiring geometric proof. Students are also asked to induce definitions of new terms such as *equilateral triangle*, from examples. Students frequently work problems on the blackboard. The teacher uses completed homework assignments to detect any conceptual problems. The fast-paced class meets only once a week for two to two and a half hours.

DT–PI is a method of individual or small-group instruction and provides an effective vehicle for accelerating a single student or small numbers of students, as may be necessary in rural areas. The teacher assesses the student's knowledge through a standardized diagnostic test—for example, a test covering Algebra I for a student who has not yet taken an algebra class. Comparing missed test items with an item content classification chart, the teacher determines which concepts the student has not mastered. A program is then prescribed to help the student learn rapidly only those concepts within Algebra I that the student does not know; the student is not required to go through the entire Algebra I text. The student learns the new concepts at a rapid pace, and unnecessary repetition is eliminated. When the student has completed the "course," the teacher administers a standardized test to ensure that the student has mastered all the Algebra I concepts. DT–PI can be used in heterogeneous classes divided into small groups based on ability. The teacher works with each group separately, pacing the groups. While the teacher instructs one group, the others work on given problems. Group interaction is encouraged, and students who master concepts more rapidly than other group members can be moved to a higher group.

Recent evaluations have indicated that students in fast-paced mathematics classes learn precalculus well and three or four times more quickly than pre-scribed in the standard, unaccelerated curriculum. The DT–PI programs pro-duced similar results (Bartkovich and Mezynski, 1981). Both programs require well-qualified mathematics teachers and excellent texts.

Other Models for Mathematics Education

For gifted students in the regular elementary classroom, several authors have suggested enrichment activities such as puzzles, games, and projects (Gibney, 1982; Tucker, 1982; Wagner and Penner, 1982). Sirr (1984) proposed a learning centers approach to differentiating mathematics for gifted elementary students. Such an approach permits acceleration in computation skills, problem solving using manipulatives, and experience with topics not available in the regular program (for example, number theory, logic, and probability). While such activities provide short-term practice in logical thinking and calculating, a well-sequenced curriculum provides more appropriate skill development and un-derstanding for gifted students. Wavrik (1980) has described a mathematics curriculum for gifted elementary students that follows an enrichment rather than an acceleration model and emphasizes creativity. Wavrik's curriculum includes topics such as geometry, probability and statistics, number theory, functions and graphs, topology, combinatorics, scientific and business appli-cations, and use of computers.

Hersberger and Wheatley (1980) have argued that an elementary mathe-matics curriculum for gifted students should not focus on computation but rather on building (*a*) a sound conceptual base for higher mathematics, (*b*) the computational proficiency necessary for studying higher mathematics, (*c*) highly developed problem-solving skills, and (*d*) thinking and learning skills. More recently Wheatley (1983) designed a mathematics curriculum for gifted ele-mentary students based on the assumption that mathematics problem solving can be practiced simultaneously with learning of computational skills, thus increasing motivation and learning. Wheatley's curriculum is divided into strands as follows:

STRAND TOPIC	TIME ALLOCATION
Problem solving	20%
Estimation/mental arithmetic	6%
Numeration	6%
Geometry and measurement	15%
Spatial visualization	5%
Probability and statistics	6%
Arithmetic/algebra concepts	12%
Facts and computations	15%
Applications	5%
Computer programming	10%

Wheatley (1983) also provided a list of instructional materials for strand topics. Although the strands were selected to prepare students for the new technological society, Wheatley offered no information to support their selection or time allocations. In fact, more time may be required than is allotted for facts and computations, which are prerequisite for advanced mathematics. Wheatley's curriculum, however, provides enrichment ideas that may be appropriate for some gifted students.

Several writers have developed enrichment programs in specific areas of mathematics at the secondary level. For example, Kulm (1984) described a thoughtfully constructed geometry enrichment course for gifted eight-grade students that uses a problem-solving approach. Objectives include building on factual knowledge, gaining intuitive foundations, appreciating the need for proof, and experiencing spatial visualization, reasoning, and the form and symmetry of geometry. All these objectives are aimed at developing in students a firm basis for later formal work. Topics include Pythagorean triples, projections from a point, figurate numbers, constructions, cross-sectional drawings of cubes, Euler's formula, transformations, and intersection of planes and lines. The instructor introduces each topic by posing a problem for investigation. Solutions lead to generalizations and hypotheses. Kulm offered the following sample problem from transformational geometry:

> A ball is located at point A on a billiard table, and a different ball is at point B. In what direction should A be hit so that it will hit ball B after striking (1) exactly one side of the table? (2) exactly two sides? (3) exactly three sides?
>
> — Kulm, 1984, p. 151

Shulte (1984) suggested that problems in statistics and probability are appropriate for gifted middle school students because they provide opportunities for reasoning, analyzing, decision making, and predicting and can be solved by students who have skills in computing with whole numbers, decimals, and percentages. Topics in statistics suggested by Shulte include methods for displaying, comparing, and interpreting data. Probability activities might include investigating the fairness of games, explaining paradoxes, and simulating probability situations using a die. An example of a fairness problem follows:

> Three players each flip a coin. If all the coins match (that is, if all are heads or all tails), player A wins a point. If they don't match, there are two possibilities: 2 heads, 1 tail (player B wins a point); 2 tails, 1 head (player C wins a point). Is the game fair?
>
> — Shulte, 1984, p. 154

CHAPTER SUMMARY

Attainment of knowledge in the content areas is a major goal for gifted students. Although higher-order thinking and creative thinking are important, gifted individuals cannot make significant contributions to the various disciplines without possessing a core of knowledge. This chapter has described considerations for educational planning for the gifted in social studies, language arts, science, and mathematics.

Curricula for all children contain these subject areas. However, curricula for the gifted must be differentiated to meet students' needs for more complex, broader, and deeper conceptual knowledge and their higher abilities to analyze, synthesize, and evaluate. Programs for students gifted in specific talent areas should be differentiated from those for gifted students whose abilities lie in other areas. For example, a student gifted in science might require a more intensive science program than is required for a gifted child who has little talent or interest in science.

Language arts curricula for gifted students can be differentiated through telescoping of content, incorporation of higher-level thinking and creative-thinking processes, emphasis on great literature, and demands for excellence in oral and written communication. Social, natural, and physical science programs for the gifted aim at both attainment of knowledge and application of the discipline's specific methods of inquiry. For students gifted in mathematics, carefully planned acceleration appears to be the most appropriate instructional mode.

ACTIVITIES FOR THOUGHT AND DISCUSSION

1. As a consultant on gifted education, would you recommend a social studies or a social science approach to a school district that has expressed a need for a K–12 social studies program for gifted students? Why?

2. Develop a list of readings you might recommend for gifted students in a literature course at a specific grade level. What criteria would you use for selecting readings?

3. Identify the major issues and problems in providing appropriate science education to gifted students. Recommend solutions to the problems.

4. Compare the advantages and disadvantages of acceleration and enrichment in mathematics for mathematically precocious students.

5. Outline goals and instructional procedures for a program for gifted students in one of the following areas: social studies, language arts, science, or mathematics.

SECTION VI

Ecological Perspectives

Chapter Twelve

SPECIAL POPULATIONS

In her presidential address to the Association for the Gifted, Joyce Van Tassel (1980) outlined several trends and issues in gifted education for the eighties, including a need for identification of subpopulations of gifted and talented that have not received appropriate attention: young gifted children, low-income gifted, handicapped gifted, female gifted, and underachieving gifted. To these special populations we add the rural gifted and the extremely gifted since both groups may require considerations different from those of the general population of gifted and talented students.

Extreme caution against overgeneralizing is warranted in any discussion of categories of special learners. Every gifted individual—irrespective of ethnicity, sex, age, or degree of giftedness or disability—is unique in terms of characteristics and needs. When determining the most appropriate placement, services, and objectives for gifted children, teachers must make decisions based on each child's individual profile of strengths and weaknesses. We cannot assume that because a child falls into a specific category (for example, low-income gifted), he or she possesses characteristics and needs ascribed by educators or social scientists to that category. Within each group is a broad range of individual differences due to differences in parenting practices, child personality traits, ability levels, and home, community, and school experiences.

A review of literature on special populations has relevance for educators because (a) knowledge of potential characteristics can help educators understand potential needs of special learners and (b) failure to focus attention on special populations may result in their being ignored and unserved. This chapter describes characteristics, needs, identification issues, and instructional programs for special populations of gifted and talented learners: preschool, low-income and culturally different, handicapped, female, underachieving, rural, and extremely gifted.

YOUNG GIFTED CHILDREN

Increasing interest has been focused on early identification of gifted children and early intervention to encourage development of the child's potential and to prevent later underachievement. Several authors (Fox, 1971; Isaacs, 1963; Whitmore, 1979, 1980) have pointed to lack of support in the early years as one source of underachievement among gifted adolescents. Children who find their first formal school experiences unchallenging and boring may form a chronic antipathy toward school and may evidence poor work habits. Identifying gifted children in the early years also permits early interaction between parents and professionals, which can promote supportive parenting practices and parent advocacy (Karnes, Shwedel, and Linnemeyer, 1982). Parents can learn to foster independence, creativity, leadership, and thinking skills by involving children in decision making, giving rational explanations for rules, applying rules consistently, and demonstrating warmth, achievement values, and appropriately high standards. Early identification and parent training are particularly critical for gifted children from economically disadvantaged backgrounds. Karnes, Shwedel, and Linnemeyer (1982) suggested that parents who gain in-depth understanding of their gifted children during the preschool years will be better advocates for their children in subsequent years.

Despite the need, few special programs exist for gifted children below kindergarten age (Roedell, Jackson, and Robinson, 1980). Jenkins (1979) conducted a nationwide survey of preschool and primary programs for gifted children. Of the 113 programs from twenty-nine states that responded, only 15 were considered preschool; only 8 served preschool or kindergarten children exclusively. Reasons for the sparsity of preschool programs for gifted children include (a) scarcity of funding, (b) lack of preschool personnel trained in gifted education, (c) lack of parent and community awareness of gifted characteristics and special needs, and (d) problems with identification procedures.

Because preschool education generally is not mandated for nonhandicapped children, no systematic procedures exist for identifying gifted children at a young age. Parents from group-oriented cultures whose values mitigate against recognition of individual achievement, as well as parents from cultures that view education as the prerogative of the schools, may not view their gifted children as exceptional or seek assistance outside the home. Parents and preschool teachers who suspect that certain children have exceptional potential often have no resources available for assessment and instructional guidance. Moreover, educators have been reluctant to identify young children as gifted because currently available procedures may not differentiate between nongifted children who are rapid developers and children who are truly precocious. Current measures may also fail to identify gifted children who are late bloomers. In a retrospective study of approximately one hundred gifted children (IQ over 140), Willerman and Fiedler (1974, 1977) found that performance on the Bayley Scales of mental and motor development at eight months of age did not predict intellectual giftedness at ages four or seven. Intelligence tests given in the early years may not accurately predict later intelligence. Despite these problems, we can identify a high proportion of gifted children during the preschool years (ages three to five), and many of these children will benefit from special programs.

Characteristics and Needs of Young Gifted Children

Checklists have been developed by a number of writers (e.g., Karnes and Associates, 1978a, 1978b) to help teachers identify young gifted children in the several talent areas. The characteristics described in the following list are similar to those presented in Chapter 4. In general, young gifted children display these traits, which should be considered in relation to characteristics displayed by other children of the same age, sex, and cultural group:

___ advanced vocabulary and store of information
— early interest in books, numbers, clocks, calendars, puzzles
— preference for being with older children

— long attention span
— possession of extensive collections
— high ability, persistence, and creativity in solving problems
— unusual imagination
— high level of curiosity
— broad or intense interests
— independence and ability to keep busy
— high level of empathy for others
— mature sense of humor
— unusual memory for detail

Not every gifted preschool child displays all these characteristics. For example, the development of information and interests depends to a great extent on the variety and richness of opportunities in the environment. One of the authors met an eighteen-month-old boy who had not yet developed expressive language but whose receptive language was outstanding. The child also demonstrated perfect pitch by picking out on the piano notes sung by the mother. He watched the author intensely as she spoke to the mother and extended his right hand for a handshake as the author was about to leave!

Because of their age, gifted preschool children may evidence uneven development. For example, a three-year-old may read at third-grade level but may not possess the fine motor coordination necessary to form legible letters. A child's advanced speaking vocabulary may mask a lower level of conceptual understanding (Safford, 1978). Uneven development requires that assessment and programming in the basic skill areas constitute an integral part of programs for young gifted children. Gifted preschool children may also experience frustration when they want to pursue some interesting project but need an afternoon nap. Daily schedules should vary indoor and outdoor play periods, exploration time, basic skill development, and academic activities, as well as provide larger blocks of time for long-term independent and group projects.

As in all educational programs, the goals of programs for gifted young children derive from the characteristics and concomitant needs of the children. General goals for the New Mexico State University Preschool for the Gifted are that children will do the following:

— develop a positive attitude toward themselves and toward learning
— develop positive social values and interaction skills, including independence, responsibility, and leadership
— develop competency in the basic skills (expressive and receptive language, fine and gross motor skills, reading readiness and reading, and quantitative concepts)
— broaden interests
— pursue special talents and interest areas
— advance in breadth and depth of knowledge in the academic disciplines (social studies, science, math, humanities)

— develop and utilize effective thinking skills, convergent and divergent
— develop an appreciation and acceptance of different cultures and lifestyles

Programs for Young Gifted Children

Several programs have been developed around the country to serve specific populations of gifted preschool children. Each program follows an established model or combination of models that gives the program direction and consistency in curriculum planning.

New Mexico State University Preschool for the Gifted. The preschool serves twenty minority and majority children, ages three to five, in a half-day program. Under the direction of certified diagnosticians, university students assess children from the community each spring for the coming fall semester. The battery consists of the Stanford–Binet or the Leiter Intelligence Test, the Peabody Individual Achievement Test, the Raven Coloured Progressive Matrices, and Thinking Creatively in Action and Movement by Torrance. A selection committee composed of university and public school personnel in gifted education, a certified diagnostician, and a parent determine (*a*) whether the child can be considered gifted according to state guidelines and (*b*) whether the child would benefit from the preschool program. State guidelines generally require that the child perform at a level of two standard deviations above the mean, or above the ninety-fifth percentile on at least two of four measures.

The instructional program is organized around three components: basic skill development, thematic units, and multicultural education. These components are designed to accommodate the developmental, advanced intellectual, and cultural/linguistic needs of the target population. Criterion-referenced assessment conducted at the beginning of the school year provides a baseline for development of an individualized educational program in the basic skills. Thematic units, each four to six weeks long, combine process and content objectives in a logically sequenced curriculum of humanities, arts, and sciences. Unit topics have included The Self, Sound, Computers, Careers, and Energy. Each unit activity combines content and process objectives with instructional procedures based on an established teaching model—for example, Bloom's taxonomy, Taba's inductive methods, Suchman's inquiry approach, or Torrance's creative questioning techniques (see Kitano, 1982, for sample units). The multicultural component consists of (*a*) sharing of cultural experiences through social studies, art, music, and cooking activities and (*b*) daily bilingual (Spanish and English) discussion of the calendar and other events of group interest. A sample schedule follows:

8:30	Self-selected activities and projects, such as dramatic play, water or block play, toys and games, art, cooking, or reading; individual instruction
9:20	Calendar and sharing; creative movement
9:25	Unit studies (whole group)

9:50	Outdoor play
10:15	Snacks
10:25	Individual or small-group work (basic skill development); continuation of unit activities
11:00	Story time
11:15	Dismissal

The children's progress is evaluated through teacher observation, parent questionnaire reports, and end-of-year performance on the Peabody Individual Achievement Test and the Raven Coloured Progressive Matrices.

Seattle Child Development Preschool. Under the direction of the late Halbert Robinson, the Child Development Preschool of the University of Washington became in 1976 a center for research and curriculum development in the education of gifted preschool children (Robinson and Roedell, 1980; Robinson, Roedell, and Jackson, 1979; Roedell, Jackson, and Robinson, 1980). In 1982 the preschool was incorporated as a nonprofit organization under parent direction. Children are selected on the basis of a comprehensive parent questionnaire, the short-form Stanford–Binet, an informal reading assessment, and various subtests from the Wechsler intelligence scales. Children are grouped by competence levels for structured activities in language arts, reading, science, mathematics, social skills, art, drama, and creative movement. The development of social skills constitutes an important component of the preschool curriculum and emphasizes independence, assertiveness, social sensitivity, formation of friendships, and problem solving.

University of Illinois, Champaign–Urbana Programs. The University of Illinois Preschool Gifted Project serves ten gifted children mainstreamed with ten children of average ability (Karnes and Bertschi, 1978; Karnes, Shwedel, and Linnemeyer, 1982). The assessment battery includes a test of intelligence (Stanford–Binet), a test of creativity (Thinking Creatively in Action and Movement), and a test of perceptual-motor-cognitive ability (Harris Draw-a-Man). Children qualify for the program by scoring two standard deviations above the mean on any single test, or one and one-half standard deviations above the mean on any two. The Seattle Gifted Preschool Project's parent questionnaire is also used. Program goals focus on development of self-concept, interpersonal skills, attitudes toward school, task commitment, risk taking, and creative and higher-level thinking skills. The project combines the open-classroom approach for pursuit of interests and independent projects with Guilford's structure-of-intellect model to encourage thinking processes.

The Retrieval and Acceleration of Promising Young Handicapped and Talented Project (RAPYHT), also at the University of Illinois, was developed for young gifted and talented handicapped preschoolers. Handicapped children are referred on the basis of the preschool talents checklists (Karnes and Associates,

1978a, 1979b). Follow-up data include information from teacher interviews, individual child assessment, and consultation and trial programming. One RAPYHT classroom uses an open-classroom approach, while a second employs a teacher-directed model. The project has developed separate curriculum guides for nurturing intellectual, creative, academic, leadership, artistic, and psychomotor talent (Karnes and Associates, 1978c). Parents play an integral role as members of the interdisciplinary team that determines each child's educational plan. Evaluation studies of RAPYHT indicate short-term gains in self-concept, motivation, creativity, and talent-area functioning (Karnes, Shwedel, and Lewis, 1983b), as well as long-term benefits (Karnes, Shwedel, and Lewis, 1983a).

Hunter College Elementary School. The Hunter College Elementary School is located at Hunter College in New York City. Children are screened for the gifted preschool program according to performance on the Stanford–Binet Intelligence Test administered by a private agency and according to descriptions of test-taking behavior. The highest-scoring majority children and the highest-scoring minority children (ratio 60:40) are invited to spend half a day at the school, where they are observed by specialists and administered a creativity scale and a task commitment measure (McCarthy, 1982, personal communication). The curriculum emphasizes traditional academic skills and second-language learning in a playfully creative atmosphere and involves children in independent projects and unit activities (Camp, 1963; Roedell, Jackson, and Robinson, 1980).

The Astor Program. The Astor Program, Level I, is a public school program in New York City that serves four- and five-year-old gifted children. Identification procedures include a telephone screening interview of the parents and psychological testing using the Stanford–Binet, the Wide Range Achievement Test, a figure-drawing test (Goodenough), and others as indicated. The Astor program focuses on the higher-level skills of Bloom's taxonomy as well as on academic skills and creative investigation (Ehrlich, 1980; Roedell, Jackson, and Robinson, 1980).

Experiences with these and other programs (e.g., Bauer and Harris, 1979; Vantassel-Baska, Schuler, and Lipschutz, 1982) indicate that young gifted children make academic and social-affective gains in preschool programs designed to meet their needs. Karnes (1980) described thirteen elements of exemplary preschool/primary programs for gifted children: program advocates, a specialist consultant, well-defined identification procedures, a conceptual model, flexible administrative arrangements, clearly defined program goals with appropriate instructional methods, an environment conducive to learning, ample and appropriate instructional materials, competent teachers, parent involvement, program evaluation, in-service training, and program continuity after "graduation."

THE LOW-INCOME AND CULTURALLY DIVERSE GIFTED

Although ethnic minorities are represented in every social class, a disproportionately high number of certain minority groups, such as blacks and Hispanics, come from low-income backgrounds. Therefore, it is difficult to separate out the effects of economic class and racial origin. However, several points must be kept in mind in any discussion of low-income and culturally diverse populations. First, in many performance areas middle-class minorities behave more similarly to middle-class whites than to lower-class minorities. Second, many middle- and upper-class minority families retain cultural values and behaviors different from the values and behaviors of the majority culture. Third, although cultural groups such as black, Hispanic, Native American, and Asian can be described in terms of recognizable sets of values and child-rearing practices, wide differences exist within each group. These intragroup differences may stem from a number of variables, including generation in the United States, geographical location, density of the minority population, social class, education level, variety of life experiences, and perhaps the intellectual and personality characteristics of the individual. Finally, many low-income homes provide a quality learning environment and are not disadvantaged. In sum, a major problem to avoid is the indiscriminate application of stereotypical descriptions to each minority or low-income individual encountered.

Despite these caveats, recognition of the special challenges presented in educating low-income and culturally diverse gifted children is critical both to the children's development and to the nation's development of human resources. Before its repeal in 1981, the Gifted and Talented Children's Education Act of 1978 specified as a priority the funding of projects to identify and meet the needs of disadvantaged gifted and talented children from low-income families. The urgency of this objective is easily recognized when one considers that innate potential is not immutable; lack of appropriate stimulation over the formative years will suppress intellectual capacity.

Ethnic minority children continue to be underrepresented in classes for the gifted, especially in regions highly populated by minorities. For example, Baca and Chinn (1982) cited the following data:

— In a 1980 Office of Civil Rights study, blacks constituted 15.7 percent of the surveyed sample but only 10 percent of the gifted within the sample.
— In the South, blacks constitute 26.8 percent of the total school population but only 12 percent of the gifted population.
— In the western states, the number of Hispanics in gifted classes is less than half of what would be expected from their numbers in the general population.

Likewise, High and Udall (1983) found that in a southwestern school district whose minority population was 42.6 percent, minorities constituted only 11 percent of students in the gifted program.

Gifted migrant children form a highly neglected subpopulation of the low-income and culturally different gifted. A migrant child is defined as a child of a worker in agriculture or food processing related to agriculture or a child of a fisherman who has moved from one district to another within a twelve-month period (Hamilton, 1984). Gifted migrant children are particularly difficult to identify and serve due to their high mobility and linguistic differences, and to the difficulty of obtaining the support of their parents, who frequently lack high school educations. Migrant children may evidence significant disadvantages due to the absence of possessions such as toys and books, educational television, and writing materials, which provide experience for academic readiness.

Identifying Low-Income and Minority Gifted Children

The obstacle to achieving more representative percentages of low-income and minority children in programs for the gifted continues to lie in the identification process. Educators generally agree that low-income and culturally different gifted children are underidentified and underserved. One problem concerns low referral rates from parents and teachers. Even in a community heavily populated by low-income and minority families, few parents seem spontaneously to perceive their children as gifted or as requiring special educational services. By the time they reach school age, gifted children from severely economically disadvantaged homes frequently do not appear exceptionally talented. Culturally different gifted children may manifest their high abilities in ways unlike those of children from the majority culture. Culturally different gifted children may also evade recognition. Moreover, teacher attitudes toward culturally different students may affect referral rates (High and Udall, 1983).

The standardized test scores of low-income and minority children who participate in districtwide screening or who are referred for individual assessment may not reflect their exceptional potential. Due to cultural loading, traditional intelligence tests may discriminate against children from lower-class backgrounds as well as children from culturally diverse backgrounds (MacMillan, 1982).

Several arguments have been made against use of standardized tests for minority children. For example, the tests have been criticized as culturally biased in terms of content. However, efforts to develop culture-fair and culture-free tests have failed to produce instruments that eliminate bias. Minority students do not tend to perform better on culture-fair tests than on traditional intelligence measures. Moreover, culture-fair tests do not predict school success as well as do traditional intelligence instruments.

Additional criticisms of standardized tests concern (*a*) the testing of minority children on instruments that have not included children of the same minority cultures in the standardization sample, (*b*) depressed student motivation due to lack of familiarity with test situations and majority-culture examiners, and (c) the validity of traditional measures for linguistically different children. Research on the effects of examiner ethnicity has not been conclusive, but little evidence exists to show that testing in black dialect or in Spanish significantly improves test scores for bilingual children (Sattler, 1973). Obviously, monolingual non–English speakers require testing in their native language.

No perfect solutions to the problem of underidentification of low-income and culturally different gifted children currently exist. However, the suggestions that follow deserve consideration.

Recruitment through Community and Parent Awareness Programs. Coordinators of gifted programs can train community liaison persons (religious and community leaders, parents, day-care workers, health and social service personnel, pediatricians) to recognize referral characteristics and to inform parents of available programs. Awareness programs can also develop and distribute bilingual brochures explaining the rationale for gifted education, referral characteristics, and available services. Preschool screening clinics can be held in a community center and advertised in supermarkets, retail stores, and community service centers as well as on radio and television and in newspapers. Finally, awareness programs can provide in-service training for all public school personnel regarding referral characteristics and procedures.

Assessment and Selection through Multiple Measures and a Case Study Approach. Standardized individual intelligence measures should be included in the battery because some low-income, minority, and underachieving students perform well on these measures. Intelligence tests can provide useful information when their shortcomings are recognized and scores are interpreted appropriately. However, no single test score should be used as the sole criterion of giftedness or program eligibility. Eligibility criteria should permit inclusion of students who demonstrate high performance capability on any one (Bernal, 1979) or two of several measures that test abilities in areas consistent with program goals.

Proportionate Representation of Cultural and Economic Groups. Gifted programs should reflect the cultural and economic mix of the community. For example, one school district in New Mexico serves a tricultural community composed of Anglos (40 percent), Hispanics (30 percent), and Native Americans (30 percent). Spaces are reserved in the gifted program according to a 4:3:3 ratio. The district fills these spaces with the children who score highest (above minimum criteria) in each cultural group. LeRose (1978) has also described a quota system for gifted minority preschool children.

Provided that all students are screened or identified through an effective referral system, the quota approach helps ensure delivery of special services to talented students from each cultural group. One potential problem is that students in a low-scoring cultural group may be selected for the program to fill the group's quota while higher-scoring students in a different group are denied admission. Also, because scores of children who rank at the top of each group may vary from school to school, children identified for special services in one location may be denied such services in another. For additional comments on quota systems, see Hersberger and Asher (1980).

Test Measures and Procedures that Reduce Cultural Bias. The Torrance Tests of Creative Thinking and the Alpha Biographical Inventory appear to produce little or no difference in performance between black and white students (Torrance, 1977). Primarily using group measures, creativity, ability to perceive symbolic equivalence, and self-description, Chambers, Barron, and Sprecher (1980) have developed a method to identify gifted elementary-age Hispanic children. Ryan (1983) found that parent descriptions and the Leiter Intelligence Test may be more effective in identifying intellectually superior black children than teacher nomination, the Stanford–Binet test, the Draw-a-Man test, or pupil products. Use of the Scales for Rating the Behavioral Characteristics of Superior Students (SRBCSS) with culturally different children requires further study. Argulewicz, Elliott, and Hall (1982) found that Anglo gifted students score significantly higher than Mexican-American gifted students on the learning and motivation scales of the SRBCSS, although the two groups are rated similarly on the creativity and leadership scales.

Based on her work with the SOI Learning Abilities Test, Meeker (1978, 1981) has predicted development of a specific, nonbiased screening measure to identify cognitively gifted minority children. Meeker's investigations of gifted minority children through use of the Stanford–Binet with a structure-of-intellect analysis and the SOI Learning Abilities Test indicated that each group displayed a unique pattern of strengths and weaknesses. Disadvantaged Anglo boys exhibited high abilities on verbal subtests, convergent thinking, and some creativity subtests but not on evaluation. Disadvantaged blacks demonstrated strengths in arithmetic and nonverbal abilities. Hispanics scored high on comprehension subtests and showed nonverbal and spatial numerical strengths. Analysis of scores of Navajo children showed low semantic skills, high figural ability, and low classification skills in the figural dimension.

One procedure that has potential for reducing cultural bias in the identification process is the System of Multicultural Pluralistic Assessment (SOMPA) developed by sociologist Jane Mercer (Mercer, 1981; Mercer and Lewis, 1978). The SOMPA procedure utilizes (*a*) the Adaptive Behavior Inventory for Children (ABIC), (*b*) the Wechsler Intelligence Scale for Children–Revised (WISC–R), and (*c*) a measure of sociocultural characteristics. The ABIC is employed as a measure of social role behavior based on the child's role performance in the family, in the community, with peers, in nonacademic school situations, as an earner and consumer, and in self-maintenance. The WISC–R provides a measure of school functioning level. Four scales are used to measure sociocultural characteristics: urban acculturation, socioeconomic status, family structure, and family size. The child's WISC–R score is adjusted statistically based on his or her scores on the sociocultural scales. The adjusted WISC–R score yields an index of Estimated Learning Potential (ELP), which provides a comparison of the child's potential with the potential of others from precisely the same cultural and economic background.

Mercer and Lewis (1978) suggest that both the ABIC and the ELP scores may be useful in identifying gifted minority children. Case studies described by Mercer and Lewis illustrate how ELP scores may be more consistent with teacher estimates of potential and may qualify more minority children as gifted. One inner-city black child, for example, achieved a verbal score of 111, a performance score of 109, and a full-scale IQ of 111 on the WISC–R. Her estimated learning potential scores were 130 on the verbal scale, 128 on the performance scale, and 134 on the full scale.

Although SOMPA was developed to prevent mislabeling of minority children as mentally retarded, the approach may be useful in identifying gifted minority children (Mercer and Lewis, 1978). More research is needed to determine the predictive validity of estimated learning potential in identifying gifted children. Oakland (1980), for example, found that correlations between ELP and achievement were lower than correlations between WISC–R scores and achievement. As with the quota system, SOMPA's reliance on multiple norms raises the issues of using different criteria for different ethnic groups.

Another approach that may have potential in identifying culturally different gifted students is the inclusion of cognitive style measures in assessment batteries. DeLeon (1983b) has argued that culturally related differences in field independence–dependence may affect performance on standardized intelligence and achievement tests and that consideration of style differences may help in the identification of gifted minority students. For example, much of the literature on Hispanic children describes them as having a field-dependent, holistic style of responding, while traditional tests require field-independent, analytic modes of response.

Characteristics and Needs of the Low-Income and Minority Gifted

It is at best difficult to describe characteristics and needs of low-income and culturally diverse gifted children because the category encompasses a variety of distinctly different cultural groups: blacks, Hispanics, Native Americans, Asian-Americans, Pacific Americans, and disadvantaged whites. Each of these groups further includes a number of unique subgroups. For example, there are over two hundred tribes of North American Indians; Chinese, Japanese, Korean, Filipino, Vietnamese, Cambodian, Laotian, Samoan, Hawaiian, and Chamorro (from Guam) children must be counted among Asian-American and Pacific American subgroups.

Efforts have been made to pinpoint characteristics of gifted children from specific cultural groups. As noted in Chapter 4, Torrance (1977) identified a number of strengths that he suggests may be applicable to blacks, Native Americans, Hispanics, and Appalachian whites. Torrance's "creative positives" include ability to express feelings and emotions and to improvise with commonplace materials, enjoyment and ability in the visual and performing arts, figural creativity, responsiveness to the concrete and kinesthetic, humor, skills in group activity, persistence in problem solving, emotional responsiveness, and quickness of warmup. Torrance also provides suggestions for identifying these strengths and for using them to motivate learning.

Based on three hundred interviews with barrio residents in three Texas communities, Bernal (1978) reported the following to be characteristic of gifted Mexican-American children: rapid acquisition of English, leadership and interpersonal skills, play and interaction with older children, ease with adults, effective risk-taking behavior, ability to keep busy and entertained, acceptance of responsibility reserved for older children, and street-wise behavior. Perrone and Aleman (1983) have warned that gifted Mexican-American children may not ask many questions because questions are frequently discouraged by overworked parents. Moreover, the school system's expectations for individual competition and self-initiative may conflict with Mexican-American cultural values of cooperation, obedience, and group direction. Perrone and Aleman suggest that language-manipulation abilities best characterize gifted Mexican-American children. Bilingual Mexican-American children may demonstrate facility in manipulating both Spanish and English to convey more subtle and finer meanings. They also may create new words using the two languages in unique combinations.

There is some, albeit conflicting, evidence to suggest that bilingual children score higher than their monolingual peers on creativity measures. Price-Williams and Ramirez (1977) found that bilingual Mexican-American and black elementary-age boys performed better than Anglo boys on fluency and flexibility. Based on a different measure, findings from an earlier study of Chinese and Malayan children (Torrance et al., 1970) indicated that monolinguals excelled over bilinguals on fluency and flexibility but that the opposite was true for originality and elaboration.

Puerto Rican children represent a cultural group distinct from the Mexican-American. However, as with Mexican-American children, the talents of gifted Puerto Rican children may not be recognized easily because of differences between the culture of the home and that of the school. Perrone and Aleman (1983) have described the Puerto Rican culture as not valuing individualism, assertiveness, and competition so much as cooperation and interdependence of family members. Differentiation of home responsibilities based on distinct sex roles incompatible with school expectations may cause hesitancy or conflict in children's behavior. Perrone and Aleman suggest that curriculum planners take into consideration the real-life issues with which many Puerto Rican children in the United States must deal—for example, single-parent families, unemployment, discrimination, substance abuse, and crime.

American Indian values also encourage interdependence and collective decision making. Emphasis is also placed on the individual's relationship to and respect for nature. Programs for gifted Native American children should be sensitive to the conflicts produced by the desire to maintain traditional beliefs, customs, and language in the face of American technology and consumerism (Perrone and Aleman, 1983). Preliminary findings from an anthropological study of Navajo concepts of giftedness (cited in Maker, 1983) suggest that one such concept is the capacity for great or good thought, which perhaps may be manifested by listening without being distracted, by having questions about what is heard, by exhibiting awareness of what is on another's mind, and by comprehending.

Little information is available concerning characteristics of gifted Asian-American and Pacific American students. Kitano (1983) has described cultural values, child-rearing practices, and learning attributes of seven subgroups, finding both intergroup and intragroup differences. In a study of disadvantaged gifted Asian-American children, Chen and Goon (1976) interviewed teachers and guidance counselors at seven elementary schools located in the greater Chinatown area of New York. Compared to gifted non-Asian children, gifted Asian children were described as getting along better with others, especially adults; working more diligently; demonstrating humor and sarcasm without viciousness; and being strong in math. Although English was the children's second language, their verbal ability was reported as equal to or greater than that of their non-Asian gifted peers. The seven participating schools had Asian enrollments ranging from 11.12 to 99.04 percent. Within these schools the proportion of sixth-grade Asian children recommended for gifted programs ranged from 38.9 to 100 percent. Among the total number of Asians in the sixth grade, 11.8 to 26.9 percent were referred as gifted. One concern of Asian-American educators is whether some Asian-American children labeled as gifted are instead high achievers who conform to teacher expectations of behavior. Such children may experience pressure for performance to an unhealthy extent (Kitano, 1975).

The literature rarely separates characteristics of low-income gifted children from those of gifted minorities. However, in one study Frierson (1965) compared characteristics of four groups of elementary school children matched according to age, grade, ethnic background, and school experience. The children were grouped as (a) upper socioeconomic status (SES) gifted, (b) lower SES gifted, (c) upper SES average, and (d) lower SES average. Results indicated significant differences between lower and upper SES gifted groups. Upper SES gifted demonstrated (a) greater desire to read during nonschool hours, (b) reading of more educational magazines, and (c) knowledge that their parents wanted them to go to college. The lower SES gifted indicated (a) greater preference for adventure-hero comics, (b) lower grades in science, (c) greater dislike of school, (d) greater preference for competitive sports, and (e) higher creativity scores.

The lower SES gifted children differed from lower SES average children in that the lower SES gifted (a) were more likely to play musical instruments, (b) aspired to higher-status occupations, (c) were more likely to read the news sections of the newspaper, (d) made up more games to play, (e) tended to read more "classic" and "true" comic books, and (f) earned their highest grades in reading.

Curriculum and Instructional Planning for the Low-Income and Minority Gifted

Little agreement exists regarding what constitutes the best program for low-income and culturally different gifted students. Obviously, monolingual non–English speakers require special instructional methods and materials. Bilingual–bicultural instruction would be appropriate for bilingual gifted children who desire to maintain their home language and culture. Diaz et al. (1983) have developed a curriculum guide for gifted and talented Hispanic and Haitian limited-English-proficient students, supported by a Title VII bilingual exceptional student education demonstration grant. The curriculum takes into consideration gifted students' ability to learn language rapidly and through unconventional methods. The curriculum encourages cooperative work as well as independence and task commitment.

For gifted low-income and minority children whose dominant language is English, program recommendations do not differ substantively from those for other gifted children. Sato (1974), Strobert and Alvarez (1982), and the National/State Leadership Training Institute on the Gifted and Talented (1981) provide descriptions of specific programs and suggestions for working with the culturally different gifted. Several program components require special emphasis for low-income and culturally diverse gifted students; these components are listed in the following paragraphs.

1. *Teachers who are sensitive to cultural differences.* Such teachers recognize that low-income and culturally different children do not differ from middle-income majority students in basic abilities and potential but rather in the contexts in which these abilities and potential are expressed (Cole and Bruner, 1971). Sensitive teachers structure the learning environment to bring out students' already existing abilities and to help students generalize their skills to other situations.

2. *Broad exposure.* Children whose home lives have been limited by economic conditions or who lack familiarity with a variety of cultures need exposure to a range of experiences. For example, some gifted children in the inner-city areas of Los Angeles have never seen the Pacific Ocean. Depending on the individual child, experiences may include visits to zoos, museums, libraries, art galleries, concerts, science centers, and geological sites.

3. *Multicultural awareness.* The program should expose children to a variety of cultural lifestyles, traditions, and beliefs. Instruction in academics might incorporate culturally relevant examples—for example, a unit on American literature might include works by black, Hispanic, Native American, and Asian-American authors and poets along with the works of Whitman, Emerson, Mel-

ville, and Dickinson. Multicultural awareness is also important for programs composed primarily of middle-class majority students.

4. *Role models.* Where possible, guest speakers, mentors, and other program participants should be representatives of the target cultural groups. Role models help students realize that people from backgrounds similar to their own have made outstanding achievements.

5. *Use of cultural strengths.* Torrance (1977) has suggested ways in which teachers can capitalize on the strengths of culturally diverse children to motivate learning. For example, a talent for improvisation with commonplace materials can be an asset in arts-and-crafts and drama projects. Group orientation, common to many minority children, can be effectively utilized in group projects and group competitions.

6. *Counseling and instruction for skill development.* For students who need to upgrade their academic skills (especially oral and written communication) and to increase self-direction and control, the program should provide a combination of counseling and direct instruction (Frasier, 1979).

THE GIFTED HANDICAPPED

Recent years have witnessed a growing awareness of the special needs of handicapped children who are also gifted. Handicapping conditions generally include speech impairments, mental retardation, specific learning disabilities (normal intelligence with inability to read, spell, calculate, or perform in other academic areas), behavior disorders/emotional disturbances, hearing impairment, visual impairment, physical (orthopedic or health) impairment, and multiple disabilities such as deafness-blindness. Eligibility for special education services usually requires that the impairment prevent the student from being appropriately accommodated in the regular program without special assistance. Individuals having any handicap except mental retardation can possess exceptional talent in intellectual, academic, creative, leadership, and/or artistic areas. However, mentally retarded individuals can be gifted in the visual and performing arts. For example, Yoshihiko Yamamoto, considered "a Van Gogh of Japan," has an estimated IQ of 40 and severe speech and hearing impairments (Morishima, 1974).

One has only to think of Helen Keller (deaf-blind), Albert Einstein (learning-disabled), Itzhak Perlman (physically impaired), and Mel Tillis (speech-impaired) to realize that people can possess both talent and handicapping conditions. However, the exceptional potential of many gifted handicapped children goes unrecognized and/or undeveloped because of several factors. First, when working with handicapped children, parents and educators often focus on remediating weaknesses, sometimes to the virtual exclusion of improving strengths. Given a profile of a gifted student's abilities, teachers of the handicapped often tend to perceive areas of lower functioning as "weaknesses" to be remediated, even though all abilities are depicted at or above chronological age-expectancy level. Special classes for the handicapped tend to focus on basic skills, omitting science, social studies, and creative problem solving from the curriculum. Placed in such classrooms, gifted handicapped students have limited opportunities to demonstrate and develop their superior abilities. Yet, given training in gifted characteristics, needs, and teaching methods, teachers of the handicapped can be effective providers of services to gifted handicapped students because of their sensitivity to individual differences and their already existing skill in individualizing instruction.

A second problem is that gifted handicapped children's physical or perceptual impairments may hinder their performance on traditional assessment devices; thus, scores may fail to reflect the children's actual potential. For example, the performance of learning-disabled children who have visual perception and reading difficulties will be negatively affected on tests that require visual perception and reading skills. Similarly, a gifted child who has cerebral palsy and severe speech impairments will do poorly on tests requiring traditional oral or written responses. Temporary developmental delays in young children as a consequence of specific handicaps may also impede accurate assessment of potential in young gifted handicapped children (Whitmore, 1981). For example, a blind three-year-old child may exhibit a delay in abstract thinking due to inability to perceive and hence process visual images. The exceptional abilities of behavior-disordered children are frequently not discovered until these children are assessed after referral for behavior problems.

Maker (1977) has suggested a combination of three approaches to improve identification of gifted handicapped students: (a) look for potential rather than demonstrated abilities by using, for example, a biographical inventory; (b) compare handicapped students' performance with the performance of members of their own subgroup; and (c) observe how students compensate for the handicapping condition and give more weight to characteristics that enable them to adapt. With deaf children, for example, nonverbal communication skills may provide the best indicators of potential; for learning-disabled children, abstract thinking and problem solving might be given more weight than reading or writing skills.

A third obstacle to providing appropriate services to gifted handicapped children concerns inflexible funding formulas. Some school districts have regulations that prohibit funding the same child in two categories of exceptionality, such as gifted and emotionally disturbed. Where no services specifically for the gifted handicapped are available, school personnel and parents often are asked to choose between two placements—a program for gifted students or one for the emotionally disturbed—neither of which provides services geared to the needs of the gifted handicapped student. In such districts the gifted handicapped frequently are placed according to their handicapping condition. Providing the teacher with a resource specialist in gifted education can help ensure individual programming suitable to the student's unique needs. Where the gifted handicapped receive instruction in a program for gifted students, a resource specialist in handicapped education can serve in a similar way.

Because of the relatively small numbers and heterogeneous nature of gifted handicapped students, many school districts do not find it financially feasible to offer special programs for the gifted handicapped. The Department of Education reported that the number of handicapped individuals (under age twenty-one) served in 1980–81 under P.L. 94–142 and P.L. 89–313 was 4,177,934 (Haring, 1982). Considering that the actual number of handicapped individuals exceeds the number served, the number of gifted handicapped individuals under twenty-one can be conservatively estimated at 41,779 to 125,338 (1 to 3 percent of the total handicapped population). Estimates based on 1976 figures were 120,000 to 180,000 (Whitmore, 1981).

A small school district will have proportionately few gifted handicapped students, each with uniquely different needs. For example, one child may be artistically gifted and mentally retarded, another scientifically gifted and orthopedically impaired, and a third highly intelligent and deaf. Obviously, the same placement or services would not be appropriate for each student. Rather, the gifted handicapped require special provisions based on individual strengths and weaknesses (Maker, 1977).

Another factor that hinders identification and appropriate program development for gifted handicapped students is the scarcity of personnel knowledgeable in both handicapped and gifted education. Whatever the student's placement, a transdisciplinary approach must involve regular teachers, special education teachers, support personnel as required (speech, physical, or occupational therapists), teachers of the gifted, and parents in the formulation and implementation of individualized educational plans (Pledgie, 1982).

Characteristics and Needs of the Gifted Handicapped

Several checklists have been developed specifically for identifying gifted handicapped students (Ford and Ford, 1981; Karnes and Associates, 1978a, 1978b; Pledgie, 1982). Identifying characteristics of giftedness in handicapped students are the same as those for nonhandicapped students, except that expression of the characteristics will be limited to their intact modalities. For example, gifted learning-disabled children who have specific deficiencies in reading, writing, spelling, arithmetic, and/or perceptual–motor skills may exhibit (a) high abilities in oral language, comprehension, memory, problem solving, or creativity; (b) advanced knowledge; (c) keen interests; and/or (d) superior sensitivity and humor (Whitmore, 1981).

In a study of thirty learning-disabled children with superior intelligence (at least one IQ score over 120), Schiff, Kaufman, and Kaufman (1981) found that the children exhibited strengths in verbal comprehension, expression, and conceptualization, as well as creative talents. Their relative weaknesses were in sequencing, distractibility, and motor coordination. Many of the students demonstrated talent in art, music, poetry, electronics, business, and science. The authors mentioned one child who built computer boards by age ten and another who served on the high school debate team despite severe writing and spelling disabilities. Ellis-Schwabe and Conroy (1983) compared small samples of learning-disabled, gifted, and gifted learning-disabled students. They found that the gifted learning-disabled performed well on creativity measures.

Gifted students whose handicapping conditions limit oral communication (for example, students with cerebral palsy or deafness) may evidence (a) strong desire to communicate through alternative modes, such as gesturing, writing, or using a communication board; (b) superior problem solving and memory; and (c) exceptional interest and motivation in response to challenge (Whitmore, 1981). For example, a junior high student embarrassed by his speech impediment responded little in his classes. A serious illness kept him out of school for several months, and upon his return school administrators suggested grade retention. His parents protested, arguing that their son was highly capable of being promoted. A thorough assessment by the school psychologist revealed outstanding intellectual abilities that were corroborated by his written work.

Gifted students with behavior disorders may display (a) high verbal skills, (b) exceptional capacity to manipulate others, (c) high problem-solving ability, and (d) outstanding general knowledge and memory (Whitmore, 1981). One of the authors worked with an adolescent behavior-disordered girl who, inspired by a drama unit, "performed" as an angry, hateful stepdaughter during a videotaped counseling session. So convincing was the performance that, after reviewing the tape, her psychiatrist diagnosed the girl as a potential murderess. It took further interviews and investigations to reveal that the girl had been using the videotaped counseling sessions as a chance to try out her acting talents. After finishing high school, the girl enrolled in an acting academy.

Teachers should be aware that other gifted handicapped students in addition to the behavior-disordered develop skills in manipulating others. One verbally gifted quadriplegic high school student convinced his regular-classroom teachers that his handicap prevented him from doing written assignments. His sympathetic teachers permitted oral and taped reports and exams until the resource teacher explained that the student was quite capable of legible, if slow, writing.

Program Coordination for the Gifted Handicapped

The most salient characteristics of gifted handicapped students are scattered profiles of strengths and weaknesses and wide discrepancy between potential and achievement. Based on these characteristics, the goals and program considerations listed in the following paragraphs appear appropriate for many gifted handicapped students.

1. *Setting of realistic expectations and goals.* Because other people perceive and treat gifted handicapped students as handicapped, these students tend to set their objectives too low (Maker, 1977). Teachers, parents, and the student

need to develop an accurate picture of the student's individual strengths and limitations. Career education should be introduced early to help students understand the range of occupations open to them, to provide realistic appraisals of their potential for success, and to prescribe knowledge and skill requirements that must be mastered. Becoming acquainted with successful handicapped adults through readings and guest presentations can provide handicapped students with encouragement and realistic understanding of obstacles.

2. *Provision for means of coping with feelings and frustrations.* Maker (1977) has emphasized the need for affective development in programs for gifted handicapped students to help them deal with the frustrations of having high potential limited by handicapping conditions. Schiff, Kaufman, and Kaufman (1981) found that their sample of highly intelligent learning-disabled students displayed more exaggerated emotional problems than did typical learning-disabled students. The "uneven gifted," as the authors called the gifted learning-disabled, tended to be emotionally upset and disorganized and to express feelings of unhappiness, of not fitting in, of being isolated, corroded, dumb, and powerless. Individual and group counseling should constitute an integral component of programs for gifted handicapped students.

3. *Compensation for handicapping conditions.* Teachers can help gifted handicapped students find specific ways to compensate for limiting conditions through curricular adaptations (Elkind, 1973; Wolf and Gygi, 1981). For example, learning-disabled students may become highly frustrated when they have something crucial to contribute on a written assignment but find writing painfully slow because of spelling, composition, or handwriting deficiencies. Teachers might permit such students to present oral or taped reports. Similarly, when gifted nonreaders are eager for information, volunteers can tape record resource materials or serve as readers. Many books are available on audiotape from the American Printing House for the Blind.

4. *Development of strengths.* Most experts in the area of gifted handicapped education agree that programs for such students must focus on developing strengths. Although each student will present a unique profile of strengths and weaknesses, common areas to be considered in developing the curriculum include (*a*) specific academic subjects, including special talent and interest areas; (*b*) creativity; (*c*) problem solving; (*d*) higher-level thinking skills; and (*e*) communication. Ford and Ford (1981) emphasized the special value of creative problem solving for handicapped children. Jaben (1983) demonstrated that specific instruction can lead to improvements in tested creativity of learning-disabled students.

5. *Remediation of weaknesses.* To develop potential and provide challenges, programs for the gifted handicapped should emphasize students' strong areas. However, it would be an error to ignore deficiencies where improvement is both possible and potentially gratifying. For example, although a gifted student with a specific reading disability may glean information most effectively in an aural manner, he or she will still require "survival" skills in reading, such as those needed for filling out applications. Understanding the need for literacy in a high-information society, some learning-disabled students will undertake the struggle to improve reading proficiency.

GIFTED GIRLS

Although the incidence of giftedness in boys and girls is equal, the number of males clearly exceeds the number of females in terms of adult achievers. As Callahan (1981) has pointed out, the literature on gifted adults suggests that a substantially greater proportion of creative, productive adults are males. One study of four hundred historically eminent individuals included only fifty-two women (Goertzel and Goertzel, 1962). A more recent examination of three hundred contemporary individuals of eminence mentioned only seventy-eight women (Goertzel, Goertzel, and Goertzel, 1978). Solmon (1976) reported that although approximately equal numbers of men and women enter college, women constitute only one-third of the students admitted to graduate school. Moreover, women fill less than one-fourth of the academic positions in this country. Even with the advent of the women's liberation movement, the proportion of women holding top positions in business, academia, science, journalism, literature, the arts—virtually all professional fields—continues to be small. Society's loss of the potential contributions of many gifted women makes critical an understanding of sex differences and their origins and implications.

Sex Differences in Achievement

One hypothesis that attempts to explain male superiority in adult achievement concerns innate differences in intellectual abilities between males and females. However, several decades of research have failed to substantiate differences in general intelligence between the sexes, although evidence exists for differences in specific abilities. From their comprehensive review of sex differences, Maccoby and Jacklin (1974) concluded that (a) boys and girls are similar in basic intellectual processing, problem solving, concept mastery, reasoning, and creativity; (b) after age eleven girls outperform boys on tests of verbal performance; and (c) by adolescence boys begin to demonstrate superiority on measures of spatial ability.

More recent reviews (Goleman, 1978; Burstein, Bank, and Jarvik, 1980) support the conclusions of Maccoby and Jacklin that boys and girls perform similarly on measures of general intelligence but differ in verbal and spatial performance. While a number of studies support differences in cognitive style, with girls being more field-dependent and boys more field-independent (analytic), the evidence is inconsistent and inconclusive (Burstein, Bank, and Jarvik, 1980).

Burstein, Bank, and Jarvik (1980) explored several alternative explanations for sex differences in specific abilities. One hypothesis is that sex hormones differentially influence the organization and functioning of the brain. A second explanation concerns possible genetic factors. A third explanation (supported by Goleman, 1978) is differences in neuroanatomy—that is, differential organization of male and female brains. Goleman reviewed preliminary evidence that women's hemispheres are less specialized for spatial and linguistic functions and that women seem better able than men to selectively activate one center in the brain while keeping others quiet.

A fourth explanation for sex differences in specific abilities is sociocultural. The evidence for differential socialization of males and females is widely accepted. However, Burstein, Bank, and Jarvik (1980) argued that little concrete support exists for differential socialization with respect to development of sex differences in cognitive style, verbal ability, or visual–spatial ability. They concluded that while sex differences in cognitive functioning clearly exist, further research is needed to determine the origins of these differences.

Sex Differences in Personality

Maccoby and Jacklin (1974) found differences in aggressive behavior for the general population. Males displayed more physical and verbal aggression as early as age two. Some evidence suggests that girls exhibit more fear, timidity, anxiety, compliance, and nurturance, while boys display greater activity, competitiveness, and dominance. However, Maccoby and Jacklin concluded that the findings with regard to these personality patterns are ambiguous. Clearly, some girls demonstrate timidity, compliance, and anxiety, but others are competitive, independent, and dominant. Baumrind's (1972) investigations suggest that differences in socialization practices contribute to differences in instrumental competence, independence, achievement orientation, and task commitment. She found that authoritative parents have the most achievement-oriented and independent daughters, although permissive parents who do not inhibit tomboy behavior and more masculine pursuits have daughters who are nearly as achievement oriented and independent. However, a study examining gifted adults' perceptions of their early home environment suggested that while maternal warmth is sufficient for enabling gifted men to achieve, gifted women need support from both parents—perhaps to validate their combination of femininity and intellectuality (Groth, 1971).

Baumrind (1972) concluded that instrumental competence in girls and boys is facilitated when parents act in the following ways: (a) exhibit socially responsible and self-assertive behavior, especially when the parent, as a model, is perceived as powerful and reinforcing to the child; (b) systematically reward socially responsive behavior and punish deviant behavior and offer explanations and reasons; (c) have nonrejecting but not overprotective attitudes; (d) make high demands for achievement but remain receptive to the child's rational demands; (e) provide opportunities for children to exercise independent judgment; and (f) provide a stimulating environment offering both challenge and security, plus encouragement of divergent and convergent thinking.

Differential socialization practices also occur outside the home. Callahan (1979, 1981) has suggested that the schools' failure to provide examples of successful professional women contributes to girls' lower achievement as adults. Callahan also points to sex bias in readers and in textbooks that portray men as professionals and women as wives and mothers. Moreover, there is evidence that school counselors, male and female, frequently advise girls according to sex role stereotypes (Fox, 1977). For example, one study indicated that counselors often discouraged gifted girls from enrolling in advanced placement courses. Female counselors projected their own fear of failure onto their counseling strategies, while male counselors tended to feel that available positions in mathematics and science fields should go to men. A recent study of elementary school teachers' responses to descriptions of gifted students found no significant sex biases (Handel, 1983). However, this study did not include observations of actual teacher behavior with gifted students.

Characteristics of Gifted Females

It is not known to what extent the findings on differences between males and females generalize to gifted populations. Fox (1977) has suggested that differential values and interests contribute significantly to sex differences in mathematics achievement at high levels of ability. Although gifted girls have higher theoretical interests related to science than nongifted girls, they are less theoretically oriented than gifted boys. Fox also found that while gifted and nongifted girls express similar interests in conventional pursuits (domestic arts and office work), gifted girls also show more interest than their average-ability peers in more "masculine" fields such as science, mathematics, and mechanical activities. Because gifted girls have both masculine and feminine interests, Fox suggests that they experience more conflict than boys in making career choices. Moreover, with regard to the traditionally male-dominated fields of advanced mathematics and science, girls face both fear of failure and the possibility of rejection if they succeed. Schwartz (1980) has also described fear of success and conflict between achievement and the feminine role as barriers to gifted women's success.

While more gifted males achieve professional success than gifted females, gifted females generally display more achievement-oriented characteristics than do their nongifted peers, and some gifted females are highly successful. Several authors have described the personality traits of different samples of gifted females (Blaubergs, 1978; Bruch and Morse, 1972; Werner and Bachtold, 1969). For example, Werner and Bachtold found gifted girls in middle childhood to be more outgoing, conscientious, venturesome, forthright, self-assured, and self-disciplined than their peers of average ability. Adolescent gifted girls displayed greater enthusiasm, nonconformity, and individualism than nongifted adolescent girls.

Comparisons of successful and less successful gifted females indicate that successful females display higher achievement motivation, self-confidence, ego strength, and independence (Callahan, 1981). Faunce (1968) compared 723 gifted women who graduated from college with 526 who did not graduate. The nongraduates had less insight into their own personality structures, more problems with impulse control, and greater inner tensions. The graduates were found to be more insightful, conventional, temperate, and self-confident and to have better ego strength and psychological integration. Faunce concluded that the different patterns of personality characteristics and vocational interests of the two groups led to differences in persistence. More recently Hollinger and Fleming (1984) found personality differences in work orientation and mastery between gifted female adolescents who evidenced internal barriers to realization of career potential (for example, fear of success or low self-esteem) and gifted adolescent girls who evidenced no internal barriers.

Although few studies are available on child-rearing practices in the families of successful and less successful gifted women, one study of creative female mathematicians indicated that these women tended to be the eldest daughters, to have no brothers, and to have fathers who were professional men and who exercised considerable dominance in the family (Helson, 1971). Compared to less creative women mathematicians, the creative subjects were more likely to have identified with their fathers than with their mothers. These findings suggest that gifted girls from families that do not emphasize traditional sex roles may be more achieving, perhaps because they develop more "masculine" traits such as independence and assertiveness.

A recent study suggested that sex role stereotyping in families still occurs. Burns (1983) found that despite efforts to avoid sex stereotyping, parents of middle- and upper-class junior high gifted students generally favored essentially male characteristics for male students and female characteristics for female students. However, the gifted students themselves tended to cross traditional sex lines.

A follow-up study of Terman's intellectually gifted women at average age sixty-two indicated that positive parent–child relationships did not predict work pattern satisfaction of gifted daughters, although these relationships did correspond to general life satisfaction (Sears and Barbee, 1977). Helpfulness of parents, encouragement of independence by parents, parent perceptions of child self-confidence, and lack of inferiority feelings were related to gifted women's general life satisfaction. Early feelings of self-confidence and ambition also predicted later satisfaction with life, but early self-confidence did not distinguish gifted women who became professionals from those who chose to be homemakers.

Program Considerations for Gifted Girls

The foregoing discussion of sex differences and the characteristics of gifted females does not indicate that gifted females lack achievement motivation, independence, and competitive tendencies. Rather, the fact that fewer women enter professions and achieve eminence may be attributable to a variety of factors related to differential socialization practices for boys and girls. Resulting differences, particularly in interests and values, deserve consideration in program development. Specific considerations can be suggested for assessment practices, administrative arrangements, and instructional planning.

Assessment. Systematic sex biases on cognitive measures do not appear to be a problem; boys and girls perform similarly on measures of general intelligence and creativity. However, evidence shows (*a*) test bias in specific academic areas, (*b*) failure of traditional measures to identify nonacademic talents, and (*c*) differences in predictive validity of instruments for adult achievement. Callahan (1981) has discussed evidence that test bias may affect measured achievement in mathematics and science. In physics, for example, boys perform better on tests with predominantly visual–spatial items, while girls perform better on tests with primarily verbal items. Girls also tend to improve their performance in mathematics when problems are worded to involve feminine rather than masculine tasks, even though the solutions require identical processes. Fleming and Hollinger's (1981) study of 1,141 female high school sophomores suggests a need for a multidimensional approach to identify talent in this population. Traditional academic indicators such as standardized test scores and grades were relatively independent of self-reported accomplishments in nontraditional areas (home related, athletic, community, employment, arts, cocurricular, leadership, and other activities). The authors concluded that reliance on academic measures would fail to identify women talented in nontraditional areas.

Studies of many characteristics and relationships have indicated more variability among females than among males. For example, it is apparently more difficult to predict adult creative achievement for women than for men (Torrance, 1972b; Torrance, Bruch, and Morse, 1973). A twelve-year follow-up study of gifted girls indicated that combined use of biographical information (the Alpha Biographical Inventory) and creativity measures (the Torrance Tests of Creative Thinking) predict the adult creative achievement of young women better than either measure used alone (Torrance, Bruch, and Morse, 1973). Data from the follow-up also indicated that (*a*) no sex differences were apparent on measures of quantity and quality of creative achievement and creativeness of aspirations and (*b*) creativity measures are better predictors of women's adult achievement than are IQ measures (Torrance, 1972b). A twenty-one year follow-up study suggested that the Torrance Tests of Creative Thinking administered in elementary school were useful in predicting the adult creative performance of women (Rieger, 1983).

A final consideration regarding assessment of gifted females concerns teacher referral of potentially gifted students for special services. Gifted girls frequently derive their reinforcement from high grades and may behave in a docile, conforming way in academic classes. They appear to be successful in regular classes and hence not in need of special services. Gifted boys, socialized to be more aggressive, may manifest their boredom and frustration in verbal and physical behaviors that cause teachers to perceive a lack of adjustment to the regular class and a need for services beyond the regular curriculum. As a result, while gifted boys and girls may have similar needs for extra support, more boys than girls may be referred for special services.

Administrative Arrangements. Much of what we know about the utility of various administrative options for gifted girls comes from the Study of Mathematically Precocious Youth (SMPY) at Johns Hopkins University. While the samples were limited to mathematically gifted students, the findings indicate the need to consider carefully the relative merits of various types of programs for gifted girls. Fox's (1977) summary of the findings on gifted girls is given in the following paragraphs.

1. Early admission to kindergarten or first grade, moderate grade skipping during the elementary years, and early college entrance (by one or two years) appear valuable for gifted girls and boys. Radical early admission (before age fourteen) may be more favorable for boys than for girls.

2. Grade skipping, subject-matter acceleration (that is, being accelerated only in a specific content area), and advanced placement programs in mathematics and science in junior high appear more acceptable to gifted boys than to gifted girls. Fox sampled gifted seventh- and eighth-grade students who entered a mathematics competition at Johns Hopkins University and found that girls held less favorable attitudes toward acceleration for themselves than did boys. Only 54 percent of the girls favored acceleration, as compared to 73 percent of the boys. The SMPY staff found girls more fearful than boys of possible peer rejection because of academic acceleration and of possible failure. Gifted adolescent girls were less likely than their male counterparts to take advantage of options for subject-matter acceleration—for example, taking college courses while in secondary school. Schools that enroll sizable numbers of girls in advanced placement programs have (*a*) teachers who actively recruit girls and demand high performance from both sexes and/or (*b*) early tracking of students (by fourth grade) into homogeneous or accelerated programs.

3. Homogeneously grouped accelerated programs in mathematics can promote achievement in gifted girls and boys under some conditions. Girls are more likely to participate if the classes are conducted as part of the regular school program than if the classes are extracurricular or Saturday programs. Girls are more likely to achieve as well as or better than boys when taught by women instructors in classes where all students or a large number of students are girls.

Fox (1977) concluded that grade skipping, subject-matter acceleration, advanced placement programs, and Saturday courses at the junior high level are not necessarily less effective for girls than for boys, but these arrangements are less likely to be tried by girls. Again, contributing factors may be adolescent girls' fear of estrangement from their peer group and fear of academic failure (or success). Such self-perceptions merit serious consideration; evidence shows that mathematically talented female adolescents' perceptions of their own ability contribute to their career aspirations (Hollinger, 1983).

The findings of the SMPY investigations on administrative options suggest that, where appropriate for the individual gifted girl, the following should be encouraged: (*a*) early admission to kindergarten or first grade; (*b*) early ability grouping; (*c*) instructors who serve as appropriate role models; and (*d*) a variety of acceleration options, including advanced placement courses within the regular school program. For example, Hall (1982) reported higher enrollments of girls than boys in a program sponsored by the University of Wisconsin–Green Bay. Courses for university credit were held in high schools and taught by high school teachers who qualified as ad hoc instructors of the university. Although the subject matter (English) may explain the higher enrollment of girls, the model represents an administrative option consistent with SMPY findings.

Instructional Planning. Whatever the administrative arrangement selected, programs should include the instructional components described in the following paragraphs. These components are aimed at supporting the specific needs of gifted girls.

1. *Teacher, counselor, and administrator in-service training.* Such training is necessary to cultivate awareness of the special needs of gifted girls and the subtle, unintentional ways in which sex stereotyping occurs in the schools. Carrelli (1982) has listed a number of resources on sex equity that can help educators become positive models and raise their own and their students' level of awareness regarding stereotyping, bias, and discrimination.

2. *Parent awareness training.* Such training helps parents understand the consequences of early sex role stereotyping and recognize the ways in which stereotypes are supported through differential reinforcement, media, and printed material.

3. *Opportunities to interact with role models.* Gifted girls can benefit substantially from interacting with gifted women who have succeeded in a variety of traditionally male as well as traditionally female professions (Shakeshaft and Palmieri, 1978). Literature depicting women's accomplishments also provides examples of successful women.

4. *Teacher reinforcement of risk taking, independence, and self-confidence for boys and girls.* Teachers should encourage gifted children of both sexes to explore new fields, try different activities, and understand their high abilities.

5. *Guidance for all students regarding the various administrative options available throughout their school years.* Girls and boys need realistic appraisal of their abilities relative to grade skipping, acceleration, subject-matter acceleration, and advanced placement programs. Students also need to know how each of these options might affect their social and extracurricular plans.

6. *Career counseling for all students.* Because of recent efforts to break down traditional sex role stereotypes, men and women have more socially acceptable choices open to them. However, traditions are slow to change, and it is still less acceptable for men to be homemakers than for women. Hence, women continue to face more choices than men: Women must choose between homemaking and a career, they must choose a type of career, and they must choose whether to balance family and career simultaneously or to sequence one before the other. While more men today are single parents, most men face this situation as a result of divorce rather than as an initial, free choice. Girls have special need for counseling regarding single parenthood, and girls who plan to have families before careers need special information regarding career development and continuing education. Boys whose interests lie in traditionally female areas, such as the visual and performing arts (especially dance and costume design) and culinary arts, face parent, teacher, and peer pressures similar to those faced by girls who want to pursue careers in mathematics and the sciences. Unbiased career counseling and encouragement are important for these students.

One issue regarding sex bias is inherent in the premise that creative and productive adults are those who achieve success in the academic, artistic, and/or leadership fields. By this definition far fewer gifted girls reach their potential than gifted boys. But if excellence in homemaking and lower-level careers constitutes success, then the differences in success rates between males and females are not so well defined. In practical terms, the issue is whether educators should counsel gifted girls to become professionals when the girls express a preference for homemaking.

It is not clear that gifted women who choose to be homemakers are less happy or satisfied than gifted women who select professional careers. Birnbaum (1975) compared married and single women faculty from a prestigious university with married women who had graduated from the same university fifteen to twenty years earlier, who were not working, and who had children. She found that the homemakers exhibited lower self-esteem and sense of personal competence and felt less attractive, less challenged, and less creatively involved. She concluded that "we cannot in good conscience continue to raise girls to seek their *primary* personal fulfillment and self-identity within the family" (Birnbaum, 1975, p. 418).

In contrast, a follow-up of 430 gifted women (average age sixty-two) out of the 671 originally selected in 1922–1928 by Terman concluded: "Clearly, there is no single path to glory. . . . The life style which brings happiness to one woman with one kind of life experience does not necessarily bring it to another woman with a different experiential background" (Sears and Barbee, 1977, p. 60). Using a measure of work satisfaction and a more general measure of life satisfaction, Sears and Barbee found that gifted women employed outside the home reported greater work satisfaction than did gifted homemakers. However, homemakers reported greater measures of life satisfaction. Moreover, marriage and children appeared to be important aspects of life satisfaction.

Differences in findings between the two studies may be due to differences in the times and to the greater selectiveness of the Birnbaum sample. Teachers

and counselors who prefer to withhold value judgments about whether professional careers or homemaking careers result in greater personal happiness and/
or more significant contributions to society can still present the choices and
describe the options.

THE UNDERACHIEVING GIFTED

A number of operational definitions of gifted underachievement appear in the
literature (Dowdall and Colangelo, 1982). However, definitions of giftedness
such as Renzulli's (1978), which limit the gifted to those who combine intelligence, creativity, and task commitment, automatically exclude underachievers
from the gifted category.

Most educators generally define underachievement among gifted students
as performance significantly below potential. In her comprehensive volume on
gifted underachievers, Whitmore (1980) estimated that as many as 25 percent
of the gifted may be considered underachievers. Past estimates based on academic records of students identified as gifted have ranged from 15 to 50 percent,
depending on the definition of "significantly below potential." These estimates
do not include gifted individuals who perform under par on both aptitude and
achievement measures or individuals who perform satisfactorily in class but are
never referred as having high potential. Available estimates nonetheless indicate
that underachievement constitutes a major problem in education, both for the
individual and for society. Fortunately, researchers and practitioners have become increasingly aware of the phenomenon of underachievement, and more is
becoming known about characteristics of underachievers and possible causes of
and solutions to the problem.

Characteristics of Gifted Underachievers

Students identified as gifted underachievers tend to be males who have IQ scores
of 145 or above and who evidence personal and social maladjustment (Whitmore,
1980). Although some gifted girls are also underachievers, the ratio of underachieving males to females appears to be greater than two to one. As a group,
gifted underachievers tend to manifest the following characteristics (Clark, 1983;
Fine and Pitts, 1980; Pirozzo, 1982; Whitmore, 1980; Zilli, 1971):

— social immaturity manifested by feelings of rejection by peers, antagonism,
  and hostility
— negative attitudes toward school work resulting in or associated with poor
  study habits, failure to complete assignments, failure to master basic skills,
  poor test performance, distractibility, school phobia, weak motivation except for special-interest areas, high ability in verbal rationalization, lack of
  persistence, tendency to set unrealistic standards, and low aspirations
— feelings of inferiority evidenced by defensiveness, tendency to blame others,
  and aggressive or withdrawn behavior

Causes of Underachievement

Much of the early literature on the origins of underachievement blamed students' personality maladjustment resulting from negative family dynamics (e.g., Purkey, 1969). In other words, the gifted students themselves and their parents received most of the blame for underachievement. Since the late 1960s, however, several researchers have proposed "ecological" models that depart from the "disordered child" model by explaining problem behaviors as a result of interactions between the child and many features of the environment. For example, Rhodes (1967) described emotional disturbance as a consequence of interactions between characteristics of the individual and those of the ecology, which included parents, teachers, and community. Adelman (1971) defined learning problems as the result of a failure to match the learner's characteristics (motivation, abilities, personality) with those of the classroom situation (teachers and instructional approaches). An ecological model of underachievement suggests that several factors contribute to the development of underachievement among gifted students: child characteristics, parent behaviors, teacher behaviors, school curriculum characteristics, and community values.

Child Characteristics. Based on a study of elementary-age underachieving gifted students, Whitmore (1979) concluded that the personality and social adjustment problems of gifted underachievers are symptoms rather than causes of underachievement. She suggested that three characteristics of gifted students underlie their adjustment problems: perfectionism, frustration, and acute sensitivity. Whitmore found that some underachieving students demanded perfection of themselves and experienced anxiety regarding achievement. They set unrealistically high goals for themselves and often stopped trying to achieve so that they might avoid failure. Frustration occurred when the students perceived a large gap between their ideal selves and their level of functioning on specific tasks. The gifted students manifested acute sensitivity to the needs and feelings of other individuals and groups and agonized over problems such as world hunger, overpopulation, and the possibility of nuclear warfare. The same sensitivity caused such students to respond to pressure by exhibiting intense emotions, including feelings of guilt for their perceived failure to live up to parents' or teachers' standards. The importance of raising the self-esteem of low-achieving gifted students is suggested by research supporting a relationship between self-concept and learning among gifted children (Dean, 1977).

Whitmore (1979) also found that physical–developmental factors contributed to underachievement in 35 percent of the students studied, although the students felt that physical factors were problems of a secondary nature. Physical–developmental factors included discrepancies between mental ability and physical or social maturity; specific psychomotor or perceptual motor immaturity, which affected writing and reading; and learning problems possibly related to neurologically based learning disabilities.

Parent Behaviors. The literature on parent–child interactions indicates that certain patterns of behaviors differentiate families of high achievers from families of low achievers (Martin, 1975; Pirozzo, 1982; Radin, 1982; Thiel and Thiel, 1977; Zilli, 1971). In general, parents of high achievers tend to be warm, nurturing, and affectionate; to make demands for mature, independent behavior; to give reasons and explanations for their demands; and to state their expectations and apply consistent sanctions. In contrast, parents of low achievers tend to be more rejecting, authoritarian, restrictive, and punitive; to set unrealistic goals; and to fail to reward achievement or to apply pressure for achievement.

Teacher Behaviors. Pirozzo (1982) suggests that teachers can contribute to a gifted child's underachievement by expecting too little, by aiming activities at the average child, and by being satisfied with average achievement. Some teachers may have hostile feelings toward gifted children and may react to these children's demands with strict and repressive actions. Teachers who feel threatened by gifted children's knowledge, who set unrealistic standards, who use threat and ridicule, who are cold and impersonal, or who fail to provide challenge and stimulation also contribute to gifted children's dissatisfaction with school and their consequent underachievement (Evans, 1965). Evidence shows that schools that provide intellectual stimulation and challenge and value high achievement have fewer underachievers among the gifted (Zilli, 1971).

School Curriculum Characteristics. In Whitmore's (1979) study, gifted underachievers reported that the structure of the school curriculum did not meet their needs for independent investigation and analytic discussion. As early as grades one and two, these students rebelled against the school's emphasis on conformity to precise directions, excessive repetition, memorization, drill, and failure to individualize assignments. Likewise, Goertzel and Goertzel (1962) found that the biographies of a number of eminent individuals indicated frustration with their school's inability to provide opportunities to pursue interests and to work independently.

Community Values. Modern American society values achievement as a measure of success. As agents of acculturation, parents and teachers may expect and demand high accomplishments from gifted students. Consequently, students may come to perceive their worth as contingent on school achievement (Whitmore, 1979). One of the authors worked with an adolescent boy in an upper-class neighborhood where achieving at grade level was perceived as academic retardation. As a result of intense pressures to try harder, the boy developed overwhelming feelings of inadequacy and guilt about displeasing his parents and teachers. He also exhibited low self-esteem due to obesity that resulted from nervous overeating.

Social values may play a significant role in the underachievement of gifted girls, whose pattern of underachievement differs from that of gifted boys. In a retrospective study of underachieving high school students, Shaw and McCuen (1960) found that male subjects had entered school with a predisposition to underachieve. Among the girls, those who were underachievers in high school had tended to do better than the high school achievers had done during the first five grades, although the differences were not statistically significant. More recently, Fitzpatrick (1978) replicated Shaw and McCuen's finding of no significant differences between female high school achievers and underachievers during their earlier school years. Fitzpatrick suggested that the onset of underachievement in gifted adolescent girls may be attributed to the importance of sex role conformity.

Potential Solutions for Underachievement

The literature suggests three major strategies for ameliorating the problems of underachievement among gifted students: prevention, counseling, and education intervention.

Prevention. Educators agree that early intervention is critical for preventing and remediating underachievement among gifted students. The tendency to underachieve, especially for boys, may be present at the time of school entrance, and the discrepancy between aptitude and achievement increases at each grade level (Shaw and McCuen, 1960). Unfortunately, most programs for underachievers do not begin until high school. Programs aimed at prevention of underachievement must include at least three components: early identification, appropriate instructional services, and parent education. Gifted children should be identified at the preschool or kindergarten level to ensure their placement in challenging educational programs from their first school experience. These programs should be flexible, enriching, challenging, and individualized and should provide opportunities for pursuing interests and independent projects. Parents should receive support and guidance in (*a*) establishing a stimulating, challenging environment at home; (*b*) modeling achievement behavior; (*c*) showing interest in their child's activities; (*d*) setting realistic goals; (*e*) displaying warmth and affection; and (*f*) providing reasons for decisions and involving their child in decision making.

Counseling. Because underachievement has been viewed as due at least partially to the student's social and personality characteristics and to family interactions, most programs for gifted underachievers contain a counseling component. Types of counseling include individual, group, and family counseling. For example, Gurman (1970) has emphasized concurrent counseling of underachieving students and their parents in separate groups. Fine and Pitts's (1980) guidelines for intervention with gifted underachievers involve the child, the parents, and school personnel in a counseling program aimed at opening communication and maintaining consistency. Fine and Pitts recommend intervention to reduce the symptoms of underachievement and to foster self-control through provision of structure and support. Structure is decreased as the child increasingly assumes responsibility for his or her own behavior.

Unfortunately, the literature offers few empirical investigations of the efficacy of counseling for underachievers in general or for gifted underachievers. Available studies focus almost exclusively on high school students and present inconsistent results (Pirozzo, 1982; Whitmore, 1980; Zilli, 1971). For example, Baymur and Patterson (1960) compared the effects of individual counseling, group counseling, a one-session motivational talk, and a no-counseling control situation on adjustment and academic performance of underachieving high school students. Counseling sessions were held weekly for ten to twelve weeks. Results tended to favor individual and group counseling over the two no-counseling conditions, although differences between groups in adjustment and grade point average were not strong. Interestingly, the one-time inspirational talk, an approach commonly used by parents and teachers to motivate underachievers, failed to produce any positive changes.

Raths (1961) reported that having an adult work individually with underachieving high school students on clarifying values, attitudes, and beliefs (for twelve twenty-minute sessions over one semester) improved student achievement. Doyle, Gottlieb, and Schneider (1979) found improvements in reading scores for low-achieving remedial high school students who participated in ten to twelve small-group or individual counseling sessions. However, average or above-average underachievers did not show significant gains.

Studies specifically aimed at bright underachievers also present conflicting results. Broedel et al. (1960) studied the effects of group counseling on gifted underachievers in the ninth grade. The groups met for one class period twice a week for eight weeks. Broedel and associates found greater gains in acceptance of self and of others for counseled than for control students. However, achievement test scores and grades of counseled students declined, while those of control students increased or remained the same. Among academically gifted underachieving high school sophomores who received four semesters of weekly group counseling, Finney and Van Dalsem (1969) found small improvements in attitude but no significant increase in grade point average compared to controls. In one of the few investigations of counseling with elementary students (fifth grade), Ohlsen and Gazda (1965) reported no improvements in achievement test scores or grade point averages for bright underachievers who participated in twice-weekly group counseling sessions over eight weeks, with concurrent group counseling for parents. The authors noted that where significant gains were obtained, they tended to relate to increased congruence between perceptions of actual self and ideal self or to increased acceptance of peers.

Where underachievement stems from personality problems and family conflicts, a combination of individual, parent, and family counseling appears to be a logical intervention. However, because underachievement is a chronic problem, counseling programs of brief duration may produce few positive results. Research to date has not demonstrated clearly the effectiveness of counseling for improving the academic performance of underachieving gifted students. Additional studies, which will consider counseling over longer time periods and specific counseling techniques, are still required.

Educational Intervention. Where underachievement has its roots in curricular inflexibility, educational modifications may be appropriate intervention methods. Educational modifications for gifted underachievers have generally consisted of (*a*) grouping gifted underachievers with gifted achievers or (*b*) grouping gifted underachievers together. Karnes et al. (1963) compared the efficacy of placing elementary-age gifted underachievers in homogeneous classes of high achievers with the efficacy of placing gifted underachievers in heterogeneous classes. The researchers found greater achievement and fluency gains for underachievers in the homogeneous classes, as well as greater gains in perceived acceptance by parents. However, underachievers in both placements decreased in perceived peer acceptance. Whitmore (1980) has argued that placing underachievers in classes of gifted achievers results in the underachievers making comparisons of themselves with their achieving peers, which consequently may produce feelings of guilt and of not belonging.

Pirozzo (1982) concluded that grouping gifted underachievers together may result in negative modeling. However, Whitmore (1980) reported positive results from the Cupertino Project for Highly Gifted Underachievers, an elementary-level program in which students were grouped in self-contained classrooms for full-time intervention for one to two years. Whitmore suggested that because underachievement stems from rebellion against oppressively structured classrooms, a program for gifted underachievers should (*a*) be student centered, challenging, and flexible; (*b*) involve students in planning, organizing, and evaluating; (*c*) provide success experiences; (*d*) focus on advanced thinking skills (the students' strengths); (*e*) develop social skills and leadership; and (*f*) involve parents. Whitmore's suggestions appear most consistent with the literature, which suggests that ameliorating the problem of gifted underachievement requires early identification, family involvement, and long-term commitment (Dowdall and Colangelo, 1982).

In any discussion of intervention, an issue deserving consideration is a student's right to make choices about his or her own performance. The literature urges teachers and parents to encourage student decision making. Yet if a student with the potential to be a fine surgeon expresses instead a desire to study auto mechanics, should the teacher discourage such a goal? Clearly, teachers, parents, and students must work together to investigate options, examine possible consequences, and make judgments.

THE RURAL GIFTED

Rural areas are generally defined by sparse populations, isolation from population centers, and an agrarian way of life that centers on farming, mining, or forestry. Technically a rural community has a population of 2,500 or less and lies twenty-five miles or more from a county that contains a standard metropolitan area of 50,000 or more inhabitants. The 1980 census indicated that 35.6 percent of the U.S. population resides in rural areas. An estimated 15,896,619 are of school age (five through nineteen), and 1 to 5 percent, or 158,966 to 794,831, are potentially gifted (all figures extrapolated from the U.S. Department of Commerce, Bureau of the Census, 1983). Evidence suggests that the majority of gifted students in rural areas can be considered underachieving (Plowman, undated). The unique features of rural areas result in specific program needs, and the characteristics of rural gifted students result in specific instructional needs.

Features of Rural Areas and Implications for Program Development

Birnbaum (undated) described three features of rural areas and their implications for program development in gifted education: sparse population, provincial attitudes, and parental reluctance.

1. *Sparse population.* The sparse population of rural areas results in a correspondingly low number of gifted students, who may be separated from each other by wide geographic distances. The school district may face difficulty in securing special funding for the small number of gifted students and in obtaining personnel and material resources in a cost-effective manner. For example, districts isolated from universities, cultural centers, and major industries encounter obstacles in obtaining in-service training for teachers of the gifted and in providing mentors and field trip sites. Distances separating gifted students also limit the number of opportunities for interaction.

2. *Provincial attitudes.* Birnbaum (undated) described the attitude of many rural and remote communities as provincial, conservative, and resistant to change. Loss of gifted individuals to urban centers helps support negative attitudes toward gifted programs. Although achievement in the arts and subject areas relevant to local industry (for example, agronomy) may be lauded, the general population may be unsympathetic to academic excellence.

3. *Parental reluctance to acknowledge giftedness.* The third, related characteristic of rural areas identified by Birnbaum is parental reluctance to have children identified as gifted. In small communities, being identified for special services marks a child as different or unusual.

Program Needs in Rural Areas

The special features of rural communities make essential three program needs: professional leadership, trained personnel, and access to resources (Birnbaum, undated).

Leadership. Overcoming problems of apathy and antipathy among school personnel, parents, and the community requires leadership from the teachers and administrators responsible for educating gifted learners in rural areas. Leadership is required if these groups are to understand the rationale for gifted education and be aware of the identifying characteristics and special educational needs of the gifted. Administrators can support programs for the gifted by (*a*) selecting appropriate teachers, (*b*) providing released time for professional development and for locating external resources, (*c*) helping secure community and school involvement and support, (*d*) providing in-service training to all school personnel, and (*e*) establishing a roster of resource persons.

Trained Personnel. Teachers who work with the gifted in rural areas need specialized learning experiences to identify gifted students, assess their needs, and provide appropriate services. Witters (1979) conducted a survey of regular-class teachers of gifted elementary and secondary students, facilitators of gifted programs, and resource and special-class teachers of the gifted from rural districts in a midwestern state. The fifty-three participants were all enrolled in college courses in gifted education. At least 75 percent of the respondents desired help in the following areas: (*a*) knowledge of the needs and problems of gifted and talented children; (*b*) competencies in using formal and informal identification procedures; (*c*) preparation of curriculum materials and activities; (*d*) evaluation of teaching skills and pupil achievement in cognitive and affective areas; and (*e*) development of instructional methods for gifted underachievers.

Goodrum and Irons (1981) reported positive results from one effort to assess the efficacy of a model for training rural teachers in Appalachia. The in-service program provided three workshops, each three hours long, on Bloom's taxonomy and monthly follow-up sessions for reviewing knowledge and sharing instructional materials and activities. The students of participating teachers used a student workbook based on Bloom's taxonomy. A preassessment and a postassessment of teaching styles indicated a shift to clearer emphasis on both lower- and upper-level processes of Bloom's taxonomy. Although specific variables contributing to change were not isolated in the study, Goodrum and Irons suggested that focus on a single teaching model and follow-up/reinforcement of in-service activities may be useful approaches.

Access to Resources. The third program need, access to resources, stems from the isolation of rural communities from a broad range of scientific, cultural, and human service centers and the experts who staff such centers. Strategies for providing access to services in rural and remote areas include those listed in the following paragraphs.

1. *Busing of students to a central location.* Such a location could be a media center, a university, a natural history museum, or a science and industry complex. This strategy has the additional advantage of bringing gifted students together for stimulating interaction.

2. *Correspondence courses with another school or university or correspondence with a mentor.* Both types of correspondence result in a wider range of curricular offerings to gifted students.

3. *Televised courses broadcast from a central location.* New communications technology enables students to "interact" with the instructor and other students while each person works at his or her own location.

4. *Telephone conferencing.* Students can interact with each other and with a teacher or mentor through telephone conferences arranged after students have had opportunities to do independent investigations on a common topic.

5. *Computer conferencing.* Microcomputers at home or in school can provide access to computer conference systems that enable users to carry on short- or long-term discussions. For example, the CONFER system (Heydinger, 1979) permits users to leave messages for another student, for the teacher, or for the entire class. A complete transcript of the conference is maintained and is available to any member. Discussions can be organized under topical items, allowing students to access topics that interest them. Computer conferences can involve individuals across the country, permitting inclusion of experts in the topic area. A major advantage over telephone conferencing is that users can participate at the time most convenient for them.

6. *Audiocassette tape and videotape exchange.* Communications among students, teachers, and mentors can be facilitated through use of audiocassette tapes and, where taping and playback equipment is available, videotape cassettes. More sophisticated systems for interfacing computer-aided instruction with videotapes, slides, and videodisks are also becoming available and can provide instruction to individuals in rural and remote areas (Caldwell, 1981).

7. *Mobile enrichment units.* Many libraries, zoos, and mechanical shops for vocational training operate self-contained programs brought to students on a van, truck, bus, or other vehicle. For example, New Mexico State University operates a van carrying microcomputers to provide instruction in computer literacy to students in rural and remote areas.

Characteristics of Rural Gifted Students

As a result of being isolated by geography from intellectual stimulation, gifted students in rural areas may demonstrate lack of sophistication, lack of general information, and lower levels of social and cognitive skills compared to their urban counterparts. On the positive side, rural gifted students may be more open to a variety of learning experiences, free from pseudosophistication, and in possession of a unique understanding of the natural environment (Plowman, undated).

The case study approach described in Chapter 5 would be an appropriate method for identifying gifted students in rural areas. Plowman (undated) has suggested several characteristics common to such students: (*a*) early school-related learning, maturation, active and persistent exploration of the environment, imitation of adult behavior, and questioning of established ways of doing things; (*b*) unusual resourcefulness in coping with home, school, work, and community responsibilities; (*c*) playfulness with materials and ideas; (*d*) sense of humor; and (*e*) products, achievements, and skills of high quality.

Instructional Needs of the Rural Gifted

Based on their characteristics, gifted students in rural areas need (*a*) a broad range of learning experiences to make up for lack of variety in the environment and (*b*) opportunities for interaction with intellectual peers and for stimulation, competition, and realistic appraisal of personal abilities. Program alternatives to meet the needs of gifted students in rural areas include those listed in the following paragraphs.

1. *Internship or apprenticeship experiences.* For example, students can intern as legislative aides, researchers to the governor, technicians in science laboratories, or trainees in businesses, schools, or hospitals. Internship experiences should constitute only one part of the special program.

2. *Guest experts.* Experts from urban areas—for example, senators, scientists, artists, university faculty—are often willing to spend time in the country to work with gifted students. Resident experts, such as painters, musicians, and craftspeople, can also discuss their work with students.

3. *Saturday seminars and weekend exploration trips.* Gifted students can be brought together on weekends for classroom seminars or for field trips led by experts. Plowman (undated) described a weekend exploration trip that included discussions with a geologist, a forest ranger, a fish hatchery director, and a water utility engineer. The trip included tours of the forest, the fish hatchery, and the water system.

4. *Exchange programs with urban schools.* Students can expand their experiences by participating in week-long exchange programs with their counterparts in large cities. Participants have the opportunity to compare settings in terms of physical ecology, social systems, and formal and informal institutions.

5. *Summer institutes and seminars.* Rural gifted students can participate in intensive residential programs aimed at a variety of interest areas or focused on one specific topic, such as leadership training. Many such institutes are held on university campuses and taught by university faculty.

Other program options described for the gifted in general can be equally appropriate to the rural gifted—for example, independent projects, mentors, acceleration, special schools and classrooms, itinerant teachers, and regular-classroom enrichment. Within the regular classroom, teachers can provide stimulating materials, higher-level books, do-it-yourself projects, independent study opportunities, challenging problems related to an ongoing unit, guidance with hobbies and special interests, and practice with higher-level and creative-thinking processes. Gear (1984) has suggested that rural districts provide an assortment of services based on school and community cooperation, relying on existing resources as well as new extensions as needs emerge. Lupkowski (1984) has described several ideas for innovative teaching in small rural schools.

Programs for gifted students in rural areas must include programs for parents that will help them understand the need for gifted education, help them cope with their children's special characteristics and problems, and help enlist their support. Communication between teachers and parents can be facilitated through group meetings arranged through car pools, frequent note writing, telephoning, weekly or monthly newsletters, and audiotaped messages.

EXTREMELY INTELLIGENT CHILDREN

Society tends to view children of moderately superior intelligence (IQ 120 to 155) as bright but essentially normal. However, children with IQs above 170 are frequently regarded as odd or even freakish. Rarity may account in part for this perception; only 1 child in 100,000 scores between 170 and 180; only 1 in 1 million scores above 180 (Gallagher, 1975). For these children the stereotype of the social misfit persists. Available data on extremely intelligent individuals challenge this stereotype but do indicate a need for special educational considerations.

Characteristics of the Extremely Intelligent

Hollingworth's (1942) classic investigation of twelve children who scored above 180 on the Binet indicated that extremely intelligent children have needs substantially different from the needs of moderately bright children. Hollingworth's subjects began talking at a median age of fourteen months and began reading at thirty-six months. Some rebelled against schooling, while others eagerly accepted it, depending on how early they were identified as exceptional and adjustments were made. Hollingworth concluded that these children are so far above their age peers and so rare in number that they become isolated and may consequently develop social adjustment problems.

Findings from the Terman studies suggest that difficulties in social adjustment of extremely intelligent children may be outgrown. Terman and Oden's (1947) follow-up investigations of Terman's gifted subjects at average age thirty-five included examination of forty-seven men and thirty-four women who, as children, had tested on the Stanford–Binet at 170 or above. The IQs ranged from 170 to 194 for men (mean of 177.7) and from 170 to 200 for women (mean of 177.6). Comparisons with the total group of gifted subjects indicated no substantive differences in age of walking or talking, physical health, mental health, or marriage and divorce rates. The group with IQs above 170 more often learned to read at an early age, more often were accelerated in school, and received higher grades in college. However, 25 percent of this group had college records that were fair to poor. Men in this group generally achieved higher occupational status than men in the total group. The extremely intelligent women did not differ from the total group of women on occupational status. Some individuals within the high-IQ group had lower occupational histories than would have been expected from their IQ scores.

The social adjustment of the extremely intelligent did not differ from that of the total group except in one respect. Data taken during the middle teen years indicated some maladjustment, but the problems appeared to correct themselves with age. Like Hollingworth, Terman and Oden concluded that extremely intelligent children face more difficult problems with social adjustment. They gave an example of a seven-year-old boy with a mental age of thirteen whose vocabulary was unintelligible to the average child of his age. Roedell (1984) listed several types of difficulties to which highly gifted children are vulnerable: uneven development, perfectionism, heightened adult expectations, intense sensitivity, identity problems, alienation, and role conflict. On the positive side, these children have superior intelligence with which to deal with their social difficulties. The authors recall one extremely gifted ten-year-old who conversed with adults much like a gifted thirty-year-old, especially about meteorology. However, we observed that when he interacted with his chronological-age peers, he modified his vocabulary level and discussion topics and changed his physical behavior, becoming more playful.

Educational Modifications for the Extremely Intelligent

Goertzel and Goertzel (1962) described several eminent individuals whose accomplishments demonstrated their extremely high intelligence. Some of them, such as John Stuart Mill and Thomas Edison, received their education outside the formal system. Mill was tutored by his father, Edison by his mother. Feldman (1979) concluded from his study of precocious children that to achieve prodigiously, such children need intensive education from a master teacher. One might infer from these cases, and from the small proportion of extremely gifted children in any given geographic area, that special tutoring may be the most appropriate educational modification.

The Terman findings suggest an alternative approach: rapid acceleration through the regular school system. However, rapid acceleration results in social difficulties due to the gifted student's age—for example, inability to compete in athletics, inability to drive, inability to participate in social events, such as dating, and conspicuousness in classes. Lewis (1984) cautioned that radical acceleration does not guarantee quality teaching and may not be the best method of educating highly gifted students, especially in fields that require experience for understanding, even though the children's high intelligence enables them to understand and adjust to their situation. On the positive side, rapid acceleration may prevent the development of serious problems of underachievement and rebellion due to extreme boredom in the regular grades. Consider the following examples:

> The father of a shy, solemn 12-year-old who became the youngest college-graduate in U.S. history says his two other children show promise of matching their brother's academic feats. . . . [The boy] earned a degree in mathematics. . . . He will enter graduate school at Stanford University as early as the summer. . . . [He] spent fewer than three years in college and skipped high school entirely. He maintained a B-plus average while carrying more than a full college class schedule.
>
> — *Las Cruces Sun News*, May 17, 1982

> ———, who enrolled at the University of Southern California when she was only 11 years old, Thursday became its youngest graduate at 16. . . . [The girl], whose IQ is somewhere around 200, was talking when she was 8 months old and reading, writing, and computing math at 2. . . . She hates the word "genius." "It insinuates you don't work for what you get, that it all comes easily. I've burned a lot of midnight oil. The only thing that sets me aside is that I got it at a younger age."
>
> [The parents] wanted their daughter to take five years to complete college in order to allow her to pace her studies with a developing maturity. Being with older students was awkward for a while, she said. "Here I was, 11, suddenly in a totally adult environment. Then they began to regard me as a younger sister," she said. About two years ago, she said, "The attitude changed from more of a little sister to more of an equal—as a friend." [She] speaks English, Spanish, Tagalog . . . as well as some French, Japanese, and Chinese.
>
> —*Las Cruces Sun-News*, May 16, 1982

As a group, the extremely intelligent men and women in Terman and Oden's (1947) study were well adjusted and vocationally more successful compared to the total group of intellectually gifted subjects. Yet some did not achieve at the level predicted by their intelligence scores. Based on a comparison follow-up of twenty-six of Terman's subjects with IQ scores above 180 and twenty-six randomly selected Terman subjects, Feldman (1984) concluded that the difference in IQ points had little effect on educational attainments, careers, marriage and family, and life satisfaction. Not all extremely intelligent children grow up to be socially adjusted, productive adults. Educational provisions for extremely intelligent students should include individual counseling to help students accept and adjust to their differences from the general population and to capitalize on their strengths.

CHAPTER SUMMARY

Preschool, low-income and culturally different, handicapped, female, underachieving, rural, and extremely intelligent gifted constitute special subpopulations that may require educational considerations different from those of the general population of gifted and talented learners. Early identification of young gifted children may help prevent later underachievement and promote supportive parenting practices. Through flexible grouping and enriching environments, programs for gifted preschool children focus on the development of positive self-concepts and attitudes toward learning, independence, competency in basic skills, special interests, and divergent- and convergent-thinking skills. Additional goals include parent participation and effective transitions to kindergarten and first grade.

As indicated by their proportionately low enrollments in programs for the gifted and talented, low-income and culturally different gifted children continue to be underidentified and underserved. Active recruitment and use of carefully selected multiple measures can aid in identifying low-income and culturally different gifted students. Although these students' specific needs depend on their individual cultural, economic, and experiential backgrounds, program considerations generally include sensitive teachers, broadening experiences, multicultural emphasis, and use of the children's strengths.

Handicapped students can also be gifted. The gifted handicapped represent a heterogeneous group requiring highly individualized educational provisions. Program goals include helping students set realistic self-expectations, cope with frustrations, compensate for handicapping conditions, develop their strengths, and remediate their weaknesses.

Although there are equal numbers of gifted boys and gifted girls, the number of males who actually achieve success—defined as eminence in the professions—vastly exceeds the number of females who achieve success. Differences between the sexes in adult achievement stem primarily from differences in socialization practices and societal values that, for girls, result in conflicts between perceived sex roles and high achievement. Recent research suggests that gifted girls may prefer administrative arrangements different from those preferred by gifted boys. Teachers, counselors, and parents need to be aware of sex discrimination practices and of the special needs of gifted girls.

Underachievement among gifted students constitutes a significant problem that, without intervention, results in tragic waste of human potential. Although the early literature attributed the cause of underachievement to personality and family conflict, more recent writers point to inflexible curricula and rigid teachers. The most effective strategy for dealing with underachievement is prevention through early identification and intervention. Unfortunately, most programs for gifted underachievers begin in high school. Although commonly recommended, counseling has not demonstrated its efficacy for improving achievement. A more promising approach appears to be intervention during the elementary years through student-centered, flexible programs aimed at using students' strengths. However, the most effective intervention for a given student may depend on the source of the individual's underachievement.

Gifted students living in rural and isolated areas may demonstrate less sophistication and general knowledge than their urban peers. Programs for these students should offer a broad range of learning experiences and opportunities for interacting with intellectual peers. Leadership and advocacy for gifted programs are critical in rural areas for developing community awareness and securing access to resources for teachers and students.

Extremely intelligent gifted children constitute the smallest subpopulation of the gifted and talented. Contrary to popular opinion, longitudinal studies of individuals with IQs over 170 indicate adequate social adjustment, especially as they "grow into" their advanced abilities and become adults. As children, the extremely intelligent face social problems due to their highly advanced verbal and problem-solving skills. If they are placed in accelerated programs, they also face problems arising from chronological age differences between themselves and their classmates. Individual tutoring, counseling, and rapid acceleration may constitute appropriate educational modifications.

Although the general characteristics and needs of different subpopulations of the gifted can be described, it is important not to overgeneralize these characteristics and needs with respect to individuals. A wide range of individual differences exists *within* each group. Decisions concerning placement, services, and objectives must be made on the basis of each student's individual profile of strengths and weaknesses.

ACTIVITIES FOR THOUGHT AND DISCUSSION

1. Interview the director of the local gifted program to determine how special populations are served. What suggestions, if any, might you make for improving services to students in special populations?

2. What agency should be responsible for providing services to gifted preschool children? Should public schools provide free education programs to all preschool children? Beginning at what age?

3. Interview leaders of ethnic minority groups at a university or in the community regarding their views on quota systems for identifying the culturally different gifted.

4. Describe specific goals, administrative arrangements, and instructional procedures for a seventh-grade intellectually gifted student who is totally blind.

5. As a high school teacher of gifted students, how would you react to the aspirations of (*a*) an intellectually gifted girl who wants to marry and raise a family after high school graduation and (*b*) a mathematically gifted boy who wants to attend trade school to become a tool-and-die man like his father.

6. How would you respond to the concern of a rural parent who fears that enrolling his daughter in a program for the gifted will result in her eventual emigration from the rural community?

7. As the parent of a preschool child who has just been tested at 185 IQ, what plans would you make for the child's future? What would you expect of the public schools? How would you approach the school if you felt your child was not receiving appropriate services? (For example, whom would you approach? Would you go as an individual parent, or would you organize an advocacy group? Would you attempt to be a "partner" with the school in planning for your child, or would you place yourself in an adversarial relationship with the school?)

Chapter Thirteen

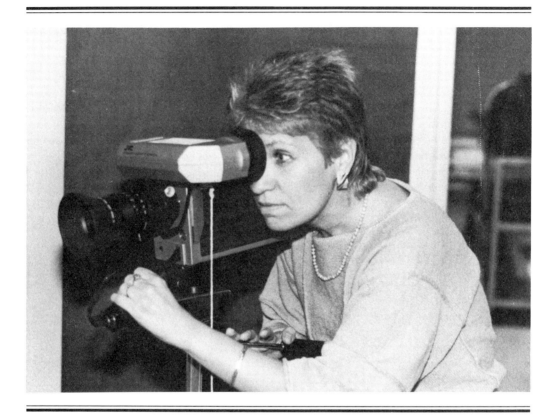

IMPLEMENTING PROGRAMS FOR THE GIFTED

Establishing (or renovating) programs for the gifted and talented can generate challenge, excitement, creative energy, and feelings of satisfaction for improving services to students. But initiators of programs can also meet with resistance, frustration, disillusionment, and unsatisfactory compromise. Careful planning and effective communication can minimize obstacles and create conditions for successful implementation. Previous chapters provided information on general definitions and characteristics of giftedness, identification procedures, program options, curriculum design, and instructional methods. This chapter describes steps and considerations for developing a successful program geared to the needs of individual schools and districts. The steps include (*a*) establishing an advisory committee, (*b*) assessing needs, (*c*) developing a philosophy, (*d*) establishing a definition, (*e*) selecting identification procedures consistent with the stated philosophy and definition, (*f*) deriving program goals, (*g*) designing a curriculum plan and administrative arrangements to meet the goals, (*h*) developing an evaluation plan, (*i*) selecting effective teachers, (*j*) providing in-service training to administrators and teachers, and (*k*) involving the community.

ESTABLISHING AN ADVISORY COMMITTEE

Overall plans for a gifted program should be generated through the cooperative efforts of several key individuals who can provide different perspectives and thereby contribute to the development of a well-considered program. These key individuals serve in an advisory capacity to the school board and might include administrators, teachers, support personnel, and representatives of the broader community.

Administrators

The administrator whose involvement in planning is most critical is the administrator who will have direct responsibility for the gifted program. Frequently, the assistant superintendent for instruction is the key administrator. In states where gifted education forms a part of special education, the director of special education would be the key participant. Alternatively, or in addition, a district may identify a special coordinator or director for gifted education. Other districts might assign the administration of gifted programs to an individual in an already existing position—for example, the curriculum supervisor. A higher administrator, such as the superintendent or assistant superintendent, with strong interest in the education of gifted and talented students—may also provide leadership.

Teachers

Even in districts that do not have formal programs for gifted students, teachers can be identified who have worked effectively with superior students and enjoy working with them. Teachers who have instructed bright youngsters can contribute many ideas regarding appropriate services. Excellent teachers who prefer to work with heterogeneous regular classes should also be represented on the advisory committee because the establishment of a strong relationship between regular teachers and special-class teachers constitutes a critical element of successful gifted programs.

Support Personnel

Depending on the nature of the gifted program being considered, the advisory committee may invite input from additional support personnel. For example, diagnosticians or school psychologists can make suggestions regarding appropriate assessment and identification procedures. Districts that want to include a counseling component will want a representative of the counseling staff on the advisory committee. School counselors may also have ideas to contribute regarding scheduling arrangements. The assistant superintendent of business or finance plays a critical role in advising the committee about the availability of resources.

Parents

Parents of gifted students often serve as the strongest supporters of efforts to develop programs for the gifted. In many cases parent activism provides the impetus for establishment of districtwide programs. The most effective parent members of the advisory committee will be those who can communicate and exchange ideas with a large group of parents—for example, the president of the local parents' association for the gifted, members of the schools' parent–community advisory board, or officers of the parent–teacher organization. Parents of children of average ability may provide viewpoints representative of the larger school community. However, while parent input is critical to effective program planning, the development of new programs remains a responsibility and prerogative of the district as an agency of the state.

Community Leaders

Members of the advisory committee representing the broader community can be extremely helpful in program planning, especially when the program will be enriched by community resources. For example, where programs for the artistically talented are being planned, representatives of community art councils and art centers can play important roles. Leaders of business and industry may have suggestions regarding fund raising and internship placements for students. Districts that serve several ethnic groups may find it useful to involve leaders of the ethnic communities to help secure community support and ensure that services will be consistent with community needs. A priest in a Catholic–Hispanic neighborhood or the chief of a native Hawaiian community are examples.

A study by Orenstein (1984) emphasized the importance of district committees and parent and community support. Orenstein compared programs in New York that were included in a catalog of effective programs with programs that were not included. Among other characteristics, programs included in the catalog had a higher level of parent involvement and frequent district committee meetings. Moreover, committee membership consisted of a more diverse group of individuals from both within and outside the formal organization. Orenstein concluded that community support aids program viability and that lay influence should be encouraged in all phases of programming for the gifted.

Responsibilities of the Advisory Committee

The committee's overall task will be to plan the program, estimate costs, and provide the leadership necessary to secure long-term school and community support. To be successful, members must be or must become knowledgeable about gifted education, and to this end they may hire consultants, tap available resources in the community (including higher-education faculty, if available), visit model programs, and request assistance from the state department of education. The committee then directs the establishment of a program for gifted students according to the steps described in the sections that follow.

ASSESSING NEEDS

The advisory committee's first step is to examine the district's existing curriculum to determine whether and where aspects of gifted education are currently operating. It would be insulting to excellent teachers in the district to assume that the needs of gifted students are not already being considered. An evaluation of the current situation can help identify personnel who have already devised methods for working effectively with superior students. A needs assessment questionnaire can be a valuable tool to determine at the outset (a) how, by whom, and to what extent the needs of gifted children are being met; (b) administrator and teacher attitudes toward gifted education; (c) student needs and resource requirements; and (d) potential in-service training areas.

While recognizing the important contributions of excellent regular-classroom teachers, experts in the field generally agree that teachers of the gifted benefit substantially from training focused on methods and materials specifically for the gifted. In his comparison of programs for the gifted, Orenstein (1984) found that effective programs tended to (a) be staffed with individuals experienced in gifted education, (b) provide more frequent in-service training, and (c) use consultants more often.

Administrators of gifted programs sometimes begin with a defensive posture arising from the untested assumption that principals and teachers will balk at yet another special program involving more time, paperwork, and scheduling hassles. Indeed, some studies have indicated that teachers express ambivalent views toward gifted education (Weiss and Gallagher, 1980). However, other investigations reveal more positive attitudes toward special services to gifted students. For example, Rubenzer and Twaite (1979) analyzed questionnaire responses of 1,220 kindergarten through twelfth-grade educators in eleven public school districts in Wisconsin; those surveyed strongly favored provision of appropriate alternatives for gifted and talented students. Most preferred serving gifted students within the regular classroom or through grouping procedures rather than through acceleration.

In Weiss and Gallagher's (1980) survey of 586 faculty members from five major universities in various parts of the country, responses indicated a strongly positive attitude toward gifted programs but ambivalence concerning implementation procedures. For example, while acknowledging the difficulty of meeting individual needs in heterogeneous classrooms, the educators expressed concern about the isolation and elitism that might result from removal of the gifted students from the peer group. Respondents who indicated that they had participated in special programs expressed more positive attitudes than those who lacked personal experience with gifted programs. The results of this study, along with the results of the Rubenzer and Twaite (1979) study, suggest that although some education is needed regarding methods for accommodating gifted students, educators at all levels generally possess positive attitudes toward special provisions for gifted children.

Advisory committees may have to work harder in rural areas, where less positive attitudes toward academic pursuits in general may exist. Colangelo and Kelly (1983) chose a consolidated junior high school serving six rural Iowa communities and surveyed the attitudes of the general student body, the students who participated in the school's gifted program, the parents, and the teachers. The researchers used an activities questionnaire that asked respondents to rank the school's fourteen extracurricular activities. Students in the gifted program ranked the program third in importance after chorus and basketball. Parents, teachers, and general students ranked the gifted program eighth, tenth, and tenth, respectively—lower than their ranking of athletics programs but consistent with their ranking of other academic activities (minicourses, speech club, and school newspaper). Although respondents seemed to consider the gifted program as valuable as other academic programs, academically oriented pursuits in general ranked low in importance.

Rubenzer and Twaite (1979) have developed an easily administered, quickly completed needs assessment instrument based on questions suggested by the 1971 U.S. Office of Education report to Congress on the status of gifted education. The thirteen items in their questionnaire, which was approved by a panel of experts and piloted on 145 educators, are contained in the following list, along with one addition (question 12) designed to assess accommodations currently being made for gifted students. (Items 1 through 10 are forced choice, to be answered yes or no. Items 11 through 14 are open ended.)

1. Is there a gifted student in your class?
2. Are gifted students easily identified?
3. Are academically gifted students creative, and vice versa?
4. Are alternative provisions required for the gifted?
5. Does exceptional talent require special nurturance?

6. Is enrichment within the regular classroom a preferred alternative for the gifted?
7. Does acceleration (grade skipping or subject advancement) cause academic or social difficulties?
8. Is elitism a by-product of special programming for the gifted?
9. Are gifted students usually enthusiastic and conforming?
10. Are gifted dropouts proportionately rare?
11. What are the observable characteristics you used for gifted nomination?
12. What accommodations, if any, are you currently making for gifted students in your classroom?
13. What provisions for the gifted would you consider most desirable?
14. What should the emphasis be for in-services on the gifted/talented?

Questions 1, 2, 3, 9, 10, and 11 provide information concerning respondents' knowledge of characteristics and referral traits. Questions 4 and 5 tap attitudes about the need to provide special services. Questions 6, 7, 8, and 13 examine perceptions regarding programming. Responses to item 14 specifically indicate perceived in-service needs. However, the total questionnaire provides information about respondents' knowledge of characteristics, false stereotypes, identification procedures, and program alternatives that can serve as the basis for in-service activities. Questionnaire results can also be analyzed by grade level, since perceived needs may differ for students in various age groups.

DEVELOPING A PHILOSOPHY

A survey of programs for gifted students within and across states will indicate a wide variety despite relatively similar populations. One source of the variation lies in the differing philosophies of program planners. In the absence of definitive empirical data supporting specific program models for specific populations of gifted students, administrators are left to base many decisions on the predominant philosophy of the district. Prior to designing specifics, planners must make philosophical or value judgments in at least four major areas: program status, program aims, program participants, and program models. The philosophy thus developed will provide guidelines for many subsequent decisions.

Program Status

The success of any program depends to no minor extent on the financial and moral support granted by district administrators. In times of prosperity, the priority rankings of various programs may lack significance. However, under stressful economic conditions district priorities have great relevance, especially where programs must compete for limited funds. A major task of the advisory committee will be to communicate to district personnel and to the greater community its perception of the importance of special programs for gifted students and to secure a favorable written policy for the implementation and continuance of the programs. The committee's task is sometimes made difficult by the widespread feeling that gifted students (and their parents) do not need special help. A basic message must constantly be reiterated: Gifted students must have the same opportunity for academic and personal fulfillment as all other students. Anything less constitutes a denial of a fundamental premise of American public education. States that mandate appropriate services to all exceptional children, handicapped and gifted, with funding formulas for each, can generally fund programs for gifted students without detracting from programs for other special needs children.

Program Aims

A second value-laden decision concerns the overall aim of the gifted program. In helping students develop their potential, is the aim of the program self-fulfillment for the students, benefit for society, or both? Setting priorities with regard to the program's overall purpose will guide subsequent decisions about curricular goals. Another question regarding program aims is the extent to which the curriculum will focus on developing students' strengths or ameliorating relative weaknesses. A third question concerns the extent to which the interests of the gifted student should influence the curriculum. For example, if a child's primary talent and interest lie in astronomy, should astronomy form the major emphasis of this child's curriculum?

Program Participants

Few districts can afford to provide appropriate programs for all grade levels, all categories of giftedness (intellectual, academic, creative, leadership, and artistic), and all types of learners (for example, the underachieving or the handicapped gifted), especially during the early stages of implementation. Therefore, decisions must be made regarding the types of students to be served.

Many districts begin with one grade level, and later expand the gifted program to serve additional grade levels. Districts commonly select grade four as a starting point. Standardized assessments appear relatively reliable at this age level, and in grade four the curriculum begins to broaden after having focused primarily on basic skills, thus allowing for more flexibility in content. However, the psychological literature suggests that children's development reaches a temporary plateau at about the fourth-grade level. Moreover, gifted children whose needs for challenge have not been met during the first four years of schooling may be underachievers by the time they reach fourth grade and thus escape identification. Thus, screening for giftedness (and for risk, in the case of handicapping conditions) ideally should begin at school entrance. Special programming should start for these children at the very beginning and should then expand to progressively higher grade levels.

Categories of giftedness to be targeted for the initial implementation period will depend on the district's resources. Most districts traditionally have focused on the intellectually gifted and later expanded their programs to include additional categories—for example, the creatively gifted. All types of gifted learners, including the underachieving gifted, deserve immediate appropriate services; from an administrative viewpoint, however, it makes sense to select as the initial group students who are most likely to succeed in the new program. A beginning program must often prove itself since success may be critical for its continuation and expansion.

Program Models

The program models selected are necessarily based on the type of students and the resources available. For example, a grouping or an acceleration model would be consistent with the needs of districts that elect to serve only the top 1 percent of students. Similarly, districts that prefer a more inclusive selection criterion (for example, the top 25 percent) might consider models designed to serve heterogeneous ability levels, such as Renzulli's enrichment triad model, Meeker's SOI, or Taylor's multiple talent approach (see Chapter 6).

ESTABLISHING A DEFINITION AND IDENTIFICATION PROCEDURES

A number of states have regulations that define gifted and talented learners and specify identification procedures. When funding is tied to these regulations, individual districts generally adopt the state definition and procedures. However, some state regulations provide only very general guidelines, permitting individual districts wide flexibility in interpretation and application. States with strict guidelines sometimes allow waivers on certain regulations for individual districts that propose innovative procedures appropriate to the needs of children whom they serve. State regulations have the benefit of providing consistency across districts within the state, which promotes but does not ensure continuous services to children who move within the state. In states that permit local initiative, individual school districts have autonomy to develop their own definitions and assessment procedures.

Both the definition of giftedness and the identification procedures must derive from and demonstrate consistency with the district's established philosophy. Thus, one element to consider in establishing a definition concerns the categories of giftedness to be included—that is, intellectual, specifically academic, social, or creative giftedness or giftedness in the visual or the performing arts. An alternative might be to define giftedness as a combination of traits— for example, Renzulli's (1978) description of above-average intellectual ability, creativity, and task commitment. Another consideration is whether the definition will include potential for high performance in addition to demonstrated high performance and thereby include underachieving gifted students. Considerations in designing identification procedures include those listed in the following paragraphs.

1. An identification model must be selected that is consistent with the district's philosophy regarding degree of inclusiveness or exclusiveness of the program. For example, districts that support the idea that virtually every individual can benefit from enriched programming might use the revolving-door model described in Chapter 5. Districts that consider only the top 1 percent of the school population as gifted could design a more traditional psychometric model where eligibility is determined by specific cutoff scores on standardized assessment devices. The psychometric model can be made more inclusive by lowering cutoff scores and/or including more informal assessment data.

2. Screening and referral procedures must be established that are consistent with age groups and categories of giftedness to be served.

3. Reliable and valid standardized instruments and/or informal assessment devices (for example, biographical inventories, expert appraisal, or teacher rating scales) must be selected for each category of giftedness included in the definition.

4. Appropriate selection criteria must be determined. Establishment of criteria requires value judgments related to philosophical issues, such as degree of inclusiveness. Also, judgments regarding the use of quota systems will affect determination of criteria since quota systems may imply different criteria for different subgroups of gifted students (for example, culturally different or handicapped).

5. Available resources must be matched to assessment needs. For example, psychometric assessment models may require additional certified diagnostic personnel.

A clear, written policy for selection and identification of students for the gifted program provides a standard set of operating procedures for all personnel involved. Moreover, having such a policy helps teachers and administrators of programs for the gifted explain procedures to the public. For example, administrators and teachers often encounter parents who have difficulty accepting their children's ineligibility for the program. Showing parents their children's scores in comparison to (*a*) criteria defined by policy and (*b*) scores of other children in the program helps parents realize the relative standing of their children. Program personnel should explain that scores can be affected by situational variables, previous experience, and language differences and that retesting at a later time may be useful. However, written procedures should not be considered immutable; they do require evaluation and updating as new information becomes available.

DERIVING PROGRAM GOALS

A program's goals are the broad aims the program intends to accomplish. The goals of a program differ from student objectives in that the latter state specific skills, knowledge, and processes to be acquired by individual students. Goals derive logically from the institution's philosophy and the perceived needs of program participants. Goals may therefore differ from program to program, depending on such factors as age group served, category of giftedness, and characteristics of students.

A review of gifted programs suggests that there exists a common core of goals that planners have deemed appropriate to gifted students at all age levels. Goals for students include helping them to (a) develop and pursue interests; (b) increase academic knowledge; (c) improve leadership skills; (d) develop self-confidence, task commitment, intelligent risk taking, and positive attitudes toward learning; (e) practice creative and high-level thinking skills; and (f) develop humanistic understanding. Goals for program implementors describe the inputs that will be provided to accomplish student goals, such as interest centers, unit studies, field trips, guest speakers, mentors, guided independent investigations, and specific administrative arrangements (acceleration, grouping, or enrichment, as needed).

DESIGNING A CURRICULUM PLAN

Based on the established philosophy, student characteristics, needs assessment data (review of current curriculum), and available resources, the advisory committee establishes a curriculum plan designed to accomplish program goals. The advisory committee frequently assigns this task to district administrators in charge of curriculum development and to selected teachers, such as those identified through the needs assessment as successfully meeting the needs of superior students. (Steps for developing a curriculum for gifted students are detailed in Chapter 6.)

Designing the curriculum occurs in tandem with (a) selection of administrative arrangements that will be used to implement the curriculum and (b) selection of instructional models or strategies. Administrative arrangements (described in Chapter 5) include various enrichment, grouping, and acceleration options (see Chapters 7, 8, and 9 for a variety of specific instructional methods for enhancing inductive, creative, and evaluative thinking). Planners at the New Mexico State University Preschool for the Gifted selected a homogeneous grouping arrangement through a self-contained special class. They selected a unit approach to content presentation that also incorporates higher-level and creative-thinking processes through use of such instructional models as Taba's inductive methods, Suchman's inquiry strategies, and Bloom's taxonomy. In another example, one school district in New Mexico serves all grade levels through an acceleration model that includes telescoping within the regular classroom, grade skipping, advanced placement in single subjects, early college entrance, and special grouping arrangements such as summer institutes and seminars to foster special interests and interaction with gifted peers.

DEVELOPING AN EVALUATION PLAN

Design of an evaluation plan should occur prior to program implementation for two reasons. First, data for the evaluation must often be collected during several phases of the implementation period. Even annual evaluations necessitate planning and preparation of procedures and measures before the end of the year. Funding agencies generally require a well-formulated evaluation plan prior to program implementation, as well as an analysis of evaluation data. Annual data collection provides a *summative* evaluation—that is, an assessment of overall program effectiveness often used for decisions about program continuance.

The second reason for designing an evaluation plan prior to program implementation is that ongoing, or *formative*, evaluation can provide information that will lead to improvements during the implementation period. Continuous feedback provides direction for modifying the program as it progresses. Summative evaluation results can also provide formative information for the subsequent implementation period.

Although the program director can conduct the summative evaluation, an external evaluator frequently provides more objectivity and insight than an individual closely involved with the program. Many programs call upon their advisory committee to design and conduct the evaluation or to select an external evaluator who reports to the advisory committee. Summative evaluation should occur at least annually.

Renzulli and Smith (1979b) have suggested that programs can be evaluated in terms of (*a*) product or outcome (for example, did the program increase student creativity?); (*b*) process or input (for example, did the teachers provide opportunities for risk taking?); and (*c*) presage or concerns related to the design of the program (for example, are the program goals appropriate?). Product evaluation generally assesses student growth, while process and presage evaluation examine the efficacy with which the program accomplishes its stated purposes. An effective evaluation design should include attention to all three components. The following sections describe some of the difficulties encountered in evaluating programs for the gifted and suggest one useful evaluation planning model.

Considerations in Evaluating Programs for the Gifted

Several authors (e.g., Archambault, 1984; Callahan, 1983; Renzulli, 1975; Renzulli and Smith, 1979b) have described problems peculiar to the evaluation of programs for gifted students. One major problem is that institutions that support gifted programs usually require annual evaluations of program effectiveness, including evidence of student progress. Yet the goals of many programs for the gifted have long-term rather than short-term consequences. For example, having students become independent investigators may first require unlearning of dependence on the teacher and acquisition of content knowledge and inquiry skills (Callahan, 1983). Depending on the student's entry level, the process can reasonably require more than one year.

A second major difficulty in evaluating programs for the gifted concerns the availability of reliable and valid instruments for measuring student change. The content of standardized measures rarely matches a program's particular goals and objectives. For example, the New Mexico State University Preschool for the Gifted has as one goal that children will increase their knowledge in content areas presented through units, such as computers or communication. Yet available standardized achievement measures, such as the Peabody Individual Achievement Test, are limited to assessment of reading, spelling, arithmetic, and general information. As an alternative, projects can develop their own measures specifically matched to program objectives. However, such measures generally lack supportive reliability and validity data. Use of multiple measures, both standardized and project developed, to assess each program element can strengthen the evaluation by providing several sources of data on the same component. Aylesworth (1984) provides some useful guidelines for selecting instruments to evaluate programs for the gifted.

A third issue in program evaluation concerns the use of one set of measures for all students, which presupposes that all students have the same achievement objectives. Programs that encourage students to pursue their own interests cannot be expected to demonstrate uniform student gains on a single achievement measure. Another problem particularly relevant to the evaluation of gifted student progress by means of pretesting and posttesting involves regression toward the mean—that is, upon second testing, initially high scores tend to decrease, while initially low scores increase; both types of scores move toward the mean. High pretest scores of gifted students theoretically can be expected to decrease toward the mean upon posttesting. A related consideration is that students who score high on pretests, as do many gifted students by definition, are more limited in the amount of improvement they can demonstrate than students who initially score low.

Special educators of the handicapped frequently use a behavioral objectives model in which evaluation consists primarily of determining whether criteria established in behavioral objectives for each student have been met. An example of a behavioral objective is this: Given ten states, the student will list corresponding capitals within thirty seconds with 90 percent accuracy. A rigid behavioral objectives model can impede appropriate programming for the gifted because it encourages program developers to focus on simple behaviors that can be easily measured rather than on higher mental processes (Renzulli and Smith, 1979b).

A Suggested Model for Evaluation Planning

Callahan (1983), Renzulli (1975), and Renzulli and Smith (1979b) have suggested several evaluation models specifically for programs for the gifted. Another useful model is an abbreviated version of the Discrepancy Evaluation Model (DEM) (Yavorsky, 1976). The DEM defines evaluation as a comparison between performance and predetermined standards. The standards by which performance is judged are subjectively determined and derived from experience, knowledge, and values. The DEM helps solve some of the difficulties associated with evaluating programs for the gifted by (a) focusing on broader components rather than on specific objectives for each student and (b) encouraging use of multiple measures for evaluating each component.

Steps for designing a DEM evaluation plan are outlined in the following paragraphs. The steps are based on the evaluation plan of the New Mexico State University Preschool for the Gifted and on a revised version of the evaluation planning matrix of the Evaluation Training Consortium (1979) and Brinkerhoff et al. (1983). The revised matrix is shown in Table 13.1.

Step 1: Identify evaluation concerns, or those areas of the program that require evaluation. These areas should include concerns related to product, process, and presage. At the planning stage, developers of the preschool envisioned six major components to be evaluated:

A. Identification procedures
B. Program inputs
C. Program effectiveness: child performance
D. Parent programs
E. Teacher training (use of the preschool as a training site)
F. Impact (on state, regional, and national levels)

Step 2: Formulate evaluation questions for each evaluation concern identified in step 1. That is, what questions, if answered, will determine the degree of success for each program component? For example, the evaluation questions for evaluation concern C (program effectiveness in terms of child performance) arethe following:

C1. Do children demonstrate a positive attitude toward learning?
C2. Do children demonstrate effective thinking processes?
C3. Do children develop wide interests and pursue identified interests?
C4. Do children demonstrate affective development?
C5. Do children demonstrate basic skill development?
C6. Do children develop an appreciation and acceptance of various cultures?

Step 3: Further define each evaluation question by specifying variables or indicators that can be measured. Variables for evaluation concern C, evaluation

Table 13.1 Evaluation planning matrix

MEASUREMENT PROCEDURES	A. Identification procedures		B. Program inputs		C. Program effectiveness: child performance						D. Parent programs		E. Teacher training		F. Impact		INSTRUMENTS
EVALUATION QUESTIONS	A1. How accurate is screening?	A2. How accurate is identification?	B1. How appropriate are methods?	B2. Are varied experiences given?	C1. Do children show positive attitudes toward learning?	C2. Do children show effective thinking processes?	C3. Do children show development and pursuit of interests?	C4. Do children show affective development?	C5. Do children show basic skill development?	C6. Do children show appreciation and acceptance of various cultures?	D1. Do parents show interest?	D2. Do programs communicate essential information?	E1. How useful is training for preservice?	E2. How useful is training for in-service?	F1. How effective is dissemination?	F2. How effective is replication?	
Canvass project records	abcd	abc									ab		a	a	b	ab	
Diagnostician reassessment		d				ab			abcd								Muller's Self-Concept, PIAT, Raven's, TCAM
Follow-up in public schools		d			a			a									
Outside evaluation by experts		d	a		a	ab									a		Modified Evaluation of Identification Process*
Teacher daily log of activities				ab													
Observation of children					a	ab	ab	abc		abc							Videotape Ratings
University student evaluation of practicum													b				
Parent questionnaire											c	abc					Parent Evaluation of Pupil*

											Modified Student Questionnaire*	Teacher Evaluation of Pupil*	Student Self-Esteem Inventory*	Teacher's Appraisal of Creative Problem-Solving Lesson*	
Child interview							ac		ab						
Teacher rating of children					a			abcd	ab	ab	a				
Child inventory									abc				abc		
Teacher evaluation of lessons/methods			ab												ab
Consumer evaluation															a
Public school teacher/administrator inventory						b									

VARIABLES

Question A1: a. ethnic distribution; b. sex; c. socioeconomic status; d. sources.
Question A2: a. ethnic distribution; b. sex; c. socioeconomic status; d. accuracy.
Question B1: a. consistency with model; b. effectiveness.
Question B2: a. number, and type of trips; b. number, and type of speakers.
Question C1: a. motivation.
Question C2: a. problem solving; b. creativity.
Question C3: a. attitude; b. area of interest.
Question C4: a. self-concept; b. responsibility; c. respect for authority.
Question C5: a. math; b. reading; c. language; d. motor skills.
Question C6: a. attitude; b. play; c. second-language acquisition.
Question D1: a. number of visits; b. attendance; c. subjective impressions.
Question D2: a. definition and characteristics of giftedness; b. parents' legal rights; c. implementation.
Question E1: a. number of students; b. quality of practicum.
Question E2: a. number of visits; b. quality of visits.
Question F1: a. quality of manual; b. number of workshops.
Question F2: a. number of requests; b. number of sites.

*Available from Renzulli, 1975.

question C4 (Do children demonstrate affective development?) are as follows:

a. realistic self-concept
b. responsibility
c. respect for authority

Step 4: Relate the variables to measurement procedures by determining what types of data sources will provide information on each variable. It can be helpful to begin by simply listing available data sources or measurement procedures (see the leftmost column in Table 13.1) and matching appropriate ones to the variables. For example, measurement procedures for variable C4a, realistic self-concept, can include formal testing through diagnostic reassessment and use of a parent questionnaire, teacher rating scale, or child inventory.

Step 5: Relate the variables and measurement procedures to instruments. After variables and measurement procedures have been defined, specific existing instruments may suggest themselves as appropriate assessment tools (see the final column in Table 13.1). Where no instruments exist, the variables and measurement procedures serve as a basis for constructing new instruments. For example, the matrix indicates that a parent questionnaire can provide data to assess variables C1a, C2ab, C3ab, C4abc, C6abc, D1c, and D2abc. An already existing instrument, the Parent Evaluation of Pupil (Renzulli, 1975), can be modified to include questions relevant to these variables. It is critical that each measure (*a*) appropriately assess the information desired and (*b*) be administered to individuals representative of the population sampled.

The completed evaluation planning matrix provides an overall picture of program components and evaluation procedures, permitting planners to see areas of overlap as well as gaps. Instruments can be constructed that provide evaluation information for several program components, eliminating the need to devise separate measures for each component. Moreover, as stated earlier, the multiple sources of information help answer evaluation questions. As can be seen from the matrix, formal assessment, parent questionnaires, and teacher evaluations provide separate sources of data for evaluating the extent to which the program had helped children to use effective thinking skills (C2).

The planning matrix is flexible and designed for change as needs dictate. Next steps for implementing the evaluation design include (*a*) collecting and/ or developing the instruments, (*b*) establishing a timeline for data collection, (*c*) assigning data collection to appropriate personnel, and (*d*) collecting, analyzing, and reporting the data.

SELECTING EFFECTIVE TEACHERS

The most crucial factor in the success of any educational program is the selection of teachers who work directly with targeted students. Even poorly conceived programs can be salvaged by excellent teachers, while the most carefully planned programs cannot succeed in the absence of such teachers. Teacher selection ranked highest in a study in which experts identified key features of programs for the gifted (Renzulli, 1981). The critical role played by teachers requires that administrators carefully match teachers to student needs. Unfortunately, some administrators select teachers for gifted programs on the basis of seniority, while others rotate teachers in and out of gifted programs to ensure teachers an equal distribution of fair, good, and excellent students. Although characteristics of the best teachers of the gifted have yet to be empirically validated, samples of gifted students and teacher trainers describe effective teachers in similar terms. The following sections summarize the literature on the characteristics of excellent teachers of the gifted and the professional competencies required.

Teacher Characteristics

Bishop (1981) compared the characteristics of 109 high school teachers identified as successful by intellectually gifted students with the characteristics of 97 teachers not so identified. Bishop found that the two groups did not differ according to marital status, type of undergraduate institution attended, highest degree earned, course work preparation, or extent of association with professional organizations. However, teachers perceived as successful tended (a) to be mature and experienced; (b) to be mentally superior (among the top 3 percent of scorers on the WAIS); (c) to pursue more intellectual interests, such as literature and the arts; (d) to have high achievement needs; (e) to pursue teaching because of a desire for intellectual growth; (f) to possess more favorable attitudes toward students and to take a personal interest in them; (g) to encourage and accept student participation in the classroom; (h) to be systematic, orderly, businesslike, stimulating, and imaginative; and (i) to support special educational provisions for the gifted and to prefer to teach gifted students.

Sisk (1978), former director of the Office of Gifted and Talented of the U.S. Office of Education, characterized excellent teachers of the gifted as enthusiastic about teaching, highly intelligent, scholarly, artistic, mature and unthreatened, possessed of a keen sense of humor, student centered, tending to seek advanced study, and interested in a wide range of subjects. In short, effective teachers of the gifted demonstrate many qualities associated with giftedness.

Professional Competencies

Experts in the field appear to agree that teachers of the gifted and talented require master's-level training, expertise in curriculum development and modification for the gifted, and knowledge of instructional strategies and materials appropriate to the gifted population. Beyond competencies in working with gifted students, teachers also require the ability to communicate effectively with the larger educational community.

To identify competency areas for training teachers of gifted students, Seeley (1979) surveyed teacher trainers at thirty institutions of higher education that offer programs in gifted education. A sample of principals and teachers who work with gifted students in Colorado were also included in the study. Although some differences occurred among the groups, teacher trainers, principals, and teachers of the gifted tended to concur in rating the following competencies most highly: higher cognitive teaching and questioning, curriculum modification strategies, special curriculum development strategies, diagnostic prescriptive teaching skills, and student counseling strategies. Seeley concluded that teachers assigned to the gifted should hold a master's degree in the field, have one or two years of successful prior teaching experience, and possess a strong content area emphasis. In addition, all teachers should receive some training in gifted education, and state certification and endorsement standards should be mandatory, with flexibility for phase-in of the standards.

Most experts in the field call for mandatory state certification for teachers of the gifted to help ensure quality control and consistency. However, a recent survey of certification practices (Karnes and Parker, 1983) reported that certification standards for teachers of the gifted have been established in only thirteen states: Alabama, Florida, Georgia, Illinois, Indiana, Kansas, Louisiana, Mississippi, New Mexico, North Carolina, North Dakota, Tennessee, and West Virginia.

The National Association for Gifted Children and the Association for the Gifted, a division of the Council for Exceptional Children, have proposed two certification models—Model A for teachers of gifted students and Model B for those who teach the fine and performing arts (see Figure 13.1). Model A calls for a planned graduate degree program (master's level or above), including twelve credit hours of gifted education, a course on research procedures, nine credit hours in a content area, and a practicum. Model B offers two options for teachers of the fine and performing arts. The first incorporates the arts into Model A's nine-hour content area. The second permits certification of individuals with demonstrated records of achievement in the arts.

A critical competency not directly addressed thus far concerns the ability of teachers of the gifted to work with regular classroom teachers. Establishing positive relationships with regular classroom teachers is particularly important for teachers of the gifted whose students spend part of their time in the regular classroom. Failure to develop supportive interaction and effective communication can result in defensiveness and resentment on both sides. One common source of strain between regular and special teachers is potential or actual overlap in experience provided in the two programs. For example, a problem frequently encountered at the fourth-grade level occurs when regular classroom teachers resent acceleration programs that use fourth-grade materials (readers or textbooks) at earlier grade levels, forcing the regular teachers to find different materials when the gifted students reach fourth grade. Another problem occurs when regular classroom teachers require gifted students to make up work missed while they attended special classes. Requiring gifted students to complete the work of both programs can be penalizing and can lead to student frustration and resentment. Teachers of the gifted must be able to work cooperatively with

Figure 13.1 Proposed teacher certification models* from the National Association for Gifted Children and the Association for Gifted (Karnes and Parker, 1983, p. 19)

**Certification for
Teachers of the Gifted**

Complete an approved program in gifted education, culminating in (or at a level beyond) the master's degree and including at least the following components:

1. A minimum of 12 semester hours of credit involving the following course contents:
   Nature and needs/psychology of the gifted
   Assessment of gifted students
   Counseling of the gifted
   Curriculum development for the gifted
   Strategies and materials for teaching the gifted
   Creative studies
   Program development and evaluation
   Parent education and advocacy training
   Special populations/problems of gifted students
   Cognitive and affective processing

2. At least one graduate course in research procedures;

3. A minimum of 9 semester hours (or equivalent) of credit in an approved content area designed to develop a specialization appropriate to the level of teaching or the anticipated professional role of the individual;

4. A practicum involving university-supervised instruction of gifted students, geared to the anticipated future teaching role.

MODEL A

**Certification for
Teachers of the Fine
and Performing Arts**

Option One. Certification for teachers of the fine and performing arts may be incorporated into Model A through the nine-hour content block. In such a case, graduate program coordinators would have the responsibility of guiding students in the selection of appropriate course work to support the anticipated teaching role.

Option Two. Certification for persons with demonstrated records of achievement in the fine and performing arts may be earned as follows:

There must be substantive evidence of artistic and/or creative accomplishment over an extended period of time.

There must be evidence of professional recognition in the arts area for which certification is sought.

Qualification of an individual in the above areas must be judged by a committee of three recognized experts in the area to be credentialed, appointed by the State Department of Education.

MODEL B

*Models represent the recommendations of the NAGC Professional Training Institute's Subcommittee on Teacher Certification and have not been officially endorsed by NAGC or TAG.

regular classroom teachers to find solutions for such problems. For example, the student might be permitted to test out of regular classroom work or to incorporate the skill areas missed into the special-program activities.

In a study undertaken to identify key factors that affect relationships between teachers of the gifted and regular classroom teachers (Frasier and Carland, 1980), teachers of the gifted, administrators, teacher trainers, and counselors agreed that open communication, awareness and respect for the responsibilities of both regular and special teachers, and mutual concern for the appropriate education of gifted students contribute to positive relationships. Other factors cited by respondents included strong administrative support, in-service training for regular classroom teachers, careful scheduling, communication regarding the student's performance, sharing of teaching strategies, understanding of the goals of both programs, and involvement of regular teachers in the selection process. A survey by Meyers (1984) supported these suggestions and emphasized the need for shared ownership of gifted programs as well as improved communication and scheduling. Meyers recommended involving classroom teachers in selection of students for the resource room program, in discussing independent study projects, and in planning and sharing committees.

Berghoff and Berghoff (1979) have offered several suggestions for resource teachers of the gifted to use in establishing open communication with regular-classroom teachers. Suggestions included (a) informing the regular teacher of specific services offered in the gifted program (for example, teaching strategies, supplementary materials, assistance in using community services and designing learning centers, and direct instruction of small groups); (b) expressing appreciation for the regular teacher's interest; (c) conveying feelings of respect by listening to the regular teacher; (d) showing support by praising the regular teacher's accomplishments and offering encouragement after perceived failures; and (e) offering follow-up support.

PROVIDING IN-SERVICE TRAINING

In-service training plays a significant role in schools and districts that plan to implement a program for gifted students. If, as in many districts, regular classroom teachers, counselors, and principals act as the major referral sources for identifying gifted students, these individuals need a firm understanding of special services for gifted students and a thorough knowledge of referral characteristics. One challenge in instituting new programs is securing support across all school buildings in a given district and across all teachers within a building. In districts that have attempted to establish programs in, for example, all elementary schools, availability of services is often uneven for the first several years because of differences among principals and teachers in degree of support for the new program.

In-service activities should be carefully planned, developmentally sequenced, and professionally approached. Provision of salary incentives and/or college or recertification credit can help ensure participation. Topics important for in-service training directed at all school personnel include (a) rationale and need; (b) federal, state, and local definitions; (c) referral characteristics; (d) specific referral, identification, and selection procedures for the district and school; and (e) methods for enriching the regular curriculum. In-service activities aimed specifically at personnel directly associated with the program for the gifted (for example, teachers, counselors, diagnosticians/psychologists) depend on needs identified as the program is planned and implemented. Generally, topics requested by staff members of gifted programs are specific to their responsibilities—for example, science methods for the gifted, curriculum adaptations, guiding of independent investigations, and identification and modification of materials. Where possible, opening in-service training opportunities to all school personnel can support positive public relations.

INVOLVING THE COMMUNITY

Although the planning committee may already include key representatives of the larger community, the new program will benefit from the involvement of a greater proportion of the community through planned public awareness activities. Increased public awareness has several advantages. First, community awareness of the availability of programs for gifted students, of the rationale for special services, and of referral characteristics and procedures results in increased interest and demand for services. Thus, it becomes apparent that the program serves a community need. Second, positive press helps create a favorable image for the program and for the district, which does not hurt relations with higher administrators. Third, large-scale community awareness increases the number of individuals and organizations that will volunteer their support as mentors, guest speakers, field trip sponsors, internship supervisors, and donors.

Effective community awareness activities can take many forms. The most common and effective activities are media campaigns through newspaper write-ups, local television talk shows, and radio spots (usually free for nonprofit organizations). Other projects include open house with formal invitations to key individuals, multilingual fliers distributed at supermarket counters, and information tables at shopping malls and community events.

CHAPTER SUMMARY

Establishing new programs to serve gifted and talented students can be a rewarding endeavor for school personnel and students alike. Careful planning by the advisory committee is crucial to effective program development and includes assessing current status and perceived needs, developing a philosophy, establishing a working definition, selecting identification procedures, deriving program goals, designing the curriculum plan and administrative arrangements, developing an evaluation plan, selecting teachers, providing in-service training, and involving the community. Consistency among all these elements constitutes a most important factor for program success.

Effective teachers also play a critical role in program implementation. Effective teachers of the gifted appear to possess many traits associated with giftedness—high intelligence, maturity, sense of humor, and wide interests. Training programs for teachers of the gifted should be offered at the graduate level, should provide important competencies, and should require subject matter knowledge. The number and quality of teacher training programs will increase as more states pass appropriate regulations requiring specific certification or endorsement for teachers of the gifted.

ACTIVITIES FOR THOUGHT AND DISCUSSION

1. Develop a philosophy for planning a program for gifted students that reflects your personal views. Try to articulate a rationale for each judgment you make in developing your philosophy.

2. Develop an evaluation plan for a program with which you are familiar.

3. Make a list of competencies you feel are important for teachers of the gifted. Then outline a program for training teachers of the gifted, listing course titles and descriptions. If your state specifies certification standards for teachers of the gifted, compare your plan with these standards.

4. Outline a total program plan following the steps presented in this chapter.

Chapter Fourteen

PARENTS AND FAMILIES

Parents of gifted and talented children have received relatively little attention in the literature on gifted education. Callahan (1982) has suggested that the lack of emphasis on parents of the gifted may be due to erroneous beliefs that (*a*) gifted children succeed without intervention and (*b*) the parents of gifted children are also gifted and employ effective child-rearing strategies. However, while many parents of gifted children possess above-average ability, some do not. Moreover, no evidence exists to show that parents of gifted children necessarily use effective parenting strategies. In fact, little research is available on what constitutes effective parenting strategies for the gifted (Colangelo and Dettman, 1983).

Despite the sparsity of information on programs for parents of gifted children, several assumptions support the development of such programs. First, parents influence their children's behaviors, values, and attitudes. Parents are the first teachers of their children; it is commonly under the tutelage of parents that children develop language, establish self-care habits, and learn motor and social skills. A substantial body of literature indicates that interactions and processes within the home, such as maternal responsiveness, stimulation of language and of academic behavior, variety of stimulation, and type of discipline, are related to children's cognitive development and school achievement (Freund, Bradley, and Caldwell, 1979). Based on a review of cross-sectional, longitudinal, and intervention studies on the role of parents in the educational process, Schaefer concluded that parents have "great influence upon the behavior of their children, particularly their intellectual and academic achievement" (Schaefer, 1972, p. 198). Therefore, parent education programs can have a positive effect on children's achievement.

A second assumption supporting the value of programs for parents is that education is more effective when parents and schools support the same objectives. Although Callahan and Kauffman (1982) found little empirical evidence to show that parent involvement in school programs for the gifted results in higher achievement, other writers have suggested that such involvement may have positive outcomes. For example, Bloom and Sosniak (1981) found in retrospective analysis that parents of highly accomplished individuals received detailed information from their children's teachers, monitored their children's practice, and encouraged and corrected their children's performance. Programs that encourage parents to reinforce at home specific goals being worked on at school may conceivably help in the attainment of those goals.

Two other assumptions supporting the development of programs for parents of gifted children are compelling but difficult to test empirically. The first is that parents of the gifted are interested in their children's education and will represent their best interests. This assumption implies that programs that include parents as integral contributors to a gifted child's educational plan may help ensure the plan's appropriateness for that child. The second assumption is that parents have an inherent right to involvement in decisions about their gifted child's curriculum goals and placement.

As discussed in Chapter 5, only two-fifths of the states extend to parents of the gifted the rights of parents under P.L. 94–142. In these states, education regulations encourage parents to participate in the development of their gifted child's individualized education program and provide due process procedures that permit parents a strong voice in the assessment, evaluation, and placement of their gifted child. In states whose regulations do not provide for parent involvement in the decision-making process, parents' inherent rights and responsibilities regarding their children's education must be considered. Programs that include parents of the gifted as members of the decision-making team encourage the production of educational plans more appropriate to the individual child and stronger accountability on the part of the school.

Parent involvement, then, should constitute an important component of educational programs for gifted and talented students. In the absence of a body of controlled research regarding effective parenting strategies for gifted children and parent involvement programs, models for working with parents of the gifted must be derived from theory and research on parenting practices in general, descriptive research on families of gifted children, and experience. This chapter begins by providing a broad theoretical perspective on parent–child interactions and then describes the characteristics and child-rearing practices of parents of gifted and achieving children. The chapter ends with a discussion of parent involvement in school programs, with specific reference to the needs of parents of gifted children and the ways in which parents can contribute to their children's progress.

THEORETICAL PERSPECTIVES: A BIDIRECTIONAL MODEL OF SOCIALIZATION

Socialization refers to the process by which children acquire the knowledge, skills, attitudes, and values necessary for membership in the society and culture in which they live. Socialization theory prior to the 1950s tended to emphasize the role of parents in the socialization process to the virtual exclusion of child contributions. Data indicating significant correlations between parent and child behaviors were interpreted as unidirectional—that is, the emphasis was on the parents influencing the child. Bell (1971) attributed neglect of the child's role in parent–child interactions to early notions equating the child's contribution with biological and genetic factors. However, the prevailing American political and social philosophies of egalitarianism and opportunity promote the idea that human beings are flexible, adaptable, and capable of improvement rather than limited by fixed biological determinants. In sociology and psychology, reaction against biological determinism has resulted in a focus on external sources (parents) as agents in modifying children's behaviors.

Limiting the child's contributions in the socialization process to biological factors precluded the idea that children exhibit behaviors that are based on *experience* and can modify parent behaviors. During the 1950s and 1960s, researchers who recognized the importance of child contributions to the socialization process began to reinterpret the data to demonstrate that children's behavior also affects that of their parents. For example, one early study (cited in Bell, 1968) found that parents of adolescent male repeat offenders used more physical punishment than did parents of nondelinquents, and the authors concluded that physical punishment leads to delinquent behavior. However, Bell reinterpreted the data to suggest that the boys' congenital tendency to hyperactivity led to parents' efforts to control their sons' behavior and thus to increased use of physical punishment. Additional studies cited by Bell (1971) support the theory that children play an active role in the socialization process. For example, one investigation indicated that increased frequency of smiling in infants changed the behavior of caretakers.

Socialization, then, is an interactional, bidirectional process. Parents both direct and react to their children's behaviors; children influence and are affected by the behaviors of their parents. A child's contributions to the interaction may be based on biological and genetic factors—for example, physical appearance or intellectual capacity—as well as on temperament, personality, and knowledge gained from previous experience with the environment. Radin (1982) described six ways in which parents directly influence child behavior: (*a*) by acting as models for the child to observe and imitate; (*b*) by using verbal and physical rewards and punishments; (*c*) by providing direct instruction (for example, teaching colors or numbers); (*d*) by stating expectations through rules; (*e*) by using cognitive modification strategies (for example, labeling behaviors, reasoning with the child, and arousing feelings of guilt or empathy); and (*f*) by establishing the physical setting (for example, opportunities for exploration, manipulation, or academic learning). It would be difficult to isolate the specific contributions of parents and children to the socialization process since socialization is continuous and interactive. The parent, for example, may stimulate a certain behavior on the part of the child, which in turn may elicit a different behavior in the parent.

For the gifted, the major implication of an interactive theory of socialization is that research on parents and families of gifted children must be interpreted within an interactive framework. Much of the research on parents of gifted children focuses retrospectively on parental behaviors and attitudes that may have fostered achievement and creativity in the children. An interactive interpretation, however, would suggest that the gifted child's inherent genetic superiority, temperament, or learned behaviors (positive and negative) may have helped produce the observed parental behaviors and attitudes. One father, for example, did not recognize his two-year-old son's intellectual precocity until an adult friend, reading a newspaper with the child on his lap, discovered that the boy was reading the paper. The father reacted by providing more reading materials, spending more time listening to the child read, and attending more to other indications of the child's exceptional abilities.

Peterson (1977) noted that the presence of a gifted child can affect the family by inducing (a) competition among family members, (b) sibling jealousy, and (c) parental failure to recognize and respect each family member's unique gifts and differences. The gifted child's influence may be more pronounced when great discrepancy exists between his or her abilities and those of other family members. The literature suggests that giftedness may have greater effects on sibling relationships than on parent–child relationships (Ballering and Koch, 1984).

Hackney (1981) reported from a program for parents of gifted children that having a gifted child in the family is not necessarily perceived as a positive experience. Based on parents' written observations and oral discussions, Hackney identified five ways in which gifted children impact significantly on family life. First, having a gifted child in the family can alter normal family roles. For example, a gifted child's adultlike ways may interfere with discipline and, from a sibling's perspective, lead to having a third "parent" in the family. Second, parents' feelings about themselves can change. They may feel a heavy burden of responsibility and pressure to provide extra materials and experiences. Feelings of guilt may ensue as they wonder whether they should be doing more. Third, a gifted child may require the family to make special adaptations, such as budget allocations for out-of-school lessons and trips. Fourth, family–neighborhood problems can arise if other children tease the gifted child. Finally, having a gifted child in the family often gives rise to issues that divide family and school. For example, a socially adept, manipulative gifted child can have the parents and the school blaming each other for the child's disinterest or lack of achievement.

PARENT CHARACTERISTICS AND CHILD-REARING PRACTICES

Examining the characteristics and child-rearing behaviors of parents of gifted children is particularly interesting in light of long-range practical implications. Theoretically, can we maximize a child's potential by replicating the parenting behaviors of mothers and fathers whose children are gifted achievers? Our theoretical discussion, however, cautions that while child behavior is seen as a result of the interaction between parent and child, as the child matures, other factors within and outside the home (siblings, television, school, and the community) also exert powerful influences on the developing child's behavior. The relative strengths and specific consequences attributable to each influence are difficult, if not impossible, to isolate. Nevertheless, parenting of gifted and talented children remains an intriguing means of furthering our understanding of such children. The following sections summarize the literature on parents of highly intelligent children, creative children, children with specific talents, and high and low achievers. Parent–child interactions in minority and low-income families are also discussed.

Parents of Highly Intelligent Children

Much of the information available on characteristics of parents of intellectually gifted children comes from the early Terman studies on children with IQs generally of 140 or above (see Chapter 3). Terman's (1926) data characterized his subjects' parents and their homes as described in the following paragraphs.

1. *Father's occupation.* A high proportion of fathers (31.4 percent) had professional occupations, and 50.0 percent had semiprofessional or business occupations. Skilled workers constituted 11.8 percent of the fathers included, semiskilled workers constituted 6.6 percent, and common laborers constituted 0.13 percent. The professional category included lawyers, engineers, teachers, professors, architects, and artists. The semiprofessional and business designation referred generally to executives, business managers, brokers, retail dealers, store owners, clerical workers, druggists, and civil service clerks. Skilled labor included, among others, carpenters, mechanics, butchers, barbers, and policemen.

2. *Income.* Although a few families lived at poverty level, the median income of a subsample of 170 families was reported as more than twice the California average at the time.

3. *Home conditions.* Homes were rated on inclusion of necessities, neatness, size, and degree of parental supervision. Ratings of 288 homes of gifted children were slightly higher than those for unselected homes and considerably higher than those for homes of delinquent boys. The homes of gifted children also contained between 0 and 6,000 books, with a median of 202 volumes.

4. *Marital stability.* The divorce rate among parents of gifted children was 5.2 percent—lower than the divorce rate among comparable families in California (8.75 percent).

5. *Parent education.* Fathers and mothers of gifted children completed an average of twelve grades, about twice as many grades as was the nationwide average at the time. One-fourth of the gifted children had at least one parent who had completed college. In a later survey of Los Angeles parents (Groth, 1975), mothers of intellectually gifted students reported lower divorce rates and higher educational levels than was true for the general population.

6. *Reported parenting techniques.* Although few parents described themselves as employing a systematic scheme of child training, most said they encouraged their children by answering questions and taking an interest in the things that concerned them.

A follow-up report of Terman's gifted subjects studied men who were then at least twenty-five years old. The 150 men rated highest for success (the A's) and the 150 rated lowest (the C's) were compared on a number of variables (Terman, 1954). During their elementary years the groups did not differ in achievement. Despite intellectual capacities equal to those of the A's, the C's began a scholastic decline after entering high school. Of the A's, 97 percent entered college, and 90 percent graduated. Only 68 percent of the C's entered college, and only 37 percent graduated. Terman noted that the differences in the educational histories of A's and C's reflected differences in family backgrounds: 50 percent of the fathers of A's, but only 15 percent of the fathers of C's, had completed college; homes of A's contained nearly 50 percent more books than did homes of C's; more than twice as many of the parents of C's had divorced as of 1928, when the gifted subjects' average age was sixteen.

Terman also reported differences between the groups in childhood data that had been collected years before the A and C groups were formed. The early data described A's as higher in prudence, self-confidence, perseverance, desire to excel, leadership, popularity, and sensitivity to approval and disapproval. In the follow-up study, the A group was rated higher than the C group on persistence, integration toward goals, self-confidence, and freedom from feelings of inferiority. Keeping in mind that the relative contributions of the parents and the gifted child to the make-up of the gifted adult are hard to discern, the following questions remain: Did the A group's superiority as adults result from a more enriched family background or from their own strong personality characteristics evident from their childhood years? Did parents of A's react to their young children's self-confidence and perseverance by providing more enrichment, or did home enrichment produce the childhood self-confidence and perseverance? Again, it appears that adult performance reflects an interaction of personal characteristics and parent practices.

The Terman studies generally indicate that compared to parents of children with average IQs, parents of the intellectually gifted tend to have attained higher educational, professional, and economic levels. This conclusion, however, must be viewed against the limitations of Terman's sample, which was identified in the early 1920s and consisted mainly of middle-class Anglo children. Compared to the population of the cities in which the children lived, the Terman sample contained a disproportionately large number of Jews and a small number of Hispanics and blacks. Hence, it is not clear whether the Terman studies compared children with high IQs to those with average IQs, as intended, or whether they compared middle-class children to children of low socioeconomic status.

A more recent comparison of upper-middle-class parents of gifted and of average children (Karnes, Shwedel, and Steinberg, 1984) indicated that although many similarities existed, the parents of the gifted tended to (a) spend more time with their children on school-related activities, (b) be more likely to report unconditional love for their children, and (c) be more willing to encourage independence.

Parents of Creative Children

Studies comparing personality characteristics and child-rearing practices of parents of the intellectually gifted to characteristics and practices of parents of creative children present a consistent picture. Getzels and Jackson (1961) examined the behaviors and family environments of twenty-six adolescent boys and girls who scored high in intelligence and lower in creativity and twenty-eight who demonstrated high creativity but lower intelligence. Compared to a larger sample, the high-intelligence group scored among the top 20 percent on an IQ test but below the top 20 percent on creativity. Their mean IQ was 150. The high-creativity group scored among the top 20 percent on creativity but below this range on IQ. The mean IQ of this group was 127.

Parents of high-IQ and high-creativity subjects differed in several ways. First, although both groups of parents evidenced a higher level of education than was true for the general population, parents of high-IQ children tended to have achieved higher educational status than parents of high-creativity children and to have had more specialized training. Also, a greater proportion of mothers of high-IQ children held full- or part-time jobs. A second difference between the groups concerned parents' vigilance over their children's activities. Parents of the high-IQ adolescents tended to be more critical of their children and their children's schools. A third difference was found in the values of the parents as reflected in the types of friends they preferred for their children. Parents of the highly intelligent students focused on external characteristics such as cleanliness, good manners, and studiousness, while parents of the creative students focused on internal traits such as interests, sense of values, and openness. Based on their findings, Getzels and Jackson characterized families of high-IQ students as encouraging conformity and minimalizing risk. Parents of highly creative students, in contrast, encouraged diversity and accepted risk.

Nichols's (1964) investigation of maternal child-rearing attitudes yielded results generally consistent with the findings of Getzels and Jackson, particularly with regard to parental vigilance. Nichols examined the relationship between the creativity scores of high school National Merit Scholarship finalists and their mothers' attitudes. He found that mothers' authoritarian child-rearing attitudes were negatively related to children's originality and creativity but positively related to school grades and favorable teacher ratings. Acknowledging the potential bidirectionality of parent–child relationships, Nichols concluded that mothers' attitudes influence children's behavior. One generalization may be that authoritarian parenting practices tend to foster conformity but stifle creativity.

Domino (1969) used a psychological inventory to compare thirty-three mothers of creative high school boys with thirty-one mothers of noncreative controls. Mothers of creative boys exhibited greater self-assurance, initiative, and interpersonal competence; preferred change and unstructured demands; were more insightful and more tolerant of others; and valued autonomy and independence. However, they were also less sociable, conscientious, dependable, and inhibited than the controls, as well as less concerned about creating a favorable impression and less nurturant and obliging toward others. According to Domino, a picture emerges of a highly independent and perceptive woman who can adapt to change but cares little about the impression she makes on others and who may not be consistently dependable. Domino further postulated that mothers of creative boys may be themselves more creative than the general population and that their characteristics help foster creativity in their children.

Dewing (1973) conducted a similar study in western Australia to compare the parents of high-creative and low-creative seventh-grade students matched for intelligence. She further divided the creative group into creative performers and the potentially creative. Her findings corroborated many of those from previous studies conducted in the United States. Mothers of creative children tended to have achieved higher levels of education than control mothers, and more mothers in the creative group held full- or part-time jobs. Parents of creative children reported more interests and hobbies than parents of noncreative children. With regard to personality traits, mothers of creative children, especially mothers of creative daughters, were more complex and less dogmatic than their control peers. Fathers' personality was more related to creativity in sons. On child-rearing attitudes, mothers of creative children were more egalitarian, less authoritarian, more permissive of children's contact with influences outside the home, and somewhat more likely to reject the homemaking role. Like the mothers in Getzel and Jackson's (1961) study, mothers of creative children in Dewing's study expressed greater concern about the internal characteristics of their children's friends than about socially desirable, conforming behaviors.

These studies suggest that parents of highly creative children tend to (a) express democratic and permissive as opposed to authoritarian child-rearing attitudes; (b) value internal rather than external, socially desirable characteristics; and (c) be themselves more independent but less sociable than parents of less creative children. The studies also suggest that parent characteristics are more closely related to the creativity of a child of the same sex and that parents of creative children are themselves creative.

Parents of Children with Specific Talents

Few studies are available concerning parents and families of children gifted in specific talent areas. Schaefer and Anastasi (1968) compared family patterns of high school boys selected as creative in graphic arts, literary expression, science, or mathematics with family patterns of control students. The authors reported that parents of creative boys tended to (a) act as role models of creative expression in the child's field of interest, (b) have more education (especially the mothers), (c) have available in the home political commentary or cultural–intellectual magazines, (d) play a musical instrument or encourage their child to play one, (e) read more books, and (f) have more hobbies. Fathers of creative boys had won more honors or awards in literary and artistic fields than had fathers of controls. Mothers had more creative hobbies and more frequently visited art museums and galleries. For students creative in the arts, relationships with parents centered more on shared interests in the special field than on warm, personal interactions. Anastasi and Schaefer (1969) reported similar findings for artistic girls. They also reported that girls seemed to have been more influenced by their fathers, boys by their mothers.

Bloom and Sosniak (1981) reported preliminary findings from a study of the development of more than 120 individuals who had demonstrated excellence in one of six different artistic, psychomotor, or cognitive fields: piano, sculpture, swimming, tennis, research mathematics, and research neurology. Their report, based on the data from pianists, swimmers, and mathematicians, can be summarized as follows:

1. In the majority of cases, one or both parents (or a sibling or other relative) had a personal interest in the talent area and greatly supported and encouraged the subject's development in that area.
2. Some of the parents were above average in the talent area, and most provided a model of the qualities and lifestyle related to the specific talent area.
3. In some cases the parents expected all members of the family to participate in the talent area from an early age.
4. In their early years (ages three to seven), many of the children were encouraged to explore and participate in the activity within or outside the home and were rewarded for signs of interest and ability.
5. In the early years of talent development, the child's teacher generally gave some instruction to the parents regarding follow-up activities, such as observing the child's practice, requiring the appropriate amount of practice time, referring the child to procedures suggested by the teacher, and rewarding the child's progress.
6. In later years of talent development, the family continued to supply encouragement and resources, provided outside aid if needed, and helped the subject consider options for the future.

The findings of Bloom and Sosniak indicate that parents and families of individuals who excel in specific talent areas begin at an early age to supply material and emotional support for exploring the talent area, take an active role in training, and reward progress. However, superior achievement in a talent area will probably not occur in the absence of a child's inherent potential. Moreover, the behaviors of parents whose children do excel may stem in part from an early recognition of the child's potential. Yet the parental role in talent development should not be underestimated. Feldman (1979) has suggested with regard to early prodigious achievement in specific talent areas that such achievement is not inevitable and does not occur spontaneously; it requires specialized resources and intensive instructional efforts. Bloom (1982) concluded that the accomplishments of his subjects could not have been predicted from early signs of talent alone but required a supportive home environment as well as personal commitment and excellent teaching.

Parents of High Achievers and Low Achievers

The literature on parents of high achievers and low achievers, though not specifically focused on gifted students, offers some insight into interaction patterns related to cognitive development and achievement. Radin (1982) has summarized research with regard to parental influences on young children's cognitive development. One conclusion drawn from her review is that parental warmth and nurturance foster the child's identification with the parent and increase the likelihood that the child will imitate adult problem-solving strategies and vocabulary. Supportive parents help the child perceive the environment as reinforcing and thus encourage the child to explore the environment.

Radin also concluded that when nurturance is accompanied by demands for mature, independent behavior, intellectual competence is fostered. Authoritarian parenting practices—being restrictive, intrusive, and punitive—tend to hinder development of intellectual competence, especially in families of low socioeconomic status. However, a certain amount of parental abrasiveness may foster self-direction and independence in young girls, perhaps because it forces the child to assert herself in the environment. Radin pointed to four specific parenting practices that appear to be positively related to young children's intellectual development: (a) offering explanations for rules and restrictions, sometimes allowing input from the child; (b) stating expectations and using sanctions; (c) providing stimulating materials in the home; and (d) having fathers work with their sons in academic areas.

Martin (1975) conducted an extensive review of literature on parent–child relations, including studies on the achievement behavior of older children and adults. His findings are consistent with those of Radin. Martin cited one study reported in 1970 by Crandall and Battle on adult academic effort (course work at school) and intellectual effort (self-chosen intellectual pursuits outside school). Adult academic effort was found to be related to early childhood help-seeking and proximity-seeking dependency behavior. Intellectual effort, in contrast, was not associated with childhood dependency but with maternal independence training. For females, adult intellectual effort was related to low maternal protectiveness and babying in childhood and to high rejection by fathers in early adulthood. These findings suggest that school-oriented academic achievement (good grades), as opposed to independent intellectual effort, may be related to needs for adult approval.

Martin's review indicates that (a) independent behavior is related to demands for age-appropriate behavior, firm and consistent enforcement of rules, encouragement, affection, and approval; (b) achievement behavior is associated with demands for and reinforcement of such behavior; and (c) high achievement in girls may be related to relatively low levels of parental acceptance. The literature on parents of high achievers and low achievers, then, generally suggests that achievement behavior is positively related to parental nurturance and expectations for achievement and negatively related to parental authoritarianism, especially for males. Low parental nurturance may foster achievement behavior in girls, perhaps causing girls to seek acceptance through academic accomplishment. Another possible explanation for achievement behavior among girls is that low-nurturant mothers may be more achievement oriented and may serve as models for their daughters (Martin, 1975).

A common assumption is that underachievement among gifted children is caused by parent or family problems. Whitmore (1980), however, found no significant common thread in the home situations of a group of underachieving gifted students, except that most of the parents possessed above-average intellectual ability. The causes of underachievement in students of gifted or of average ability appear to be a number of interacting factors, including child characteristics (perfectionist personality or immaturity), parent expectations and behaviors, teacher behaviors, school curriculum and its flexibility, and community pressures.

Parent–Child Interactions in Minority and Low-Income Families

Little information is available concerning parenting practices specific to families of gifted minority children. The findings so far discussed may also apply to minority groups. But because many of the studies were conducted with majority samples, differences may exist for families of different cultural backgrounds. The literature on parent–child interactions within minority families must be viewed with caution, separating out the factors of culture, economic status, and unintended cultural bias on the part of the researcher. The literature on parent–child interactions among low-income families is more definitive but also requires care in interpretation.

Social Class Differences in Child Rearing.
Several studies have been conducted on methods used by parents of different socioeconomic status for teaching their young children. These studies controlled for ethnicity by selecting all participants from a single ethnic group. In one classic study Hess and Shipman (1965) compared the teaching strategies that middle-class and lower-class black mothers used with their young children. The middle-class mothers used more elaborate speech, explanation, reasoning, praise, and specific feedback. Lower-class mothers tended to give more negative feedback, use more imperatives, and offer less explanation or reasoning. Maternal teaching strategies appeared to be related to children's cognitive functioning.

A study by Bee et al. (1969) yielded similar results, although social class and ethnicity were confounded. The authors found that middle-class mothers used more instruction, less physical intrusion, less negative feedback, and more complex speech patterns. Middle-class mothers also allowed their children to work at their own pace and offered suggestions on how to search for solutions to problems. Lower-class mothers gave highly specific suggestions and were more critical and controlling in their interactions with their children. These findings are consistent with the observations of Mitchell (1975), who examined the "poverty culture" with respect to development of creativity. He described low-income parents as typically not fostering their children's language skills, not asking or answering questions, disciplining by force, and being unsupportive of fantasy play.

More recently, Laosa (1978) examined the relationship between maternal teaching behavior and educational level (another socioeconomic status variable) among Chicano families. He found that more highly educated mothers used more inquiry and praise. Mothers with less formal education tended to use modeling, visual cues, and directives. For boys, the data indicated a relationship between lower levels of parental formal education and use of physical punishment and control.

These studies suggest that the teaching strategies of middle-class mothers, involving nurturance and the offering of explanations and reasons, are more consistent with parent–child practices related to achievement behavior in children. Maternal teaching strategies may thus mediate between socioeconomic status and achievement behavior, with the result that more gifted children are identified among middle-income than among lower-income families.

Studies investigating social class differences in verbal behavior have been criticized for applying a deficit interpretation to lower-class unelaborated or restricted speech. Hess and Shipman (1965), for example, suggested that the restricted, authoritarian verbal behavior of lower-class mothers may result in child learning styles incompatible with reflective problem solving. Hilliard and Vaughn-Scott (1982) have argued that such a deficit interpretation reflects cultural ignorance—specifically, failure on the part of researchers to recognize the linguistic equivalence between nonstandard and standard speech. In other words, an expression in a dialect and an expression in standard English can have the same intellectual meaning; the standard English expression is not intellectually superior to the equivalent expression in dialect. Hilliard and Vaughn-Scott warn that ignorance about linguistic equivalence may result in lower expectations on the part of the schools for children with nonstandard dialects. Thus, middle-class-oriented schools may fail to recognize and identify low-income children as gifted.

Child-Rearing Practices in Minority Cultures. The findings of Hess and Shipman (1965) and Laosa (1978) suggest that child-rearing practices may relate more to socioeconomic status than to ethnic origin. Yet culture may still be an important factor in understanding parent and child behavior independent of income level. Arciniega, Casaus, and Castillo (1977) noted that upwardly mobile members of ethnic groups do not necessarily become assimilated into the mainstream culture. Mexican-Americans, for example, are acculturated with regard to material benefits but not with regard to the values of the dominant culture; they have a collective cultural identity characterized by family interdependence and close personal relationships, cooperation as opposed to competition, and acceptance of what is. With regard to specific parenting behaviors, Steward and

Steward (1973) observed that Mexican-American mothers tended to teach their children at a slower pace, give more negative feedback, and use more nonverbal instruction than comparison groups of Chinese and Anglo mothers. Mexican-American mothers did not perceive themselves as teachers but relegated that responsibility to the schools. Anglo mothers, in contrast, perceived teaching as one of several roles they performed, and Chinese-American mothers considered teaching an important part of their role.

Parents who belong to the same economic group but who have different cultural backgrounds may be more similar to each other in child-rearing practices than to parents who are from the same ethnic group but who belong to a different economic class. However, certain cultural values, attitudes, and behaviors may be pervasive across income levels. In interpreting and planning for interaction with parents, educators who work with parents of gifted children from minority backgrounds must be sensitive to cultural differences.

In sum, the literature on parents of intelligent, creative, and achieving children suggests that these parents tend to be supportive and nurturant, to spend time with their children on achievement-related activities (for example, reading, hobbies, field trips, and specific talent areas), to provide models of confidence and independence, and to establish a democratic atmosphere characterized by reasoning, explanations, and opportunities to participate in decision making. However, cultural and economic differences may affect specific child-rearing practices.

PARENTS AND THE SCHOOLS

Interactions among teachers, school administrators, and parents of gifted students can produce constructive change in the lives of gifted and talented children at home and at school. Such interactions can also result in mutual distrust and defensiveness. Colangelo and Dettman (1982) have described four general types of parent–school interactions. Type I, cooperation, is characterized by open sharing of information about the child, cooperation between the parents and the school, and agreement that the school should provide special programs for gifted and talented students. Type II, conflict, occurs when parents desire special school programs for their gifted children, but the school believes that the regular curriculum can meet the children's needs. Conflict interactions can result in continued parent demands, parent hopelessness and withdrawal, or parent provision of services to gifted children. Type III interaction, interference, occurs when the school desires to provide special services but the parents are opposed. Type IV, natural development interactions, occur when both the parents and the school agree that the regular curriculum is sufficient for the gifted. Positive, cooperative interaction is facilitated when schools are aware of (a) the unique needs of parents in coping with a gifted child, (b) the ways in which schools can meet parental needs, (c) the contributions parents as individuals can make to school programs, and (d) the role of parent organizations.

Needs of Parents of the Gifted

Parents of gifted children are often stereotyped as overly assertive individuals who attempt to gain personal recognition through the placement of their children in programs for the gifted. While every professional in gifted education has no doubt encountered this type of parent, the number of such parents appears to be very small. For example, the staff of New Mexico State University's Preschool for the Gifted could classify as self-interested the parents of only three of over one hundred children screened. Many parents were self-effacing and apologetic about their concerns, hoping only to find a way to obtain special help for what appeared to be an exceptionally bright youngster. Although such parents are frequently criticized as trying to "make" their child special, a more accurate interpretation is that these parents are *reacting* to a child whose exceptional behavior (rapid learning, inquisitiveness, varied and deep interests, and frustration with the ordinary) requires special attention.

Our experiences with the Preschool for the Gifted, together with reports by other professionals who work with parents of gifted children (Debinski and Mauser, 1978; Malone, 1975), indicate that such parents have valid concerns and unique needs as a result of having a gifted child in the family. These needs fall into the following categories and are typically expressed by parents as questions.

1. *Referral and assessment.* To whom do I refer my child for testing to determine whether he or she is gifted? How soon after referral will my child be tested? What can I do if no one will make or accept the referral? What types of tests are given? What are the criteria or cutoff scores my child must meet to qualify as gifted? Is there a different set of criteria for minority children? How do I interpret the test results? What should I do if there are no provisions for referral, assessment, or special services?

2. *Placement.* What types of placements or programs are available for my gifted child? Which, if any, would be the most appropriate for my child? What are my options if I disagree with available placements or with the school's preferred placement alternative? Who are the best teachers for my child? What happens to the social adjustment of children who are accelerated? What services are available for gifted children in the community?

3. *Support at home.* How can I help my gifted child at home? What kind of things can I do to ensure motivation and progress? How can I facilitate my child's individual learning style? How can I handle my gifted teenager's rebelliousness? How should I deal with sibling rivalry? How should I guide my child's heightened sensitivities? Does my child need professional counseling? Should I be concerned about discrepancies between my child's reading and mathematics performance? How can I support my child without imparting the idea that he or she is special or superior to others?

4. *Parent contributions.* What can I do to help in my child's program? How can I participate?

Problems in Parent–School Relationships

Many schools have taken on the responsibility of providing information to answer parents' questions and concerns. Several states, for example, require that meetings be held, with parents invited, to determine the most appropriate placement for the child and to develop an individualized education program as outlined in Chapter 5. Mathews, however, has pointed out some problems with this approach:

> . . . many of these conferences consist of a monologue in which parents are given few opportunities to offer any real input or to talk about their child. Parents are often hustled out the door at the end of a 15-minute session because the conference is slotted into an already too-tightly scheduled day. It is rare for any previous parent education to have taken place before the conference. Single facets of a program, such as assessment results, administrative arrangements, or procurement of a parental signature on the individual educational plan, are frequently the only outstanding features of these sessions. These experiences can be frustrating to parents and do little to enhance their knowledge or attitudes about various dimensions of the program.
>
> — Mathews, 1981, pp. 207–208

Several factors work to produce the ineffective, frustrating type of school–parent interaction described by Mathews. First, programs for the gifted are frequently understaffed, and teachers may have little time to devote to parent conferences. Second, teachers and administrators may feel threatened by parents of gifted students, who may be themselves highly educated, articulate, and assertive. Third, programs for gifted and talented students may be unevenly implemented throughout the district. The quality and types of programs available may depend on the attitudes and training of individual principals and teachers. Parents may find that the school their child currently attends does not offer the same type program available in a school the child attended earlier.

Parents sometimes contribute to troubled relationships between themselves and the schools in several ways. First, not all parents desire the same things for their children. Some parents prefer acceleration; others request self-contained classrooms or enrichment within the regular program. School personnel and parents both desire what is best for an individual child, but no objective methods exist for determining what constitutes the most appropriate placement for any given child. Parents also may not agree on how the schools may best meet parental needs for information. Mathews (1981) surveyed research on the most effective format for parent programs and found conflicting results. One study indicated that readings alone were effective; another, that parents preferred personal contact plus supplementary readings. A third study indicated that parents preferred interaction with teachers to printed materials. Some parents of gifted children, being highly intelligent themselves, feel competent to determine the best methods for serving their child, failing to recognize the school's professional expertise and vast amount of experience in gifted education.

Goals and Components of Effective Programs for Parents

To facilitate positive, mutually helpful interactions between parents of gifted and talented children and the school staff, every district should provide a well-planned program for parents. The goals of such a program should be as follows:

— to establish open communication between parents and teachers
— to establish mutually agreeable goals and objectives for each child based on his or her individual needs
— to inform parents regarding (*a*) state and district regulations governing the program; (*b*) parent and child rights; (*c*) federal, state, local, and program definitions of giftedness; (*d*) effective parenting practices; and (*e*) alternatives for the future
— to invite parent participation in the program

Schools can establish several program components to meet these goals. The components described in the following subsections are based on our experience with private and public school programs and on the recommendations of Mathews (1981).

Orientation Meetings. For parents of all children attending the school, meetings should be held to describe the characteristics of gifted children, programs available to serve their needs, and procedures for referral, assessment, identification, and placement. Some gifted children are overlooked because their parents are not aware of special services, and the teacher for whatever reason has not referred the child for assessment. Schools must make a concerted effort to encourage minority and low-income parents to attend orientation meetings because for cultural reasons these parents may not perceive or recognize their children as gifted or as having unique needs. Some parents may be unaware of gifted programs because they lack access to information sources such as professional organizations, parent magazines, and social cliques where such information is exchanged (Marion, 1980). All printed materials should be written in a form understandable to all parents, with appropriate adaptations for linguistic differences. Parent orientation meetings should be held at least annually, at the beginning of the school year.

Often orientation meetings are not held because of the belief that most parents think their children are gifted and will therefore refer more children than can be reasonably assessed. A second reason why meetings are not held is the assumption that teachers can more acccurately identify potentially gifted students. However, although parents do tend to overrefer, their assessments may be more accurate than those of teachers. Ciha et al. (1974) administered intelligence measures to a stratified sample of 465 children. They sent a list of characteristics of intellectual giftedness to parents and asked them to determine whether they thought their child was gifted. Teachers were also asked to nominate the children they believed to be gifted. Of the 58 children identified as gifted on intelligence measures, parents correctly nominated 39, or 67 percent.

Teachers correctly nominated only 22 percent. Parents, however, nominated a total of 276 children, teachers only 54. These data suggest that compared to parents, teachers nominate fewer (and miss more) potentially gifted children.

Printed Materials. Information packets or booklets should be given to parents as soon as a child is identified as gifted. Specific information should be included describing the program's definition of giftedness, goals and objectives, placement options available in each school within the district, general curriculum plans, teacher qualifications, and sample projects done by children. A bibliography of readings and resources and a questionnaire about the child's interests and learning style should also be included.

A monthly parent newsletter can keep parents informed about units and projects currently under study, meetings, and readings of interest. The newsletter can also disseminate children's written products, such as poetry. Parents of young gifted children often ask to be informed of current units of study so that they can reinforce their children's learning at home.

Parent Awareness Meetings. Evening meetings can be scheduled to provide parents with answers to their concerns about gifted education in general, specific parenting practices, and school programs. A frequent error in promoting parent awareness is to give parents lists of general tips, such as "encourage creativity." Generalizations have much less utility than training in specific techniques, such as creative-questioning models (for example, Bloom's taxonomy or Torrance's divergent questioning). Meetings should be limited to parents and relatives of gifted children. Sometimes school districts invite teachers to such meetings as part of in-service training, but the presence of large numbers of teachers can preclude candid interactions between the parents and the speaker.

Individual Parent–Teacher Conferences. Conferences should be held at least twice a year. The first should occur at the beginning of the year and should be used for the cooperative establishment of objectives for the child and the exchange of information about learning styles, special interests, and needs. A conference should also be held at the end of the year to help the parent understand the child's progress and program for the future. Additional conferences may be necessary and desirable, especially when problems arise or when a new idea is being implemented and requires monitoring.

Our experience has shown that structuring parent–teacher conferences around an individualized educational program (IEP) has benefits for all parties involved. IEP objectives, formulated on the basis of criterion-referenced assessment and teacher observation, give the teacher a concrete place from which to begin the conference. The steps described in the following paragraphs are suggested for the teacher's use in structuring a successful initial conference.

1. Develop a tentative IEP, including a summary of the child's strengths and weaknesses, annual goals, specific objectives, and proposed methods for meeting the objectives.

2. Begin the conference by clearly stating its purpose—for example, to jointly define objectives and methods for meeting the needs of the child.

3. If you have specific concerns about the child, ask the parents to describe their observations with regard to the behavioral area. Their observations can help you understand more about the child's abilities in the area in question. In one case, for example, a teacher was concerned about the expressive language abilities of an otherwise highly creative child. The teacher asked the parents whether the child talked at home and what he talked about. Analysis of the parents' responses (for example, "I work late and sometimes don't see him") and their mode of responding (for example, saying "He talks about *things*," and pointing to objects the child talks about rather than describing the objects) suggested that the child had limited exposure to adult language and was modeling parents whose mode of communication was heavily nonspecific and nonverbal.

4. Briefly describe the results of your observations and assessment and summarize the child's strengths and weaknesses. Clearly define terms. For example, a child may be above age expectancy in all areas but reading, where he or she is performing at age level. "Weakness" in reading is therefore only relative to the child's high performance in other areas. It is generally better to identify as "weak" only those areas where performance is below age expectancy. Do not omit information on the assumption that parents do not possess the sophistication required to understand the material. It is the educator's responsibility to ensure that parents understand.

5. Ask the parents whether your findings are consistent with their observations. We have found that some children perform differently at school than they do at home. One child, for example, would discuss at home the day and date but respond incorrectly during calendar activities at school. Having such information is important if you are to establish appropriate objectives. Instead of teaching calendar facts, the teacher in this case needed to change the physical and emotional setting to make the child feel comfortable in responding. It is also helpful to seek advice from the parent regarding any behavioral problems. For example, one three-year-old child would occasionally revert to baby talk at school. The mother indicated that telling the child to "talk like a four-year-old" was generally successful, because the child wanted to be four. The method worked in the classroom and provided consistency between home and school in objective and method.

6. Ask parents whether there are any objectives they would like to add to the IEP. Sincerely consider the appropriateness of their requests and your ability to implement them. One parent, for example, wanted to improve her child's self-confidence by having the child serve as a tutor for other children in the class. Although the teacher initially felt the parent was "telling her how to teach," she implemented the suggestion. The child seemed more confident, the parent was happy, and the teacher learned that teachers can learn! When parent requests are not appropriate or cannot be met, be candid in telling the parent why you cannot implement the request. Parents will respect honesty more than insincere promises. In one case, for example, parents requested daily foreign language lessons but were told that providing the lessons was not financially feasible. Another parent requested that her daughter be directly helped rather than asked to "think of what *you* can do to solve the problem." This request was also denied, but the teacher took time to explain the program's philosophy and its goal of fostering independence and personal responsibility. The parent responded that although she did not agree with the technique, she understood the philosophy. Working with parents requires sincere efforts at give-and-take. Parents need to recognize that the teacher is a professional, trained to make educational decisions, and teachers must recognize that parents have extensive knowledge of their own children and can offer legitimate suggestions.

7. Briefly describe the methods you will use to help the child accomplish the objectives of the IEP. For example, you might explain which objectives will be addressed through whole-group, small-group, and individual activities. It is generally not necessary to give detailed explanations of instructional methods unless parents request such information.

8. If you would like to have parents work on an objective at home, ask whether they would be willing to do so. Be prepared to give precise instructions. In the case of the child with low expressive language, for example, both parents were instructed on how to ask open-ended questions and have the child describe objects in detail (color, shape, size, texture, and use).

9. Ask the parents whether they have any questions or comments they would like to make about the program or the child. Parents may express surprise that your observations are so consistent with their own. Many will ask what they can do at home to reinforce the child's school learning or to handle specific behavioral difficulties. Some will offer to share their specific areas of expertise with the class.

10. Write on the IEP itself any agreed-upon changes. Tell the parents what you are doing as you write. If they have not already done so, give them time to read the document.

11. Sign the IEP. Explain that you would like the parents' signatures on the document to verify that the meeting has occurred and that the IEP was discussed. Explain also that the IEP is a flexible, guiding plan and will be changed as the child's needs change. If you have agreed to try out a new program that needs monitoring, set a date for a follow-up conference.

Although the amount of time needed for a parent–teacher conference will vary, it is a good idea to structure a definite beginning and ending time so that parents and teachers focus their discussion on the points at hand. Scheduling half-hour sessions, with fifteen to thirty minutes between sessions, provides structure while allowing flexibility in cases where unexpected topics may arise and require more time.

Although IEPs are one means of providing structure for parent–teacher interaction, two points should be kept in mind. First, other, less structured approaches are available for program planning and parent conferencing. Second, parents and teachers must avoid interpreting the IEP as a rigid contract in which every item must be fulfilled as initiated.

Regular parent–teacher conferences are highly recommended, even in states and districts that do not require individualized educational programs. Although individual parent meetings take a great deal of planning and organization, they are valuable for opening communication, increasing parent and teacher understanding of the child, and planning instruction.

Parent Contributions to Programs for the Gifted

The schools have a professional responsibility to serve the parents of gifted children. Schools will find that many parents are equally willing to contribute to school programs. Especially in light of recent funding cutbacks, parents realize that the schools cannot meet every need and that the community is obligated to help fill the gaps. Parents can contribute as individuals or can organize for concerted efforts toward achieving agreed-upon goals.

Individual Contributions. Cassidy (1981b) has listed five roles that schools can encourage parents to develop. The first is the advisor role in program planning, which can be developed through such vehicles as the teacher–parent conference. Second, parents can serve as guides at home, carrying over instructional goals and organizing supportive field trips. A third role for parents is to act as mentors. Many parents of gifted children are professionals willing to serve as models for gifted students who wish to study in their field of expertise. Parents can help such students by discussing job prerequisites and training and by engaging them in the field. Fourth, parents who are free during the day can function as classroom aides, helping in small-group and individual instruction. Parents are generally reliable classroom helpers who free teachers to provide more individualized instruction. Like any other aides, parents need specific instruction so that their work will be consistent with the goals and methods of the program. A fifth role for parents is that of material developers. For example, a parent may construct an inquiry package consisting of materials needed to build an electric circuit.

In addition to Cassidy's suggestions, another highly beneficial role is that of classroom presenter. A simple questionnaire can be given to parents when their children are enrolled in the gifted program, asking the parents to specify their own areas of interest and expertise (vocation, avocation, travel, cultural background, or various life experiences) and to state whether they would be willing to share these areas with the children. Teachers are then able to integrate the skills and knowledge of willing parents into ongoing units. As part of a unit on sound, for example, a geophysicist father discussed seismology and simulated an earthquake for the children. As part of a career education unit, another parent, a Tony Award–winning playwright, discussed the acting profession and took the students to the theater to demonstrate the contributions of make-up artists, set designers, and lighting technicians. A Native American mother presented Navajo dances, music, costumes, and foods as part of a multicultural awareness unit. Parents will often volunteer to conduct specific activities without being solicited.

Parent Organizations. Although individual parents can make needed contributions to specific classrooms or schools, some goals are more effectively accomplished when parents are organized. Parent groups originally developed at the local level as a means for achieving recognition for gifted students in local communities where no services were available (Nathan, 1979). A few parent organizations, such as the California Parents for Gifted, were able to lobby at the state level to establish large-scale programs for gifted students. Nathan has suggested that such organizations are important because parents operating alone are frequently unsuccessful and "do more harm than good by antagonizing professionals who sometimes retaliate by making school life difficult for the children involved" (Nathan, 1979, p. 258). Organizations that are separate from the school district provide more objectivity than individual school personnel or parents and can serve to support both parties.

Parent organizations can improve the education of gifted students in several ways. Often the first role played by new organizations is that of advocacy. Parent organizations often develop specifically to encourage the local school board to initiate services to gifted students. The Las Cruces Association for Gifted Children, for example, began with a local newspaper advertisement of a meeting for parents interested in programs for gifted children. After sharing their personal frustrations about securing special services, the parents organized to launch awareness meetings, provide speakers on parent rights and due process, make their needs known to the school district, and provide their own summer program for gifted students. The school district took over the successful summer program and soon initiated its own program for the academic year. Once programs were established, the advocacy role became one of monitoring programs and providing information to parents new to the community and parents of recently identified gifted students. One helpful resource that parent organizations can provide is a videotape simulation of school–parent placement and IEP meetings. The tape helps parents understand their own role and the types of questions they should ask.

A second function best performed by parent organizations is to provide parent support. Parents who have recently agonized over placement decisions, sibling rivalry problems, and adolescent adjustment concerns can lead small groups of other parents in problem-solving discussions.

A third role of parent organizations is to provide direct out-of-school services to gifted students. Despite sincere efforts on the part of schools to serve all gifted children, some deserving students will not fit the district's definitional criteria, and some important services will not be provided to identified gifted children. Parent organizations can provide field trips and lyceum courses to round out gifted students' experiences. Parents can arrange for museums, libraries, and cultural centers to provide well-articulated, continuing seminars and field trips that will encourage learning in areas not covered by the school curriculum. Such activities also give gifted students from diverse neighborhoods an opportunity to interact with and be stimulated by each other.

A final role of parent organizations is fund raising. When programs are underfunded, parents may volunteer to seek external funding sources or may organize their own fund-raising activities. Parents of gifted children are often respected, influential members of the community who act effectively as public relations people. Fund-raising activities are particularly important in traditionally underfunded programs, such as fine arts, where equipment, material, and attendance at camps require extra resources. The role of parents as fund raisers has as a precedent parents' booster clubs for athletics and groups of band parents for musical activities.

In planning parent organizations, several potential problems should be anticipated and precluded. One problem often faced by parent organizations is maintaining visibility as an organization after major goals have been effected. Both the statewide California Parents for the Gifted and the local Las Cruces Association for Gifted Children found membership dwindling after programs had been established in the schools. Parent organizations should establish commitment to several goals at the outset and should schedule priorities in advance.

A second potential problem for parent organizations concerns roles as direct service providers and fund raisers. Parent efforts should be directed at filling in gaps after the school district has established essential programs; parent contributions should not be used as a substitute for programs that are the legitimate responsibility of the schools.

Another problem arises from the usual constituency of parent organizations for gifted children. As Nathan (1979) has observed, parents active in these organizations tend to be affluent, well educated, articulate, and white. Hence they can become a target for accusations of elitism. The accusations may be partially justified; few organizations make efforts to include parents from low-income or minority backgrounds. However, because of cultural differences, some parents have been socialized to feel that parenting is their major role and that education is the province of the schools. Such parents are much less likely to attend parent meetings, express concerns about their children's education, or refer their children for assessment as potentially gifted. Parent organizations for gifted students need to seek out parents from different cultural and economic backgrounds to serve as advocates for children in their communities. Parents struggling to meet basic survival needs may have difficulty joining dues-paying organizations and may feel like outsiders in terms of income and family structure. Organizations can encourage such people to become members by providing dues waivers for families experiencing financial difficulties. Teachers can encourage parents of minority children to join parent organizations and can give them coping skills for maintaining membership (Marion, 1980). Including parents and children of different backgrounds will ultimately lead to better community representation, improved credibility, and richer experiences for the children.

CHAPTER SUMMARY

Because parents of gifted children have special needs, influence their children's academic performance, and contribute positively to program planning, schools are beginning to recognize the importance of involving parents in programs for gifted students. School personnel and other professionals have criticized parents for overemphasizing their children's talents and for creating situations demanding special treatment at home and at school. Theories regarding the bidirectional nature of parent–child interactions, however, support the idea that gifted children's unique characteristics may influence their parents' behavior. Most parents' concerns are legitimate responses to their gifted children's special needs.

The literature on parents of gifted individuals, mostly retrospective, suggests that such parents display a common constellation of characteristics and behaviors that may have affected (or been affected by) their children's achievements. Early data on parents of the intellectually gifted suggested that such parents tend to be more highly educated and to have larger incomes and more stable marriages than unselected parents. Failure of standard assessment procedures to identify gifted children from low-income and culturally different backgrounds must be considered in evaluating early data.

Parents of creatively gifted children tend to be more permissive in child-rearing practices, to value internal characteristics, and to be more independent than parents of less creative children. Individuals who excel in specific talent areas appear to have parents who began to support their children's talent development at an early age. High achievement among children and adolescents tends to be related to parent encouragement, nurturance, approval, rewarding of achievement behavior, and consistent reinforcement of rules, especially for boys. Girls' high achievement may be related to less nurturant parent behavior.

Child-rearing practices may differ among parents of different income levels and cultural backgrounds. Specific parenting practices related to giftedness among minority and low-income families have not been defined. Differences among cultural values with regard to parental roles and linguistic behavior are important considerations in working with parents.

Parent involvement in school programs can take various forms. To facilitate communication and serve parent needs, schools can provide orientation meetings for parents, printed information, training sessions, and individual parent–teacher conferences. Parents can contribute to school programs by helping with program planning, reinforcing concepts in the home, acting as mentors and classroom presenters, functioning as teacher aides, and developing needed materials.

Parent involvement programs administered through the schools cannot function effectively in an advocacy or parent-support capacity. Independent parent organizations are needed to serve advocacy functions and to monitor existing programs, provide out-of-school services, share parenting techniques, and secure involvement of parents from many different backgrounds. When open communication and mutual respect exist, parent organizations and school personnel minimize adversary roles and progress toward the common goal of providing the best possible services to gifted and talented students.

ACTIVITIES FOR THOUGHT AND DISCUSSION

1. Do you think we can help parents foster giftedness by teaching them parenting behaviors that parents of gifted children have used? Why or why not? What would you need to know to develop such a program?

2. Interview parents of a gifted child from an ethnic or income group different from your own regarding their child-rearing attitudes and behaviors. Try to observe their interactions with the gifted child in a teaching situation.

3. Draft a brochure for informing parents about a gifted program (real or hypothetical). What information would you need to include?

4. As a teacher, list all the ways in which parents of gifted students might contribute to your program. How would you secure their help? What types of training might they need?

5. You are a teacher in a regular classroom in which nongifted and gifted children are integrated. How could you establish a program for parents? What would be your objectives? How would you implement the program?

SECTION VII

Perspectives for the Future

Chapter Fifteen

CURRENT ISSUES AND FUTURE DIRECTIONS

ISSUES AND ASSUMPTIONS

This book represents an effort to describe the state of the art in gifted education, particularly with regard to promising practices for curriculum development and instruction. We have selected and described certain methods and techniques that have a basis in some coherent theory of intelligence or of learning. Ideally, curricula and methods for specific populations of learners such as the gifted (*a*) derive from well-established theories of the way these students learn and (*b*) yield empirical evidence of efficacy.

Unfortunately, many programs and methods have been established for gifted and talented learners in the absence of theoretical and empirical foundations. Such efforts are often the result of having to establish programs quickly to meet local, state, or federal directives and deadlines. Lacking a coherent theory of the nature of giftedness, educators have based these programs primarily on assumptions about the characteristics of gifted learners and on historical precedent, social pressures, and philosophic/value orientations.

In short, the state of the art of gifted education encompasses a variety of program models and instructional methods derived from several untested assumptions about the nature of giftedness. These models and methods have benefited educators and students by providing direction to meet immediate demands for special services. The field now requires thoughtful analysis and evaluation of current practices as well as development of a comprehensive theory of the nature of giftedness. A first step may be to study empirically the validity of the following assumptions, from which present practices derive.

1. *Gifted individuals require special considerations because they differ qualitatively from average individuals.* Unless neuropsychology proves otherwise, it appears safe to conclude that the salient difference between gifted and average individuals is quantitative in nature. Intellectual, academic, creative, leadership, and artistic ability each can be conceived as part of a continuum along which individuals fall. Institutions establish arbitrary cutoff points along the continuum to define exceptionality. It would be absurd to conclude that a person who scores 129 in a school district with an IQ criterion of 130 differs qualitatively from the person who scores 130 and therefore qualifies as gifted.

The implication is that some students who do not qualify formally for gifted programs can benefit from the challenging experiences proposed for the gifted. Nonetheless, society's need for individuals of exceptional ability and motivation in every field and the right of every individual to opportunities that help realize his or her potential demand that attention be paid to gifted education. The case for gifted education does not preclude the fact that bright children in regular programs also deserve services that meet their individual needs.

2. *The special classroom constitutes the least restrictive environment for gifted learners.* Studies on the effects of educational provisions for gifted students

conducted since the 1950s have indicated that (*a*) gifted children do not suffer detrimental effects from special groupings, (*b*) gifted learners given special provisions demonstrate greater achievement gains than gifted controls, (*c*) removing gifted students from the regular classroom does not disadvantage regular-class peers, and (*d*) the gifted may benefit most from homogeneous grouping (Whitmore, 1980). Although empirical research supports acceleration and ability grouping as having positive effects on the achievement and personal–social development of gifted learners as a group, some gifted children experience academic and/or social difficulties under some special provisions. Case study and observational research may be useful for formulating hypotheses for predicting which types of program arrangements will best meet the needs of gifted learners with specific characteristics.

3. *A program should be based on an instructional model.* Adopting a model, such as the enrichment triad model or the multiple talent approach, provides direction for planning and decision making about curriculum, structure, and teaching methods. However, most existing program models have been based primarily on the creator's particular philosophical orientation regarding the needs of gifted learners (for example, need for exploration or for product orientation). A need now exists for models derived from sound theories of intellectual functioning and supported by research data. For example, Sternberg's work on information-processing approaches to problem solving (see Chapter 3) has potential for providing a theoretical foundation for development of a program model.

4. *Programs for gifted students should differ from programs for their average peers through greater emphasis on development of creative and higher-level thinking processes.* Determining that a group is "special" rests on the observation that members of the group exhibit characteristics unique from the general population. Identifying special populations of students makes sense only if special services are to be provided to meet the population's needs. Hence, differentiating programs for gifted students from programs for nongifted students constitutes a primary educational goal. One means of providing differentiated instruction for gifted students is to increase opportunities for engaging in creative and higher-level thinking skills, such as planning, predicting, analyzing, synthesizing, evaluating, and inducing. Additional research is needed to support the assumptions that (*a*) gifted individuals benefit more from such opportunities than do their average peers, (*b*) gifted individuals require instruction and/or practice in such thinking processes to be productive, and (*c*) nongifted individuals can be successful without added opportunities to engage in creative and higher-level thinking.

5. *Instructional methods for the gifted should avoid rote learning and emphasize inductive, discovery-oriented techniques.* We have emphasized inductive strategies for the gifted that require students to derive concepts, hypotheses, rules, and generalizations from raw information rather than requiring the teacher to present generalizations and rules and then ask students to apply them to given information. The rationale for focusing on inductive strategies is that inductive exercises simulate the process of scientific discovery and that gifted students will be the generators of new knowledge. Research is needed to support the assumption that practice in inductive thinking encourages the pursuit of inquiry and new discoveries. Didactic instruction and simple memorization may be more efficient methods for some learning objectives, such as arithmetic facts and foreign-language vocabulary. Moreover, even gifted students do not have time to rediscover all existing knowledge. Having mastered available information, gifted students should aim at adding new insights and syntheses.

FUTURE DIRECTIONS

The last decade has witnessed a new surge of interest in gifted individuals as a national resource and a concomitant increase in the number of programs designed to serve gifted individuals. However, like most new programs, programs for the gifted currently face the developmental stage in which increased quality and excellence lag behind increased demand for services and program proliferation. Yet the outlook for gifted education is highly optimistic. The next task for educators of the gifted is to improve the quality of services while expanding the number of students served. Future trends in gifted education will primarily involve renewed efforts in the areas described in the following paragraphs.

1. National guidelines must be established for defining, identifying, and serving the gifted. National guidelines are needed to (a) provide consistency among states in serving gifted students and (b) permit flexibility on a regional and local level to meet the specific needs of different populations of gifted learners.

2. Funds must be appropriated in both the federal and the private sector to support theory development, research on learning, curriculum development and evaluation, and efficacy research, including longitudinal studies of program outcomes.

3. Increased efforts are needed to discover neurophysiological indicators (for example, accelerated synaptic activity) and infant predictors (for example, visual attention) of giftedness. Such efforts may ultimately result in the development of early identification methods that are culturally unbiased and permit intervention for infants whose socioeconomic environments might otherwise depress their potential.

4. Local efforts are needed to ensure program articulation from the preschool to the postsecondary level. For example, leadership at the district level will enable children identified as gifted at any age to enter an appropriate program and continue to receive services coordinated from one grade level to the next. Development of comprehensive K–12 curricula specifically for gifted students will support the development of articulated services.

5. Cooperative teacher training efforts must involve special and general educators and content area specialists in the development of quality teachers who (*a*) provide instruction at students' current functioning levels rather than at a single, preestablished level; (*b*) employ homogeneous and heterogeneous grouping as the task demands; (*c*) design instructional units that provide a range of activities to accommodate a range of abilities and interests; and (*d*) recruit and manage community resources that extend and enrich the curriculum. Concurrently, high standards for certification of teachers of the gifted will be required.

Perhaps the most positive sign for gifted education is the general public's increased awareness of the need for excellence in education, as manifested by the establishment in 1981 of the National Commission on Excellence in Education. The commission's findings have been widely disseminated. Should a coordinated national effort be made to ensure quality education in every classroom, pressure for additional special programming for the gifted may decrease, except in the case of the extremely gifted and students highly gifted in a specialized area. Excellence in education would then be defined as including provisions for the following:

— manageable teacher–pupil ratios that permit planning for individualization with regard to pacing and pursuit of interests
— comprehensive, articulated K–12 curricula
— enrichment activities that increase the depth and variety of explorations and experience
— maintenance of high standards for academic achievement and general problem solving
— encouragement of creative thinking and creative production
— opportunities for developing leadership and sensitivity to human needs
— guidance by excellent teachers

Educational programs incorporating these provisions for excellence would help *all* students develop their potential and would hence fulfill the charge for which schooling was created.

References

Abeles, S. 1977. "Science Education for the Gifted and Talented." *Gifted Child Quarterly* 21:75–80.

Abroms, K. I., and Gollin, J. B. 1980. "Developmental Study of Gifted Preschool Children and Measures of Psychosocial Giftedness." *Exceptional Children* 46:334–41.

Ackerman, P. R., and Weintraub, F. J. 1969. "Summary Analysis of State Laws for Gifted Children." *Exceptional Children* 35:569–76.

Adelman, H. S. 1971. "The Not So Specific Learning Disability Population." *Exceptional Children* 37:528–33.

Alexander, P. A. 1984. "Training Analogical Reasoning Skills in the Gifted." *Roeper Review* 6:191–93.

Alexander, P. J., and Skinner, M. E. 1980. "The Effects of Early Entrance on Subsequent Social and Academic Development: A Follow-up Study." *Journal for the Education of the Gifted* 3:147–50.

Altman, R. 1983. "Social–Emotional Development of Gifted Children and Adolescents: A Research Model." *Roeper Review* 6:65–68.

Anastasi, A., and Schaefer, C. E. 1969. "Biographical Correlates of Artistic and Literary Creativity in Adolescent Girls." *Journal of Applied Psychology* 53(4):267–73.

Anderson, R. S. 1975. *Education in Japan: A Century of Modern Development*. Washington, D.C.: U.S. Government Printing Office.

Andrews, M. F. 1980. "The Consonance between Right Brain and Affective, Subconscious, and Multisensory Functions." *Journal of Creative Behavior* 14(2):77–87.

Archambault, F. X., Jr. 1984. "Measurement and Evaluation Concerns in Evaluating Programs for the Gifted and Talented." *Journal for the Education of the Gifted* 7:12–25.

Arciniega, M., Casaus, L., and Castillo, M. April 1977. "Parenting Models and Mexican–Americans: A Process Analysis." Paper prepared by the Bureau of Educational Research and Evaluation, School of Education, San Diego State University.

Argulewicz, E. N., Elliott, S. N., and Hall, R. 1982. "Comparison of Behavioral Ratings of Anglo-American and Mexican-American Gifted Children." *Psychology in the Schools* 19(4):469–72.

Arnold, A., et al. 1981. *Secondary Programs for the Gifted/Talented*. National/State Leadership Training Institute on the Gifted and the Talented. Ventura, Calif.: Office of the Ventura County Superintendent of Schools.

Asher, S. R., Oden, S. L., and Gottman, J. M. 1981. "Children's Friendships in School Settings." In *Contemporary Readings in Child Psychology*, 2d ed. Edited by E. M. Hetherington and R. D. Parke, 277–94. New York: McGraw-Hill.

Asian Pacific American Concerns Staff. March 1982. *APACS Briefing*. (Commission hears of science, mathematics gap.) Washington, D.C.: U.S. Department of Education.

Assembly of National Arts Education Organizations. 1979. "The Arts for Gifted and Talented Students." In *Someone's Priority*. Edited by E. Larsh, 71–79. Denver: Colorado Department of Education.

Atamian, G. C., and Danielson, E. W. 1977. "Programs for the Gifted at Talcott Mountain Science Center." *Gifted Child Quarterly* 21:69–74.

Austin, A. B., and Draper, D. C. 1981. "Peer Relationships of the Academically Gifted: A Review." *Gifted Child Quarterly* 25:129–33.

Ausubel, D. P. 1961. "In Defense of Verbal Learning." *Educational Theory* 11:15–25.

Aylesworth, M. 1984. "Guidelines for Selecting Instruments in Evaluating Programs for the

Gifted." *Journal for the Education of the Gifted* 7:38–44.

Baca, L., and Chinn, P. C. 1982. "Coming to Grips with Cultural Diversity." *Exceptional Education Quarterly* 2(4):33–45.

Bailey, D. B., and Leonard, J. 1977. "A Model for Adapting Bloom's Taxonomy to a Preschool Curriculum for the Gifted." *Gifted Child Quarterly* 21:97–103.

Baldwin, A. Y. 1978. "The Baldwin Identification Matrix." In *Educational Planning for the Gifted: Overcoming Cultural, Geographic, and Socioeconomic Barriers.* Edited by A. Y. Baldwin, G. H. Gear, and L. J. Lucito, 33–36. Reston, Va.: Council for Exceptional Children.

Ballering, L. D., and Koch, A. 1984. "Family Relations When a Child Is Gifted." *Gifted Child Quarterly* 28:140–43.

Barron, F., and Welsh, G. S. 1952. "Artistic Perception as a Possible Factor in Personality Style: Its Measurement by a Figure Preference Test." *Journal of Psychology* 33:199–203.

Bartkovich, K. G., and George, W. C. 1980. *Teaching the Gifted and Talented in the Mathematics Classroom.* Washington, D.C.: National Education Association.

Bartkovich, K. G., and Mezynski, K. 1981. "Fast-Paced Precalculus Mathematics for Talented Junior High Students: Two Recent SMPY Programs." *Gifted Child Quarterly* 25:73–80.

Bartz, W. 1982. "The Role of Foreign Language Education for the Gifted and Talented Student." *Foreign Language Annals* 15(5):329–34.

Bass, B. M. 1981. *Stogdill's Handbook of Leadership: A Survey of Theory and Research.* New York: The Free Press.

Bauer, H., and Harris, R. 1979. "Potentially Able Learners (P.A.L.s): A Program for Gifted Preschoolers and Parents." *Journal for the Education of the Gifted* 2:214–19.

Baumrind, D. 1972. "Socialization and Instrumental Competence in Young Children." In *The Young Child: Reviews of Research*, vol. 2. Edited by W. W. Hartup, 202–24.

Washington, D.C.: National Association for the Education of Young Children.

Baymur, F. B., and Patterson, C. H. 1960. "A Comparison of Three Methods of Assisting Underachieving High School Students." *Journal of Counseling Psychology* 7:83–90.

Bear, G. G. 1983. "Moral Reasoning, Classroom Behavior, and the Intellectually Gifted." *Journal for the Education of the Gifted* 6:111–19.

Beckwith, A. H. 1982. "Uses of the Ross Test as an Assessment Measure in Programs for the Gifted and a Comparison Study of the Ross Test to Individually Administered Intelligence Test." *Journal for the Education of the Gifted* 5:127–40.

Bee, H. L., Van Egeren, L. F., Streissguth, A. P., Nyman, B. A., and Leckie, M. S. 1969. "Social Class Differences in Maternal Teaching Strategies and Speech Patterns." *Developmental Psychology* 1:726–34.

Bell, R. Q. 1968. "A Reinterpretation of the Direction of Effects in Studies of Socialization." *Psychological Review* 75:81–95.

———. 1971. "Stimulus Control of Parent or Caretaker Behavior by Offspring." *Developmental Psychology* 4:63–72.

Berghoff, B. K., and Berghoff, P. J. 1979. "Communication Techniques for Gifted/Talented Support Teachers." *Journal for the Education of the Gifted* 3:105–7.

Bernal, E. M., Jr. 1978. "The Identification of Gifted Chicano Children." In *Educational Planning for the Gifted.* Edited by A. Y. Baldwin, G. H. Gear, and L. J. Lucito, 14–17. Reston, Va.: Council for Exceptional Children.

———. 1979. "The Education of the Culturally Different Gifted." In *The Gifted and the Talented: Their Education and Development.* Edited by A. H. Passow, 395–400. Chicago: University of Chicago Press.

Biehler, R. F. 1981. *Child Development: An Introduction*, 2d ed. Boston: Houghton Mifflin.

Birch, J. W. 1984. "Is *Any* Identification Procedure Necessary?" *Gifted Child Quarterly* 28:157–61.

Birnbaum, J. A. 1975. "Life Patterns and Self-

Esteem in Gifted Family-Oriented and Career-Committed Women." In *Women and Achievement: Social and Motivational Analyses.* Edited by M. T. S. Mednick, S. S. Tangri, and L. W. Hoffman, 396–419. New York: Wiley.

Birnbaum, M. J. Undated. "Educational Problems of Rural Education for the Gifted." In *Ideas for Urban/Rural Gifted/Talented.* National/State Leadership Training Institute on the Gifted and the Talented, 67–69. Ventura, Calif.: Office of the Ventura County Superintendent of Schools.

Bishop, W. E. 1981. "Characteristics of Teachers Judged Successful by Intellectually Gifted, High-Achieving High School Students." In *Psychology and Education of the Gifted,* (3d ed. Edited by W. B. Barbe and J. S. Renzulli, 422–32. New York: Irvington.

Blaubergs, M. 1978. "Personal Studies of Gifted Females: An Overview and Commentary." *Gifted Child Quarterly* 22:539–47.

Bloom, B. S. 1956. *Taxonomy of Educational Objectives: The Classification of Educational Goals. Handbook I: Cognitive Domain.* New York: David McKay.

———. 1982. "The Role of Gifted and Markers in the Development of Talent." *Exceptional Children,* 48:510–22.

———, ed. 1985. *Developing Talent in Young People.* New York: Ballantine.

Bloom, B. S., and Sosniak, L. A. 1981. "Talent Development vs. Schooling." *Educational Leadership* 39(2):86–94.

Bogen, J. E., and Bogen, G. M. 1976. "Creativity and the Bisected Brain." In *The Creativity Question.* Edited by A. Rothenberg and C. R. Hausman, 256–61. Durham, N.C.: Duke University Press.

Boothby, P. 1979. "Tips for Teaching Creative and Critical Reading." *Roeper Review* 1:24–25.

———. 1980. "Creative and Critical Reading for the Gifted." *The Reading Teacher* 33(6):674–76.

Borland, J. 1978. "Teacher Identification of the Gifted: A New Look." *Journal for the Education of the Gifted* 2:22–32.

Braga, J. L. 1971. "Early Admission: Opinion vs. Evidence." *The Elementary School Journal* 72(1):35–46.

Brain, R., Sir. 1960. "Some Reflections on Genius." In *Some Reflections on Genius and Other Essays.* Philadelphia: J. B. Lippincott.

Brandwein, P. 1981. *The Gifted Student as Future Scientist.* Ventura, Calif.: Office of the Ventura County Superintendent of Schools. Originally published by Harcourt Brace Jovanovich, 1955.

Brickman, W. W. 1979. "Educational Provisions for the Gifted and Talented in Other Countries." In *The Gifted and the Talented: Their Education and Development.* Edited by A. H. Passow, 308–29. Chicago: University of Chicago Press.

Brinkeroff, R. O., et al. 1983. *Program Evaluation: A Practitioners Guide for Trainers and Educators.* Boston: Kluwer-Nijhoff.

Broedel, J., Ohlsen, M., Proff, F., and Southard, C. 1960. "The Effects of Group Counseling on Gifted Underachieving Adolescents." *Journal of Counseling Psychology* 7(3):163–70.

Bronfenbrenner, U. 1972. "Is 80% of Intelligence Genetically Determined?" In *Influences on Human Development.* Edited by U. Bronfenbrenner, 118–27. Hinsdale, Ill.: The Dryden Press.

Brown, D. S. 1973. *Teaching Gifted Students Art in Grades Seven through Nine.* ERIC Document Reproduction Service No. ED 088 253. Sacramento, Calif.: California State Department of Education.

Brown, J. E. 1982. "Supplementary Materials for Academically Gifted English Students." *Journal for the Education of the Gifted* 5:67–73.

Bruch, C. B., and Morse, J. A. 1972. "Initial Study of Creative (Productive) Women under the Bruch–Morse Model." *Gifted Child Quarterly* 16:282–89.

Bruner, J. S. 1960. *The Process of Education,* 8th ed. Cambridge, Mass.: Harvard University Press.

———. 1964. "The Course of Cognitive Growth." *American Psychologist* 19:1–15.

———. Undated. *Man: A Course of Study.* Cambridge, Mass.: Social Studies Curriculum Project, Educational Services, Inc.

Buhler, C. 1931. "The Social Behavior of the Child." In *A Handbook of Child Psychology.* Edited by C. Murchison. Worcester, Mass.: Clark University Press.

Burke, J. P., Haworth, C. E., and Ware, W. B. 1982. "Scales for Rating the Behavioral Characteristics of Superior Students: An Investigation of Factor Structure." *Journal of Special Education* 16(4):477–85.

Burns, F. D. 1983. "Sex Differences—A Silent Message? A Comparison Study of Parents' Assessment and Junior High School Students' Self-Assessment of Learning Strengths and Weaknesses." *Journal for the Education of the Gifted* 6:195–212.

Burstein, B., Bank, L., and Jarvik, L. F. 1980. "Sex Differences in Cognitive Functioning: Evidence, Determinants, Implications." *Human Development* 23:289–313.

Busse, T. V., and Mansfield, R. S. 1980. "Theories of the Creative Process: A Review and a Perspective." *Journal of Creative Behavior* 14(2):91–103, 132.

———. 1981. "The Blooming of Creative Scientists: Early, Late, and Otherwise." *Gifted Child Quarterly* 25:63–66.

Buttermore, P. H. 1979. "Arts in Gifted Education." *Gifted Child Quarterly* 23:405–14.

Caldwell, R. M. 1981. "Computer-Based Medical Education: New Ways to Meet Persistent Needs." *Performance and Instruction* 20(10):11–14.

Callahan, C. M. 1979. "The Gifted and Talented Woman." In *The Gifted and the Talented: Their Education and Development.* Edited by A. H. Passow, 401–23. Chicago: University of Chicago Press.

———. 1981. "The Gifted Girl: An Anomaly?" In *Psychology and Education of the Gifted,* 3d ed. Edited by W. B. Barbe and J. S. Renzulli, 498–510. New York: Irvington.

———. 1982. "Parents of the Gifted and Talented Child." *Journal for the Education of the Gifted* 5:247–57.

———. 1983. "Issues in Evaluating Programs for the Gifted." *Gifted Child Quarterly* 27:3–7.

Callahan, C. M., and Corvo, M. L. 1980. "Validating the Ross Test for Identification and Evaluation of Critical Thinking Skills in Programs for the Gifted." *Journal for the Education of the Gifted* 4:17–26.

Callahan, C. M., and Kauffman, J. M. 1982. "Involving Gifted Children's Parents: Federal Law Is Silent, but Its Assumptions Apply." *Exceptional Education Quarterly* 3(2):50–55.

Camp, L. T. 1963. "Purposeful Preschool Education." *Gifted Child Quarterly* 7:106–7.

Carlson, N. N. 1981. "An Exploratory Study of Characteristics of Gifted and Talented Foreign Language Learners." *Foreign Language Annals* 14(5):385–91.

Carrelli, A. O. 1982. "Sex Equity and the Gifted." *G/C/T* (25):2–7.

Carroll, K. L. 1976. "Alternative Programs in the Arts for Gifted and Talented Students." *Gifted Child Quarterly* 20:414–21.

Carter, K. R. 1985. "Cognitive Development of Intellectually Gifted: A Piagetian Perspective." *Roeper Review* 1:180–84.

Carter, K. R., and Ormrod, J. E. 1982. "Acquisition of Formal Operations by Intellectually Gifted Children." *Gifted Child Quarterly* 26:110–15.

Cassidy, J. 1981a. "Inquiry Reading for the Gifted." *The Reading Teacher* 35:17–21.

———. 1981b. "Parental Involvement in Gifted Programs." *Journal for the Education of the Gifted* 4:284–87.

Cassidy, J., and Vukelich, C. 1980. "Do the Gifted Read Early?" *The Reading Teacher* 33(5):578–82.

Cattell, R. B. 1963. "Theory of Fluid and Crystallized Intelligence." *Journal of Educational Psychology* 54:1–22.

Cavedon, J. F. Undated. "Leadership, the Gifted Population, and the Center for Creative Leadership: A Network System." In *A New Generation of Leadership.* National/State Leadership Training Institute on the Gifted and the Talented, 25–32. Ventura, Calif.: Office of the Ventura County Superintendent of Schools.

Chambers, J. A., Barron, F., and Sprecher, J. W. 1980. "Identifying Gifted Mexican-American Students." *Gifted Child Quarterly* 24:123–28.

Chen, J., and Goon, S. W. 1976. "Recognition of the Gifted from among Disadvantaged Asian Children." *Gifted Child Quarterly* 20:157–64.

Chetelat, F. J. 1981. "Visual Arts Education for the Gifted Elementary-Level Art Student." *Gifted Child Quarterly* 25:154–58.

Chittenden, G. E. 1942. "An Experimental Study in Measuring and Modifying Assertive Behavior in Young Children." *Monographs of the Society for Research in Child Development* 7.

Ciha, T. E., Harris, R., Hoffman, C., and Potler, M. W. 1974. "Parents as Identifiers of Giftedness, Ignored but Accurate." *Gifted Child Quarterly* 18:191–95.

Clark, B. 1983. *Growing Up Gifted*, 2d ed. Columbus, Ohio: Charles E. Merrill.

Clark, G., and Zimmerman, E. 1982. "The Indiana University's Summer Arts Institute." *Journal for the Education of the Gifted* 5:204–8.

———. 1983. "At the Age of Six, I Gave Up a Magnificent Career as a Painter: Seventy Years of Research about Identifying Students with Superior Abilities in the Visual Arts." *Gifted Child Quarterly* 27:180–84.

———. 1984. "Toward a New Conception of Talent in the Visual Arts." *Roeper Review* 6:214–16.

Clark, H. F., and Davis, J. C. 1981. "Ability and Access to Advanced Training in Selected Countries." In *The Gifted Child, the Family, and the Community*. Edited by B. S. Miller and M. Price, 206–15. New York: Walker and Co., with the American Association for Gifted Children.

Cleveland, H. 1980. "Learning the Art of Leadership." *Twin Cities* (August).

Cohen, E. 1981. "The Arts from the Inside Out: Developing a Performing Arts Curriculum." *G/C/T* (20):38–42.

Colangelo, N., and Dettmann, D. F. 1982. "A Conceptual Model of Four Types of Parent–School Relationships." *Journal for the Education of the Gifted* 5:120–26.

———. 1983. "A Review of Research on Parents and Families of Gifted Children." *Exceptional Children* 50:20–27.

Colangelo, N., and Kelly, K. R. 1983. "A Study of Student, Parent, and Teacher Attitudes toward Gifted Programs and Gifted Students." *Gifted Child Quarterly* 27:107–10.

Colby, A., Kohlberg, L., Gibbs, J., and Lieberman, M. 1983. "A Longitudinal Study of Moral Development." *Monographs of the Society for Research in Child Development* 48:1–2.

Cole, M., and Bruner, J. 1971. "Cultural Differences and Inferences about Psychological Processes." *American Psychologist* 26(10):867–75.

Coleman, J. M., and Fults, B. A. 1982. "Self-Concept and the Gifted Classroom: The Role of Social Comparisons." *Gifted Child Quarterly* 26:116–20.

———. 1985. "Special-Class Placement, Level of Intelligence, and the Self-Concepts of Gifted Children: A Social Comparison Perspective." *Remedial and Special Education (RASE)* 6(1):7–12.

Collier, D. 1972. "Pierre and Marie Curie." In *100 Great Modern Lives*. Edited by J. Canning. New York: Beekman House.

Collis, H. 1981. "The British National Association for Gifted Children." In *The Gifted Child, the Family, and the Community*. Edited by B. S. Miller and M. Price. New York: Walker and Co., with the American Association for Gifted Children.

Cooke, G. J. 1980. "Scientifically Gifted Children." *G/C/T* (12):17–18.

Council of State Directors of Programs for the Gifted. 1984. *TAG Update* 8(1).

Covington, M. V., Crutchfield, R. S., Davis, L., and Olton, R. M. 1974. *The Productive Thinking Program: A Course in Learning to Think*. Columbus, Ohio: Merrill.

Cox, C. 1926. *Genetic Studies of Genius*. Vol. 2, *The Early Mental Traits of Three Hundred Geniuses*. Stanford, Calif.: Stanford University Press.

Cox, J., and Daniel, N. 1983. "Options for the

Secondary-Level G/T Student (Part II)." *G/C/T* (27): 24–30.

Crabbe, A. B. 1982. "Creating a Brighter Future: An Update on the Future Problem-Solving Program." *Journal for the Education of the Gifted* 5:2–11.

Crabtree, C. 1970. "Inquiry Approaches: How New and How Valuable?" In *Readings on Elementary Social Studies*. Edited by J. McLendon et al., 324–31. Boston: Allyn and Bacon.

Creighton, H. C. 1961a. "Facilities for the Talented in the USSR." In *Concepts of Excellence in Education: The Yearbook of Education*. Edited by G. Z. F. Bereday and J. A. Lauwerys, 317. New York: Harcourt, Brace, and World.

———. 1961b. "The Bolshoi Ballet School." In *Concepts of Excellence in Education: The Yearbook of Education*. Edited by G. Z. F. Bereday and J. A. Lauwerys, 467. New York: Harcourt, Brace, and World.

Crockenberg, S. B. 1972. "Creativity Tests: A Boon or Boondoggle for Education?" *Review of Educational Research* 42(1):27–45.

Cropley, A. J. 1972. "A Five-Year Longitudinal Study of the Validity of Creativity Tests." *Developmental Psychology* 6:119–24.

Crovitz, H. F. 1970. *Galton's Walk*. New York: Harper & Row.

Daddario, E. O. 1977. "Science, the Future, and the Gifted Child." *Gifted Child Quarterly* 21:32–36.

Darlington, R. B., Royce, J. M., Snipper, A. S., Murray, H. W., and Lazar, I. 1980. "Preschool Programs and Later School Competence of Children from Low-Income Families." *Science* 208(1):202–8.

Davidson, J. E., and Sternberg, R. J. 1984. "The Role of Insight in Intellectual Giftedness." *Gifted Child Quarterly* 28:58–64.

Davis, G. A. 1976. "Research and Development in Training Creative Thinking." In *Cognitive Learning in Children: Theories and Strategies*. Edited by J. R. Levin and V. L. Allen, 219–40. New York: Academic Press.

Dawkins, B. 1978. "Do Gifted Junior High School Students Need Reading Instruction?" *Journal for the Education of the Gifted* 2:3–9.

Dean, R. S. 1977. "Effects of Self-Concept on Learning with Gifted Children." *Journal of Educational Research* 70(6):315–18.

DeAvila, E. A., and Havassy, B. 1974. "The Testing of Minority Children: A Neo-Piagetian Approach." *Today's Education* 63(4):72–75.

———. 1975. "Piagetian Alternatives to IQ: Mexican-American Study." In *Issues in the Classification of Children*, vol. 2. Edited by N. Hobbs. San Francisco: Jossey Bass.

Debinski, R. J., and Mauser, A. J. 1978. "Parents of the Gifted: Perceptions of Psychologists and Teachers." *Journal for the Education of the Gifted* 1:5–14.

DeFries, J. C., Johnson, R. C., Kuse, A. R., McClearn, G. E., Polovina, J., Vandenberg, S. G., and Wilson, J. R. 1979. "Family Resemblance for Specific Cognitive Abilities." *Behavior Genetics* 9:23–43.

DeFries, J. C., Vandenberg, S. G., and McClearn, G. E. 1976. "Genetics of Specific Cognitive Abilities." *Annual Review of Genetics* 10:179–207.

DeLeon, J. 1983a. "A Study in the Modification of Aggressive Behavior of Three Gifted Preschool Children." Unpublished manuscript. Las Cruces, N.M.: New Mexico State University.

———. 1983b. "Cognitive Style Difference and the Underrepresentation of Mexican-Americans in Programs for the Gifted." *Journal for the Education of the Gifted* 6:167–77.

Delisle, J. R., Reis, S. M., and Gubbins, E. J. 1981. "The Revolving Door Identification and Programming Model." *Exceptional Children* 48:152–56.

Delisle, J. R., and Renzulli, J. S. 1982. "The Revolving Door Identification and Programming Model: Correlates of Creative Production." *Gifted Child Quarterly* 26:89–95.

Devall, Y. L. 1982. "Some Cognitive and Creative Characteristics and Their Relationship to Reading Comprehension in Gifted and Nongifted Fifth Graders." *Journal for the Education of the Gifted* 5:259–71.

Dewey, J. 1933. *How We Think*, rev. ed. Lexington, Mass.: D. C. Heath.

Dewing, K. 1970. "Family Influences on Creativity: A Review and Discussion." *Journal of Special Education* 4(4):399–404.

———. 1973. "Some Characteristics of the Parents of Creative Twelve-Year-Olds." *Journal of Personality* 41:71–85.

Diaz, V. T., Martin, T., Patterson, P., and Stringfellow, M. 1983. *Bilingual Gifted/Creative and Talented Curriculum Guide.* Davie, Fla.: School Board of Broward County.

Diessner, R. 1983. "The Relationship between Cognitive Abilities and Moral Development in Intellectually Gifted Children." *G/C/T* (28):15–17.

Dirks, J. 1979. "Parents' Reactions to Identification of the Gifted." *Roeper Review* 2:9–11.

Dole, J. A., and Adams, P. J. 1983. "Reading Curriculum for Gifted Readers: A Survey." *Gifted Child Quarterly* 27:64–72.

Domino, G. 1969. "Maternal Personality Correlates of Sons' Creativity." *Journal of Consulting and Clinical Psychology* 33:180–83.

Domino, G., Walsh, J., Reznikoff, M., and Honeyman, M. 1976. "A Factor Analysis of Creativity in Fraternal and Identical Twins." *Journal of General Psychology* 94:211–21.

Dorhout, A. 1982. "Identifying Musically Gifted Students." *Journal for the Education of the Gifted* 5:56–66.

Dorn, C. M. 1976. "The Advanced Placement Program in Studio Art." *Gifted Child Quarterly* 20:450–58.

Dowdall, C. B., and Colangelo, N. 1982. "Underachieving Gifted Students: Review and Implications." *Gifted Child Quarterly* 26:179–84.

Doyle, R. E., Gottlieb, B., and Schneider, D. 1979. "Underachievers Achieve: A Case for Intensive Counseling." *The School Counselor* 26:134–43.

Ehrlich, V. Z. 1980. "The Astor Program for Gifted Children." In *Educating the Preschool/Primary Gifted and Talented.* National/State Leadership Training Institute on the Gifted and the Talented, 248–50. Ventura, Calif.: Office of the Ventura County Superintendent of Schools.

Elkind, J. 1973. "The Gifted Child with Learning Disabilities." *Gifted Child Quarterly* 17:96–97.

Ellis-Schwabe, M., and Conroy, D. 1983. "A Discussion of the Creative Abilities of Learning-Disabled, Gifted, and Learning-Disabled/Gifted Children." *Journal for the Education of the Gifted* 6:213–21.

Ellison, R. L., Abe, C., Fox, D. G., Coray, K. E., and Taylor, C. W. 1976. "Using Biographical Information in Identifying Artistic Talent." *Gifted Child Quarterly* 20:402–13.

Ennis, R. H., and Millman, J. 1971. *Cornell Critical Thinking Test.* Creative Thinking Project, University of Illinois.

Evans, E. D. 1965. "Pupil Achievement: Are We Responsible?" *Instructor* 75(4).

Evans, E. D., and Marken, D. 1982. "Multiple Assessment of Special Class Placement for Gifted Students: A Comparative Study." *Gifted Child Quarterly* 26:126–32.

Evaluation Training Consortium. March 1979. "Type II Workshop, Phoenix, Arizona." Kalamazoo, Mich.: Evaluation Center, Western Michigan University.

Ewart, A. 1972. "Bertrand Russell." In *100 Great Modern Lives.* Edited by J. Canning. New York: Beekman House.

Eysenck, H. J. 1979. *The Structure and Measurement of Intelligence.* New York: Springer-Verlag.

Faunce, P. S. 1968. "Personality Characteristics and Vocational Interests Related to the College Persistence of Academically Gifted Women." *Journal of Consulting Psychology* 15(1):31–40.

Feldhusen, J. 1978. *Leadership Training for the Gifted*. West Lafayette, Ind.: Purdue Gifted Program.

Feldhusen, J., and Reilly, P. 1983. "The Purdue Secondary Model for Gifted Education: A Multiservice Program." *Journal for the Education of the Gifted* 6:230–44.

Feldhusen, J. F., Treffinger, D. J., and Bahlke, S. J. 1970. "Developing Creative Thinking: The Purdue Creativity Program." *Journal of Creative Behavior* 4:85–90.

Feldman, D. 1979. "The Mysterious Case of Extreme Giftedness." In *The Gifted and the Talented: Their Education and Development*. Edited by A. H. Passow, 335–51. Chicago: University of Chicago Press.

———. 1984. "A Follow-up of Subjects Scoring above 180 IQ in Terman's 'Genetic Studies of Genius.'" *Exceptional Children* 50:518–23.

Finch, A. J., Jr., and Spirito, A. 1980. "Use of Cognitive Training to Change Cognitive Processes." *Exceptional Education Quarterly* 1(11):31–39.

Fine, M. J., and Pitts, R. 1980. "Intervention with Underachieving Gifted Children: Rationale and Strategies." *Gifted Child Quarterly* 24:51–55.

Finney, B. C., and Van Dalsem, E. 1969. "Group Counseling for Gifted Underachieving High School Graduates." *Journal of Counseling Psychology* 16(1):87–94.

Fitzpatrick, J. L. 1978. "Academic Underachievement: Other-Direction and Attitudes toward Women's Roles in Bright Adolescent Females." *Journal of Educational Psychology* 70(4):645–50.

Fleming, E. S., and Hollinger, C. L. 1981. "The Multidimensionality of Talent in Adolescent Young Women." *Journal for the Education of the Gifted* 4:188–98.

Ford, B. G., and Ford, R. D. 1981. "Identifying Creative Potential in Handicapped Children." *Exceptional Children* 48:115–22.

Foster, W. 1981. "Leadership: A Conceptual Framework for Recognizing and Educating." *Gifted Child Quarterly* 25:17–25.

Fox, A. E. 1971. "Kindergarten: Forgotten Year for the Gifted?" *Gifted Child Quarterly* 15:42–48.

Fox, L. H. 1977. "Sex Differences: Implications for Program Planning for the Academically Gifted." In *The Gifted and the Creative: A Fifty-Year Perspective*. Edited by J. C. Stanley, W. C. George, and C. H. Solano, 113–38. Baltimore: Johns Hopkins University Press.

———. 1979. "Programs for the Gifted and Talented: An Overview." In *The Gifted and the Talented: Their Education and Development*. Edited by A. H. Passow, 104–26. Chicago: University of Chicago Press.

Fraenkel, J. R. 1977. *How to Teach about Values: An Analytic Approach*. Englewood Cliffs, N.J.: Prentice-Hall.

Frasier, M. M. 1979. "Rethinking the Issues Regarding the Culturally Disadvantaged Gifted." *Exceptional Children* 45:538–42.

Frasier, M. M., and Carland, J. 1980. "A Study to Identify Key Factors That Affect the Establishment of a Positive Relationship between Teachers of the Gifted and Regular Classroom Teachers." *Journal for the Education of the Gifted* 3:225–27.

Frasier, M. M., and McCannon, C. 1981. "Using Bibliotherapy with Gifted Children." *Gifted Child Quarterly* 25:81–85.

Freund, J. H., Bradley, R. H., and Caldwell, B. M. 1979. "The Home Environment in the Assessment of Learning Disabilities." *Learning Disability Quarterly* 2(4):39–51.

Friedman, P. G. 1980. *Teaching the Gifted and Talented Oral Communication and Leadership*. Washington, D.C.: National Education Association.

Frierson, E. C. 1965. "Upper and Lower Status Gifted Children: A Study of Differences." *Exceptional Children* 32:83–90.

Fu, V. R. 1979. "Preschool Leadership–Followership Behaviors." *Child Study Journal* 9(2):133–40.

Furman, W., Rahe, D. F., and Hartup, W. W. 1979. "Rehabilitation of Socially Withdrawn Preschool Children through Mixed-Age and Same-Age Socialization." *Child Development* 50(4):915–22.

Galasso, V. G., and Simon, M. 1981. "Program for Developing Creativity in Science at the Bronx High School of Science." In A. Arnold et al., *Secondary Programs for the Gifted/Talented*, 55–57. National/State Leadership Training Institute on the Gifted and the Talented. Ventura, Calif.: Office of the Ventura County Superintendent of Schools.

Galbraith, B. W. 1985. "Interlochen Arts Academy: Its Guidelines for Success." *Journal for the Education of the Gifted* 8:199–210.

Gallagher, J. J. 1975. *Teaching the Gifted Child*, 2d ed. Boston: Allyn and Bacon.

———. 1979. "Issues in Education for the Gifted." In *The Gifted and the Talented: Their Education and Development*. Edited by A. H. Passow, 28–44. Chicago: University of Chicago Press.

Gallagher, J. J., Weiss, P., Oglesby, K., and Thomas, T. 1983. *The Status of Gifted/Talented Education: United States Surveys of Needs, Practices, and Policies*. National/State Leadership Training Institute on the Gifted and the Talented. Ventura, Calif.: Office of the Ventura County Superintendent of Schools.

Gallagher, J. M., and Quandt, I. J. 1981. "Piaget's Theory of Cognitive Development and Reading Comprehension: A New Look at Questioning." *Topics in Learning and Learning Disabilities* 1(1):21–30.

Gardner, H. 1982. "Giftedness: Speculations from a Biological Perspective." *New Directions for Child Development* 17:47–60.

———. 1983. *Frames of Mind: The Theory of Multiple Intelligences*. New York: Basic Books.

Gear, G. H. 1976. "Accuracy of Teacher Judgment in Identifying Intellectually Gifted Children: A Review of the Literature." *Gifted Child Quarterly* 20:478–89.

———. 1978. "Effects of Training on Teachers' Accuracy in the Identification of Gifted Children." *Gifted Child Quarterly* 22:90–97.

———. 1984. "Providing Services for Rural Gifted Children." *Exceptional Children* 50:326–31.

Gelman, R. 1979. "Preschool Thought." *American Psychologist* 34(10):900–905.

Getzels, J. W. 1975. "Problem-Finding and the Inventiveness of Solutions." *Journal of Creative Behavior* 9:12–18.

———. 1979. "From Art Student to Fine Artist: Potential, Problem Finding, and Performance." In *The Gifted and the Talented: Their Education and Development*. Edited by A. H. Passow, 372–87. Chicago: University of Chicago Press.

Getzels, J. W., and Dillon, J. T. 1973. "The Nature of Giftedness and the Education of the Gifted." In *Second Handbook of Research on Teaching*. Edited by R. M. W. Travers, 689–731. Chicago: Rand McNally.

Getzels, J. W., and Jackson, P. W. 1961. "Family Environment and Cognitive Style: A Study of the Sources of Highly Intelligent and of Highly Creative Adolescents." *American Sociological Review* 26(3):351–59.

———. 1962. *Creativity and Intelligence: Explorations with Gifted Students*. New York: Wiley.

Gibney, T. 1982. "The Gifted as Problem Solvers in Elementary Schools." *Roeper Review* 4:13–14.

Gibson, J., and Chennells, P., eds. 1976. *Gifted Children: Looking to Their Future*. London: Latimer New Dimensions, with the National Association for Gifted Children.

Gilbert, J. P., and Beal, M. R. 1982. "Music Experiences for the Gifted and Talented: Adapting the Renzulli Enrichment Triad Model." *G/C/T* (24):50–51.

Goertzel, M. G., Goertzel, V., and Goertzel, T. G. 1978. *Three Hundred Eminent Personalities*. San Francisco: Jossey-Bass.

Goertzel, V., and Goertzel, M. G. 1962. *Cradles of Eminence*. Boston: Little, Brown.

Goldschmid, M. L., and Bentler, P. M. 1968. *Manual: Concept Assessment Kit—Conservation*. San Diego: Educational and Industrial Testing Service.

Goleman, D. 1978. "Special Abilities of the Sexes: Do They Begin in the Brain?" *Psychology Today* (November).

Good, H. G. 1960. *A History of Western Education*, 2d ed. New York: Macmillan.

Goodrum, S., and Irons, V. 1981. "Monitoring Programmed Inservice Preparation of Teachers for Rural Gifted Students." *Journal for the Education of the Gifted* 4:270–77.

Gordon, E. E. 1980. "The Assessment of Music Aptitudes of Very Young Children." *Gifted Child Quarterly* 24:107–11.

Gordon, W. J. J. 1961. *Synectics*. New York: Harper.

———. 1972. "On Being Explicit about Creative Process." *Journal of Creative Behavior* 6:295–300.

Gordon, W. J. J., and Poze, T. 1971. *The Basic Course in Synectics*. Cambridge, Mass.: Porpoise Books.

———. 1980. *The New Art of the Possible*. Cambridge, Mass.: SES Associates.

———. 1981. "Conscious/Subconscious Interaction in a Creative Act." *Journal of Creative Behavior* 15(1):1–10.

Gowan, J. C. 1979. "The Production of Creativity through Right-Hemisphere Imagery." *Journal of Creative Behavior* 13(1):39–51.

Gregory, A. 1982. "Applying the Purdue Three-Stage Model for Gifted Education to the Development of Art Education for G/C/T Students." *G/C/T* (25):23–26.

Groth, N. J. 1971. "Differences in Parental Environment Needed for Degree of Achievement for Gifted Men and Women." *Gifted Child Quarterly* 15:256.

———. 1975. "Mothers of Gifted." *Gifted Child Quarterly* 19:217–22.

Grusec, J. E., and Arnason, L. 1982. "Consideration for Others: Approaches to Enhancing Altruism." In *The Young Child: Reviews of Research*, vol. 3. Edited by S. G. Moore and C. R. Cooper, 159–74. Washington, D.C.: National Association for the Education of Young Children.

Guilford, J. P. 1959. "Three Faces of Intellect." *American Psychologist* 14:469–79.

———. 1967. *The Nature of Human Intelligence*. New York: McGraw-Hill.

———. 1973. "Theories of Intelligence." In *Handbook of General Psychology*. Edited by B. B. Wolman, 630–43. Englewood Cliffs, N.J.: Prentice-Hall.

———. 1975. "Creativity: A Quarter-Century of Progress." In *Perspectives in Creativity*. Edited by I. A. Taylor and J. W. Getzels. Chicago: Aldine.

Gurman, A. S. 1970. "The Role of the Family in Underachievement." *Journal of School Psychology* 8(1):48–53.

Hackney, H. 1981. "The Gifted Child, the Family, and the School." *Gifted Child Quarterly* 25:51–54.

Hall, E. G. 1982. "Accelerating Gifted Girls." *G/C/T* (25):48–50.

Hallahan, D. P., and Kauffman, J. M. 1978. *Exceptional Children*. Englewood Cliffs, N.J.: Prentice-Hall.

Hamilton, J. 1984. "The Gifted Migrant Child." *Roeper Review* 6:146–47.

Handel, R. D. 1983. "Teachers of Gifted Girls: Are There Differences in Classroom Management?" *Journal for the Education of the Gifted* 6:86–97.

Haring, N. G. 1982. *Exceptional Children and Youth*, 3d ed. Columbus, Ohio: Charles E. Merrill.

Harvey, S. 1982. "A New View of the Relationship between Creativity and Intelligence." *Journal for the Education of the Gifted* 5:295–307.

Haskell, A. L. 1961. "The Royal Ballet School: Education for the Dancer." In *Concepts of Excellence in Education: The Yearbook of Education*. Edited by G. Z. F. Bereday and J. A. Lauwerys, 461. New York: Harcourt, Brace, and World.

Hatch, A. 1974. *Buckminster Fuller at Home in the Universe*. New York: Crown Publishers.

Helson, R. 1971. "Women Mathematicians and the Creative Personality." *Journal of Counseling and Clinical Psychology* 36(2):210–20.

Hersberger, J., and Asher, W. 1980. "Comment on 'A Quota System for Gifted Minority Children.'" *Gifted Child Quarterly* 24:96.

Hersberger, J., and Wheatley, G. 1980. "A Proposed Model for a Gifted Elementary School Mathematics Program." *Gifted Child Quarterly* 24:37–40.

Hershey, M. 1980. "Individual Educational Planning for Gifted Students: A Report from Kansas." *Journal for the Education of the Gifted* 3:207–13.

Hess, R. D., and Shipman, V. C. 1965. "Early Experience and the Socialization of Cognitive Modes in Children." *Child Development* 36:869–86.

Hessler, G. L. 1985. "Review of the Kaufman Assessment Battery for Children: Implications for Assessment of the Gifted." *Journal for the Education of the Gifted* 8:133–47.

Heydinger, R. B. 1979. "Computer Conferencing: Its Use as a Pedagogical Tool." *Journal of Educational Computing* (Spring):6–29.

High, M. H., and Udall, A. J. 1983. "Teacher Ratings of Students in Relation to Ethnicity of Students and School Ethnic Balance." *Journal for the Education of the Gifted* 6:154–66.

Hilliard, A. G., III, and Vaughn-Scott, M. 1982. "The Quest for the 'Minority' Child." In *The Young Child: Reviews of Research*, vol. 3. Edited by S. G. Moore and C. R. Cooper, 175–89. Washington, D.C.: National Association for the Education of Young Children.

Hillman, S., and Smith, G. 1981. "Development of Leadership Capacities in Children." *Elementary School Journal* 82(1):59–65.

Hirsch, S. P. 1976. "Executive High School Internships: A Boon for the Gifted and Talented." *Teaching Exceptional Children* 9:22–23.

Hollinger, C. L. 1983. "Multidimensional Determinants of Traditional and Non-traditional Career Aspirations for Mathematically Talented Female Adolescents." *Journal for the Education of the Gifted* 6:245–65.

Hollinger, C. L., and Fleming, E. S. 1984. "Internal Barriers to the Realization of Potential: Correlates and Interrelationships among Gifted and Talented Female Adolescents." *Gifted Child Quarterly* 28:135–39.

Hollingsworth, L. S. 1939. "What We Know about the Early Selection and Training of Leaders." *Teachers College Record* 40:575–92.

———. 1942. *Children above 180 IQ, Stanford–Binet*. Yonkers-on-Hudson, N.Y.: World Book.

Honzik, M. P. 1973. "The Development of Intelligence." In *Handbook of General Psychology*. Edited by B. B. Wolman, 644–55. Englewood Cliffs, N.J.: Prentice-Hall.

Howieson, N. 1981. "A Longitudinal Study of Creativity—1965–1975." *Journal of Creative Behavior* 15(2):117–34.

Hubert H. Humphrey Institute of Public Affairs. 1981. *Education for Reflective Leadership*. Minneapolis: University of Minnesota.

Hunt, J. McV. 1961. *Intelligence and Experience*. New York: Ronald Press.

Hurwitz, A. 1976. "The US and USSR! Two Attitudes towards the Gifted in Art." *Gifted Child Quarterly* 20:458–65.

———. 1981. "Arts: New Recognition for the Gifted in Art." *School Arts* 81(1):32–33.

Institute for Behavioral Research in Creativity (IBRIC). 1968. *Alpha Biographical Inventory*. Greensboro, N.C.: Prediction Press.

Isaacs, A. F. 1963. "Should the Gifted Preschool Child Be Taught to Read?" *Gifted Child Quarterly* 7:72–77.

Iwahashi, B. 1961. "Problems of Educating the Gifted in the Primary and Secondary Schools in Japan." In *Concepts of Excellence in Education: The Yearbook of Education*. Edited by G. Z. F. Bereday and J. A. Lauwerys, 284. New York: Harcourt, Brace, and World.

Jaben, T. H. 1983. "The Effects of Creativity Training on Learning-Disabled Students' Creative Written Expression." *Journal of Learning Disabilities* 16(5):264–65.

Jackson, D. M. 1979. "The Emerging National and State Concern." In *The Gifted and the Talented: Their Education and Development*. Edited by A. H. Passow, 45–62. Chicago: University of Chicago Press.

Jackson, N. E., Famiglietti, J., and Robinson, H. B. 1981. "Kindergarten and First Grade Teachers' Attitudes toward Early Entrants, Intellectually Advanced, and Average Students." *Journal for the Education of the Gifted* 4:132–42.

Jacobs, J. 1971. "Effectiveness of Teacher and Parent Identification of Gifted Children as a Function of School Level." *Psychology in the Schools* 8:140–42.

Jarecky, R. K. 1959. "Identification of the Socially Gifted." *Exceptional Children* 25:415–19.

Jenkins, R. C. W. 1979. *A Resource Guide to Preschool and Primary Programs for the Gifted and Talented*. Mansfield Center, Conn.: Creative Learning Press.

Jennings, K. D. 1975. "People versus Object Orientation, Social Behavior, and Intellectual Abilities in Preschool Children." *Developmental Psychology* 11(4):511–19.

Jensen, A. R. 1969. "How Much Can We Boost IQ and Scholastic Achievement?" *Harvard Educational Review* 39:1–123.

———. 1970. "Hierarchical Theories of Mental Ability." In *On Intelligence*. Edited by W. B. Dockrell. London: Methuen.

Jensen, S. A. 1979. "A Reading Program for Gifted High School Students." *Roeper Review* 1:25–27.

Johnson, M., Jr. 1967. "Definitions and Models in Curriculum Theory." *Educational Theory* 17:127–40. Cited in *Contemporary Thought on Public School Curriculum: Readings*. Edited by E. C. Short and G. D. Marcounit. Dubuque, Iowa: Wm. C. Brown.

Jones, H. E. 1983. "Developing Social Studies Units for the Gifted: A Conceptual Model." *G/C/T* (28):32–34.

Judkins, P. A. Undated. "Certain Criteria Lead toward Leadership." In *A New Generation of Leadership*. National/State Leadership Training Institute on the Gifted and the Talented. Ventura, Calif.: Office of the Ventura County Superintendent of Schools.

Jung, C. G. 1923. "On the Relation of Analytic Psychology to Poetic Art." Translated by H. G. Baynes. *British Journal of Medical Psychology* 3:219–31.

Kaplan, S. N. 1975. *Providing Programs for the Gifted and Talented: A Handbook*. Reston, Va.: Council for Exceptional Children.

———. 1979a. *Inservice Training Manual: Activities for Developing Curriculum for the Gifted/Talented*. National/State Leadership Training Institute on the Gifted and the Talented. Ventura, Calif.: Office of the Ventura County Superintendent of Schools.

———. 1977b. "Language Arts and Social Studies Curriculum in the Elementary School." In *The Gifted and the Talented: Their Education and Development*. Edited by A. H. Passow, 155–68. Chicago: University of Chicago Press.

———. 1980. "Curricular and Programmatic Concerns." In *Educating the Preschool/Primary Gifted and Talented*. National/State Leadership Training Institute on the Gifted and the Talented, 61–101. Ventura, Calif.: Office of the Ventura County Superintendent of Schools.

———. 1981. "The Should Nots and Shoulds of Developing an Appropriate Curriculum for the Gifted." In *Psychology and Education of the Gifted*. Edited by W. B. Barbe and J. S. Renzulli, 351–58. New York: Irvington.

Kaplan, S. N., et al. 1982. "Curricula for the Gifted." Selected proceedings of the First National Conference on Curricula for the Gifted/Talented, National/State Leadership Training Institute on the Gifted and the Talented. Ventura, Calif.: Office of the Ventura County Superintendent of Schools.

Karnes, F. A., and Brown, K. E. 1981. "Moral Development and the Gifted: An Initial Investigation." *Roeper Review* 3:8–10.

Karnes, F. A., and Chauvin, J. C. 1982. "A Survey of Early Admission Policies for Younger than Average Students: Implications for Gifted Youth." *Gifted Child Quarterly* 26:68–73.

Karnes, F. A., and Karnes, M. R. 1982. "Parents and Schools: Educating Gifted and Talented Children." *The Elementary School Journal* 82(3):236–48.

Karnes, F. A., and Parker, J. P. 1983. "Teacher Certification in Gifted Education: The State of the Art and Considerations for the Future." *Roeper Review* 6:18–19.

Karnes, M. B. 1980. "Elements of an Exemplary Preschool/Primary Program for Gifted and Talented." In *Educating the Preschool/Primary Gifted and Talented*. National/State Leadership Training Institute on the Gifted and the Talented, 103–37. Ventura, Calif.: Office of the Ventura County Superintendent of Schools.

Karnes, M. B., and Associates. 1978a. *Preschool Talent Checklists Manual*. Urbana, Ill.: Institute for Child Behavior and Development, University of Illinois.

———. 1978b. *Preschool Talent Checklists Record Booklet*. Urbana, Ill.: Institute for Child Behavior and Development, University of Illinois.

———. 1978c. *RAPYHT Curriculum Guides for Nurturing Talent in Early Childhood*. Urbana, Ill.: Institute for Child Behavior and Development, University of Illinois.

Karnes, M. B., and Bertschi, J. D. 1978. "Teaching the Young Gifted Handicapped Child." *Teaching Exceptional Children* 10:114–19.

Karnes, M. B., McCoy, G., Zehrbach, R. R., Wollersheim, J. P., and Clarizio, H. F. 1963. "The Efficacy of Two Organizational Plans for Underachieving Intellectually Gifted Children." *Exceptional Children* 29:438–46.

Karnes, M. B., Shwedel, A. M., and Lewis, G. F. 1983a. "Long-Term Effects of Early Programming for the Gifted/Talented Handicapped." *Journal for the Education of the Gifted* 6:266–78.

———. 1983b. "Short-Term Effects of Early Programming for the Young Gifted Handicapped Child." *Exceptional Children* 50:103–9.

Karnes, M. B., Schwedel, A. M., and Linnemeyer, S. A. 1982. "The Young Gifted/Talented Child: Programs at the University of Illinois." *Elementary School Journal* 82(3):195–213.

Karnes, M. B., Schwedel, A. M., and Steinberg, D. 1984. "Styles of Parenting among Parents of Young Gifted Children." *Roeper Review* 6:232–35.

Karnes, M. B., and Strong, P. S. 1978. *Nurturing Leadership Talent in Early Childhood*. Urbana, Ill.: Institute for Child Behavior and Development, University of Illinois.

Katz, A. N. 1978. "Creativity and the Right Cerebral Hemisphere: Towards a Psychologically Based Theory of Creativity." *Journal of Creative Behavior* 12(4):253–64.

Katz, E., and Seeley, K. 1982. "The University of Denver's University for Youth." *Journal for the Education of the Gifted* 5:160–69.

Kaufman, A. S. 1984. "K–ABC and Giftedness." *Roeper Review* 7:83–88.

Kaufmann, F. A., Tews, T. C., and Milam, C. P. 1985. "New Orleans Center for the Creative Arts: Program Descriptions and Student Perceptions." *Journal for the Education of the Gifted* 8:211–19.

Keating, D. P. 1979. "Secondary-School Programs." In *The Gifted and the Talented: Their Education and Development*. Edited by A. H. Passow, 186–98. Chicago: University of Chicago Press.

Kelly, K. R., and Colangelo, N. 1984. "Academic and Social Self-Concepts of Gifted, General, and Special Students." *Exceptional Children* 50:551–54.

Kester, E. S. 1982. "SOI: A Qualitatively Different Program for the Gifted." *G/C/T* (21):21–25.

Khatena, J. 1978. "Identification and Stimulation of Creative Imagination Imagery." *Journal of Creative Behavior* 12(1):30–38.

Kilpatrick, W. H. 1925. *Foundations of Method*. New York: Macmillan.

King, E. J. 1973. *Other Schools and Ours*, 4th ed. New York: Holt, Rinehart and Winston.

Kitano, H. 1975. "Cultural Diversity and the Exceptional Child: Asian Component." In *Promising Practices: Teaching the Disadvantaged Gifted*. National/State Leadership

Training Institute on the Gifted and the Talented, 20–21. Ventura, Calif.: Office of the Ventura County Superintendent of Schools.

Kitano, M. K. 1982. "Young Gifted Children: Strategies for Preschool Gifted." *Young Children* 37(4):14–24.

———. 1983. "Early Education for Asian-American Children." In *Understanding the Multicultural Experience in Early Childhood Education.* Edited by O. N. Saracho and B. Spodek, 45–66. Washington, D.C.: National Association for the Education of Young Children.

Kitano, M. K., and Kirby, D. F. In press. "The Unit Approach to Curriculum Planning for the Gifted." *G/C/T.*

Kitano, M. K., and Tafoya, N. 1982. "Preschool Leadership: A Review and Critique." *Journal for the Education of the Gifted* 5:78–89.

Knutsen, L. 1979. "Teaching Fifty Gifted Science Units in Two Easy Steps." *Science and Children* 16(6):51–52.

Kogan, N., and Pankove, E. 1974. "Long-Term Predictive Validity of Divergent Thinking Tests: Some Negative Evidence." *Journal of Educational Psychology* 66(6):802–10.

Kohlberg, L. 1964. "Development of Moral Character and Moral Ideology." In *Review of Child Development Research*, vol. 1. Edited by M. L. Hoffman and L. W. Hoffman, 383–431. New York: Russell Sage Foundation.

———. 1967. "Moral and Religious Education and the Public Schools: A Developmental View." In *The Role of Religion in Public Education.* Edited by T. R. Sizer, 164–83. Boston: Houghton Mifflin.

———. 1968. "The Child as a Moral Philosopher." *Psychology Today* 2(4):25–30.

———. 1969. "Stage and Sequence: The Cognitive-Developmental Approach to Socialization." In *Handbook of Socialization Theory and Research.* Edited by D. A. Goslin, 347–480. Chicago: Rand McNally.

———. 1976. "Moral Stages and Moralization: The Cognitive-Developmental Approach."

In *Moral Development and Behavior.* Edited by T. Lickona, 31–53. New York: Holt, Rinehart, and Winston.

Kopelman, M., Galasso, V. G., and Strom, P. 1977. "A Model Program for the Development of Creativity in Science." *Gifted Child Quarterly* 21:80–84.

Krathwohl, D., Bloom, B., and Masia, B. 1964. *Taxonomy of Educational Objectives: The Classification of Educational Goals. Handbook II: Affective Domain.* New York: David McKay.

Krech, D. 1971. "The Chemistry of Learning." In *Modern Philosophies of Education.* Edited by J. P. Strain, 258–64. New York: Random House.

Kreitner, K., and Engin, A. W. 1981. "Identifying Musical Talent." In *Psychology and Education of the Gifted.* Edited by W. B. Barbe and J. S. Renzulli, 192–204. New York: Irvington.

Kreuger, M. L., and Newman, E., comps. 1974. *Perspectives on Gifted and Talented Education.: Arts and Humanities.* ERIC Document Reproduction Service Number ED 101 491. Reston, Va.: Council for Exceptional Children.

Kris, E. 1952. *Psychoanalytic Explorations in Art.* New York: International Universities Press.

Kubie, L. S. 1958. *Neurotic Distortion of the Creative Process.* Lawrence, Kans.: University of Kansas Press.

Kulm, G. 1984. "Geometry Enrichment for Mathematically Gifted Students." *Roeper Review* 6:150–54.

Labuda, M., ed. 1974. *Creative Reading for Gifted Learners: A Design for Excellence.* Newark, Del.: International Reading Association.

Lajoie, S. P., and Shore, B. M. 1981. "Three Myths? The Overrepresentation of the Gifted among Dropouts, Delinquents, and Suicides." *Gifted Child Quarterly* 25:138–43.

Laosa, L. M. 1978. "Maternal Teaching Strategies in Chicano Families of Varied Educational and Socioeconomic Levels." *Child Development.* 49:1129–35.

Larsh, E. 1979a. "Historical Perspective." In *Someone's Priority: The Issues and Recommendations of the State of the Arts and Gifted in America.* Edited by E. Larsh, 4–11. Denver, Colo.: Colorado Department of Education.

———. 1979b. "Issues and Recommendations." In *Someone's Priority: Issues and Recommendations of the State of the Arts and Gifted in America.* Edited by E. Larsh, 12–29. Denver, Colo.: Colorado Department of Education.

Lehman, E. B., and Erdwins, C. J. 1981. "The Social and Emotional Adjustment of Young, Intellectually Gifted Children." *Gifted Child Quarterly* 25:134–37.

Lerner, J., Mardell-Czudnowski, C., and Goldenberg, D. 1981. *Special Education for the Early Childhood Years.* Englewood Cliffs, N.J.: Prentice-Hall.

LeRose, B. 1978. "A Quota System for Gifted Minority Children: A Viable Solution." *Gifted Child Quarterly* 22:394–403

Lewis, G. 1984. "Alternatives to Acceleration for the Highly Gifted Child." *Roeper Review* 6:133–36.

Lombroso, C. 1895. *The Man of Genius.* London: Charles Scribner's Sons.

Luca, M. C., and Allen, B. 1973. *Teaching Gifted Children Art in Grades Four through Six.* ERIC Document Reproduction Service Number ED 088 254. Sacramento, Calif.: California State Department of Education.

———. 1974. *Teaching Gifted Children Art in Grades One through Three.* ERIC Document Reproduction Service Number ED 100 102. Sacramento, Calif.: California State Department of Education.

Ludwig, G., and Cullinan, D. 1984. "Behavior Problems of Gifted and Nongifted Elementary Girls and Boys." *Gifted Child Quarterly* 28:37–39.

Lupkowski, A. E. 1984. "Gifted Students in Small Rural Schools Do Not *Have* to Move to the City." *Roeper Review* 7:13–16.

Maccoby, E. E., and Jacklin, C. N. 1974. *The Psychology of Sex Differences.* Stanford, Calif.: Stanford University Press.

Maccoby, M. 1981. *The Leader.* New York: Simon & Schuster.

MacMillan, D. L. 1982. *Mental Retardation in School and Society,* 2d ed. Boston: Little, Brown.

Maddux, C. D., Scheiber, L. M., and Bass, J. E. 1982. "Self-Concept and Social Distance in Gifted Children." *Gifted Child Quarterly* 26:77–81.

Magoon, R. A. 1980. "Developing Leadership Skills in the Gifted, Creative, and Talented." *G/C/T* (12):40–43.

Maker, C. J. 1977. *Providing Programs for the Gifted Handicapped.* Reston, Va.: Council for Exceptional Children.

———. 1982. *Curriculum Development for the Gifted.* Rockville, Md.: Aspen Systems Corp.

———. 1983. "Quality Education for Gifted Minority Students." *Journal for the Education of the Gifted* 6:140–53.

Malone, C. E. 1975. "Education for Parents of the Gifted." *Gifted Child Quarterly* 19:223–25.

———. 1976. "Parents as Facilitators of Talent in the Arts." *Gifted Child Quarterly* 20:447–50.

Manaster, G. J., and Powell, P. M. 1983. "A Framework for Understanding Gifted Adolescents' Psychological Maladjustment." *Roeper Review* 6:70–73.

Mansfield, R. S., Busse, T. V., Krepelka, E. J. 1978. "The Effectiveness of Creativity Training." *Review of Educational Research* 48(4):517–36.

Marion, R. L. 1980. "Communicating with Parents of Culturally Diverse Exceptional Children." *Exceptional Children* 46: 616–23.

Marland, S. P. 1972. *Education of the Gifted and Talented. Report to Congress.* Washington, D.C.: U.S. Office of Education.

Martin, B. 1975. "Parent–Child Relations." In *Review of Child Development Research,* vol. 4. Edited by F. D. Horowitz, 463–540. Chicago: University of Chicago Press.

Martin, C. E., and Cramond, B. 1983. "Creative Reading: Is It Being Taught to the Gifted in Elementary Schools?" *Journal for the Education of the Gifted* 6:70–79.

Martinson, R. A. 1975. *The Identification of the Gifted and Talented*. Reston, Va: Council for Exceptional Children.

Maslow, A. H. 1968. *Toward a Psychology of Being*. New York: Van Nostrand Reinhold.

Master, D. L. 1983. "Writing and the Gifted Child." *Gifted Child Quarterly* 27:162–68.

Mathews, F. N. 1981. "Effective Communication with Parents of the Gifted and Talented: Some Suggestions for Improvement." *Journal for the Education of the Gifted* 4:207–10.

Maxwell, S. 1980. "Museums Are Learning Laboratories for Gifted Students." *Teaching Exceptional Children* 12(4):154–59.

Mayer, R. E., 1977. *Thinking and Problem Solving: An Introduction to Human Cognition and Learning*. Glenview, Ill.: Scott, Foresman.

McCall, M. W., Jr., and Lombardo, M. M., eds. 1978. *Leadership: Where Else Can We Go?* Durham, N.C.: Duke University Press.

McCallum, R. S., and Glynn, S. M. 1979. "Hemispheric Specialization and Creative Behavior." *Journal of Creative Behavior* 13(4):263–73.

McCallum, R. S., Karnes, F. A., and Edwards, R. P. 1984. "The Test of Choice for Assessment of Gifted Children: A Comparison of the K–ABC, WISC–R, and Stanford–Binet." *Journal of Psychoeducational Assessment* 2:57–63.

McCormick, S., and Swassing, R. H. 1982. "Reading Instruction for the Gifted: A Survey of Programs." *Journal for the Education of the Gifted* 5:34–43.

McKay, M. D. 1983. "Is Music a Trap for the Academically Gifted?" *Music Educators Journal* 69(8):32–33.

Mednick, S. A. 1962. "The Associative Bases of the Creative Process." *Psychological Review* 69:220–32.

Meeker, M. 1977. *SOI Learning Abilities Test*. El Segundo, Calif.: SOI Institute.

———. 1978. "Nondiscriminatory Testing Procedures to Assess Giftedness in Black, Chicano, Navajo, and Anglo Children." In *Educational Planning for the Gifted*. Edited by A. Y. Baldwin, G. H. Gear, and L. J. Lucito, 17–26. Reston, Va.: Council for Exceptional Children.

———. 1981. "The Status of Nondiscriminatory Testing Procedures to Assess Giftedness in Blacks, Chicanos, Navajos, and Anglos: An Answer to Jensen and Shockley on Truth in Testing." In *Balancing the Scale for the Disadvantaged Gifted*. National/State Leadership Training Institute on the Gifted and the Talented, 91–99. Ventura, Calif.: Office of the Ventura County Superintendent of Schools.

———. 1984. *The Structure of Intellect: Its Interpretation and Uses*. Los Angeles, Western Psychological Services.

Meichenbaum, D. 1975. "Enhancing Creativity by Modifying What Subjects Say to Themselves." *American Educational Research Journal* 12:129–45.

Meier, N. C. 1942, 1963. *Meier Art Tests*. Iowa City: University of Iowa, Bureau of Educational Research and Service.

Mercer, J. R. 1981. "The System of Multicultural Pluralistic Assessment: SOMPA." In *Balancing the Scale for the Disadvantaged Gifted*. National/State Leadership Training Institute on the Gifted and the Talented, 29–57. Ventura, Calif.: Office of the Ventura County Superintendent of Schools.

Mercer, J. R., and Lewis, J. F. 1978. "Using the System of Multicultural Pluralistic Assessment (SOMPA) to Identify the Gifted Minority Child." In *Educational Planning for the Gifted*. Edited by A. Y. Baldwin, G. H. Gear, and L. J. Lucito, 7–14. Reston, Va.: Council for Exceptional Children.

Meyer, A. E. 1965. *An Educational History of the Western World*. New York: McGraw-Hill.

Meyers, E. 1984. "A Study of Concerns of Classroom Teachers Regarding a Resource Room Program for the Gifted. *Roeper Review* 7:32–36.

Michael, W. B. 1977. "Cognitive and Affective

Components of Creativity in Mathematics and the Physical Sciences." In *The Gifted and the Creative: A Fifty-Year Perspective*. Edited by J. C. Stanley, W. C. George, and C. H. Solano, 141–72. Baltimore: Johns Hopkins University Press.

Michaelis, C. T. 1980. *Home and School Partnerships in Exceptional Education*. Rockville, Md.: Aspen Systems Corp.

Mierke, K. 1962. "Educability and Endowment." In *The Gifted Child: The Yearbook of Education*. Edited by G. Z. F. Bereday and J. A. Lauwerys, 106–14. New York: Harcourt, Brace, and World.

Miller, M. S. 1982. "Using the Newspaper with the Gifted." *G/C/T* (23):47–49.

Mitchell, B. 1975. "Creativity and the Poverty Child." In *Promising Practices: Teaching the Disadvantaged Gifted*. National/State Leadership Training Institute on the Gifted and the Talented, 46–50. Ventura, Calif.: Office of the Ventura County Superintendent of Schools.

———. 1984. "An Update on Gifted/Talented Education in the U.S." *Roeper Review* 6:161–63.

Moller, H. J. 1983. "Retrieval from Long-Term Memory of Semantic Information by High and Average Intelligence Children." Unpublished doctoral dissertation, New Mexico State University, Las Cruces, New Mexico.

Morgan, H. J., Tennant, C. G. and Gold, M. J. 1980. *Elementary and Secondary Level Programs for the Gifted and Talented*. New York: Teachers College, Columbia University.

Morishima, A. 1974. " 'Another Van Gogh of Japan': The Superior Artwork of a Retarded Boy." *Exceptional Children* 41:92–96.

Moses, N. 1981. "Using Piaget Principles to Guide Instruction of the Learning Disabled." *Topics in Learning and Learning Disabilities* 1(1): 11–19.

Musser, P. H., Conger, J. J. and Kagan, J. 1969. *Child Development and Personality*, 3d ed. New York: Harper & Row.

Myers, J. T. 1982. "Hemisphericity Research:

An Overview with Some Implications for Problem Solving." *Journal of Creative Behavior* 16(3):197–211.

Nathan, C. N. 1979. "Parental Involvement." In *The Gifted and the Talented: Their Education and Development*. Edited by A. H. Passow, 255–71. Chicago: University of Chicago Press.

National Commission on Excellence in Education. 1983. *A Nation at Risk*. Washington, D.C.: U.S. Department of Education.

National Society for the Study of Education. 1958. *Education of the Gifted*. Fifty-seventh yearbook of the National Society for the Study of Education. Edited by N. B. Henry. Chicago: University of Chicago Press.

———. 1979. *The Gifted and Talented: Their Education and Development*. Seventy-eighth yearbook of the National Society for the Study of Education. Edited by A. H. Passow. Chicago: University of Chicago Press.

National/State Leadership Training Institute on the Gifted and the Talented. 1981. *Balancing the Scale for the Disadvantaged Gifted*. Ventura, Calif.: Office of the Ventura County Superintendent of Schools.

Navarre, J. 1983. "How the Teacher of the Gifted Can Use the SOI." *G/C/T* (26):16–17.

Newcomer, P. L. and Goldberg, M. A. 1982. "The Relationship between Written Expression and Reading in Gifted Adolescents." *Journal for the Education of the Gifted* 5:90–97.

Newell, A. and Simon, H. A. 1972. *Human Problem Solving*. Englewood Cliffs, N.J.: Prentice-Hall.

Newland, T. E. 1976. *The Gifted in Socioeducational Perspective*. Englewood Cliffs, N.J.: Prentice-Hall.

Nichols, R. C. 1964. "Parental Attitudes of Mothers of Intelligent Adolescents and Creativity of Their Children." *Child Development* 35:1041–49.

Oakland, T. 1980. "An Evaluation of ABIC, Pluralistic Norms, and Estimated Learning Potential." *Journal of School Psychology* 18:3–11.

Oden, M. H. 1968. "The Fulfillment of Promise: 40-Year Follow-up of the Terman Gifted Group." *Genetic Psychology Monographs* 77:3–93.

Ohlsen, M. M., and Gazda, G. M. 1965. "Counseling Underachieving Bright Pupils." *Education* 86(2):78–81.

Olson, L. 1985. "Programs for Gifted Students Fragmented, Inadequate, Study Says." *Education Week* (January 16).

Orenstein, A. J. 1984. "What Organizational Characteristics Are Important in Planning, Implementing, and Maintaining Programs for the Gifted?" *Gifted Child Quarterly* 28:99–105.

Osler, S. F., and Fivel, M. W. 1961. "Concept Attainment: I. The Role of Age and Intelligence in Concept Attainment by Induction." *Journal of Experimental Psychology* 62:1–8.

O'Tuel, F. S., Ward, M., and Rawl, R. K. 1983. "The SOI as an Identification Tool for the Gifted: Windfall or Washout?" *Gifted Child Quarterly* 27:126–34.

Parker, J. P. 1983. "The Leadership Training Model." *G/C/T* (29):8–13.

Parker, J. P., and Kreamer, J. T. 1983. "A Picture Is Worth a Thousand Words." *G/C/T* (26):38–39.

Parnes, S. J. 1977. "Guiding Creative Action." *Gifted Child Quarterly* 21:460–76.

———. 1981. *The Magic of Your Mind.* Buffalo, N.Y.: Creative Education Foundation.

Parnes, S. J., and Brunelle, E. A. 1967. "The Literature of Creativity (Part 1)." *Journal of Creative Behavior* 1(1):52–109.

Parnes, S. J., Noller, R. B., and Biondi, A. M. 1977. *Guide to Creative Action.* New York: Scribners.

Passow, A. H. 1977. "Fostering Creativity in the Gifted Child." *Exceptional Children* 43:358–64.

———. 1978. "Styles of Leadership Training." *G/C/T* (5):9–12.

Paulus, P. 1984. "Acceleration: More than Grade Skipping." *Roeper Review* 7:98–100.

Pearce, N. 1983. "A Comparison of the WISC-

R, Raven's Standard Progressive Matrices, and Meeker's SOI Screening Form for Gifted." *Gifted Child Quarterly* 27:13–19.

Pegnato, C. W., and Birch, J. W. 1959. "Locating Gifted Children in Junior High Schools: A Comparison of Methods." *Exceptional Children* 25:300–304.

Perrone, P. A. and Aleman, N. 1983. "Educating the Talented Child in a Pluralistic Society." In *The Bilingual Exceptional Child.* Edited by D. R. Omark and J. G. Erickson. San Diego: College Hill Press.

Peterson, D. 1977. "The Heterogeneously Gifted Family." *Gifted Child Quarterly* 21:396–408.

Petzold, R. G. 1979. "Identification of Musically Talented Students." In *Someone's Priority.* Edited by E. Larsh, 58–65. Denver, Colo.: Colorado Department of Education.

Pfeffer, J. 1978. "The Ambiguity of Leadership." In *Leadership: Where Else Can We Go?* Edited by M. W. McCall, Jr. and M. M. Lombardo, 13–34. Durham, N.C.: Duke University Press.

Piaget, J. 1950. *The Psychology of Intelligence.* Translated by M. Percy and D. E. Berlyne. London: Routledge and Kegan Paul.

———. 1958. *The Growth of Logical Thinking from Childhood to Adolescence.* Translated by A. Parsons and S. Seagrin. New York: Basic Books.

Pines, M. 1979. "Superkids." *Psychology Today* 12(8):53–63.

Pirozzo, R. 1982. "Gifted Underachievers." *Roeper Review* 4:18–21.

Pizzini, E. L. 1982. "Appropriate Experiences for the Gifted Science Student." *Roeper Review* 4:7–8.

Pledgie, T. K. 1982. "Giftedness among Handicapped Children: Identification and Programming Development." *Journal of Special Education* 16(2):221–27.

Plomin, R., and DeFries, J. C. 1980. "Genetics and Intelligence: Recent Data." *Intelligence* 4:15–24.

Plowman, P. Undated. "What Can Be Done for Rural Gifted and Talented Children and Youth?" In *Ideas for Urban/Rural Gifted/*

Talented. National/State Leadership Training Institute on the Gifted and the Talented, 71–87. Ventura, Calif.: Office of the Ventura County Superintendent of Schools.

Ponder, G., and Hirsch, S. A. 1981. "Social Studies Education for the Gifted: Lessons from other Pasts?" *Roeper Review* 4:17–19.

Power, C., and Reimer, J. 1978. "Moral Atmosphere: An Educational Bridge between Moral Judgment and Action." *New Directions for Child Development* 2:105–16.

Price-Williams, D. R., and Ramirez, M., III. 1977. "Divergent Thinking, Cultural, Differences, and Bilingualism." *Journal of Social Psychology* 103:3–11.

Purkey, W. W. 1969. "Project Self-Discovery: Its Effect on Bright but Underachieving High School Students." *Gifted Child Quarterly* 13:242–46.

Pyryt, M. C. 1979. "Helping Scientifically Gifted Students." *Science and Children* 16(6): 16–17.

Radin, N. 1982. "The Unique Contribution of Parents to Child Rearing." In *The Young Child: Reviews of Research*, vol. 3. Edited by S. G. Moore and C. R. Cooper, 57–76. Washington, D.C.: National Association for the Education of Young Children.

Raths, J. 1961. "Underachievement and a Search for Values." *Journal of Educational Sociology* 34:422–24.

Raths, L., Harmin, M., and Simon, S. 1966. *Values and Teaching.* Columbus, Ohio: Charles E. Merrill.

Reis, S. M., and Cellerino, M. 1983. "Guiding Gifted Students through Independent Study." *Teaching Exceptional Children* 15(3): 136–39.

Rellas, A. J. 1969. "The Use of the Wechsler Preschool and Primary Scale (WPPSI) in the Early Identification of Gifted Students." *California Journal of Educational Research* 20(3):117–19.

Renzulli, J. S. 1975. *A Guidebook for Evaluating Programs for the Gifted and Talented.* Ven-

tura, Calif.: Office of the Ventura County Superintendent of Schools.

———. 1977. *The Enrichment Triad Model: A Guide for Developing Defensible Programs for the Gifted and Talented.* Wethersfield, Conn.: Creative Learning Press.

———. 1978. "What Makes Giftedness? Reexamining a Definition." *Phi Delta Kappan* 60(3).

———. 1981. "Identifying Key Features in Programs for the Gifted." In *Psychology and Education of the Gifted*, 3d ed. Edited by W. B. Barbe and J. S. Renzulli, 214–19. New York: Irvington Publishers.

Renzulli, J. S., and Callahan, C. M. 1976. *New Directions in Creativity.* New York: Harper & Row.

Renzulli, J. S., and Hartman, R. K. 1971. "Scale for Rating Behavioral Characteristics of Superior Students." *Exceptional Children* 38:243–48.

Renzulli, J. S., Hartman, R. K., and Callahan, C. M. 1971. "Teacher Identification of Superior Students." *Exceptional Children* 38:211–14.

Renzulli, J. S., and Smith, L. H. 1977. "Two Approaches to Identification of Gifted Students." *Exceptional Children* 43:512–18.

———. 1979a. *A Guidebook for Developing Individualized Educational Programs (IEP) for Gifted and Talented Students.* Mansfield Center, Conn.: Creative Learning Press.

———. 1979b. "Issues and Procedures in Evaluating Programs." In *The Gifted and the Talented: Their Education and Development.* Edited by A. H. Passow, 289–307. Chicago: University of Chicago Press.

———. 1980. "Revolving Door: A Truer Turn for the Gifted." *Learning* (October):91–93.

Renzulli, J. S., Smith, L. H., White, A. J., Callahan, C. M., and Hartman, R. K. 1976. *Scales for Rating the Behavioral Characteristics of Superior Students.* Mansfield Center, Conn.: Creative Learning Press.

Reynolds, B. 1981. "College-Level Writing Skills for the Early-Adolescent Verbally Gifted: Philosophy and Practice." *G/C/T* (15):48–51.

Reynolds, B., Kopelka, K., and Durden, W. G. 1984. *Writing Instruction for Verbally Talented Youth: The Johns Hopkins Model.* Rockville, Md.: Aspen Systems Corp.

Reynolds, C. R., and Torrance, E. P. 1978. "Perceived Changes in Styles of Learning and Thinking (Hemisphericity) through Direct and Indirect Training." *Journal of Creative Behavior* 12(4):247–52.

Rhodes, W. C. 1967. "The Disturbing Child: A Problem of Ecological Management." *Exceptional Children* 33:449–55.

Rieger, M. P. 1983. "Life Patterns and Coping Strategies in High and Low Creative Women." *Journal for the Education of the Gifted.* 6:98–110.

Rindfleisch, N. 1981. "In Support of Writing." In *Respecting the Pupil: Essays on Teaching Able Students.* Edited by D. B. Cole and R. H. Cornell. Exeter, N.H.: Phillips Exeter Press.

Riner, P. S. 1983. "Establishing Scientific Methodology with Elementary Gifted Children through Field Biology." *G/C/T* (28):46–49.

Roberson, T. G. 1984. "Determining Curriculum Content for the Gifted." *Roeper Review* 6:137–39.

Robinson, H., and Roedell, W. C. 1980. "Child Development Preschool." In *Educating the Preschool/Primary Gifted and Talented.* National/State Leadership Training Institute on the Gifted and the Talented, 237–41. Ventura, Calif.: Office of the Ventura County Superintendent of Schools.

Robinson, H. B., Roedell, W. C., and Jackson, N. E. 1979. "Early Identification and Intervention." In *The Gifted and the Talented: Their Education and Development.* Edited by A. H. Passow, 138–54. Chicago: University of Chicago Press.

Robinson, N. M., and Robinson, H. B. 1976. *The Mentally Retarded Child: A Psychological Approach,* 2d ed. New York: McGraw-Hill.

Roe, A. 1951. "A Psychological Study of Physical Scientists." *Genetic Psychology Monographs* 43(2):121–35.

Roedell, W. C. 1984. *Vulnerabilities of Highly Gifted Children." Roeper Review* 6:127–30.

Roedell, W. C., Jackson, N. E., and Robinson, H. B. 1980. *Gifted Young Children.* New York: Teachers College Press.

Rogers, C. R. 1959. "Toward a Theory of Creativity." In *Creativity and Its Cultivation,* Edited by H. H. Anderson. New York: Harper & Brothers.

Romey, W. D. 1980. *Teaching the Gifted and Talented in the Science Classroom.* Washington, D.C.: National Education Association.

Rose, L. H., and Lin, H. 1984. "A Meta-analysis of Long-Term Creativity Training Programs." *Journal of Creative Behavior* 18(1):11–22.

Rosen, J. C. 1955. "The Barron-Welsh Art Scale as a Predictor of Originality and Level of Ability among Artists." *Journal of Applied Psychology* 39(5):366–67.

Rosen, S. 1969. *Wizard of the Dome.* Boston: Little, Brown.

Rosenberg, H. 1974. "Theatre in Education: The Belgrade Team." In *Perspectives on Gifted and Talented Education: Arts and Humanities.* Compiled by M. L. Kreuger and E. Newman, 37–38. ERIC Document Reproduction Service Number ED 101 491. Reston, Va.: Council for Exceptional Children.

Ross, A., and Parker, M. 1980. "Academic and Social Self-Concepts of the Academically Gifted." *Exceptional Children* 47:6–10.

Ross, J. D., and Ross, C. M. 1976. *Ross Test of Higher Cognitive Process.* San Rafael, Calif.: Academic Therapy Publications.

Rothenberg, A., and Hausman, C. R., eds. 1976. *The Creativity Question.* Durham, N.C.: Duke University Press.

Royer, R. 1982. "Creative Writing Assignments for the Gifted." *G/C/T* (21):29–30.

Rubenzer, R. L., and Twaite, J. A. 1979. "Attitudes of 1,200 Educators toward the Education of the Gifted and Talented: Implications for Teacher Preparation." *Journal for the Education of the Gifted* 2:202–13.

Rubin, K. H., and Everett, B. 1982. "Social Perspective-Taking in Young Children." In *The Young Child: Reviews of Research*, vol. 3. edited by S. G. Moore and C. R. Cooper, 97–113. Washington, D. C.: National Association for the Education of Young Children.

Ryan, J. S. 1983. "Identifying Intellectually Superior Black Children." *Journal of Educational Research* 76(3):153–56.

Ryder, V. P. 1972. "A Docent Program in Science for Gifted Elementary Pupils." *Exceptional Children* 38:629–31.

Safford, P. L. 1978. *Teaching Young Children with Special Needs*. Saint Louis: C. V. Mosby.

Sakiey, E. 1980. "Reading for the Gifted: Instructional Strategies Based on Research." Paper presented at the Annual Meeting of the Eastern Regional Conference of the International Reading Association, Niagara Falls, New York. ERIC Document Reproduction Service Number ED 186 881.

Salvia, J., and Ysseldyke, J. E. 1981. *Assessment in Special and Remedial Education*, 2d ed. Boston: Houghton Mifflin.

Sato, I. S. 1974. "The Culturally Different Gifted Child—The Dawning of His Day?" *Exceptional Children* 40:572–76.

Sattler, J. M. 1973. "Intelligence Testing of Ethnic Minority Group and Culturally Disadvantaged Children." In *The First Review of Special Education*, vol. 2. Edited by L. Mann and D. Sabatino, 161–201. Philadelphia: JSE Press.

Scarr-Salapatek, S. 1975. "Genetics and the Development of Intelligence. "In *Review of Child Development Research*, vol. 4. Edited by F. D. Horowitz, 1–57. Chicago: University of Chicago Press.

Schaefer, C. E., and Anastasi, A. 1968. "A Biographical Inventory for Identifying Creativity in Adolescent Boys." *Journal of Applied Psychology* 52(1): 42–48.

Schaefer, E. S. 1972. "Parents as Educators: Evidence from Cross-Sectional, Longitudinal, and Intervention Research. In *The Young Child: Reviews of Research*, vol. 2. Edited by W. W. Hartup, 184–201. Washington, D. C.: National Association for the Education of Young Children.

Schiff, M. M., Kaufman, A. S., and Kaufman, N. L. 1981. "Scatter Analyses of WISC–R Profiles for Learning-Disabled Children with Superior Intelligence." *Journal of Learning Disabilities* 14(7):400–404.

Schlichter, C. L. 1981. "The Multiple Talent Approach in Mainstream and Gifted Programs." *Exceptional Children* 48:144–50.

Schultz, H. A. 1953. "Review of Meier Art Test 1—Art Judgment." In *The Fourth Mental Measurements Yearbook*. Edited by O. K. Buros. Highland Park, N.J.: Gryphon Press.

Schwartz, L. L. 1980. "Advocacy for the Neglected Gifted: Females." *Gifted Child Quarterly* 24:113–17.

Scobee, J., and Nash, W. R. 1983. "A Survey of Highly Successful Space Scientists Concerning Education for Gifted and Talented Students." *Gifted Child Quarterly* 27:147–51.

Scruggs, T. E., and Mastropieri, M. A. 1984. "How Gifted Students Learn: Implications from Research." *Roeper Review* 6:183–85.

Seagoe, M. 1975. "Some Learning Characteristics of Gifted Children." In *The Identification of The Gifted and Talented*. Edited by R. A. Martinson, 20–21. Reston, Va.: Council for Exceptional Children.

Sears, P. S., and Barbee, A. H. 1977. "Career and Life Satisfactions among Terman's Gifted Women." In *The Gifted and the Creative: A Fifty-Year Perspective*. Edited by J. C. Stanley, W. C. George, and C. H. Solano, 28–65. Baltimore: Johns Hopkins University Press.

Sears, R. R. 1977. "Sources of Life Satisfaction of the Terman Gifted Men." *American Psychologist* 32(2):119–28.

Seeley, K. R. 1979. "Competencies for Teachers of Gifted and Talented Children." *Journal for the Education of the Gifted* 3:7–9.

———. 1984. "Perspectives on Adolescent

Giftedness and Delinquency." *Journal for the Education of the Gifted* 8:59–72.

Shachter, J. 1979. "Profiles in Literature." Video cassettes. *Journal for the Education of the Gifted* 3:108–10.

Shakeshaft, C., and Palmieri, P. 1978. "A Divine Discontent: Perspective on Gifted Women." *Gifted Child Quarterly* 22:468–77.

Shantz, C. U. 1975. "The Development of Social Cognition." In *Review of Child Development Research*, vol. 5. Edited by E. M. Hetherington, 257–323. Chicago: University of Chicago Press.

Shaw, M. C., and McCuen, J. T. 1960. "The Onset of Academic Underachievement in Bright Children." *Journal of Educational Psychology* 51(3):103–8.

Shermis, S. S., and Clinkenbeard, P. R. 1981. "History Texts for the Gifted: A Look at the Past Century." *Roeper Review* 4:19–21.

Shulte, A. P. 1984. "Statistics and Probability for Gifted Middle School Students." *Roeper Review* 6:152–54.

Silverman, L. 1980. "Secondary Programs for Gifted Students." *Journal for the Education of the Gifted* 4:30–42.

Sirr, P. M. 1984. "A Proposed System for Differentiating Elementary Mathematics for Exceptionally Able Students." *Gifted Child Quarterly* 28:40–44.

Sisk, D. 1977. "The Use of Creative Activities in Leadership Training." *Gifted Child Quarterly* 21:477–86.

———. June 1978. "Initiative." Presentation at the National Institute on Leadership Training and the Gifted, Chicago, Illinois.

———. 1979. "Unusual Gifts and Talents." In *Children with Exceptional Needs*. Edited by M. S. Lilly, 362–97. New York: Holt, Rinehart, and Winston.

———. 1982. "Caring and Sharing: Moral Development of Gifted Students." *Elementary School Journal* 82(3):221–29.

Skeels, H. M. 1966. "Adult Status of Children with Contrasting Early Life Experiences:

A Follow-up Study." *Monographs of the Society for Research in Child Development* 31(3), series 105.

Skeels, H. M., and Dye, H. B. 1939. "A Study of the Effects of Differential Stimulation on Mentally Retarded Children." *Proceedings and Addresses of the American Association on Mental Deficiency* 44:114–36.

Skinner, B. F. 1972. "A Lecture on 'Having' a Poem." In B. F. Skinner, *Cumulative Record: A Selection of Papers*, 3d ed. Englewood Cliffs, N.J.: Prentice-Hall.

Smith, J. C. 1983. "Ethical Concerns in the Moral Education of the Gifted." *Roeper Review* 6:100.

Solman, L. C. 1976. *Male and Female Graduate Students: The Question of Equal Opportunity*. New York: Praeger.

Spearman, C. 1927. *The Abilities of Man*. New York: Macmillan.

Sperry, R. W. 1973. "Lateral Specialization of Cerebral Function." In *The Psychophysiology of Thinking*. Edited by F. J. McGuigan and R. A. Schoonover. New York: Academic Press.

Spicker, H. H., and Southern, W. T. 1982. "Indiana University's College for Gifted and Talented Youth." *Journal for the Education of the Gifted* 5:155–59.

Stacey, M., and Mitchell, B. 1979. "Preparing Gifted Leaders for a Futuristic Society." *G/C/T* (10):7–9.

Stank, L. A. 1983. "Reading Programs for the Gifted: A Necessity." *G/C/T* (28):39–41.

Stanley, J. C. 1977. "Rationale of the Study of Mathematically Precocious Youth (SMPY) during Its First Five Years of Promoting Educational Acceleration." In *The Gifted and the Creative: A Fifty-Year Perspective*. Edited by J. C. Stanley, W. C. George, and C. H. Solano, 75–112. Baltimore: Johns Hopkins University Press.

———. 1985. "A Baker's Dozen of Years Applying All Four Aspects of the Study of Mathematically Precocious Youth (SMPY)." *Roeper Review* 7:172–75.

Stanley, J. C., and Benbow, C. P. 1983. "SMPY's

First Decade: Ten Years of Posing Problems and Solving Them." *Journal of Special Education* 17(1):11–25.

Stark, J. B. 1978. "Promoting Leadership." *Early Years* 8(6):12–13, 36–37.

Sternberg, R. J. 1977. *Intelligence, Information Processing, and Analogical Reasoning: The Componential Analysis of Human Abilities.* New York: Wiley.

———. 1981. "A Componential Theory of Intellectual Giftedness." *Gifted Child Quarterly* 25:86–93.

———. 1982. "Teaching Scientific Thinking to Gifted Children." *Roeper Review* 4:4–6.

Steward, M., and Steward, D. 1973. "The Observation of Anglo-, Mexican-, and Chinese-American Mothers Teaching Their Young Sons." *Child Development* 44:329–37.

Stoddard, E. P., and Renzulli, J. S. 1983. "Improving the Writing Skills of Talent Pool Students." *Gifted Child Quarterly* 27:21–27.

Stoddard, H. 1970. *Famous American Women.* New York: Thomas Y. Crowell.

Stogdill, R. M. 1974. *Handbook of Leadership: A Survey of Theory and Research.* New York: The Free Press.

Stone, B. G. 1980. "Relationship between Creativity and Classroom Behavior." *Psychology in the Schools* 17:106–8.

Stone, S. M. 1976. "NCSA: North Carolina's Venture into Professional Arts Training." *Gifted Child Quarterly* 20:422–26.

Strickland, B. 1982. "Parental Participation, School Accountability, and Due Process." *Exceptional Education Quarterly* 3(2):41–49.

Strobert, B., and Alvarez, F. R. 1982. "The Convocation Model Project: A Creative Approach to the Study of Science for Gifted Disadvantaged Students." *Elementary School Journal* 82(3):230–35.

Suchman, J. R. 1966. "A Model for the Analysis of Inquiry." In *Analysis of Concept Learning.* Edited by H. J. Klausmeier and C. W. Harris, 177–87. New York: Academic Press.

———. 1977. "Heuristic Learning and Science Education." *Journal of Research in Science Teaching* 14(3):263–72.

Superka, D. 1974. "Approaches to Values Education." *Social Science Education Consortium Newsletter* 20:1–4.

Switzer, C., and Nourse, M. L. 1979. "Reading Instruction for the Gifted Child in First Grade." *Gifted Child Quarterly* 23:323–31.

Szekely, G. 1981. "The Artist and the Child—A Model Program for the Artistically Gifted." *Gifted Child Quarterly*, 25:67–72.

———. 1982. "Art Partnership Network: A Supportive Program for Artistically Gifted Children." *Elementary School Journal* 83(1):59.

Taba, H. 1962. *Curriculum Development Theory and Practice.* New York: Harcourt, Brace, and World.

———. February, 1966. *Teaching Strategies and Cognitive Functioning in Elementary School Children.* Cooperative Research Project No. 2404. Washington, D.C.: U.S. Office of Education.

Taba, H., Durkin, M. C., Fraenkel, J. R., and McNaughton, A. H. 1971. *A Teacher's Handbook to Elementary Social Studies: An Inductive Approach*, 2d ed. Menlo Park, Calif.: Addison-Wesley.

Taft, R., and Gilchrist, M. B. 1970. "Creative Attitudes and Creative Productivity: A Comparison of Two Aspects of Creativity among Students." *Journal of Educational Psychology* 61(2):136–43.

Talents Unlimited. 1974. *Talent Activity Packet*, 2d ed. Mobile, Ala.: Mobile County Public Schools.

Tannenbaum, A. J. 1979. "Pre-Sputnik to Post-Watergate Concern about the Gifted." In *The Gifted and the Talented: Their Education and Development.* Edited by A. H. Passow, 5–27. Chicago: University of Chicago Press.

Tan-Willman, C., and Gutteridge, D. 1981. "Creative Thinking and Moral Reasoning of Academically Gifted Secondary School Adolescents." *Gifted Child Quarterly* 25:149–53.

Tatarunis, A. M. 1981. "Exceptional Programs for Talented Students." *Music Educators Journal* 68(3):55–60.

Taylor, C. W. 1967. "Questioning and Creating: A Model for Curriculum Reform." *Journal of Creative Behavior* 1:22–23.

———. 1968. April. "Multiple Talent Approach." *Instructor* 77(8).

———. 1985. "Cultivating Multiple Creative Talents in Students." *Journal for the Education of the Gifted* 8:187–98.

Taylor, C. W., and Barron, F. 1963. "A Look Ahead: Reflections of the Conference Participants and the Editors." In *Scientific Creativity: Its Recognition and Development.* Edited by C. W. Taylor and F. Barron, 372–89. New York: Wiley.

Taylor, C. W., and Ellison, R. L. 1983. "Searching for Student Talent Resources Relevant to All USDE Types of Giftedness." *Gifted Child Quarterly* 27:99–106.

Taylor, R. Undated. *The Gifted and the Talented.* Englewood, Colo.: Educational Consulting Associates.

Terman, L. M., ed. 1926. *Genetic Studies of Genius.* Vol. 1, *Mental and Physical Traits of a Thousand Gifted Children,* 2d ed. Stanford, Calif.: Stanford University Press.

———. 1954. "The Discovery and Encouragement of Exceptional Talent." *American Psychologist* 9:221–30.

Terman, L. M. and Oden, M. H. 1947. *Genetic Studies of Genius.* Vol. 4, *The Gifted Child Grows Up.* Stanford, Calif.: Stanford University Press.

Tews, T. C. 1981. "A High School for the Creative Arts." In A. Arnold et al., *Secondary Programs for the Gifted/Talented,* 58–67. National/State Leadership Training Institute on the Gifted and the Talented. Ventura, Calif.: Office of the Ventura County Superintendent of Schools.

Thiel, R., and Thiel, A. F. 1977. "A Structural Analysis of Family Interaction Patterns and the Underachieving Gifted Child." *Gifted Child Quarterly* 21:267–75.

Thies, C. D., and Friedrich, D. D. 1977. "Creativity: Ideational Fluency and Originality at the Verbal and Nonverbal Production and Recognition Levels." *Creative Child and Adult Quarterly* 2:213–26.

Thorndike, E. L. 1925. *The Measurement of Intelligence.* New York: Columbia University Teachers College.

Thurstone, L. L. 1938. *Primary Mental Abilities.* Chicago: University of Chicago Press.

Torrance, E. P. 1962. *Guiding Creative Talent.* Englewood Cliffs, N.J.: Prentice-Hall.

———. 1963. *Creativity.* Washington, D.C.: National Educational Association.

———. 1965. *Rewarding Creative Behavior: Experiments in Classroom Creativity.* Englewood Cliffs, N.J.: Prentice-Hall.

———. 1966. *Torrance Tests of Creative Thinking: Technical-Norms Manual.* Princeton, N.J.: Personnel Press.

———. 1967. "The Minnesota Studies of Creative Behavior: National and International Extensions." *Journal of Creative Behavior* 1(2):137–54.

———. 1972a. "Can We Teach Children to Think Creatively?" *Journal of Creative Behavior* 6(2):114–43.

———. 1972b. "Creative Young Women in Today's World."*Exceptional Children* 38:597–603.

———. 1972c. "Predictive Validity of the Torrance Tests of Creative Thinking." *Journal of Creative Behavior* 6(4):236–62.

———. 1977. *Discovery and Nurturance of Giftedness in the Culturally Different.* Reston, Va.: Council for Exceptional Children.

———. 1980. "Lessons about Giftedness and Creativity from a Nation of 115 Million Overachievers." *Gifted Child Quarterly* 24:10–14.

Torrance, E. P., Bruch, C. B., and Morse, J. A. 1973. "Improving Predictions of the Adult Creative Achievement of Gifted Girls by Using Autobiographical Information." *Gifted Child Quarterly* 17:91–95.

Torrance, E. P., and Myers, R. E. 1970. *Creative Learning and Teaching.* New York: Harper & Row.

Torrance, E. P., Reynolds, C. R., Riegel,

T. R., and Ball, O. E. 1977. "Your Style of Learning and Thinking, Forms A and B: Preliminary Norms, Abbreviated Technical Notes, Scoring Keys, and Selected References." *Gifted Child Quarterly* 21:563–73.

Torrance, E. P., Wu, J., Gowan, J. C., and Aliotti, N. C. 1970. "Creative Functioning of Monolingual and Bilingual Children in Singapore." *Journal of Educational Psychology* 61(1):72–75.

Treffinger, D. J., Speedie, S. M., and Brunner, W. D. 1974. "Improving Children's Creative Problem-Solving Ability: The Purdue Creativity Project." *Journal of Creative Behavior* 8:20–30.

Tremaine, C. D. 1979. "Do Gifted Programs Make a Difference?" *Gifted Child Quarterly* 23:500–517.

Trezise, R. L. 1977. "Teaching Reading to the Gifted." *Language Arts* 54(8):920–24.

———. 1978. "What About a Reading Program for the Gifted?" *The Reading Teacher* 31(7):742–47.

Tsuin-chen, Ou. 1961. "Some Facts and Ideas about Talent and Genius in Chinese History." In *Concepts of Excellence in Education: The Yearbook of Education*. Edited by G. Z. F. Bereday and J. A. Lauwerys, 54. New York: Harcourt, Brace, and World.

Tucker, B. F. 1982. "Providing for the Mathematically Gifted Child in the Regular Elementary Classroom." *Roeper Review* 4: 11–12.

Turnbull, H. R., III, Turnbull, A. P., and Wheat, M. J. 1982. "Assumptions about Parental Participation: A Legislative History." *Exceptional Education Quarterly* 3(2):1–8.

Tuttle, F. B., Jr. 1978. *Gifted and Talented Students*. Washington, D.C.: National Education Association.

Tyler, R. W. 1950. *Basic Principles of Curriculum and Instruction*. Chicago: University of Chicago Press.

Urberg, K. A., and Docherty, E. M. 1976. "Development of Role-Taking Skills in Young Children." *Developmental Psychology* 12(3):198–203.

U.S. Department of Commerce, Bureau of the Census. 1983. *1980 Census of the Population*. Vol. 1, *Characteristics of the Population*, Ch. B, "General Population Characteristics," Part I, "United States Summary, PC80-1-B1." Washington, D.C.: U.S. Government Printing Office.

Van Tassel, J. 1980. "TAG Presidential Address." *Journal for the Education of the Gifted* 3(4).

Vantassel-Baska, J., Schuler, A., and Lipschutz, J. 1982. "An Experimental Program for Gifted Four Year Olds." *Journal for the Education of the Gifted* 5:45–55.

Vida, L. 1979. "Children's Literature for the Gifted Elementary School Child." *Roeper Review* 1:22–24.

Volkmor, C. B., Pasanella, A. L., and Raths, L. 1977. *Values in the Classroom*. Columbus, Ohio: Charles E. Merrill.

Wagner, P. A., and Penner, J. 1982. "Games, Logic, and Giftedness." *Roeper Review* 4:14–15.

Wallach, M. A. 1970. "Creativity." In *Carmichael's Manual of Child Psychology*, vol. 1, 3d ed. Edited by P. H. Mussen, 1211–72. New York: Wiley.

Wallas, G. 1926. *The Art of Thought*. New York: Harcourt, Brace & Co.

Warmington, E. H. 1961. "Ability and Genius in Ancient Greece and Rome." In *Concepts of Excellence in Education: The Yearbook of Education*. Edited by G. Z. F. Bereday and J. A. Lauwerys, 70. New York: Harcourt, Brace, and World.

Watson, G., and Glaser, E. M. 1964. *Watson-Glaser Critical Thinking Appraisal*. New York: Harcourt Brace Jovanovich.

Wavrik, J. J. 1980. "Mathematics Education for the Gifted Elementary Student." *Gifted Child Quarterly* 24:169–73.

Weber, J. 1981. "Moral Dilemmas in the Classroom." *Roeper Review* 3:11–15.

Weiss, P., and Gallagher, J. J. 1980. "The Effects of Personal Experience on Attitudes toward Gifted Education." *Journal for the Education of the Gifted* 3:194–206.

Welsh, G. S., and Barron, F. 1963. *Barron-Welsh Art Scale*. Palo Alto, Calif.: Consulting Psychologists Press.

Wenger, W. 1981. "Creative Creativity: Some Strategies for Developing Specific Areas of the Brain for Working Both Sides Together." *Journal of Creative Behavior* 15(2):77–89.

Wenner, G. G. 1985. "Discovery and Recognition of the Artistically Talented." *Journal for the Education of the Gifted* 8:221–38.

Werner, E. E., and Bachtold, L. M. 1969. "Personality Factors of Gifted Boys and Girls in Middle Childhood and Adolescence." *Psychology in the Schools* 6:177–82.

West, W. W. 1980. *Teaching the Gifted and Talented in the English Classroom*. Washington, D.C.: National Education Association.

Wheatley, G. H. 1983. "A Mathematics Curriculum for the Gifted and Talented." *Gifted Child Quarterly* 27:77–80.

Whitmore, J. R. 1979. "The Etiology of Underachievement in Highly Gifted Young Children." *Journal for the Education of the Gifted* 3:38–51.

———. 1980. *Giftedness, Conflict, and Underachievement*. Boston: Allyn and Bacon.

Whitmore, J. R. 1981. "Gifted Children with Handicapping Conditions: A New Frontier." *Exceptional Children* 48:106–14.

Willerman, L., 1979. "Effects of Families on Intellectual Development." *American Psychologist* 34:923–29.

Willerman, L. and Fiedler, M. F. 1974. "Infant Performance and Intellectual Precocity." *Child Development* 45:483–86.

———. 1977. "Intellectually Precocious Children: Early Development and Later Intellectual Accomplishments." *Journal of Genetic Psychology* 131(1):13–20.

Witters, L. A. 1979. "The Needs of Rural Teachers in Gifted Education." *Journal for the Education of the Gifted* 3:79–82.

Witty, P. A. 1958. "Who Are the Gifted?" In *Education of the Gifted, Part II*. Fifty-seventh yearbook of the National Society for the Study of Education. Edited by N. B. Henry. Chicago: University of Chicago Press.

Witty, P. A., ed. 1971. *Reading for the Gifted and the Creative Student*. Newark, Del.: International Reading Association.

Wolf, J., and Gygi, J. 1981. "Learning Disabled and Gifted: Success or Failure?" *Journal for the Education of the Gifted* 4:199–206.

Woodman, R. W. 1981. "Creativity as a Construct in Personality Theory." *Journal of Creative Behavior* 15(1):43–66.

Yager, R. E. 1982. "Information from Students Concerning School Science: Implications for Instruction for the Gifted." *Roeper Review* 4:9–10.

Yavorsky, D. K. 1976. *Discrepancy Evaluation: A Practitioner's Guide*. Charlottesville, Va.: University of Virginia Evaluation Research Center.

Zettel, J. J. 1979a. "Gifted and Talented Education over a Half-Decade of Change." *Journal for the Education of the Gifted* 3: 14–37.

———. 1979b. "State Provisions for Educating the Gifted and the Talented." In *The Gifted and the Talented: Their Education and Development*. Edited by A. H. Passow, 63–74. Chicago: University of Chicago Press.

———. 1980. *Gifted and Talented Education from a Nationwide Perspective*. Reston, Va.: Council for Exceptional Children.

Zettel, J. J., and Ballard, J. 1978. "A Need for Increased Federal Effort for the Gifted and Talented." *Exceptional Children* 44:261–67.

Zigler, E. 1970. "The Nature-Nurture Issue Reconsidered." In *Social-Cultural Aspects of Mental Retardation*. Edited by H. C. Haywood. New York: Appleton-Century-Crofts.

Zilli, M. G. 1971. "Reasons Why the Gifted Adolescent Underachieves and Some of the Implications of Guidance and Counseling to This Problem." *Gifted Child Quarterly* 15:279–92.

Acknowledgments

(continued from copyright page)

Tables

Table 6.1: From "The Multiple Talent Approach in Mainstream and Gifted Programs" by Carol Schlichter, Exceptional Children, vol. 48, no. 2, 1981, p. 146. Copyright 1981 by the Council for Exceptional Children. Reprinted by permission.   *Table 6.2:* From Margie K. Kitano, "Young Gifted Children: Strategies for Preschool Teachers," *Young Children* 37 (1982):14–24. Reprinted by permission.   *Tables 7.1, 7.2, 7.3, 8.1, 9.2, 9.3, and 9.4:* From *A Teacher's Handbook to Elementary Social Studies*, Second Edition by Hilda Taba, Mary C. Durkin, Jack R. Fraenkel and Anthony H. McNaughton. Copyright © 1971 by Addison-Wesley Publishing Company, Inc. Reprinted by permission.   *Table 9.1:* From *Taxonomy of Educational Objectives: Handbook II: Affective Domain* by David R. Krathwohl, et al. Copyright © 1964 by Longman Inc. All rights reserved. *Table 13.1:* From R.O. Brinkerhoff, D.M. Brethower, T. Hluch- ijj, and J. Nowakowski, *Program Evaluation: A Practitioners Guide for Trainers and Educators* (Boston: Kluwer-Nijhoff, 1983).

Text

Chapter 6: Portions of the material in this chapter will appear in a forthcoming issue of *G/C/T*, the world's most popular magazine for parents and teachers of gifted, creative, and talented children, P.O. Box 66654, Mobile, AL 36606.   *Chapter 9, page 223:* From A. Colby et al., "A Longitudinal Study of Moral Judgment," *Monographs of the Society for Research in Child Development*, Serial No. 200, Vol. 48, Nos. 1–2, 1983, p. 81. © The Society for Research in Child Development, Inc. Reprinted by permission.   *Chapter 12, page 327:* Reprinted by permission of *Las Cruces Sun-News. Chapter 13, pages 335–36:* From R.L. Rubenzer and J.A. Twaite, "Attitudes of 1,200 Educators Toward the Education of the Gifted and Talented: Implications for Teacher Preparation," *Journal for the Education of the Gifted*, 2 (1979):202–213. Copyright © 1979 TAG. Reprinted by permission.

413

Index